THE GOLDEN AGE
SHTETL

THE GOLDEN AGE SHTETL

A NEW HISTORY OF JEWISH LIFE IN EAST EUROPE

YOHANAN PETROVSKY-SHTERN

PRINCETON UNIVERSITY PRESS

Princeton and Oxford

Copyright © 2014 by Princeton University Press

Published by Princeton University Press, 41 William Street, Princeton, New Jersey 08540

In the United Kingdom: Princeton University Press, 6 Oxford Street, Woodstock, Oxfordshire OX20 1TW

press.princeton.edu

ISBN 978-0-691-16074-0

Library of Congress Control Number: 2013945451

British Library Cataloging-in-Publication Data is available

Publication of this book has been aided by

This book has been composed in Minion Pro and Lithos Pro.

Printed on acid-free paper. ∞

Printed in the United States of America

10 9 8 7 6 5 4 3 2

Jacket art: *Golden Gefilte Fish,* acrylic on canvas, 2008 © Yohanan Petrovsky-Shtern.

TO MY JEWISH HISTORY MENTORS

Arthur Green
Antony Polonsky
Moshe Rosman
Shaul Stampfer

מכל מלמדי השכלתי–
אבות ד.א

("I learned from all my teachers." Mishnah Avot 4:1)

CONTENTS

MAP 1. Volhynia, Podolia, and Kiev provinces of the Russian Empire in the 1820s with the key market towns (shtetls).

Credit: Dimitri Karetnikov, on the basis of the contemporary 1818 map.

THE GOLDEN AGE
SHTETL

INTRODUCTION

WHAT'S IN A NAME?

Many of us recall Anatevka from *Fiddler on the Roof* with warmth, mercy, and grief. Anatevka was a Jewish village in dire straits, with its broken-down Jews, wooden huts, rotting shingles, clumsy wooden fences, cracked church walls, and pitiful marketplace with several crooked wooden stalls. Anything made of stone in this village—the church, a factory, the administration offices—was clearly not Jewish, except, of course, the tombstones. The hand-polished copper candlesticks and samovars of the inhabitants of Anatevka shone like rare treasures in that sepia world of decay.

The literary invention of the ingenious imagination of Sholem Alei-chem, Anatevka represented the wooden age of the shtetl, the penultimate chapter of its existence. The actual shtetl, however, had seen much better times. A century earlier, in the 1790s, it entered a fifty-year period that I shall call the golden age of the shtetl. Of course, this description sounds like an oxymoron. How could a ramshackle village in the middle of nowhere where nothing happened but pogroms and expulsions have had a golden age?

This book seeks to answer this question by inquiring into the huge archival evidence that turns upside down the received wisdom about the shtetl and demonstrates the golden age shtetl as economically vigorous, financially beneficial, and culturally influential. The shtetl between the 1790s and the 1840s was an East European market town in private possession of a Polish magnate, inhabited mostly but not exclusively by Jews and subject to Russian bureaucracy. The golden age shtetl presented fascinating opportunities for the Russian Empire to integrate its Jews, and for Jews to adapt themselves to Russia—opportunities that Russia, following a new nationalist and chauvinistic state ideology, completely lost. The golden age shtetl was the manifestation of a highly productive and promising encounter between the Russian Empire and the Jews, but an encounter ultimately ruined by the ideologically and geopolitically driven Russian administration, not without the help of some Jews.

Between the 1790s and the 1840s the shtetl went through a fifty-year period of prosperity and stability, a time of economic and cultural opportunity. During this period the shetl was very different from what we usually imagine it to have been. The beginning and the end of this little-known golden age were marked by two events. The first was the partitioning of Poland by Russia, with the help of Prussia and Austria, which began in 1772, continued in 1773, and ended in 1795. It diminished Polish presence, offered new socioeconomic opportunities, and brought about the flourishing of the shtetl. The second event was the Russian imperial iron age, with its militarization, political and economic rivalry, xenophobia, and nationalism, which after the 1840s transformed the shtetl little by little into a ramshackle town, perhaps even a village, stricken by poverty and pogroms—an Anatevka of sorts. In East European Jewish cultural memory, that later shtetl replaced the shtetl as it had been before. It is precisely this earlier shtetl that this book resurrects by digging it out from beneath layers of literary and cultural stereotypes.

As a result of the partitions, Russia inherited the shtetl with its Polish magnate town-owner and the Jews as its driving economic mechanism. The golden age shtetl was a Polish, Jewish, and Russian joint effort, and it was a proud place with a fascinating social tapestry. Russia treated the shtetl at first with caution and respect, then turned envious, suspicious, and intolerant. Seeking to suppress the Polish shtetl owners, Russia introduced laws that the Jews saw as meted out specifically against them. While the shtetl retained its delicate balance of power among Poles, Russians, and Jews, it endured through its golden age. Yet the more vigorous the shtetl was, the more dangerous it became in the eyes of the new regime, which now sought ways to undermine the shtetl's economic power. In a word, the shtetl prospered so long as the Russian regime put up with its Polish heritage, and it entered into a decline when the regime chose to eradicate it. When in the 1840s Russia finally chose ideology and protectionism over economic growth, the balance shattered, and the glorious years of the shtetl came to a halt. The shtetl's golden age tells the story of a lost struggle for freedom and survival—the early nineteenth-century understanding of survival and freedom.

For some fifty years, between the 1790s and the 1840s, the shtetl was politically no longer Polish but administratively not yet entirely Russian, and its Jews were left to their own devices. It was the unique habitat of some 80 percent of East European Jews, who constituted two-thirds of world Jewry at the time. The shtetl's unlikely golden age marked the first encounter of East European Jews with the Russian Empire.[1] The shtetl had little to no chance of surviving Russia's modernization, yet it endured as long as it withstood the attempts to reform and transform it—and as long as Russia left it in peace. Once its better days were over, the shtetl continued on in the cultural memory, folklore, literature, and phraseology of Russians, Ukrainians, Poles, and Jews. Moreover, the shtetl realities informed much of these cultural memories, as reflected in the literature, language, and folklore, which thus posthumously perpetuated, perhaps even immortalized, the shtetl.

Since this golden age had a beginning and an end, an examination of this specific period reveals not only the everyday reality but also the unrealized potential of the shtetl: who its Jews and other inhabitants were, what kind of lives they lived, why the Russian regime could not accept them as such, and how the regime hastened the shtetl's demise. The story of the golden age shtetl is a story of unfulfilled promise and myopic geopolitics. By trying to make the shtetl one of its own, Russia broke its back, destroyed its uniqueness, and triggered its transformation into Anatevka.

The shtetl could have become the economic if not sociopolitical back-bone of the western part of the Russian Empire and could have had a very different history, but because of its unique socioeconomic, political, and legal structure, it never did. This story also illuminates how the shtetl Jews changed when the regime forced them to, yet still remained who they had been. If we consider the attempts of the regime to transform the shtetl as a forced modernization, the desire of Jews to remain who they were could equally be considered as countermodernity. But the dichotomy of modernity and countermodernity only poorly conveys the vagaries and travails of the shtetl's grass roots, which is precisely what this book seeks to revive.

We will look at several dozen shtetls in Podolia, Volhynia, and Kiev, three provinces in Ukraine, in the southern part of what the Russian ad-ministrators called the Pale of Jewish Settlement in Russia, roughly coin-ciding territorially with what today is the area encompassed by Lithuania, Belarus, and Ukraine, a land representing East European Jewish life in the nineteenth century as a whole.[2] These three provinces in central Ukraine, even before they were established by the incoming Russian administra-tion, formed a distinct habitat quite different from that of other regions—Belorussia and Lithuania to the north, central Poland and Galicia to the west.

Above all, the three provinces were different demographically. Before the partitions, out of forty-four Polish towns with Jewish populations of more than one thousand, seventeen were distributed unevenly between northern, western, and central (formerly Polish) territories, while twenty-seven were located in central Ukraine, at that time a southwestern region of the Russian Empire. Economically, these central provinces of Podolia, Volhynia, and Kiev also stood out: no others had such a significant num-ber of markets and annual fairs attracting thousands of merchants.[3] In terms of their turnover, the trading firms in towns such as Radzivilov were comparable to the biggest trading firms in Moscow and St. Petersburg, whereas manufacturing in the three provinces far surpassed the manu-facturing in the Belorussian provinces in the north and the Polish prov-inces (also under the Russian Empire) in the west.[4] Also, Volhynia, Podolia, and Kiev provinces did not suffer from the devastating Napoleonic invasion and the 1812 military campaign.

Central Ukraine was a peculiar religious entity with distinct traditions of piety, mysticism, folklore, and magic. It was also precisely there that Hasidism as a movement of religious enthusiasm came into being, in Podolia and Volhynia, and moving north and west from there. Hasidism was a full-fledged socioreligious movement in central Ukraine already in the last quarter of the eighteenth century, whereas in the north, in Lithuanian and Belorussian lands, the adherents of Hasidism were marginalized, persecuted, and excommunicated by their anti-Hasidic brethren. Hasidic courts dotted the Ukrainian shtetlekh, and the names of many Hasidic dynasties and trends came from these towns, from Bratslav, Linits-Sokolovka, Radzivilov, Nesukhozh, and Chernobyl to Skvira, Talnoe, Ruzhin, and Makarov.[5] Hasidic masters shaped the shtetl as much as the shtetl shaped Hasidism. Whereas in Poland the *tsadikim*, Hasidic masters, preferred to settle in urban areas or near big cities, Ukrainian Hasidic masters preferred the shtetl, an entire community they could control, educate, and subsequently convert to their mystical worldview. The shtetls, where Hasidic masters established their courts, became centers of pilgrimage.

The Jews in central Ukraine had differences in cuisine; for example, they almost never sweetened their *gefilte* (stuffed) fish, unlike the Polish and Lithuanian Jews.[6] In addition, the Jews inhabiting these territories spoke a variant of the *mameloshn,* the Ashkenazi Jewish mother tongue, known as the Volhynian Yiddish.[7]

The three provinces are circumscribed by the Dnieper River in the west and the Dniester in the southeast, the Pripet in the north, and an imaginary line connecting Cherkas and Kamenets-Podolsk in the south.[8] Unlike other regions with a significant Jewish population in East Europe, such as Belorussia and Lithuania, our three provinces—Volhynia, Podolia, and Kiev—lie in the center of the "black soil" of modern-day Ukraine—a fertile area with lakes and rivers, mild winters and humid summers, and charming landscapes that alternate between picturesque hills and valleys, abundant pastures and vast meadows, the beauty and richness of which could not escape the eye of the Polish magnates, who established their latifundia here.

Jews settled in what is today Ukraine in the first centuries of the Common Era, along with Greek colonizers. They established trading ports along the Crimean shore, and centuries later, together with the Byzantine merchants, moved northward to the Duchy of Kiev. In the ninth and tenth centuries, Jews moved to Ukraine not only from Byzantium and the Crimea but also from the nomadic kingdom of Khazaria, which stretched between the Volga and the Dnieper rivers, and from Western Europe, and which, contrary to common knowledge, had never been a Jewish polity. There was an organized Jewish community in Kiev already in the tenth century, yet the Jews in the Duchy of Kiev—also known as Kievan Rus— left little, if any imprint on the later Jewish communities established in the same areas only after the Mongol invasion in the mid-thirteenth century, the demise of Kievan Rus, and the conquest of these territories by the Duchy of Lithuania.[9]

Of course, the expulsion of the Jews from all Western and some Central European countries (Spain, Portugal, France, England, Hungary, and several Germanic lands), the intolerant policy toward Jews in the crown Polish towns where the Catholic Church established its headquarters (such as Kraków), and the welcoming attitudes of the mercantilist-minded Polish magnates toward the infidel Judaic settlers were decisive factors for robust Jewish resettlement in what was at the time Eastern Poland. The Polish magnates gladly used the Jews as a colonizing force in these very underpopulated and economically underdeveloped territories, for the Jews helped them build and maintain their manorial estates.[10]

The manorial estates of the landlords grew into towns and came to define a unique type of settlement unknown elsewhere in Europe, the Polish private town. After the 1569 Union of Lublin (finally and formally uniting Poland and Lithuania), the Polish magnates took over the areas they called województwo (palatinate) Bracławskie, Wołyńskie, Kijowskie, and Podolskie, and established themselves there for good reason: these territories were covered in forest, convenient for the famous national sport of the Polish nobility, hunting. The forests abruptly stopped at the Dnieper, on the left bank of which stretched the steppes, while on the other side, in the west, the three provinces bordered on the Carpathian Mountains and Galicia. One of the poorest regions in all of East Europe, Galicia was placed under Habsburg rule, whereas the former Polish palatinates in central Ukraine, fertile and agriculturally rich, now became the territory of the three Russian provinces Kiev, Volhynia and Podolia.

We begin the story of the shtetl's golden age at the moment when Russia moved westward and inherited these formerly eastern Polish territories with about one million Jews, one-third of whom lived in central Ukraine. For the author, this story also began with a hunt for primary sources. That hunt brought me to the strongholds of previously classified archives, where a wealth of documents from the shtetls has lain dormant for more than two hundred years. To gain access to these documents, I sometimes disguised myself as a Ukrainian clerk, a Soviet speleologist, and a Polar explorer. This unorthodox approach yielded several thousand archival sources in seven languages, from six countries and dozens of depositories, that reveal the shtetl in its years of glory.

From the publications of my mentors, predecessors, and colleagues, much can be learned about Russia's attempts to create new legislation and introduce regulations regarding the Jews, the variety of reformist and counter-reformist efforts of the Russian tsars, the structures and functions of Jewish communal institutions and their intercessors in the government, and the voices of enlightened Jews, who encouraged the state to reform traditional shtetl life.[11] Until now, however, no one has been able to tell this story of the shtetl's Jewish tavernkeepers, international smugglers, members of Slavic gangs, traders in colonial commodities, disloyal husbands, and avid readers of books on ethics and Jewish mysticism— ordinary Jews in ordinary and extraordinary circumstances. Resorting to what Clifford Geertz called "thick description," I hope to re-create a three-dimensional, colorful, and picturesque shtetl. Even as we delve into the material culture and cultural anthropology, we will keep an eye on the social, economic, and political history, as well as on the reflection of the shtetl in the Jewish cultural memory.

To reconstruct various aspects of the shtetl and simultaneously keep the reader's interest in the story, I structured the chapters around an interplay between the case studies and a broader context. Organizationally, each chapter begins with a case study, which serves as a window on a larger sociocultural issue. The ensuing discussion of the political history provides the general context for the events in the shtetl and helps us focus clearly on the subject against its broader political backdrop. Police grassroots reports allow us a look at history from the bottom up, thereby balancing the top-down approach of the central administration to the same empirical reality. All these diverse sources come together to tell the story of the shtetl and its Jews, who both adapted to a new environment and molded this environment to suit their own needs, thus endowing it with extraordinary economic capacities and cultural longevity. This capacity for survival, however, meant that the shtetl would outlive its golden era and enter a very different period of a longlasting agony.

Although I do point out various forms of shtetl's afterlife, I do not go that far as to explore the shtetl's agony and death in the fires of the twentieth-century revolutions, two world wars, totalitarian projects of social engineering, and the Holocaust. Of course, there are books that emphasize historical change over a long period of time; there are also books that reconstruct the minutiae of everyday life and discuss how the meanings of things came into being. Some of these meanings are still carved into our cultural identities, while others have been entirely abandoned. This book seeks to combine both approaches, but emphasizes the second. We will pause sometimes on the big-name players—general governors, magnates, tsars, rabbinic leaders, Hasidic masters—yet our focus is on the ordinary people, the Ukrainians, Poles, Russians, and Jews who walked through history without leaving a footprint.

This book argues that these people did leave their imprint and made the golden age shtetl what it was. To humanize the shtetl dwellers, we deetatize the shtetl, presenting it first as a phenomenon in and of itself, with its own system of regulations, its unique legislative idiom, and its own logic of development—beyond the political, intellectual, and ideological. This does not mean that we will take the empire and its institutions out of the shtetl. On the contrary, we will discuss how the empire came in and what it did to the cultural and socioeconomic texture of the shtetl. Yet we will be concerned above all with the ordinary shtetl dwellers, through whose lives we will see why the shtetl could not have survived under Russian control as a Polish private town. Thus this book brings the reader into the shtetl and the shtetl to the reader on a journey through the high moments of shtetl life, exploring the world that Russia, Poland, and Ukraine irretrievably lost.

BEYOND COLLOQUIAL STEREOTYPES

I will use the word *shtetl* often: the shtetls each have a history, and so does the word itself. Paradoxically, we know better what the shtetl is not than what it is. The authors of a book on Jews from Luboml insist that their hometown was indeed a shtetl because it was not a metropolis, was in a bad location, and did not have even one small Talmudic academy, yet for some mysterious reason it held a "noteworthy position among the Jewish communities of Volhynia."[12] A book on Korsun claims that "Korsun was too large to be called a village (a *dorf* in Yiddish), and too small to be called a city (a *shtot*), but large enough to be called a small town, a *shtetl*."[13] As we will see, the shtetl handily becomes a kind of a synecdoche for something distant, small, and lost, and rarely for something thriving and vigorous.

We do not actually know what makes an East European locale a shtetl. The number of Jews, their hustle and bustle, or perhaps their poverty, if not their piety, all seem to play a role, yet none is constitutive. Jewish nineteenth-century writers convince us that we were not missing much in the shtetl, a shrinking, insolvent Jewish habitat on its path from decay to demise. The grandfather of Yiddish literature, Mendele Moykher Sforim, calls his imaginary shtetl "Kaptsansk," a name referring not only to destitute *kaptsonim*, "Jews without a cent to their name," but also to the town's imminent fall, *kaputs* in Yiddish or *kapets* in Russian.[14] A golden age Kaptsansk would defy common sense.

This vision of the moribund Jewish town appears in many authors, including Sholem Aleichem, who compares the shtetl houses to gravestones; Y. L. Peretz, with his portrayal of an imaginary shtetl as a "dead town"; Isaak Babel, shocked by shtetl agoraphobia; and Dovid Bergelson, who calls the shtetl a godforsaken town. The shtetl came to usher its own decline and fall, as if there were nothing in its history but agony.[15]

However, an alleged downtrodden village and a loser by definition, the shtetl looked different to some of its shtetl contemporaries, who used the word *shtetl*, a small town, and the word *shtot*, town, indiscriminately. Born and raised during the golden age of the shtetl, Yisroel Aksenfeld sketched what was perhaps the first literary portrayal of the shtetl: "A few small cabins and a fair every other Sunday." Unlike the shtetl, continued Aksenfeld, dripping with sarcasm, a Jewish town, a *shtot*, was different. He portrayed a big imaginary Loyhoyopoli with its burgeoning economy, Jewish communal institutions, and the entire gamut of Jewish social types just to make his point: Loyhoyopoli was unquestionably a town, a shtot, not a shtetl. And then, unexpectedly, Aksenfeld mocked his own definition: "in a shtetl like—oops! Pardon me, that was a slip of the tongue—in a *town*...."[16]

Today, Aksenfeld's irony and revealing slip of the tongue would be lost on us, since it is assumed—and as we will see, mistakenly—that the shtetl was a decaying Jewish nonentity. Berdichev was an epicenter of civilization and therefore, according to today's assumptions, could not possibly be a shtetl. On the contrary, Slavuta, Belaia Tserkov, or Talnoe were anything but centers of civilization and therefore correspond to what we think of as shtetls. But the shtetl *was* a civilization, in and of itself, a very specific one, and not for Jews alone.

The shtetl of Jewish literature became the embodiment of a Jewish spirituality. The famous photographer Roman Vishniac carefully selected from among his thousands of pre-Holocaust East European pictures and published only those "that advanced an impression of the shtetl as populated largely by poor, pious, embattled Jews."[17] The writer Eva Hoffman deftly captured in her book how the shtetl conveys the "idea of a loss" and summons "poignant, warm images of people in quaint black garb, or Chagall-like crooked streets and fiddlers on thatched roofs."[18] The shtetl as an impoverished yet God-fearing Jewish dwelling place has taken such a powerful hold on the common imagination that one insightful writer diagnosed our shared romantic longing for the shtetl as "nostalgia for the mud."[19] We ascribe all our warmest cultural memories to this nostalgic world—but we are never ready to confront its vigorous and flourishing past, which challenges our predispositions.

But let us make no mistake: this lethargic yet spiritualized shtetl is a historical phenomenon shaped by post-Holocaust sensibilities. In his

1945 lecture on the East European Jewish legacy, Abraham Joshua Heschel portrayed the inhabitants of the shtetl as highly spiritual, pious Jews, genuine holy martyrs. Heschel, who never lived in a shtetl, portrayed the utopian Jew as a shtetl sage, a Hasid or a Talmudist or both. Like Natan Neta Hanover, who witnessed and lamented the destruction of the Jewish communities of Eastern Poland during the mid-seventeenth-century Cossack rebellion, Heschel sought to inspire us with what he maintained was the key traditional Judaic value of the destroyed Jewish world: Torah-based study.[20] Heschel's eulogy evinces profound ethical and intellectual messages. The problem is that both black-hat and hatless Jews took this message out of its post-Holocaust context and transformed it into a new, overarching portrait of the shtetl.

The ethnographer Mark Zborowski, author of the bestseller *Life Is with People,* used this overarching portrait to describe Jewish life and people as they never were. His shtetl Jews, young and old, lived not in the multicultural and highly interactive localities portrayed in this book but on what one contemporary scholar calls "a kind of an island of unadulterated *Yiddishkayt.*" Zborowski's Jews always follow the spirit and the letter of rabbinic prescriptions and spend their every free minute learning and praying.[21]

Inhabited by pious Yiddish-speaking dwellers, Zborowski's shtetl is a Judaic monastery with a rabbi instead of an abbot. It is an immaterial phantom, a sublime feeling, "a state of mind."[22] Not only does Zborowski's book overtly spiritualize the Jews, it also sketches an imaginary and misleading map of the shtetl, empty of any Catholics, Tartars, Armenians, Lutherans, or Eastern Orthodox, making the shtetl exclusively Jewish and meriting unmitigated scholarly critique.[23] It is easy to imagine this shtetl as the epitome of Jewish traditionalism and spirituality, and these features are discussed in due course in the final chapters. Yet the real golden age shtetl revolved around its economic axis, and hence depended above all on the marketplace and money—*złoty* and *chervontsy*, Polish and Russian gold-value coins.

As I mentioned at the beginning of this introduction, in 1964 the hit Broadway show *Fiddler on the Roof* immortalized the imaginary shtetl of Anatevka as a quintessential Jewish village. Its Jews were steeped in piety and poverty. Tevye the Milkman was the only Jew with a cow. The local rabbi was as disrespectful of Russian power as one could possibly be, and his advanced students were village boors unaware of things that Jewish boys study in elementary school. In Anatevka, Jews and Gentiles lived separated by an invisible cultural wall and got together only for a drink or a pogrom or both. It will be very difficult to dispel this by now fully accepted, deeply loved, and widely known vision of the shtetl as an impoverished dump with one wealthy Jewish butcher.

This Sholem Aleichem shtetl, destroyed by intercultural sex, antisemitic politics, and international revolution, was widely accepted until the historians of early modern Poland in the 1990s dragged the fiddler off the roof by telling a shtetl prehistory rooted in the eighteenth-century Polish private ownership of towns, the landlords' protectionist trade, and a sophisticated system of leaseholding.[24] The new scholars of Polish Jewry, Gershon Hundert, Moshe Rosman, and Adam Teller, reframed our former vision of the shtetl as victim of political persecution, proving that the shtetl had a burgeoning trade and economy, as well as an oppressive and unlikable Jewish oligarchy.[25] These historians drew heavily on Isaac Levitats's unsurpassed reconstruction of East European Jewish communal life with its umbrella *kahal*, the Jewish version of a town council, and its subordinate *havurot*, voluntary confraternities.[26] Already in the twenty-first century the late historian John Doyle Klier, one of my spiritual mentors, took the study of the Old Polish shtetl into the Russian imperial realm and boldly stated that there was no such thing as a "typical" shtetl, that every shtetl was different, that the shtetl "grew from a Polish private town," and that it was the locus of economic and cultural interaction, bringing together Christians and Jews.[27]

One caveat: unlike Russian historians, the historians of Old Poland very rarely use the word "shtetl" to describe its early period. In most cases they did as the contemporary Polish, Russian, and other European travelers did, who liked local color but did not know the word shtetl. In most cases, but not all, what we today call the shtetl the nineteenth-century Poles called a *miasteczko*, the Ukrainians a *mistechko*, and the Russians a *mestechko*, Slavic for a small market town.[28] To understand the shtetl we have to consider the *mestechko*—in a sense, the shtetl's Russian bureau-cratic equivalent.

THE AVATAR OF THE SHTETL

To map out the new territorial acquisitions for economic purposes after the partitions of Poland, the Russian authorities had to make sense of the unusual Polish shtetl-based latifundia system, now geographically in Russia, and define what a *mestechko*, the key factor in this latifundia, was supposed to be. In their attempts at defining what *mestechko* meant, they help advance our deeper understanding of what the shtetl was, precisely late in the eighteenth and early in the nineteenth century.

Russian statesmen quickly became mired in a network of incom-patible intricacies that mirror modern debates about the shtetl. Why did certain formerly Polish localities, called *mestechki* (plural of *mestechko*), benefit from the privileges granted to towns, though they seemed just like villages? Why were other *mestechki* registered as small towns, whereas demographically they competed with big localities and should have been classified as cities? The Russian bureaucrats turned to their staff to collect and provide them with hard data on the rich Polish-owned lands within the Russian borders. Controlling the actual definition of those localities could help establish Russian power in the empire's western borderlands, still unknown territory, which the regime was just staring to explore.

Russian lower-ranking bureaucrats were often undertrained, corrupt, and underpaid, yet many of them were diligent and reliable. They discov-ered that regarding the *mestechki*, size did not matter. Some of them were bigger than villages, others were smaller.[29] Later they noticed that count-ing the Jewish-owned houses in the *mestechki* also signified little. In 1845, Skvira had 242 Jewish-owned houses; Shpola, 182; Smela, 239; and Tal-noe, 166, whereas Belaia Tserkov, Korostyshev, and Berdichev, each of which the imperial rosters always identified as a *mestechko*, had two, five, and six times more Jewish homes—respectively 468, 1,066, and 1,329![30]

The Russian clerks tried to define the *mestechko* as the town of the Jews, whom they often saw at the marketplace. They compiled a meticu-lous local census and found that in 1802, such localities as Makhnovka and Vasilkov were 54 percent Jewish (1,795 inhabitants out of 3,333 and 1,302 out of 2,428), Boguslav and Radomyshl were 50 percent (2,418 out of 4,769 and 703 out of 1,406), and Uman was 51 percent (2,390 out of 4,706).[31]

If other *mestechki* were roughly half Jewish and half gentile, the locality could hardly be called a "Jewish town," particularly since up until the 1840s many, such as Belaia Tserkov, retained the same pattern: in 1845, it was 50 percent Jewish (7,043 out of 14,177).[32] In 1868 the *mestechki* in Volhynia, Kiev, and Podolia provinces had 184,384 Eastern Orthodox peasants, 24,688 Eastern Orthodox of nonpeasant stock, 9,173 Catholics (Poles), 1,549 Lutherans (Germans), and 176,547 Jews—roughly half the population. Russian clerks also discovered that the ratio of Jews to gentiles helped little to explain this phenomenon because some towns, for example Kamenets-Podolsk, legally never defined as *mestechki* but statistically close to them, also had a half Jewish population (in the 1830s, 2,903 Christians vs. 2,895 Jews).[33]

Nineteenth-century Russian bureaucrats had good reason to think that somehow the presence of Jews was helpful in understanding the *mestechko*, but the number of Jews alone was insufficient to make an ethnically and socially diverse locality into a *mestechko*. After all, Shpola, Korostyshev, Makhnovka, Talnoe, and Tomashpol had two thousand to five thousand Jews; Korets, Medzhibozh, Smela, and Tulchin had between five and ten thousand; and others, such as Berdichev, Boguslav, Vasilkov, and Skvira, had more than fifteen thousand.[34] And each of these was classified as a *mestechko*. Zborowski with his *Life Is with People* was fairly accurate when he emphasized that the shtetl was "not size at all."[35] Yet he failed to mention that the shtetl was *not* a little town and could in fact be quite big!

Delving into the taxonomy of the *mestechko*, Russian clerks became the earliest historians of the shtetl. They studied the amassed evidence and realized that, by and large, almost any *mestechko* previously belonged to a Polish landlord and had been or still was a private town. This town grew out of a small manorial estate. To make their estate and surrounding settlement into a town, Polish landlords obtained special royal privileges allowing them to establish annual fairs and regular market days and to

0.1. A shtetl inn, late 18th to early 19th century, Brailov, Podolia.
Binyamin Lukin's private collection. Courtesy of Binyamin Lukin.

produce and sell liquor. In early modern times the privilege was a legal document, implying among other things a monopoly: no one else could have annual fairs on those dates and no one else in the vicinity could distill and sell vodka. Privileges shaped the protectionist economy, which enormously favored the magnates and boosted the economy of their estates.

It also, however, favored the Jews, who were invited to settle on the landlords' estates. In exchange for legal residence, Jews had to fulfill a specific obligation: they had to bring in trade and trade in liquor. They had to engage in specific occupations and perform an important function rather than just settle as passive colonizers. The *mestechko* thus emerged as the product of precisely this Jewish activity, which made private towns into prosperous, economically advantageous, and financially beneficial possessions—that is, for the magnates, of course.

For example, as occurred everywhere else with only minor differences, the 1740 agreement between a magnate and the Zaslav (Iziaslav) Jewish communal elders outlined the key function of the Jews, who would organize five annual fairs during Eastern Orthodox and Catholic holidays such as Spas (Savior) and St. Martin in the old part of the town, and another four, also on Christian holidays such as St. Peter and St. Virgin Mary, in the new part of the town, and still three more brief fairs in the town's central square.[36] Operating shtetl trade was a Jewish obligation, not a choice. As the late eighteenth-century French traveler Hubert Vautrin observed, Jews were "foreign to the state" and served "the material interests" of the Poles.[37] When they were not efficient enough from vantage point of the Polish magnate, the latter resorted to draconian measures to make them pay their dues. Therefore, what historians have called the marriage of convenience between Jews and magnates in reality was not an equal partnership and sometimes took the ugly forms of humiliation, exploitation, and abuse.[38]

Since this Jewish privilege outlived the partitions of Poland and continued to shape the Zaslav economy well into the nineteenth century, Zaslav, as well as hundreds of other shtetls, turned out to be a lingering Polish presence for the Russian regime. Still, the word *mestechko* in Russia only partially stood for what a private town, a *miastezcko,* had been earlier in the Polish-Lithuanian Commonwealth. Even half a century after the partitions of Poland, the *mestechki* still remained the private possessions of Polish landlords: Gornostaipol belonged to Gińska, Khodorkov to Swidziński, Zhabotin to Fliorkowski, Belopolie to Tyszkiewicz, Korostyshev to Olizer, Pogrebishche to Rzewuski, and Rakhmistrivka to Zalewski. Although Potocki sold parts of Uman in the 1790s and lost the town entirely by the 1830s, and Bariatinskaia sold Dubno in the 1840s, Polish magnates still controlled several of the most important shtetls in the area: Count Branicki controlled Belaia Tserkov and Boguslav, Prince Radziwiłł controlled Berdichev, and lesser-known landlords owned several hundred other *mestechki* of secondary economic significance.[39]

As a major landowners' asset, these private towns slowly but steadily changed hands from Poles to Russians, a process that intensified after the 1830–1831 Polish rebellion and the subsequent confiscation of the rebels' property, including that of disloyal magnates. But even before the rebellion, as early as the 1790s, the Russian Ministry of Finance was taking away private towns from now politically bankrupt Poles and redesignating these towns as Russian government towns—or, as they put it, treasury-owned towns (*kazennye,* from the Russian for treasury, *kazna*).

In the eyes of the government, economic control over the western borderlands signified political control. For this reason, the Russian rulers enticed the Eastern Orthodox (that is, non-Catholic) gentry to follow their lead, take advantage of the dire situation of the Polish magnates, and buy their towns out from under them. Unlike the early twentieth-century Yiddish literati and modern-day memoirists, the Russian regime found the shtetls to be a highly valuable asset.

Thus encouraged, Colonel Berezovsky purchased Gostomel, the Russian statesman Count Palen came to own Makarov and Chernobyl, Talnoe came under the ownership of Duchess Naryshkina, Starokonstantinov came under the ownership of Countess Abamalek, Duchess Bobrinskaia purchased Smela, and the landlord Uvarova purchased Pavoloch. The Russian authorities confiscated or appropriated in lieu of debts such shtetls as Balta, Dubno, Ekaterinopol, Uman, and Fastov. Later, in midcentury, the government also purchased the fortified shtetl Zhvanets from the landlord Komar and Zhinkov from Prince von Wurtenberg.[40]

Though fifty towns became the property of the Russian state, they still appeared on the government rosters as *mestechki.* The contemporary Russian clerks were no fools: they understood that little had changed economically in the *mestechko* with its overnight reclassification, although the reclassified shtetl legally was no longer a private Polish town. Through the 1850s and even later, into the 1880s, the Russians continued to identify as *mestechko* both the towns still in the private possession of a Polish magnate or a Russian landlord and the towns already belonging to the imperial treasury.[41]

The Russian bureaucrats sought a legal basis for the confiscation of the private towns from the Poles, thus reconstructing for posterity the genealogy of the shtetl. They established that Ekaterinopol, Chernobyl, and Boguslav had become *mestechki* back in the sixteenth century—respectively in 1557, 1566, and 1591. Others, such as Tetiev, Gornoistaipol, Ianovka, Zhidichin, and Vishenki, retrospectively acquired the status of *mestechko* in the seventeenth century—in 1606, 1616, 1618, 1638, and 1695.

One of the oldest private towns in the area, Brusilov, had its privilege issued and reconfirmed in 1574, 1585, and 1720, with such pivotal Polish rulers as Stefan Batory and August II the Strong confirming it. Localities such as Belaia Tserkov, Korostyshev, and Tomashgorod received privileges from Stanisław II August between 1774 and 1779, whereas Rimanov and Obukhov became private possessions according to the 1817 and 1837 decisions of the Russian Senate, and Zhashkov did so merely because it was mentioned as a *mestechko* in the 1794 papers of Count Potemkin.[42]

To make sure they had a good grasp of the history and structure of the shtetl, the Russian clerks also interrogated the town-owners: what did it mean to be or become a *mestechko*? They dispatched requests, obtained answers, and compiled the information in tables. Krasnopol, they discovered, was called a *mestechko* "only because several Jewish families settled there." Landlord Zakaszewski, the owner of the shtetl of Gorodok, explained that his locality "had always been considered a *mestechko*: Jews had settled here long ago, they had their synagogue and butchery, and also they had regular fairs." Baranovka, Korets, Liakhovtsy, Rimanov, Troianov, Shepetovka, Sudilkov, and many other localities had no papers to support their claims but were known to have acquired their special status "from old times" and, more important, "had distinct Jewish communities."[43]

This last point became crucial for the Russian clerks. They summarized: Jews were "allowed to sell liquor in the existing *mestechki*," the localities "represent[ed] the center of trade activities," and the local Jews "had already established their communities and manufacturing."[44] Thus in the *mestechko*, a productive Jewish community and economic prosperity went hand in hand, a configuration that was far removed from the imaginary shtetls of East European writers.

Both for the Polish-Lithuanian Commonwealth before the partitions and for the Russian Empire afterward, the *mestechki* came to be defined by what the Jews did there—and the shtetl Jews were seen as the backbone of the towns' economic growth. This aspect helps explain, among other things, the attempts of the Russian gentry to imitate the Polish magnates. According to the Ministry of Finance, Russian landlords inundated St. Petersburg with multiple "petitions to rename villages as *mestechki*," as did Golenishchev-Kutuzov and Dolgorukov, for example, who wanted "to establish trade usually conducted by Jews," therefore asking to rename their villages of about 200 homes as *mestechki*.[45] The shtetl was something they sought out and found profitable. Of course, the government had to accommodate the landlords: permissions were grudgingly granted, taverns opened, market days established, and the early nineteenth-century shtetls grew in number.

The shtetl received its final clarifying touch when the governor general of Kiev, Volhynia, and Podolia provinces summed up a century-long quest. By the 1880s, there were 378 *mestechki* under his auspices, 322 of which belonged to the gentry and 56 to the state treasury. Out of those 378, 92 had received their privileges from the Polish kings, another 40 had been turned into *mestechki* by the Russian administration on its own initiative, and yet another 40 applied for and were given the status of *mestechki* after the partitions. Eighty-nine localities were called *mestechki* on the basis of some scanty documental proof, and 48 had no documents at all but retained their status as *mestechki* since they had been known as such from the time of the medieval grand duchies of Kiev and Lithuania.[46]

The governor general gave two reasons for calling a locality a *mestechko*. His first reason was of Polish origin: the locality was a market-centered settlement of urban character, belonging to a member of the Polish gentry (*szlachta*), having a monopoly on liquor trade, and known for its annual fair or fairs. "Many owners," he claimed, "had sought to rename their villages as towns, asking the Polish kings for the right to establish a fair, introduce the Magdeburg law, and obtain permission to sell vodka."

But the governor also provided another reason, this one rooted in the Russian taxonomic system: many rural-like settlements had been inhabited "by merchants and townsfolk," not only by peasants; hence it was logical to call such a locality a town, a *mestechko*. Whatever its size— 2,000, 12,000, or 20,000 people—a *mestechko* was a place with ordinary taxpaying people, not serfs. The specific shtetl economy, centered on the marketplace, made it different from a village, while the unique shtetl history, centered on private ownership, made it different from a city. The shtetl was prosperous as long as the Russian authorities agreed to its intermediary status. Once they chose to reform or reclassify it, the shtetl's predicament was sealed.

The governor general acknowledged that a *mestechko* owed its status almost exclusively to the Jews. He realized that a 34 percent Jewish population in the *mestechki* of Kiev province, 45 percent in Podolia, and 44 percent in Volhynia did not answer the question of why the locality was a Jewish-made phenomenon, whereas Jewish representation among the two most economically active urban estates, the townsfolk and merchants, did.

Townsfolk or urban dweller was a legal category. Individuals covered by this category constituted a specific estate, a class, a group of people known in Russian as a *soslovie*, different from other types of *soslovia* or estates, such as landowning nobility, petty gentry, clergy, state clerks, and peasants.[47] These groups accounted for the Christian 50 percent of the *mestechki* population. Unlike these groups, the townsfolk were made up of retail traders, leaseholders and tavernkeepers, middlemen, and artisans—butchers and bakers, shoemakers and tailors, barrel makers and tanners, blacksmiths and furriers—in a word, the third estate in its original meaning.

Jews were enormously overrepresented among these urban estates. The Kiev *mestechki* had 93 percent Jewish townsfolk, Podolia had 94 percent, and Volhynia had 92 percent, with respectively 96, 95, and 99 percent Jewish merchants. In Kiev, Podolia, and Volhynia provinces, 98, 97, and 98 percent of small stores, trading stalls, and shops belonged to Jews, in numbers respectively 3,974, 4,445, and 4,007.[48] Therefore it was the activity of the Jews, not their demographics, that made a locality a *mestechko* and defined its economic power.[49]

More than anything else, it was the commercial and economic contribution of the Jews that had a definitive impact on making the *mestechki*. If there were no specifically Jewish businesses, such as tavernkeeping, then the town was not a *mestechko,* and vice versa. This connection between the burgeoning town economy and the Jews was obvious to practically every Russian provincial bureaucrat, including one who observed that in his province, "several *mestechki* bear the title of *mestechko* for no reason: hence Jews should not be dealing in alcohol there."[50] Not the ratio of Jews to gentiles but the ratio of economically active Jews to economically active gentiles from the same class or estate—this unique socioeconomic configuration and the Jews' pivotal function in it defined the *mestechko*.

The nineteenth-century shtetl emerged as a Polish economy driven by Jews and existing within the Russian administrative system. It was this unique role of the Jews that made the early nineteenth-century locality into a vibrant, energetic, and growing shtetl. The moniker "shtetl Jews" was about producing something, not just being something.

Eastern Orthodox or Catholic landlords sought to get the *mestechko* privilege precisely because it would assure them that Jewish liquor manufacturers, innkeepers, and guild merchants, however small their number, would transform the village into a town solely by virtue of their entrepreneurship and their engagement with what contemporaries understood as urban business. And since that business was profitable and beneficial, naturally it defined the shtetl's golden age, although we now need to clarify why the Yiddish-speaking contemporaries rarely called the golden age *mestechko* a shtetl.

A SHTETL THAT WAS NOT

Jews only called their locality a shtetl once they had gotten out of the shtetl. People who left their native towns voluntarily or who were banished from their father's table observed their past from the heights of the big city and from a distance separating the Russian imperial culture from a Yiddish underdog one. They pondered their birthplace through the privileged lens of an acculturated individual who spoke the language of the state, dressed in European clothes, and no longer had use for kosher food, Talmudic debates, or the pious way of life.

Their place of origin was now a thing of the despised past: a small town, a townlet, a hamlet, a shtetl. The smaller the better—thus they could explain their escape from their particular past and their desire to become part of something universalistic, imperial, mainstream, big and important. The shtetl for them was a yardstick measuring the gap separating their acculturated present from their Jewish past.

For loyal shtetl dwellers, the word shtetl was too charged with pejorative and condescending meanings. God forbid a traveling Jewish merchant from Brody would tell the Jews of Medvedovka that they lived in a shtetl, or even worse, a *shtetele*. This condescending Yiddish nickname was reserved by the townspeople of Zaslav for those of Shargorod and by the townspeople of Slavuta for those of Polonnoe—and vice versa.

If asked where they lived, they waxed superlative. They lived in a town, a *shtot*—nothing less. Consider the ways in which Jews identified their localities in *pinkasim*, the nineteenth-century record books of the Jewish communities, voluntary societies, and professional confraternities, written, as a rule, in Hebrew. Responsible for the title pages and statutes, Jewish scribes proudly identified Lutsk in Volhynia, Kamenets in Podolia, and Nesvizh in Belorussia as towns. That Berdichev in the 1830s was described as a town (*ir*) and Bar of Podolia in the 1790s as a large town encircled by a wall (*krakh*) is hardly surprising.[51] But Jews also called Baranovka, Zaslav, Ostropolie, and Starokonstantinov towns, as well as dozens of other places that we today would call a shtetl. Even the enlightened Avraam Ber Gottlober wrote in his Hebrew memoir that his father had been born in the *town* of Tarashcha and himself in the town of Starokonstantinov—both quintessential shtetls.[52]

Jews were proud of their locales and called them holy towns and holy communities, making no distinction between a settlement of about five hundred dwellers and an urban center of ten thousand. Zhinkovets and Karvasar were holy communities on a par with the large walled town of Kamenets-Podolsk, which they were on the outskirts of. In turn, Rakhmistrivka, practically a village, claimed the status of holy community on par with Volozhin, Letichev, Miropol, and Medzhibozh.[53] When Rabbi Nachman needed a new dwelling place, he established himself in what his scribe Nosson proudly called the "community of Zlatopolie," and did not mention that it was no bigger than a village.[54]

Like the Russian administrators who sought to define *mestechko*, the Jews ignored the significance of demography and statistics. What mattered for the Jews was not the size of the place but what the Jews did there. If they had a prayer quorum to read the Torah and say kaddish, a butcher to slaughter poultry, a scribe to write a mezuzah, and a warden to open the synagogue and light the candles, any locality would then be a Jewish town, a holy town. And they would also have their own *kahal* made up of the most influential representatives of the local financial and mercantile

0.2. A Holy Ark in Ruzhin synagogue.
CAHJP, P166, G5. Courtesy of the Central Archives for the History of the Jewish People.

elite. Jews, Poles, and Russians acknowledged the legal status of the *kahal* and respected its major functions—collecting taxes, distributing communal relief funds, and supervising religious and social mores. With all this available locally, Jews did not need to walk miles in the dirt behind a wagon carrying a coffin to a distant town cemetery, and they did not need to go to a bigger city to hear the Purim story of the blessed Mordekhai and the cursed Haman. Jews could pay their respects to the dead and reenact the ancient dramas at home.

Holiness stayed local. It was created by virtue of the Judaic divine commandments transforming a rustic village-like locality into a civilized place of Jewish good deeds. What looked like a provincial rural settlement to the outsider was the center of the world for its Jews. Hence, local Jews were the proud residents of what they called a town, not a townlet or a village. The Hebrew language of the communal records was one of the reasons why the word shtetl was not used there. But even Jews who wrote in Yiddish, for example the tailors from the outskirts of Berdichev on the other side of the Gnilopiat River, presented themselves as being from the "community behind the *greblia*" (the Russian for dam), living in the town of Berdichev.[55]

Rabbinic scholars, also writing in Hebrew, called most shtetls where Jews lived towns. They were particularly careful about the names of the Jews and Jewish localities in the case of divorce documents, which had to give a clear, indisputable, standardized spelling of the name of a locality. Here a mistake might invalidate an entire document, and consequently turn the woman into an *agunah*, an abandoned wife.

In a complex divorce case, a Jew from Zaslav needed to collect signatures from one hundred different town rabbis from three different countries. But what do we call a town and what a country, asked a local rabbi? Clearly, Hungary and Austria are different lands although one and the same country; language is here a decisive factor. On the contrary, although the border splits Gusiatin and Tarnorud into two parts, they still constitute a single entity, a town, because of their thriving Jewish communities.[56]

Shtetls to us today and *mestechki* to the Russian bureaucrats and the Polish nobles, these localities were all towns to the Jews at the time. Rabbi Israel Isser from Vinnitsa in his responsum was more concerned with potential mistakes invalidating a divorce document and therefore discussed how properly to write the name of a town—was it Belo Polie or Belopolie (White Plains)? He did not use the word shtetl and did not predicate the status of the town on its size.[57]

However, the proverbial preacher Yaakov Kranz, known as the Maggid of Dubno, or perhaps his editor Avraam Flahm, who published the maggid's works posthumously in the 1830s, did use the diminutive word shtetl, and used it interchangeably with the word *shtot*, town. He did it indiscriminately: as long as his wandering poor Jews were able to find a generous Jew, a welcoming household, a synagogue with a bench to lean their head on, this was a shtetl. Or a shtot.[58]

The illustrious Yekhezkel Landau from Prague reacted in a similar manner. When a rabbinic scribe asked him whether Radzivilov could serve as a town where the court could issue divorce documents, Landau focused on how to write Radzivilov—in German or in Yiddish spelling, Radziwil or Radvil. He answered: in clear Yiddish. But he never asked what Radzivilov was, a city, a town, or a village. If they had a scribe there, a rabbi in charge of marriages and divorces, two knowledgeable Jews serving on the rabbinic court, and could issue a sophisticated document, this was a definitely a town, a formidable center of Jewish life.[59] This is precisely what the shtetl was in its golden age, and this is exactly what the Russian regime both liked and disliked about it.

A LOCUS OF ACTION

The residents of modern Ukrainian towns that were once *mestechki* use the word shtetl as a memory locus, distancing themselves from it. When asked where the shtetl was located, they wave their hand toward the center of the town, somewhere around the former market square: it was over there, where the Jews lived, traded, prayed, cried, and rejoiced. The shtetl was there—in a historical and geographic distance, in an imaginary town center with its noisy, bustling trade.[60]

Today we readily call any locality in East Europe where Jews once lived a shtetl, although the Jews who lived there two hundred years ago called it a town and the Russian bureaucrats called it a *mestechko*. The shtetl thus absorbs various meanings and the tension between them: the Polish legal and economic private town, the Russian administrative *mestechko*, and the Jewish religious "holy community."

It was precisely the combination of these factors that created the triangle of power, shared by Poles, Jews, and Russians—that shaped the shtetl golden age. As we shall see, once one of these constituencies was removed, the shtetl turned into a bent, impoverished, and stuttering East European beggar, as it entered classical Yiddish literature and as it appears in some of the photographs in this book.

Whatever the meaning of the word shtetl, its Jews were the doers, not just the dwellers. A shtetl Jew could go about his business in the small shtetl of Ruzhin, the medium-size shtetl of Skvira, or the large shtetl of

0.3. A former Polish magnate's palace in Belogorodka.
IA, f. 9, spr. 43, ark. 15. Courtesy of the Institute of Archaeology of the National Academy of Sciences of Ukraine.

Uman. Perhaps at the time, the Jews of Skvira looked down on Ruzhin, an insignificant and provincial small shtetl, and referred to Uman with respect as a *shtot* (a town), but whatever their number in a certain place, Jews were the shtetl-makers as a result of their occupational pattern.

Any number of trading Jews sufficed to make a shtetl insofar as they dominated within the corresponding trading or urban estate. This book calls a settlement a shtetl if it had elements of the old Polish leaseholding economy, an established trade and a marketplace, and a liquor trade—all run predominantly by Jews, who paid taxes to the Russian state treasury and bribes to the Russian police, and who organized themselves into a traditional Jewish community. That multiethnic settlement was a shtetl.

The Russian statesmen were not mistaken about the implications of the shtetl. The shtetl Jews engaged in trade; trade brought in people; people brought in goods; goods bought in money, and money enriched the magnates, benefited the towns, and contributed to the Russian economy.

The golden age shtetl was alive and kicking. We shall see in the next chapters how the vigor of the shtetl manifested itself at the marketplace and prayer-house, at home and in the tavern—in and outside the shtetl. We shall see the shtetl in action, ponder its chances for its survival, and observe the beginning of its fall.

The shtetl was a dynamic place and a dynamic concept, moving through stages and changes, edifying and modifying itself along the way. It was Polish Jewish in the eighteenth century, Russian Jewish at the turn of the nineteenth, and found itself in a unique synergy of three powers—Russian, Polish, and Jewish—late in the eighteenth and early in the nineteenth century. Far more nuanced than just "a state of mind" or a "locus of memory," the shtetl embodied action—economic and manufacturing, religious and educational, political and civic, cultural and criminal, the complex nature and transformation of which is our focus.

The shtetl would not exist without its Jews—trading, producing, and exchanging whatever could be exchanged, traded or produced. The shtetl for us is a place, but perhaps we need to reconceptualize it also as an action, a whir of activity. After all, it was this activity that shaped the shtetl's unique golden age and its suppression that triggered the shtetl's demise.

Had Russia come to grips with the shtetls' character and activity, its relations with its Jews would have taken a different path. This did not happen. Political and ideological interests had the upper hand over common sense, and the shtetl found itself at the epicenter of a longlasting if latent war between the Russians and the Poles. Since the Russians were playing the game on their own territory, they won, at the expense of interethnic tolerance and the golden age shtetl.

Although for the Poles the shtetl was a private town and an economic category, for the Russians an administrative subdivision, and for the contemporary Jews a religiously defined community, in this book it is indiscriminately called a shtetl. After all, "shtetl" as a word is nothing but a cultural artifact, a caprice of collective memory. It signifies a vanished Jewish Atlantis, a yearning for a distant and utopian national culture and for the redeeming traditional values of East European Jerusalem, that "holy community" that we tend to strip of corporeality and then sugarcoat its imaginary residue. This book fleshes out the shtetl and adds some salt to it.

CHAPTER ONE

RUSSIA DISCOVERS ITS SHTETL

I n 1823, Andrei Glagolev defended his dissertation in literature and decided to take a trip through Europe, which would result in his famous *Notes of a Russian Traveler* and would bring him fame as a perspicacious ethnographer and geographer. Glagolev did not expect to see much once he left Kiev, yet his discovery of the shtetls in Ukraine fascinated him.

He visited Berdichev with its "eternal Jewish marketplace." He found Korets with its beautiful palace and Christian Orthodox convent to be as nice as the Russian districts' central towns. He liked the fortress and the valley around Ostrog and observed that the house in Ostrog that held the first Slavic printing press now belonged to a Jew. In Dubno, he found an impressive Catholic temple, a military depot, the castle of the Polish magnates, and an excellent hotel with top-notch cuisine.[1]

Whatever town he visited, he never failed to mention its Polish owners—the Potockis or the Lubomirskis—and to notice whether Russia had or had not already purchased the town from the magnates for its own treasury. Of course, he complained of the importunate Jews who besieged him in Radzivilov, but his encounter with them did not mar his impressions of the towns situated on the Russian lands belonging to Polish nobility where Jews served as translators, commercial intermediaries, and tour guides.

His impressions, appended with a lengthy ethnographic chapter about the Jews, transcended the travelogue genre. His was one of many early discoveries of the shtetl, quite different from the experiences of later Russian travelers, who were supercilious and xenophobic and who called the shtetl muddy and moldy.

NEW IMPERIAL BORDERLANDS

The golden age of the shtetl coincided with the period of Russia's enlightened despotism and geographic expansion. It was precisely this epoch, from Catherine II through Alexander I, that came to be known as Russia's golden age. Russian monarchs found themselves in new political and geographic circumstances.

Between 1772 and 1795 Russia, in close cooperation with Austria and Prussia, partitioned Poland and swallowed up 66 percent of its territory—about 400,000 square miles, the entire eastern part of the country with its cities, towns, townlets, villages, valleys, roads, lakes, rivers, forests, and 900,000 to 1,200,000 Jews. Yet in the early 1790s, self-indulgent Russian statesmen showed little if any interest in exploring their new domain—a strange reaction in light of the nascent Polish military resistance, the 1794 Kosciuszko rebellion, and the 1795 third partition of Poland. The newly established administrators sent Catherine II dozens of "Potemkin" reports, which unsurprisingly ignored the reality on the ground and surprisingly neglected the Jews, never before allowed into Russia.

The newly appointed rulers felt they were living in a bucolic utopia. Your Majesty, reported the administrators, in Your territories nothing extraordinary has happened: no fires, epidemics, sicknesses, or accidents. "Everything is calm and peaceful," assured the Volhynia governor. "Everything is alright here," penned a state clerk from Podolia. Oh, yes, acknowledged a Kiev official, there was a fire in Kiev's Laura monastery, a flood near the Dnieper River, and an earthquake in the Kiev region, but this was all local and had no negative impact elsewhere. True, locusts did harm crops here and there but this was really of minor concern.

In passing, a senior clerk mentioned that Count Potocki had purchased weapons—2,000 rifles, 2,000 pistols, 4,000 swords—and the Russian governor allowed him to bring this cargo to his shtetl: after all, Potocki was a magnate, and who could prevent a magnate from purchasing some hunting weapons for personal use? Overall, the Eastern Orthodox peasants were happy, and the Catholic gentry—the Poles—were not, but the optimistic Russian bureaucrats thought they could tame the Polish landlords: they'd make them take an oath of allegiance to the Russian Empire, and their further compliance would be a matter of time.[2]

More prescient than all her governors put together, Catherine knew that things were not that simple. She presented herself as a female savior who had come to redeem Poland from the vicious political threat emanating from revolutionary France. Not from the Poles in general and not from the Sejm—the Polish parliament—in particular but from the "evil-thinking party" of the "encroaching French Jacobins," who had "exhausted her patience" and triggered the partitions of the Polish-Lithuanian Commonwealth. She, Catherine the Great, had come forth to suppress a "hideous rivalry" among Poles and eradicate those "furious and corrupt French rebels who were destroying Poland."

Thanks to Catherine II, Polish patriots would thus appear in Russian discourse as alien French-inspired revolutionary mutineers, enemies of the supposedly submissive Poland, rather than fighters for Polish independence. Only half a century later did Catherine's suspicions concerning some disloyal Poles become transformed into full-fledged governmental mistrust of the Russian Poles at large. By the late nineteenth century the regime had transferred this mistrust to the Jews, dismissing their growing loyalty to the Russian crown, and eventually to other borderland ethnicities, including Eastern Orthodox Ukrainians.

Yet before Russia's rampant late nineteenth-century xenophobia came to dominate politics, Catherine addressed her newly acquired peoples— Jews included—with the same empathy a stepmother would show her foster children. She expected awe, not love. From her subjects she sought mercantilist profit, not cultural homogeneity. She ordered a manifesto declaring the results of the partitions and the incorporation of the Polish lands into Russia. She wanted the territories rearranged: Kiev, Podolia, and Volhynia provinces established in lieu of the old Bracław woewodstvo, districts introduced, and governors appointed.

All Polish crown assets were confiscated for the benefit of the Russian treasury. Combining military candor and political paternalism, Catherine warned her administrators to be "nice" in their treatment of the newly acquired borderland population. "We desire," she explained, "that these provinces be conquered not only by the power of weapons. Russia will win the hearts of the people in these lands by a kind, righteous, merciful, modest, and humane management."

Now the Jews found themselves in Catherine's field of vision, though what would be notoriously called the Russian Jewish question was treated by the tsarina as something quite secondary at best. Like many travelers of that time, she considered the Jews in the Polish private towns as a profitable asset, not a burdensome liability. With her flowery rhetoric, Catherine extended her powerful benevolence to the Jews. She loved the docile and loyal, and abhorred dissenters and rebels. She expected the Jews to be the former, never the latter.

"It goes without saying," she declared, "that Jewish communities, dwelling in the towns and lands attached to the Russian Empire, will maintain all those freedoms which they now legally enjoy, because Her Majesty's love of humanism makes it impossible to exclude them from the universal future commonwealth under Her blessed rule, while the Jews in turn as loyal subjects will dwell with appropriate humility and engage in trade and industry according to their skills."[3]

With her enlightened paternalism firm in hand, Catherine legalized Jewish residence in some fifteen western provinces of the Russian Empire, the future Pale of Jewish Settlement, or simply the Pale—a turning point in the history of the country previously intolerant of the Jews. Catherine allowed Jews to enroll in the established estates by declaring their status as merchants or townsfolk, thus administratively integrating them into the texture of the empire and extending to them the privileges granted to the Christian merchants and townsfolk. Naturally, the shtetl, the dwelling place of most Jews and the economic headquarters of the new imperial lands, became a focal point of Catherine's geopolitics.

THE SHTETL OF CONTENTION

Catherine was essentially an enlightened despot, quite often more despotic than enlightened, whose intuition did not always serve her well.[4] She committed herself to preserving the privileges of the landlords, the Polish gentry in the western borderlands included, and got herself stuck in a trap. Any town with a Polish landlord would find itself under the dual control of the Russian administration and the Polish nobleman. Catherine realized that this double management would be counterproductive and turned to political manipulations.

In 1794, she instructed two borderland governors, Saltykov and Tutolmin, to indiscriminately apply punitive measures to Polish magnates conspiring against Russian authorities. "Take the towns and estates of the secret rebels under state control," she instructed, "so that they should not turn their income into harmful actions against the Russian state."[5] These private landlords' towns were the shtetls, now becoming a point of contention between the Russian and the Polish elites.

After Catherine, subsequent Russian rulers up to Alexander II had to consider the shtetl problem again and again. In the tone set by the tsarina, they instructed the governors "to do whatever possible to get data and acquire the townlets for the state treasury by purchasing them from the owners." They would require that the magnates, the richest among Polish nobility, submit reports disclosing their regular income, number of registered taxpaying inhabitants, number of unregistered inhabitants and plans for resettling them, and the sum they would like to get for selling the town.[6]

The Polish landlords were frightened: their privileges were in jeopardy. Most avoided submitting the data. Strutinski, whose case stands for many, feigned naiveté: my town, he wrote, with the surrounding villages costs 1,025,000 złoty—and he did not provide any further information: take it or leave it.[7] Despite the ambiguous treatment of the Polish magnates, some of whom the imperial regime appointed to supervise the local

Russian administration, the internal Russian documents reiterated: we should suppress in the former Polish territories "a false concept of freedom which is nothing but arbitrariness," and therefore we should take over such and such shtetl aggressively and appropriate it from the Polish magnate.[8]

The more serious the attempts of the Poles to restore independence and separate themselves from Russia, the more decisive the Russian regime became about appropriating the shtetls, which functioned as pawns in Russian relations with Poles. As early as 1795 the Russians introduced state management and established governmental offices, magistrates, post offices, and provincial courts in such shtetls as Tulchin, Yampol, Mogilev, Makhnovka, Lipovets, Bershad, and many others, allocating impressive government funds for the purpose.

Whatever the town's economic significance, the governors named towns such as Vladimir-Volynsk, known in Jewish cultural memory as Ludmir, and Kamenets-Podolsk, known as Kamnits, as district capitals. Jews could not but benefit from these developments as legal and state institutions moved into the shtetls, previously run and ruled by the whim of a magnate.

Shtetls such as Litin, Khmelnik, and Gaisin, recently withdrawn from Polish noblemen but preserving the entirety of their *shtetldike* infrastructure, were to become district centers, with a solid presence of Russian power.[9] To this end, the governor ordered that officials "begin inventory of the assets" of the Polish crown where Russian state institutions, including but not limited to custom houses, courts, and hospitals, could be established.[10] "Very nice buildings could be used for government offices," wrote the Zhitomir governor with the Polish nobleman's palace in mind, which he was planning to expropriate.[11]

As soon as the shtetl emerged as a point of contention between the Poles and Russians, relations between the Russians and Poles came to a head. "It is harmful for the government to have its power shared between the state treasury and the town owner," argued the Zhitomir military governor in 1839. "We should replace privately-owned central district towns with state-owned ones." He recommended establishing a commission in charge of what we would call today information hijacking and insisted

1.1. Town hall (ratusha) in Kornits.
IA, f. 9, spr. 43, ark. 27. Courtesy of the Institute of Archaeology of the National Academy of Sciences of Ukraine.

that the administration "should buy out Ostrog and Starokonstantinov from Karla Jabłonska and Countess Rzewucka."[12] When Count Lubomirski suggested exchanging his Dubno for a couple of villages, the enlightened Count Kiselev wrote on his petition that the government does not bargain and that Lubomirski should "sell the town—that's it"![13] Even as late as the 1870s, the Russian administration still urged "getting whatever possessions possible from Polish hands."[14]

Still, by the 1870s, Russia, with all its resolve, had managed to take from the Poles only fifty-six shtetls, if quite significant ones, out of 378 shtetls in Kiev, Podolia, and Volhynia provinces, and transfer forty to fifty shtetls to the Russian gentry. The Russian rulers took pains to remove the shtetls from the Polish magnates, yet, bound by the promises of Catherine to maintain gentry-protective laws, they limited their own initiative. The old system of state mercantilism and protectionism coexisted with the new unifying tendencies of the enlightened and well-managed state; to an extent, they neutralized one another. This loophole is precisely what allowed the shtetls to remain for the time being in their own element and in relative peace.

This peace lasted as long as the administration, caught in its own paradoxical attitude to the shtetls, did not start aggressively undermining the economic prosperity and social stability of the shtetls. Until about the mid-1830s, administrative control of the shtetls in the borderlands remained weak; the gentry were treated with condescending negligence; police supervision was relaxed. Despite strong orders, from the 1790s to the 1830s the shtetl remained the servant of two masters and more often than not existed in a vacuum of power, a unique situation that ordinary shtetl dwellers took advantage of immediately.

Although now on Russian territory, the shtetl continued to function as an old Polish entity. The Russian regime found this intolerable but for the time being unavoidable. The moment the Russian administration turned aggressively against the Poles in general and the shtetl owners in particular coincided with efforts at undermining the shtetl economy, forcibly integrating its Jews, and therefore breaking the spine of the shtetl.

Before this trend became dominant in the later years of Nicholas I, the relatively undisturbed shtetl saw better times. In the 1790s and early 1800s, even the Russian enlightened monarchs found this situation beneficial, especially when they initiated what we might call the great geographic discovery of the shtetl.

EXPLORING THE SHTETL

The first Russian discoverers of the shtetl really liked what they saw. Contrary to the contemporary Italian diplomats, English missionaries, or French painters touring East Europe on a quest for the East European noble savage, the first Russian discoverers of the shtetl were an anonymous, modest, and diligent group of clerks: cartographers.[15] Commissioned to survey, among many other things, what the shtetl was, they discovered what it did.

In 1797 the Kiev governor dispatched twelve clerks to various localities to prepare maps and plans, an indispensable tool of control and development. The cartographers had to collect the data that, as we have seen,

Polish town-owners were reluctant to provide.[16] To conceal their true goals, the Russian clerks were called variously "cartographers" or "topographers," although the information they amassed went far beyond routine territorial measurements. These twelve were the first, between 1797 and 1801, to travel through the newly acquired Russian lands, meticulously recording what they saw and later submitting their notes for further bureaucratic use.[17]

It is no exaggeration to say that these men were the first East European ethnographers of the shtetl. Unlike the professional ethnographers who came later, such as Pavlo Chubynskyi in the 1850s or S. Ansky in the 1910s, the cartographers of the 1790s focused on economic geography, not on folklore. And unlike the Western travelers of the time with their condescending approach to the alien and enigmatic European Orient, the Russian clerks treated what they saw with the empathy of collectors discovering for the first time what the Russian Empire had come to own, its new promised land.[18]

Their encounters with the new lands were as positive as unexpected. These Russian intelligence servicemen on a scholarly mission were struck by the abundant flora of central Ukraine with its oaks, hornbeams, maples, limes, ash trees, birches, alder trees, aspens, hazel groves, and vast fields of wheat, rye, beans, and oats. Used to dealing with scarce resources in Russian villages far to the northeast, they were surprised to discover the abundant cornucopia of Ukrainian orchards and gardens where not only the standard apples, pears, and carrots grew but also exotic apricots and peaches, mulberries, plums, cherries, nuts, currants, and strawberries.[19]

They explored the towns with their private Polish noblemen, noting robust bridges, many breweries, well-managed town councils, and fire stations.[20] If we read between the lines of their reports—overall dry, clumsily written, almost illegible—we can sense the authors' amazement. The unusual locales they visited combined urban and rural features, and beside architecturally urban buildings they found peasant homes whose inhabitants grew cherries, parsley, carrots, onions, garlic, beans, cucumbers, radishes, and cabbage.

These semi-urban, semirural settlements were the shtetls, the major discovery of the cartographers. They saw the busy "privileged fairs" in

1.2. The former house of the town leaseholder in Slavuta.
IA, f. 9, spr. 42, ark. 7. Courtesy of the Institute of Archaeology of the National Academy of Sciences of Ukraine.

Letichev; beautiful churches, shabby synagogues, and decent trading stalls in Chechenik, Brailov, and Balin; the town-owner's palace, two stone Eastern Orthodox churches, and a wooden synagogue in Zhinkov; the town-owner's castle, several Catholic and Eastern Orthodox churches, and a beautiful stone trading marketplace—"arcade"—in Medzhibozh. They noticed that the houses in the shtetl stood at a comfortable distance from one another—quite different from what we find in the popular etchings of Yudovin, who visited the same Medzhibozh a hundred years later, when this shtetl was already in complete decay.[21]

The shtetl impressed them because it was a predominantly Jewish enterprise. If anything was unique about it, it was because of what the Jews did there. The Russian petty clerks found Jews leasing mills, breweries, taverns, saltpeter factories, road check-posts, pastures, central square trading stalls, marketplace weights and measures, posts of trade and customs duties collectors, lots to build houses, fish ponds, forests—to the

1.3. A mill in Krasnopol, Volhynia.
IA, f. 9, spr. 40, ark. 12. Courtesy of the Institute of Archaeology of the National Academy of Sciences of Ukraine.

extent that they diligently recorded it all and wrote, "this is all leased by the Jews from the town owners." They also filled their lengthy rosters with lists of items and produce available in the shtetl markets, prefacing the lists with the heading "in these stores Jews sell"—as if there were nobody else trading in the shtetl marketplace.[22]

Not only did the cartographers accurately portray Jews as "merchants and townsfolk engaged in trade, middleman activities, and even more in distilling and tavernkeeping," they also emphasized Jewish craftsmanship, noticing that there were "among them craftsmen of quite impressive skills." One might be unsurprised and even question these first impressions of the Russians clerks visiting the shtetls in Volhynia and Podolia. But one cannot fail to notice their sheer astonishment, particularly when they remarked on religious tolerance in the shtetls, exclaiming that "Jews were allowed to worship in their houses and conduct all the necessary life rites."[23]

These Russian clerks likely never had seen Jews before, and the only conventional wisdom at the time was that the Jews had killed Christ and served the Polish gentry; one might wonder which of those crimes the clerks considered worse. Russian travelers normally expressed squeamishness toward Jews in the Polish lands, as for example the Russian academician Nicholas Ozertsovsky, who in 1783 observed, "Suddenly there appeared along the roads the yids' taverns, to be seen nowhere in Russia, and it became obvious that these lands are those of a different state."[24] In 1810, Count Dolgorukov also found these lands alien, dubbing them "a shred of Old Poland: yids trade and swarm everywhere, like bees in bee-hives."[25]

On the contrary, the anonymous cartographers spoke of the Jews as no different from other ethnicities, Poles or Armenians, and they referred to them predominantly with a capital "J," calling them Jews (*Evrei*), although once in a while they also slipped into the lowercase *yids* (*zhidy*). The Jews of these new lands were formidable in the eyes of the Russian clerical spies. Later in the nineteenth century the state clerks would become much less tolerant, even viciously xenophobic, and would switch in their unofficial parlance to the derogatory *yids* for the Jews, *liakhy* for the Poles, and *khokhly* for the Ukrainians.

We do not know how the imperial clerks read the reports of the cartographers. More important is how the cartographers wrote them. They described villages, landscapes, bridges, roads, and forests, but put unequivocal emphasis on the shtetls, *mestechki*. The shtetls in their eyes were worthy not only of being conquered by military force but also of being appropriated administratively and economically.

The discovery of the shtetls by the Russian cartographers late in the eighteenth century to early in the nineteenth century paved the way for a systematic study of the region by the Russian regime. Unlike the cartographers, Russian statesmen were much less fascinated by the Jewish-driven Polish economy in the shtetls, and yet they saw them as an economic competitor of the interior Russian trading cities and sought to either appropriate or ruin the shtetls.

Carrying out this task implied uprooting Jewish labor from Polish capital—or more simply, separating the Jews from the Poles. This pivotal goal inspired multiple Jewish reforms of Nicholas I in the 1820s to 1850s, but there was an effort to win over the Jews for the Russian cause even earlier than that. Why did the Russians think that they would always have problems with the Christian Polish noblemen yet perhaps be able to domesticate the religiously alien shtetl Jews? Because the shtetl Jews proved to be loyal Russian subjects long before they were ordered to do so by the empire and because the "loyalty of subjects to the ruler and the dynasty was a linchpin of the Russian empire," as the historian Andreas Kappeler instructs us.[26]

It was this Jewish attitude, juxtaposed with Russian paternalism, that delayed Russian reforms of the Jews and inspired new hopes for a rapprochement between the Russians and the Jews, a never fulfilled promise of an alternative Russian Jewish development that never took shape.

MOTHER RUSSIA

Although we know little about the feelings of the shtetl Jews toward the Russians during and immediately after the three Polish partitions, Hebrew documents of the time tell fascinating stories about Jews cursing the Poles and blessing the Russians.

Let's take a look at the Jews from such Podolia shtetls as Zhvanets, Zhinkovets, Karvasar, and Orynin: expelled from Kamenets-Podolsk in 1750 by the Polish king Augustus III, they settled in these nearby shtetls.[27] In 1797, Paul I of Russia retracted the previous ban, readmitted the Jews to Kamenets, and confirmed their residential privileges.[28] The shtetl Jews from nearby could then resettle in the previously inaccessible town. And one of them, Yaakov ben Hayym from Orynin (called in the records "Oryniner"), turned for help to the temporary military ruler of the town, Colonel Dementii Semenovich Meleshchenko. Yaakov Oryniner received from Meleshchenko a commission to rebuild the walls of the pompous Kamenets fortress, while Meleshchenko helped Oryniner erect a wall around the Jewish cemetery—thus making it fit for the rigorous funeral standards of the reestablished burial society.

Inspired by the cooperation of Russians and Jews, the Kamenets Burial Society scribe recorded this story, giving it a political message and a religious tinge. He probably conveyed the feelings of the entire local

1.4. The kiddush cup of Meir Karvisar (Karvasar, near Kamenets-Podolsk). *MIK, no. 258, Odessa collection. Courtesy of MIK and the Center for Jewish Art at Hebrew University, Jerusalem.*

Jewish community, which just two years after Paul I's decision numbered some 2,650 people, including twenty-nine guild merchants. Was this not a new redemption from Babylonian bondage, a new return to the Jerusalem of Podolia?

The scribe used metaphors from the book of Lamentations to depict Jewish suffering under Polish dominion and from the book of Esther to portray Jewish redemption under the Russian tsars.[29] The Poles embodied the evil biblical Amalekites, whereas the partitions of Poland turned out to be a salvific "fateful lot." Paul I was referred to as the "blessed one Pavel Petrovich" who "allowed what they did not allow," that is, brought Jews back to Kamenets.

The communal scribe attributed the merits of the late Catherine II to the living Paul I:

And the Jews were destined to come under the auspices of the mighty and great tsar of justice and mercy Pavel Petrovich, the tsar of Russia, may God exalt His Majesty, raise his kingdom to the heights, and increase his mercy toward our brethren, the Jews. And the kingdom announced that the tsar granted the Jews permission to return to the place of their previous residence and to dwell anywhere they find fit. And the previous power vanished like the mist.[30]

The scribe undeniably put forth the feeling that the community aspired to project. The burial society records left no doubt: the Russians were not only good in Jewish eyes, they were redeemers who conveyed the Jews from bondage to freedom, and their enemies became the enemies of the Jews. If anything, the communal record expresses the hopes of the Jews, a mistreated ethnic minority, for protection and benevolence from the new power. And benevolence and protection were precisely what they found!

Perhaps the hereditary monarchy of Russia with its absolute power appealed to the Jews more than the Polish magnate oligarchy with its elected kings and looser state structure. The Jews preferred Russia as long as this new power practiced its tolerance and extended its paternalism toward its new ethnicities. Perhaps because of this preference, just after the Polish partitions—not before—the leading Hasidic masters, leaders of the pietistic movement of religious enthusiasm, made their communal power transferable on a hereditary basis and established the longlasting Hasidic dynasties, the Jewish doubles of the Romanovs. The idea of an absolute ruler with enormous power and royal pomp seems to have inspired them much more than the opulence of the Polish magnates who failed to introduce absolutism and lost the political game.[31]

If this was an attempt of the Hasidim to imitate the Russian hereditary and dynastic tsarist power, with its royal luxury, bodyguards, orchestras, côterie, arrogant palatial courts, thousands of visitors, and material abundance, it speaks volumes about the Jewish perception of the Russian tsardom. The mother of the future famous Rizhiner (or Sadigora) tsadik, Israel of Ruzhin, tacitly agreed that her son, still a child, after her husband's death should take a silver cup in his hand, say a blessing over the wine for the *ganze mishpokhe*—the entire family—and become the master, the *rebbe*, and the leader of the generation, a *tsadik*.[32] Conscious of it or not, at that moment she made her son into a Judaic version of a young Russian tsar inheriting the scepter.

One doesn't imitate what one dislikes. Whatever the Jewish suspicions of the imperial authorities in the 1890s, in the 1790s Jews admired the Russian Empire, which had, as it were, liberated them from Polish bondage. They had no way of knowing that the Russian regime would seek to exploit, undermine, and criminalize Jewish economic endeavors. This would become clear only later.

Meanwhile, the rapidly changing political situation of the early nineteenth century enabled the Jews to demonstrate their genuine loyalty to the new power. The Jewish reaction to the Napoleonic invasion of Russia proved that the Jews were supporting the empire in deeds, not only in feeling. Most likely, Jewish leaders knew about the widely circulated December 1806 Appeal of the Russian Holy Synod, which associated Jews with Napoleon and was read aloud in all Russian parish churches.

The Holy Synod condemned Napoleon Bonaparte's plans to convene the Grand Sanhedrin and presented it as "the same godless institution which in its time conspicuously condemned Our God and the Savior Jesus Christ to the Cross." Napoleon, said the Appeal, intended to "unify the Jews, whom divine rage dispersed throughout the land," while the Jews, those alleged haters of Christ, were more than eager to "assist Napoleon in his infamy."[33]

In an effort to disassociate themselves from Napoleon in general and from his messianic pretentions in particular, Jewish communal leaders in Russia called for their congregants to extend full support to the Russian army, especially once Napoleon Bonaparte's troops defeated Austria and approached the Russian borders. Rabbis and rebbes unanimously condemned Napoleon's messianic aspirations and secularizing plans. They raised their voice against Napoleon to make a point: East European Jews did not share the revolutionary fervor of their West European brethren but did share the aversion of the Russians toward the evil French beast, Napoleon Bonaparte.

Rabbi Levy Isaac went from Berdichev to a meeting with Hasidic leaders in Warsaw at which they rejected Napoleon's plans of enforced emancipation, by no means befitting the traditional East Europeans, Christians and Jews included. Rabbi Nachman from Bratslav mocked Napoleonic plans as dangerous heresy that threatened the very existence of Judaic tradition. Schneour Zalman of Liady, the founder of the Habad movement, issued an eloquent appeal to the Jews in Lithuania and Belorussia: we Jews, he argued, should fully support the Russian military efforts against Napoleon (he paraphrased the 1806 Russian patriotic appeal) who had come to destroy Judaism. The Habad rebbe cursed Napoleon and crowned Alexander I with the wreath of hope as genuine protector of the Jewish people.

The Jews articulated their anti-Napoleonic feelings in folkloric narratives about great Hasidic leaders. As legend has it, Yaakov Isaac, the Seer of Lublin, claimed that if Napoleon had known about the Hasidic efforts to foil his plans, he would have led his cavalry against the Hasidic masters and not against the armies of his political adversaries.

They also told a story of Napoleon coming for a blessing to the renowned Israel ben Shaptai Hapshtein, called the Preacher (or the Maggid) of Kożienice. Napoleon came on Purim of 1812, and appeared at the threshold of the synagogue when the maggid was reading aloud the Scroll of Esther and had reached the verse *napol tipol le-fanav*, "you will definitely fall before him," the warning of Haman's wife to her husband.[34] In this *napol* the preacher heard a prophecy of *Napol*eon's fall, which he did not hesitate to convey to his preeminent guest, refusing to give him a blessing.[35] This story could, of course, be a legend, ex post facto presenting the Hasidic master as a prophet, after the fall of Napoleon. Still, it projected the prescriptive meanings of those who composed it: reject the enforced Napoleonic secularization, stick to traditional Judaic values, and love Mother Russia.

The deeds of ordinary Jews also proved Jewish allegiance to the Russian cause. Although free from the burden of conscription, the Jews still found various ways to contribute to the victory of the Russian troops. Wealthy purveyors helped provide the army with food and donated large sums to the military; traveling merchants informed Russian commanders about the treatment of the French troops by the local populations in Austria, Prussia, and Poland; several Jews, such as Usher Zholkver from Dubno, travelled back and forth across the border on reconnaissance missions.[36]

One shtetl Jew informed a regimental commander about the French general Corsin sojourning at a Polish landlord's palace—and the Russian army unit took the general by surprise.[37] According to the informers of the Russian police, on the eve of the 1812 campaign the Jews established an extra fast to impress the Almighty and pray for the success of the Russian troops.[38]

These deeds challenged the anti-Jewish bias of many a Russian statesman. To the Russian regime, Jews were no better than Poles—suspicious religious aliens and exploiters of the Eastern Orthodox peasantry in the imperial western borderlands. To Russian officials, Poles were stereotypically unreliable, unpatriotic, hypocritical, irrational, politically unsavvy, rebellious, ungrateful, arrogant, conceited, and treacherous. Throughout the nineteenth century, imperial legislation discriminated against the Poles, prevented their social mobility, forced their petty gentry (unlike Eastern Orthodox gentry) to serve in the Russian army, segregated them in terms of upward mobility in whatever state institutions possible, adamantly insisted on the Eastern Orthodox and not Catholic education of Polish children of mixed marriages, and even relocated Poles from the western to the central parts of the Russian Empire to accelerate their russification.[39]

Unlike the reliable and patriotic Jews, the Polish gentry in the shtetls of the Pale of Settlement unnerved the Russian authorities, triggered their anxiety, and kept them constantly on the alert.[40] In the wake of the war against Napoleon, French plans to recruit Poles and a Polish ongoing supply of food to the French army added fuel to the fire. Early in 1812, Russian governors of the borderland provinces panicked when they realized that Austria could enter the war on the French side, that Polish officers could defect, and that several Polish landlords had already joined the French troops. "Volhynia is a big wooden house on the edge of town," said one of the Russian officials. "If the wind blows from the side of the house, the town can be burnt to the ground."[41] This of course was a metaphor for the latent Polish rebellion and the Napoleonic invasion.

Because they formed an economic nexus, Jews and Poles dwelling in the shtetls found themselves under close surveillance. "Military reasons necessitate paying attention to the opinions of the gentry and townsfolk," argued the war minister. We should compose two lists, echoed the minister of police, one for those considered "dubious" and another for the "definitely suspicious," and dispatch the lists to Grodno, Minsk, Volhynia, Podolia, and Kiev provinces.

These lists identified more than a hundred "highly suspicious" magnates and rank-and-file gentry: Count Chotkiewicz from Dubno, Count Jabłonowski from Ostrog, the landlords Rzyszewski and Tarnawski from Kremenets, the noblemen Kniaziewicz from Rovno, and Teodor Korzeniowski (Joseph Conrad's grandfather) from Zhitomir. The Police Ministry added Polish ladies to this impressive list, since they were "haters of everything Russian"; all those who corresponded with Poland and France; Catholic clergy; former owners of confiscated estates; and the "Radziwiłłs of all sorts."[42] Surprisingly, the Russian secret police used very different language for the Jewish dwellers of the same shtetls owned by these Polish noblemen.

Officers at all levels reported acts of Jewish patriotic behavior. One officer mentioned in his memoirs the "courage of the cowardly Jews, who despite the unclear outcome of the campaign dared accomplish a dangerous deed, caught the messenger and brought him to the Russian detachment—a brave and noteworthy act."[43] "Jewish people have demonstrated particular loyalty to Russia," a secret informer reported from Volhynia to the Ministry of Police; "they do not want any change of regime." Several shtetl Jews hurried to inform the Russian authorities of Polish gentry hiding French transports, thus proving how Jews "loved the Russian government."[44]

The Russian regime faced a dilemma: Poles were Christians but Catholics, hence unreliable; Jews were the offspring of Judas but proved loyal. If so, the Jews should be empowered. The minister of police realized that perhaps he could use the Jews to establish a network of reliable informers. "Due to their attested loyalty," he argued, "[we should] use their representatives to investigate the way of life and behavior of the gentry and peasantry." To keep things secret, Jews would take a special oath befitting their religious rituals. A month into the war against Napoleon, he formally advised using Jews for secret reconnaissance.[45]

This was a major breakthrough: for the time being, and only for the time being, Russians took expressions of Jewish commitment at face value and singled out Jews as patriotic, loyal, and reliable. The Russian tsar

Alexander I, participant in the campaign, spoke about the services the Jews provided to the Russian army and emphatically stated that the Jews "demonstrated amazing loyalty."[46]

Nicholas I, not a great lover of Jews and Poles, made this point particularly clear, comparing and contrasting Poles and Jews: "The gentry in Belorussia, almost entirely composed of wealthy Poles, showed no loyalty toward Russia, and, except for a few Vitebsk and south Mogilev landlords, everybody else swore an oath to Napoleon." At the same time, the Jews, although they were "exploiters of the poor," had surprised Nicholas, because they "in 1812 were particularly loyal to us and even helped us, wherever they could, by risking their own lives."[47]

Much later, in the 1820s, this patriotic fervor of the Jews led the Russian authorities to think that Jews would "move toward useful occupations," "submit themselves to the civil laws," and "defend the motherland." It was Nicholas I's hope that the loyal and reliable Jews could and should be integrated into the state, and not his alleged antisemitism, that caused him to start drafting them into the army, long before he allowed the allegedly untrustworthy Poles to join the conscription pool.[48]

Once the Jewish shtetl dwellers found themselves under Russian rule, their loyalties belonged to the empire, which, they hoped, would take them under its protective aegis. Of course, not everybody would write a personal letter of gratitude to the emperor, as Rabbi David Gertsenshtein from Shargorod did in 1798, and not everybody would be able to donate oxen to the Russian army during the Polish rebellion, as Aizik Rabinovich from Kamenets did in 1830.[49] But many, especially members of trading elites, would join a certain Girshberg from Uman, who, persecuted by Count Potocki for financial reasons, wrote to St. Petersburg that he was a guild merchant and "pleaded for protection."[50] Perhaps not without some exaggeration of the Jewish aversion toward the Poles and empathy toward the Russians, Yisroel Aksenfeld (himself a writer and an army purveyor) observed that Polish aristocrats were arrogant; they cursed the Jews and regularly humiliated them. But the Russian aristocrats were "quite a different breed." They were never arrogant; they treated the Jew as their little brothers and got "to love him" if Jews served them loyally. This literary image might not be historically accurate but it does convey the feelings that many Jews shared in the 1820s or 1830s.[51]

These feelings inspired the rising Russian Jewish patriotism. Take, for example, Berdichev Jews, who celebrated Nicholas I's saint's day in 1834. Local *sheyne yidn*, wealthy merchants, purveyors, leaseholders, kahal elders, and bankers, invited a Bohemian orchestra to accompany the outdoor ceremony and later a festival dinner by the Radziwiłłs. They illuminated the entire Great Prayer House and the Choral synagogue with gas lamps. A huge poster displaying his majesty's monogram adorned the Great Synagogue. About eight thousand people, mostly Jews, both men and women, gathered in the center of the town. Merchants of the first and second guilds, the town police chief, and two governors, Levashov of Kiev province and Rimsky-Korsakov of Volhynia, joined them. According to the sympathetic report of policeman Zabelin, they all recited "a prayer for the health and long life of the Emperor, His Wife the Empress and their heirs, and also for the wellbeing of the authorities of their land," according to Jewish custom. After the prayer the crowd shouted "hurrah" and "long live our emperor Nicholas I"—three times, no less.[52]

It was precisely this Jewish political reliability that pushed the Russian authorities to allow Jews to lease a strategically crucial state business, the mail service. Jews were in charge of the post offices all along the muddy roads between Kiev, Zhitomir, Rovno, and Brody. They fed and changed horses, dispatched messengers, provided transport wagons, and accommodated state officials and couriers. Andrei Glagolev called the road from Kiev to Radzivilov "a Jewish operational line," which had "only Jewish post offices."[53]

The Chernigov commercial counselor Nikolai Lazarev, an Eastern Orthodox, and Beltsy merchant Pesakh Libman, a Jew, leased post offices in Vasilkov and Lipovets districts: their horses were always ready to go, as police reports testified.[54] Jews were allowed to make bids for the lease of post offices even after the lottery was over, as for example happened with Temkin and Kleinerman from Kiev province in 1826.[55] This was politically savvy and economically advantageous—and put the Jews in regular contact with state officials, a key factor in the Russian state-surveyed economy.

Not only did Russia legalize the Jews and empower them economically, it also empowered them administratively. Representatives of Jewish mercantile elites, particularly those able to express themselves in languages other than Yiddish, were encouraged to become *ratmans*, members of the city councils.[56] This prospect seemed to have great promise, but the Jews had to make concessions.

The governor general insisted that elected Jews shave their beards, like Russian state bureaucrats, and remove their traditional Jewish kaftan and wear Polish or Russian dress, if they were uncomfortable with the German dress.[57] Whether this was enforced or not, Jews joined the state service as town council scribes, translators, heads of the economic and army quarters' commissions, and even as those responsible for the town police.

State service was a key opportunity for the Jewish and Christian local elites to master religious and cultural tolerance. In 1796, Itsko Abramovich, elected to the Volhynia provincial council, observed the local priest sprinkling holy water and sanctifying the new governmental building. He and his German colleague Samuel Gottlieb Wuttke spent time together studying state legislation, comparing translations of legal documents from Polish to Russian and training themselves to sign their names in Russian.[58] Berko Rabinovich, the third-guild merchant, felt so secure as a member of the Zvenigorodka town council that he did not hesitate to publicly scold his colleagues for sleazy dealings.[59] The entry of Jews into the Russian state service signaled a crucial moment of trust. In addition, Jewish elites could not have missed that Poland refused them any representation before the state, whereas Russia allowed the institution of communal representatives, the deputies.[60] However, this empowering of the Jews did not last long.

A BREACH OF TRUST

Russian confidence in the political reliability of the Jews and Jewish support of the Russian cause were filled with the promise of an emerging rapprochement. The associations of Jews with the French Revolution and its catastrophic upheavals, with the Napoleonic short-lived Sanhedrin and liberalism, the satanic threat to the foundations of the Eastern Orthodoxy, and other propaganda metaphors of the Napoleonic wars, were by and large dropped or marginalized. Although the idea of creating a network of Jewish secret service informers in the Pale of Settlement and across the border spying for Mother Russia never crystallized, the official attitude well up to mid-century was that Jews could be useful, useless, or economically harmful, yet they were loyal to the Russian Empire.

From the 1790s through the 1830s, Russian authorities treated the Jews as trustworthy state clerks. This was no longer the case at the height of Nicholas I's reign with its new governmentally inspired nationalism, when Russian became the official nationality, Eastern Orthodoxy the best among religions, and the Russian people the pillar of the state. Loyalty came to be viewed as a desire to join this religiously defined nationality. Being Eastern Orthodox came to signify being loyal. A Jew in state service became nonsensical. The Poles in the western borderlands had been and remained unreliable, particularly after the 1830 rebellion, when Russian administration sequestered more than a thousand Polish estates, belonging to the Polish rebels in Ukraine, into the state treasury.[61] To disassociate the Jews from the untrustworthy Poles, the Russian regime launched a series of forceful reforms aimed at Jewish integration, without, however, the previous presumption of trust.

Whatever their diplomas—and some of them were certified medical doctors with Austrian degrees—these Jews were now laid off, just for being "of Mosaic persuasion." The Zaslav doctor Grinberg and the Novograd-Volynsk doctor Rautenberg, seven magistrates of Kamenets-Podolsk, six from Proskurov, four in Letichev, three in Litin, four in Bratslav and Gaisin, six in Balta, three in Yampol, four in Mogilev and in Bar—all lost their positions with the town councils.[62] This was the beginning of the end of Russia's tolerance toward peoples of non-Eastern Orthodox creed.

Once the enlightened considerations of Catherine II ceded to the rising Russian nationalism during the late years of Nicholas I, Russia's previously benevolent treatment of the peoples in the borderlands came to naught. By the end of the nineteenth century not only the Jews, but also the Catholic Poles and even the Eastern Orthodox Ukrainians had become aliens. Of course, it would take a tumultuous half century for Russia to start singling out Jews and blaming them for the shortcomings of

Russia's modernization. And it would take a consistent merging between the ruling elites and far rightist circles for the Jews to appear as Russia's aliens, exploiters of the peasantry, subversive revolutionary elements, and Russia's traitors in World War I. By the end of the nineteenth century the Russian regime had disowned its loyal Jews.

Once the conservative ideology prevailed over economic interests and common sense, the Russian authorities blamed the Jews in the shtetls for mistreating and ruining the peasants. Shattered at the end of the century by internal social conflicts, the regime saw the Jew as a useful scapegoat accountable for all the doubts about the reform of the peasantry and declared the Jews exploiters and bloodsuckers.[63] In 1882, several hundred shtetls were reclassified as villages just to get rid of the shtetl Jews, who were no longer allowed to reside in rural and semirural areas.

Seeking a new place of residence, Jews had to move to bigger towns and cities. This is precisely what happens to Sholem Aleichem's Tevye, who must sell his hut, part with his cow, load a wagon with his scanty belongings, and move elsewhere. It was this Russian modernization, peppered with state-supported xenophobia, that transformed the shtetl into an impoverished godforsaken village. And it was Russian state nationalism that breached the trust between the state and its Jews, adopted racial discourse, and turned the Jews into disloyal aliens, no longer protected by the state.

In the late nineteenth century the Russian shtetl came to signify provincialism, timidity and stupidity, ghettoization, uncivilized manners, a coarse accent, pedestrian thoughts, and bad taste, with the Jews possessing all these qualities. By that time the era of Catherine's paternalistic benevolence was long gone. But the shtetl had known very different times, and merits a very different attitude from those who saw it at its height.

IN RUSSIAN EYES

The bustling shtetls both fascinated and offended Russian travelers, who came to the Pale of Settlement from the much slower and parsimonious provinces of interior Russia. Their scornful remarks revealed not only cultural resentment but also genuine sympathy.

If the shtetl of the later Yiddish writers was about the dearth of opportunities, economic decline, and a stiffly ghettoized atmosphere, the early nineteenth-century Russian observers, not particularly unbiased, emphasized the beauty and abundance of the shtetl. In Uman, wrote Count Ivan Dolgorukov, you can find "anything you want." And in Zlatopolie, he remarked on the trading stalls where Jews "trade in anything one can think of." He could not help admiring "the extensive trade ... in various luxurious commodities" he found there.[64]

Olimpiada Shishkina, a member of the Russian nobility, travelled from St. Petersburg through Kiev to the Crimea and passed through a number of shtetls. In Belaia Tserkov (literally White Church; the town was known in Jewish memory as *Sde Lavan*, White Plains, or *Shvartse Tume*, Black Impurity) she saw the annual fairs where nobody seemed to be trading but Jews: "Stores here are made of stone and two-storied. Jews trade in

1.5. Trading stalls (arcade) in Slavuta.
IA, f. 9, spr. 42, ark. 5. Courtesy of the Institute of Archaeology of the National Academy of Sciences of Ukraine.

them, and one can get many quality and inexpensive goods there, but one has to be cautious, especially while choosing textiles."[65]

Alexander Muraviev, a Russian officer, mason, and mystic who had been commissioned to do a topographic description of Volhynia, portrayed Berdichev as a "big trading townlet overflowing with Jews, who control not only local, but most of the southern trade."[66] Alexander Butenev from the Ministry of the Interior seconded him, describing the shtetl in the 1810s as a "dirty townlet with wooden houses and apparently poor yet very industrious Jews."[67] The army statisticians from the Russian War Ministry surveyed the shtetls in Podolia and reported that Jews engaged in tavernkeeping and liquor brewing and were engaged in "glorious trade."[68]

Jewish women were hardly secondary in their entrepreneurship to male Jews: Józef Ignacy Kraszewski, the Polish romantic writer and talented painter, found many colorful words to describe them: "Nearby industrious Jewesses sit in their little stores, aloof from the crowds of people, and with their shrieks and yells they call people in, tempt them, beg, pull in, quarrel, bargain, even fight—with astonishing multitasking astuteness and unappreciated talent."[69]

We might appreciate the opinion of the Decembrist Rozen from the Life Guard regiment, by no means a great friend of the Jewish people. Rozen traveled through the shtetls and noticed unparalleled Jewish vigor: "The middle estate—merchants, artisans, tavernkeepers—included numerous masses of trading Yids, tirelessly active. During my constant travels and transfers, neither in the daytime nor at night have I seen a sleeping Yid."[70]

And although some later travelers, as if copying one another, mentioned the dirt, stench, and poverty of the shtetls connecting these unpleasant features to the swarms of Jews, others, much more independent in their observations, described the shtetl as a decent place. A Christian missionary and biblicist from Scotland, Ebenezer Henderson, liked good looks testifying to good well-being of the Jews in Dubno, noticed that their Great Synagogue resembled the Meeting House of the Church of Scotland, and admired the landscapes of Podolia, which he compared to Devonshire.[71] Officer Alexander Muraviev loved the Podolia and Volhynia shtetls, particularly Medzhibozh and Uman, whereas Nikolai Basargin, one of the Russian officers serving in the 1820s in Ukraine, remarked on the shtetl's homey feeling, its beauty, its visual attractiveness. "At the end of May," he wrote, "my wife and I traveled to Tulchin. We passed through Belaia Tserkov, Skvira, Letichev, Nemirov, and Bratslav. Podolia province looked like a gorgeous orchard. Wonderful land, fantastic climate. Beautiful places. Willy-nilly you get amazed and start thinking: it is here that you would like to live. I particularly liked Nemirov, a nice clean townlet, with its own special freshness."[72]

This was the pleasant, vigorous, and abundant shtetl at the zenith of its provincial glory and hopes for a happy future. It was too abundant, vigorous, and independent for the Russian regime to reconcile with. In the next chapter we enter the shtetl and explore how the Russian authorities sought to dislocate one of the driving mechanisms of its prosperity, its international trade.

CHAPTER TWO

LAWLESS FREEDOM

atherine the Great spoke fluent French, corresponded with Voltaire, and adored the Enlightenment, but abhorred the French Revolution.[1] Although she introduced free trade in 1792, she also ordered a total ban on importing French goods into Russia. Born Sophie Friederike Auguste von Anhalt-Zerbst-Dornburg to the family of a Prussian prince, Catherine had not only political reasons to dislike France. The Russian empress shared the mercantilist conviction that her country should develop its own industries, produce locally, aggressively export, and not kowtow to the European West.[2] In the case of revolutionary France, however, her economic ambitions and political preferences harmoniously merged.

Catherine used the language of reason, order, peace, and stability. She did not want her subjects to purchase French merchandise and thus provide the French Revolution with financial support. Anything "made in France" would corrupt what Catherine called pristine and subservient

Christian souls. Instead of importing, her subjects should instead develop their own crafts and trades.

Catherine pretended to be an enlightened tsarina seeking to establish well-managed border control. Her plan to integrate her new territories, enhance free trade, and nurture local stability seemed a reasonable one. But when she sought to undermine the Girondists and Jacobins, manufacturers and exporters of the French Revolution, her rational aura dissipated. Her regulations had a direct side effect: instead of international trade, Russia got contraband. Legitimate Jewish merchants now found themselves among smugglers. By fighting contraband, the Russian regime threatened to break the backbone of the shtetl economy. The persecution of smugglers took the form of anti-Jewish regulations. The shtetl, however, would not surrender so easily.

WELL-MANAGED TRADE

Catherine gave strict instructions to her statesmen: establish new western borders, open new customs houses in Yampol, Zhvanets, Radzivilov, Vladimir-Volynsk, and Gusiatin, introduce customs control, impose duties, and ban certain foreign goods from Russia's trade.[3]

The goal was twofold: in addition to the radical French, there were the subversive Poles to be thwarted. The empress intended to put down the Polish landlords who welcomed the French upheavals, sought to spark the flame of rebellion, and dreamed of an independent Poland. An intrigue-plotter of the highest caliber, Catherine imagined that once she stripped the Polish landlords of the symbols of prestige, she could neutralize them. Of course, this course of action would be a huge blow to Jewish cross-border trade.

Catherine's hidden agenda manifested itself in the items she banned unconditionally. Above all, she forbade the import of luxury goods: necklaces, gold or silver earrings, signets, rings, fans, French wines, cognac and champagne, snuffboxes and pipes, buttons, gold and silver belt buckles, and gold or silver watches and chains. These items were important for Poles as consumers, but also for Jews as purveyors.

A ban on articles of craftsmanship would contribute to the development of local manufacturing, insisted Catherine. Therefore she outlawed the import of key trinkets, iron objects such as weapons, cannons, wires, anchors, and door locks, and also hand mills, copper goods, and tableware. The tsarina envisioned her subjects building up the local economy, not wasting their time on entertainments. So she banned mirrors, gold decorations, toys, chess sets, wooden cabinets, chariots, leather and leather goods, fancy short boots, bone and silver combs, brushes, candies, and sugar toys—the articles we find regularly among the merchandise Jews brought to East Europe.

A tsarina who switched lovers with impressive frequency, Catherine had strong convictions regarding family life. Women, thought Catherine, must take good care of their families. Fashion was dangerous, subversive,

2.1. A Jewess wearing a shterntikhl, a head covering for festive occasions, eastern Galicia, 19th century.
Watercolor by J. Głogowski. BHT 87.122.5. Courtesy of LNB and the Beit Hatfutsot exhibition "Treasures of Jewish Galicia—Judaica from the Museum of Ethnography in Lviv, Ukraine," Photo Archive, Tel Aviv.

and Western. On the list of forbidden goods she included clothes made of batiste, colored striped ribbons, sleeves and lace, lipstick, powder, gloves, shoelaces, silk and velvet goods, scarves, cashmere, and dolls. Finally, argued the tsarina, her subjects did not need to read and write. Rather, they should engage in manual labor. Hence she banned the import of paper, planners, and notebooks.[4] Many of these articles appeared in the ledgers of Jewish merchants.

Now the Commission on Commerce had to translate Catherine's instructions into state legislation. In 1794, the members of the commission celebrated the shift of state borders further west as the result of the two partitions of Poland in 1772 and 1793. In view of the imminent third partition, which would occur only a year later, they considered the establishment of customs duties and foreign trade limitations a particularly urgent matter. They set duties on imports in the range of 12–30 percent of the price of the merchandise—seven times higher than the duties on export.[5]

The commission included the highest Russian state bureaucrats. Senator Gavriil Derzhavin, Russia's greatest poet at the time, an influential statesman and the head of the commission, analyzed the current border control issues. Although there was no love lost between Derzhavin and the Jews, he commended the facilitators of international trade—the merchants trading actively with Leipzig, Dresden, Frankfurt, Breslau, Poznan, Gdansk (Danzig), Warsaw, Brody, and Trieste.[6] He noted in passing that these were "Jews and foreign merchants." He did not mention, however, that the "foreign merchants" were also Jewish.

An astute courtier, Derzhavin did not dare contradict the tsarina. Yet he meant no economic harm. He understood that a ban on some goods would trigger inflation and would not change the poor quality of analogous Russian products. He preached caution. Let the merchants pay a minimal customs duty in Russia since they had already paid duties crossing into Poland, he advised.[7] However, once those new regulations reached Volhynia and Podolia, the shtetl Jews destroyed the good intentions of Catherine and Derzhavin. They knew well what the authorities seemed to ignore: that protective policies would put an end to trade.

THE BORDERLAND VERSION OF THE IMPERIAL ORDER

General Timofei Tutolmin, the governor of Minsk, Bratslav, Volhynia, and Podolia provinces, ruled over Russia's new borderland, a region that today consists of half of Belarus and one-third of Ukraine. Tutolmin gained renown for his not always productive divide-and-rule style. He translated Derzhavin's caution into decisive statements. He ordered the relabeling of all merchandise already labeled and put on sale, the restamping of all foreign goods, and the collecting of duties regardless of the goods' provenance. Stores should be closed and trade banned until the merchants paid their duties. Tutolmin established customhouses along the border and imposed strict control over trade. Local governors enforced his undertakings. For example, the Podolia provincial governor general Alexander Bekleshov ordered special passports issued for crossing the border in order to monitor traffic and make sure everybody came back.[8]

These actions provoked confusion. As customs inspectors reported, traders in the lands recently attached to Russia were familiar neither with the border regulations nor with the Russian language. Most merchants spoke Yiddish and Polish and could not understand what the authorities were up to. The local clerks did not make even the slightest effort to clarify the new rules. Instead, they took advantage of the situation in the most outrageous manner. Since the state allowed gentry and officials to lease out customhouses, local bureaucrats established duties according to their whim and began taxing not only the allegedly dangerous French goods but also the most innocuous items.

The local clerks rejoiced once they inspected the marketplaces and found virtually no goods stamped by customhouses. The customs officers made Jewish merchants pay special taxes on kitchen knives, candlesticks, watch chains, snuffboxes, copper coffee mills, and many other articles. Nobody could object: only customs officers had the lists of taxable items, and they interpreted these lists as they saw fit. Jews perceived the unexpected customs duties as an imposition and the new laws as a blow against them. Take, for example, a Zlatopolie Jewish merchant who reported 31,628 rubles' worth of goods brought from Austria: he had to pay an exorbitant

8,386 rubles to the treasury (27 percent) if he wanted to keep his merchandise from being confiscated![9]

Even if some Jewish traders had to pay heavy duties on what they had imported before, they were luckier than those merchants who traded in goods now banned from import. Those traders—Armenians, Poles, Germans, and Jews among them—received orders to take their goods back to Austria or Prussia.[10] In 1798 the customs clerks forced three Jews from Berdichev to dispose of goods such as crêpe fabric, women's gloves, fans, silk and satin ribbons, and leather-bound diaries. A Jew from Vladimir-Volynsk went across the border to sell his fans, knives, mirrors, and folding combs. Another Vladimir-Volynsk Jew had to do the same with his Dutch calico, sailcloth, and muslin. Jews from Starokonstantinov, Radzivilov, and Dubno had similar items—as well as brushes, Turkish tobacco clay pipes, pins, scissors, and women's combs. They all had to take their merchandise across the border and sell it, losing even the small margin of profit, characteristic of Jewish trade, they were planning to make. For international traders with years of experience, this was devastating; they had no intention of following the orders.

Meanwhile, the state clerks misled the Chamber of Commerce, reassuring it that everything had been shipped out of Russia, while this was hardly so. Some Jews bribed the customs officers in order to get away with the goods. Others paid them off in goods. Although Russian clerks and Jewish merchants did their best to leave behind no evidence of their under-the-table agreements, it is very likely that late in the 1790s most of these hand mills, ribbons, calico, and mirrors found their way to the cabinet drawers, closets, and kitchens of the shtetl dwellers—Polish gentry, Jewish, and Eastern Orthodox included. Alexander Gertsen, nineteenth-century Russia's greatest émigré liberal, once observed that it would have been impossible to do anything in Russia had the bureaucrats not accepted bribes. Half a century before Gertsen's famous comment, Jewish traders, if they wanted to remain in business, had to master how, when, and whose palms to grease.

Russian administrators were prone to being bribed. Financial reports sent to St. Petersburg suggest that customs officers, police, and governmental inspectors overtaxed Jewish merchants more often to enrich themselves than to recompense the treasury. By 1798, clerks had finished stamping the revolving merchandise: the treasury should have received hundreds of thousands if not millions of rubles. However, in reality it obtained the ridiculously small sum of about 775 rubles from Kiev province, 782 rubles from Podolia, and 4,300 rubles from Volhynia.[11] It is easy to conclude that the difference between what the Jews paid and what the treasury received ended up in the pockets of local bureaucrats. Russian administrators grew to appreciate their new prey, the Jewish traders. They took for granted the idea that Jewish trade was a necessary evil, one that among other things lavishly fed their families.

In turn, Jewish traders did not care when the border separating Poland from Russia moved farther west—to Austrian Galicia and Bukovina at the foot of the Carpathian Mountains. They doubted that this would have much impact on what they had been successfully doing for centuries. They began worrying only when new customs duties threatened to disrupt major trading routes between Paris, Leipzig, Brody, and Berdichev.

Jews heavily depended on this route, for they crossed the border between Russia and Austria more often than anyone else. In the fall of 1796, for example, more Austrian Jewish merchants than any other ethnic minority traders passed through the border shtetl of Gusiatin into Russia. Several Jews reported going to Ostrog or to Korets on business, and the guild merchant Berman went to Starokonstantinov to sell salt, yet most Jewish merchants headed to Berdichev to sell textiles. Reports from one of the biggest customhouses in Grodno showed a similar pattern: Jews from Minsk were dominant among the international traders.[12]

The picture was the same for those crossing from Russia into Austria. Among those traveling abroad through Radzivilov customs were Russian state clerks and Polish landlords, yet most were Jewish merchants from Tulchin, Dubno, Zaslav, Bershad, Karlin, and Nezhin going on business to Prussia or Austria. In one month, 366 travelers on 620 horses moved into Russia, bringing in 245 wagonloads of merchandise, and 143 travelers on 198 horses moved out of the country with 66 wagons.[13] The merchandise was Russian, Prussian, Austrian, and French. The merchants were predominantly Jews. The horses were nomadic cosmopolitans.

Once Russia had swallowed eastern and central Poland, the respectable Jewish occupation of trade turned into illegal activity. The 1794 Polish rebellion against Russia exacerbated the situation. Revolutionary France supported rebellious Poland, marring international trade politically. Now Russian clerks grew suspicious of any merchandise brought from abroad. Border control became increasingly tight and arbitrary. Hundreds of Jewish families faced bankruptcy. However, Jews did not consider stopping cross-border trade or ending what they had been doing for centuries. Their only question was how to conduct business under the new conditions and how to persevere in what they had been doing so far.

HUNTING CONTRABAND

While the regime sought to establish well-regulated border control, local clerks expected to derive immediate financial benefit from this control. Contraband gave them a constant, practically inexhaustible source of income. They should not be blamed: even if they intended to, they could not investigate each and every case of smuggling simply for lack of qualified personnel.[14]

Underpaid, understaffed, undertrained, and lacking experience in civil responsibility, Russian clerks considered customhouses a private venture. Money, they reckoned, would appear as soon as they put anyone engaged in cross-border trading under suspicion. Customs clerks could interpret the register of forbidden goods according to their rank, social condition, and financial need. For the low-ranking semiliterate staff, cross-border Jewish traders earned too much in comparison with the Christian servants of the crown, and hence were shameless infidels.

But some of them were not smugglers. Take Iukhim and Wolf Berenshtein from Brody, wealthy, respectable, well-connected merchants. They carried letters from the Austrian emperor, valid bills of exchange, and account books, and could prove the legality of their business to the harshest clerk. Yet their credentials could not save their shipments from confiscation. Customs officers took the legally purchased and diligently stamped sable furs, a famous Russian item of export. The Berenshteins had to appeal to Vienna in order to redeem their merchandise, falsely labeled contraband. The incident so irritated them that they made up their minds to curtail their trade with Russia.[15] Between the 1790s and the 1810s dozens of respectable Jewish merchants followed their example by leaving Russia for good.

The shtetl was left to suffer, yet overall the situation changed little: Jews persisted in bringing to Russia what they had previously brought to Poland. Customs clerks unbendingly filled their books with lists of heavily taxed or confiscated goods. Found in their books were lengthy lists that included colored calico, green men's gloves, velvet and silk ribbons, white cotton and silk stockings, bolts of multicolored muslin, demi-cotton and velveteen fabric, large quantities of sashes, kerchiefs, and nightcaps, short fur coats, Saxon and Dutch cloth, and many other types of textiles and contemporary clothes.

However, the difference between the prepartitioned times and the 1790s was critical. Ten years earlier, such a respected and very wealthy first-guild merchant as Leib Berkovich would have brought his items directly across the border to the markets in Volhynia. But in 1799 he did not want to pay inflated duties, and had all his merchandise, 4,500 rubles' worth, smuggled in and hidden in the village of Ianchitsy. Indeed, the customs clerks discovered the merchandise, confiscated it, and sent it to a district court.[16]

Within a couple of years, however, the customs officers realized that merely confiscating goods was counterproductive. What to do with the stock? Should they employ the same Jews, owners of the merchandise, to sell precisely those confiscated goods? Instead, the local clerks believed it would be more productive to have Jews pay ransoms or bribe them for permission to bring both what was allowed and what was prohibited into the country.

Jews eagerly accepted this tacit proposal: the customers could not wait. Benia Maiorkovich, a tycoon from Kamenets with an international reputation, brought four wagons with an impressive 25,000 golden rubles' worth of goods from Leipzig to Berdichev. In Proskurov, his two wagons were intercepted, allegedly for contraband. Although Maiorkovich had all his goods properly stamped and the duties paid, he had to pay the local chief of police 2,000 rubles in cash and several hundred rubles' worth of goods—yet he, now an officially sheltered contrabandist, could move on.[17]

Jews like Ios Rapoport from Korets, who did not want to pay, got stuck. Ios had bought thirty mirrors from Brodetskii, a Jew from Berdichev, but a customs clerk confiscated his stock as foreign contraband. Rapoport then turned to the district court to summon Brodetskii, who testified that the merchandise had been purchased locally and from him.[18] We may ask why Rapoport did not bribe those who had detained him in the first place. Perhaps some Jewish merchants were not ready to pay bribes and relied on common sense. They expected nothing but legality from the enlightened Russian bureaucrats who had replaced the arbitrary Polish magnates.

This false expectation cost them dearly. In 1827 the Boguslav merchants Arie Leib Loktev, Iankel Aron Rapoport, and Haim Iampolsky, trading at the Praiseworthy fair in Kherson, did not realize that a modest but timely token of appreciation paid to a Kiev police inspector would have saved bolts of their demi-cotton calico worth 264 silver rubles, which they had brought all the way from Podolia province for sale. Thus they had to bail themselves out while their merchandise was confiscated.[19]

The fate of Moshko Litvak, Benyamin Katskoen, Mikhal Morgernshtern, and Haim Shor, all dwellers of Satanov, was similar. They smuggled across the border huge amounts of cloth—5,847 bolts worth about 26,322 rubles—and managed to safely cross the border and store the cloth in the Tarnorud Jewish houses, but were arrested when a Jewish informer disclosed their hiding place to the authorities. Unable to pay a fine of 424,584 rubles and unwilling to bribe the clerks, they ran away—as far as Odessa and Belaia Tserkov, five hundred miles from the Austrian border.[20] A cross-border merchant had either to practice extraordinary prudence or else let the state clerks in some way join their business.

Jewish merchants chose to share the spoils of contraband with the Russian clerks and the late 1790s marked the beginnings of an amazing process: while Russian bureaucracy was trying to tame the shtetl trade, the Jews began taming Russian bureaucracy. This Russian-Jewish symbiosis could occur only in the shtetls, whose inhabitants knew their own strength, well-being, and importance—not before and not later.

A JOINT VENTURE

This process of collaboration relied on the entrepreneurship, parsimony, and luck of Jewish smugglers. Hardly anyone was more resourceful among Jewish smugglers than Ios Volferzon from Minkovtsy and Aron Brodberg from Zhelekhov.

Those two decided that the best way to remain in business was to pass for governmental inspectors. They approached a Russian court scribe from the shtetl of Smotrich and invited him to join their gang. The scribe knew how to imitate the intimidating speech of a judge. Besides, to look more powerful, he managed to get a military officer's uniform—a trench coat with a red standing collar. He also borrowed a sword and fixed it on his belt, tucked a whip under the belt, and put on a red sheepskin top hat—exactly the same as the Russian army officers sported in winter. Now he fully looked the part: a promising new member of the Judeo-Slavic joint venture of contrabandists in an officer's disguise.

Brodberg and Volferzon looked like pious, well-to-do Jews: one had brown hair and the other was a redhead, both had sidelocks and wore sheepskin jackets. One could easily mistake them for kahal representatives accompanying a provincial inspector on a special mission. Nobody would have suspected them of being complete frauds.

From the outset, luck followed them. The three arrived in the village of Shubovtsy—as they explained, to inspect the local absinthe brewery. They accused the workers of violating one of the state regulations. Under this shaky pretext, they extracted some cash from the workers and carried away a significant amount of absinthe as an indemnity. Then they moved on to the shtetl of Slobodkovets, where they paid a visit to a local Jewish barber, conducted a search of his house, and found muslin and silk. The shocked barber did not doubt that he was dealing with a joint inspection of the Russian authorities and the Jewish community. The three condescendingly agreed to let the barber keep his goods and freedom for a modest ransom of 500 rubles. On their next journey, they met a Jewish contrabandist, and asked him to pay. Since the poor fellow did not have any money on him, they made him leave his merchandise with them as collateral.

We know the end of their long story from their Jewish driver. He deemed his new masters untrustworthy, and Ios and Aron paid him back in kind. As the driver related, the three impostors pushed their luck to the limit. They went from Minkovtsy to Dunaevtsy, then to Gusiatin through Smotrich, then back. They traveled at night, stayed with strange people, not at regular inns, acted bizarrely, and when plotting their next adventure they would send the driver to feed the horses. In one of the shtetls they went from house to house trying to sell a bolt of Swabia fabric and trap any Jew eager to buy it. In another shtetl they robbed goods from the sledge of a Jew who was staying with them at the same inn.

When the driver informed on their unsavory behavior, a search proved that the business of Brodberg, Volferzon and Co. was thriving. Brodberg specialized in textiles: he had at home a trove of colored calico, percale, poplin, cloth, demi-cotton, silk and multicolored kerchiefs. Volferzon preferred kitchenwares: the police found eighty new porcelain plates, fifty-four smaller plates, five large trays, thirty smaller trays, five teapots, and thirteen glass jars in his house—all of them ready for sale.[21] The cooperation between the Jewish contrabandists and the Russian clerk proved highly beneficial. It involved a shared interest but also trust, shared values but also a common clandestine language.

Thanks to such entrepreneurial Jews, smuggling became a joint venture based on highly intensive interactions between Slavs and Jews. One border guard stopped a Jew from bringing merchandise worth 2,000 silver rubles to Berestechko and forced him to sell his stock under duress, and the guard then became his self-appointed partner.[22] Another Jew, Gertsik, moved successfully through the Gusiatin customs house with goods banned from import because local clerks allowed him to declare his stock and pay 623 rubles' tax on his fashionable multicolored cotton.[23] The wives and daughters of the customs clerks would enjoy having a bolt of his beautiful cotton, and their husbands were anxious to bring this bonus home. Jews shared the smuggled stock precisely with those who were supposed to confiscate it and arrest the contrabandists.

Russian clerks considered contraband their own loot. They eagerly protected Jews when paid ransom and just as eagerly denounced them when bribes were not immediately proffered. Among dozens of documented cases, that of policeman Colonel Mandryka, a one-legged hero of the Borodino battle, is particularly telling. Mandryka was closely connected to Jewish leaseholders and wholesale merchants residing in Berdichev. He usually knew when the government inspector was to arrive and warned merchants in advance to hide their nonstamped goods. For years, Russian inspectors coming to Berdichev were unable to catch Jews off guard and had to leave with a modest catch. This system was effective until 1815, when Mandryka did not receive his annual bribe of approximately 1,500 rubles and decided to show the Jews what an expensive mistake they had made. He had the Jewish stores sealed and appointed police racketeers to squeeze money from those who wanted to resume their trade.[24]

Contraband was a way of life, and as such it changed the lives of the Russian clerks, not only of the Jews. Those Russian individuals who made fortunes from bribes and intercepted contraband in fact feared for their lives just as did the contrabandists themselves. One police chief who, like Mandryka, was also a colonel supervising trade was reported to have amassed a significant amount of silver dishware, foreign gold goods, and about 100,000 rubles. To make sure no one would try to touch his earnings, he slept with a Turkish dagger and two pistols under his pillow every night.[25]

Some provincial clerks eagerly shared the vagaries of contraband trade with the Jews and successfully acculturated into this Jewish business. Their cooperation brought to life a sort of an underground department of smuggling with its own codex of honor, internal police, and documentation. They issued *kvitki*, Ukrainian for "tickets": this was the invention of the town clerks in the Letichev district, who gave *kvitki* to Jewish and non-Jewish smugglers to secure an unimpeded border crossing.

An influential Russian bureaucrat from Letichev, a repenting gangster, explained how the system operated. Two Russian customs officers guarded the trade route. At a certain moment they saw two wagons on the road: six Jews in one and five peasants in the other. Jews and peasants traveled together. The clerks asked them whether they had a *kvitok*, to which both groups presented two tickets, adding that they could not be detained. And they were not: those clerks facilitated smuggling instead of stopping it.

Not all customs clerks were familiar with this system, which did not function everywhere in Volhynia and Podolia, and clerks stopped a certain Gershon, a merchant from the shtetl of Bar, who smuggled coffee, absinthe, and sugar. Gershon presented his ticket, expecting to move on without hindrance. The clerks confiscated the ticket but did not react. The astonished Gershon realized that these were the wrong clerks and promised them some 1,000 silver rubles if they let the goods go. It is fascinating that the Letichev town clerk Voitsekhovski turned to these same customs clerks and begged them not to ruin his career and give him back the *kvitok* they had received from Gershon—which he, Voitsekhovski, had most likely issued. The clerks did not heed his plea. Instead they attached the *kvitok* to the report they sent to the deputy minister of finance.

The ticket was a square piece of paper stamped with a wax seal. According to the police report, it had a small image of shaking hands and the words "till death" on one side—and the Jewish, most likely Yiddish, words for "absinthe" and "sugar," the goods found on Gershon's wagons, on the other.[26] The deputy minister was horrified when he learned that contraband had become a shared business between Jewish traders and local administrators. He was appalled to discover that state clerks, instead of regulating trade, were trading in state regulations. The situation in the other western borderlands was not too different: Grodno customs reported cooperation between local customs officers and Jewish merchants as something normal and recurrent.[27]

The robust and advantageous shtetl culture produced a mafia of Jewish contrabandists and Russian state clerks. Not only town clerks and police but even some Cossacks, notoriously present in Jewish cultural memory as cold-blooded killers of Jews, also found themselves involved in this Judeo-Slavic brotherhood. In one of several astonishing cases, two Jews moved from the annual Leipzig fair into Russia. They drove five huge wagons led by twenty horses and loaded with 8,000 kilograms of goods. Cossacks protected them and their cargo from both the Polish magnates' customs officers and the Russian customs clerks.

On their long journey, the Cossacks repeatedly resorted to arms while trying to prevent interception of the goods. According to an informant who tried to stop the caravan, one of the Cossacks turned to a Jewish

2.2. "An Attack by the Jews," a satirical pencil drawing by W. Rossdorfer celebrating and mocking Jewish bravery.
BHT 87.212.4A. Courtesy of BN and the Beit Hatfutsot exhibition "Treasures of Jewish Galicia—Judaica from the Museum of Ethnography in Lviv, Ukraine," Photo Archive, Tel Aviv.

merchant with a cheerful "Don't worry, Moshko, the goods will not be stopped!"[28] The regime was not thrilled with this Jewish-Slavic rapprochement and moved to take whatever measures necessary to stop it.

THE IMPOTENT EMPIRE

While Jewish contrabandists and state clerks were devising new forms of managing international trade, Jewish informers were thinking only of themselves. They regularly alerted St. Petersburg, denouncing what they called ubiquitous smuggling. Although the Russian highest bureaucrats knew that the informers were selfish, hence hardly trustworthy, the Minister of Finance Kankrin grew more and more irritated. In 1824 he sent secret messages in which he shared top secrets that were already common knowledge: Jews had amassed a huge amount of contraband, established secret storage places, sent merchants from Brody to Leipzig and back, and smuggled merchandise into Russia, taking advantage of the poorly controlled borders. Berdichev, he said, had become storage for contraband. He demanded that customs and border control be reinforced, which he knew would take a lot of work. He also planned to send his own envoys with an order to "uncover contraband."[29]

Yet, as Kankrin acknowledged, twenty years of restrictive regulations, confiscations, and detentions had brought meager results. In his letter to Grand Duke Konstantin, the viceroy of Poland and brother of Nicholas I, Kankrin complained about the situation on the ground. "Berdichev is the storage ground of smuggled goods," he wrote. "Local authorities can do nothing to prevent this." Confiscations proved that this trade—he meant contraband—"had become an everyday occurrence." The central administration had to fire a member of the Volhynia provincial court from the Commission on Commerce since he had connections with a Berdichev Jewish smuggler: he sheltered those administrators who protected him.[30]

Russian state bureaucrats knew well that Berdichev was at the very center of contraband activity, but for the time being they could do nothing to suppress its flourishing business. The financial benefits offered by the local trade entrapped clerks, inspectors, customs officers, and government envoys alike. To reinforce control, Colonel Freigang, a high-ranking envoy from the Third Department of His Majesty's Chancellery—the Russian secret police—came to Berdichev on a special mission.

Freigang reported heavy contraband activity in Podolia and Volhynia. Jews, he wrote, concentrated merchandise in Berdichev, storing it in stalls, basements, attics, and treasure chests. To avoid interception, they mixed stamped and legal goods with contraband. Local police leaked information about upcoming searches to the Jews so that the contrabandists would avoid bringing their stock to the marketplace. Later, they brought contraband to various fairs as far as Nizhnii Novgorod, a thousand miles from the Pale of Settlement. "The situation with trade here does not promise any success in our cause," he commented.[31] His own actions were proof enough: Freigang preferred lavish bribes from local merchants over the dirty job of contraband hunting.[32]

As Derzhavin had done in the 1790s, so Kankrin forty years later suggested proceeding cautiously against contraband. He advised against confiscating goods that did not require stamping except goods brought from abroad in large quantities. To keep policemen from taking bribes,

Kankrin required that goods be confiscated only during the day. He also advised that the revealers of contraband activity be rewarded, making the work of informers a lever in local economic competition.

At the same time, Kankrin ordered a further increase of the prohibitive duties on imported goods. In addition, he reduced the number of customs houses along the western border, seeking to secure higher state revenues. Following Kankrin's recommendations, the civil governor of Volhynia ordered informers to provide clear, proven, and signed information, bring two witnesses who would pay damages if contraband was not found, and keep their denunciations secret. In fact, he demanded the impossible. Instead of expediting the process, he intimidated the informers and made the search for contraband even more cumbersome.[33]

The proposed countersmuggling measures worked only partially. As the Balta, Dubno, and Starokonstantinov police reported, inspectors arrived and, owing to the timely cooperation of local police, managed to find some contraband. The list as they reported: tulle, calico, and cloth. They proudly stated that all local contraband had been confiscated and, eventually, eliminated. In actuality, local police would not dream of declaring all local contraband. They revealed enough to please the authorities and make sure their obedience was subsequently rewarded. But one-time obedience could not supersede the regular bonuses they obtained from smuggling. Once the inspector left the shtetl, things returned to their own place.[34] Yet contraband became costly.

Now only rich merchants could afford it. Zeilig Barats, the first-guild merchant worth hundreds of thousands of rubles, paid significant annual dues to the Russian treasury to reconfirm his estate status. But to pay additional exorbitant customs duties and bribes was not part of his plan. He realized that for his international trade he needed something of a pyramid, a network of small-scale salesmen who employed a broader network of retailers. Barats found it a much better option to operate on a small-scale level and pay small bribes for limited amounts of contraband. He slowly but steadily set up this pyramid: his twenty-two confidants or attorneys dealt with Radzivilov customs, while about six hundred agents conducted business in Austria. His was no Ponzi scheme, for every one of

Barats's employees benefited from the operations. The major revenues, however, ended up in Barats's pockets. Kankrin himself looked into Barats's smuggling case but could not outsmart him.[35]

After some thirty years unsuccessfully trying to prevent smuggling, the central authorities finally found what they considered the best solution. They decided to remove all Jewish-owned inns within fifty miles of the border because they were convinced that the inns served as shelters for contraband. They also ruled to ban entry to Russia for all those who were suspected, indirectly involved, or caught in smuggling.[36] In a word, if it could not be controlled, let there be no international trade.

Many international traders appeared on the lists of those who were absolutely forbidden to enter Russia even with a valid Austrian passport. They joined those who had decided earlier to put an end to any dealings with Russia. Now Russia banned these Jews, just as it had banned demi-cotton, calico, crêpe, muslin, French wines, hand mills, black pekoe tea, and hand mirrors. But the shtetl dwellers, both Slavs and Jews, had no desire to make do with flax, wool, and vodka.

TRICKS OF THE TRADE

The borderland dwellers responded to the growing restrictions by honing their skills. To diminish the risks, smuggled goods had to go to those who had preordered them. Preorders had to be exact, the risks manageable: nobody could assume responsibility for returning undesirable merchandise. But how could Jews preorder anything if the clerks routinely opened and read letters at the border?

Like many other smugglers—including Mrs. Zlata Nadel from Austria, suspected of smuggling letters across the border—the Radzivilov Jewess Nehamka Toper knew the answer. Someone from Russia had to smuggle lists of preordered goods. A woman such as herself was beyond suspicion. She was going back to Austria after visiting her relatives in Volhynia. When Toper arrived at the border, one Moshko Plesser, also from Radzivilov, came to see her off. Moshko put some food on her sledge, in a kind and caring manner.

But a customs officer watching the scene did not trust kind and caring Jews. At a certain moment his suspicious eye caught a strange trick.

Suddenly, a number of small notes fell from Plesser's sleeve—right on Toper's lap. She briskly covered them in the folds of her fur coat. Soon after, she was clumsily explaining to the customs officers that she knew nothing about the notes, one of which—aha!—had a sample of calico attached to it. That one, she insisted, was a toy for a child, and it was attached to a note written by a child.

This was a childish explanation indeed. The notes, written in tiny Yiddish on narrow long paper, left no doubt as to who had written them and who was the addressee. The notes contained meticulous lists of goods, most of them banned from import. "Send me," wrote an anonymous merchant, "the following items: eight bolts of the best calico, for 4.5 talers; eight of narrow blue calico with stripes and red flowers; eight of the same type, but grey, for 5 talers; eight of bright ribbons with stripes, for 0.5 taler each; eight yellow women's caps, for 4.5 talers; eight bolts of white cloth for pillowcases, for 6 talers; 18 white and multicolored cotton kerchiefs, for 1.6 taler; six red kerchiefs for 5.18; and eight bolts of crepe for 8.18." And what is more, at the end of the note: "Send only what is on the list, do not send anything else, do not send bright blue for 5.21 talers."[37]

Seeking to outwit the border clerks, smugglers invented their own paperwork, reminiscent of Nehamka Toper's detailed notes. This process proved to be so effective that large-scale smugglers resorted to it on a regular basis—relying on the experience of those Jews who routinely carried unregistered letters from Polish gentry between Berdichev, Brody, and Lemberg.[38]

For example, three wealthy Austrian merchants, Hassel, Steltser, and Gintsberg, employed a contraband gang that included Russian deserters and runaway prisoners. While Hassel and Steltser conveniently moved through regular routes, their employees smuggled the contraband through the villages and forests, avoiding major roads with their mounted inspectors and duty barriers, and cautiously moving from Kremenets to Berdichev. Instead of placing the unstamped artifacts out in the open at the market, they consulted written notes hidden in their sleeves bearing lists of items they had to deliver to various retail merchants and customers in Berdichev, secretly and personally.[39]

Once the authorities required a customs stamp on every piece of manufacture, the Jews decided to manufacture a customs stamp. This simple thought occurred to many, but only a few, including Abram Roitenberg and Leizer Golzant, among others, actually decided to commission a forged customs house stamp from a silversmith. Peisakh Berland was a highly skilled carver. It did not take him long to forge two molds with the letters "Usti. T. Konf. Poz. T. 1825"—indicating an abbreviation for the name of the Ustiluch customs house location—and cast a metal stamp. In his own opinion, he did an excellent job and fully deserved his five silver rubles.

Now Roitenberg and Goland could use the stamps to legalize any smuggled commodities. The only problem was how to keep their device a secret. Several months after they began their business, the Russian authorities became suspicious. Too many stamped goods appeared on the marketplace. Had Jews suddenly decided to pay all their duties? It was doubtful—but the stamps were in place!

A Russian customs clerk scrutinized one of them and was shocked at what he found. The stamp was *almost* genuine—with all the required details, dates, and abbreviations, neatly carved. But in one of the words the carver, while preparing the mold, had put two letters in reverse order. The Russian clerk suspected that this kind of mistake could have been made by somebody used to writing from right to left, as in Hebrew. Finding this person was now a matter of honor for the local authorities.

The Volhynia provincial authorities mobilized all available networks. One Moshko Kandel, an informer, came to their aid, directing them to two residents of Ustiluch. The police and a unit of soldiers arrived in Ustiluch to take the suspects by surprise. They rushed into the house at night and performed a search, expecting an easy catch. To their disappointment, they found nothing.

At that point, the subservient Kandel volunteered to help. He entered the house, looked around, and saw what anyone would see upon entering a shtetl house. There was a small bag for the prayer shawl and phylacteries hanging on the wall. He pointed at it—have you looked there? A policeman reached into the bag, which contained nothing but phylacteries and a prayer shawl. Open the *shel rosh,* the head phylactery, advised Kandel.

They grudgingly followed his advice. To their amazement, inside the head phylactery, instead of the five pinky-size pieces of parchment with the prayer "Hear, o Israel," there was a stamp, one with the reversed letters, exactly what the police were looking for. They then found the second smaller stamp elsewhere.

The Volhynia police were overjoyed. The owners, Roitenberg and Goland, faced charges. During the interrogations, Berland confessed that the two Jews had commissioned him to forge a stamp. The Volhynia police proudly reported to Kankrin and Kankrin informed the tsar.[40] But this was a Pyrrhic victory: elsewhere government efforts to check smuggling were seriously hampered, and not only by Jews.

JUDEO-SLAVIC BROTHERHOOD

Smuggling was not entirely a Jewish business. Like the Jews, borderland dwellers of Eastern Orthodox, Uniate, and Catholic faith felt uncomfortable about the new borders. Christian peasants smuggling oxen across the border chose to continue doing what they had been doing before: trading along the established economic routes.[41] Christian peasants and urban dwellers near the border were also actively involved in contraband.[42] However, the Christian professional contrabandists were still less numerous than Jewish ones, as there were much fewer Russian merchants in the Pale of Settlement, yet they were more influential and more harmful to the country's economy. While Jewish smugglers dealt mostly in textiles, Russian contrabandists enjoyed a richer repertoire of merchandise. Unlike Jews, they had an official cover—and could themselves be state officials.

Ivan Pestel, the scrupulous director of the Moscow post office, intercepted several letters in which he spotted Russian smugglers, Moscow-based merchants linked to one Colonel Obrezkov. They were planning how to smuggle huge quantities of caviar, fish, and wallpaper. To this end, the Russian wholesalers hired Obrezkov, who promised to use military transportation guarded by Russian soldiers. Nobody could stop Russian army guards from crossing the border. Should they succeed, lamented Pestel in his message to the head of the chamber of commerce, the state would incur damages of between 60,000 and 70,000 rubles.[43] Jews as small-scale petty contrabandists could only dream of such turnover.

Smuggling grew into a cross-cultural business involving everybody—Catholic urban dwellers and impoverished gentry, Eastern Orthodox peasants, clerks, Cossacks, Tartars, runaway prisoners, and deserters of all creeds. The Kamenets police detained the Pole Gorodnitskii when he tried to carry four sacks of smuggled merchandise through the town, about 600 rubles' worth. Or consider a group of Russian Cossacks who bumped into border guards at Orynin, near Kamenets, while crossing the border with contraband mules belonging to local Polish landlords.

Iankel Shpigel hired Nikofor Taranenko, a peasant, to help him bring about seventy pounds of copper coins (some 200 rubles' worth) hidden inside sacks of salt to the border town of Romny, most likely for subsequent resale across the border. Since Taranenko, the peasant, spoke Ukrainian and Shpigel spoke Yiddish, it is clear that Jews knew enough Russian and Ukrainian to hire, trade, bargain, and smuggle with the Eastern Orthodox population, whereas Eastern Orthodox dwellers of the shtetls and surrounding areas had sufficient Yiddish-speaking skills to join the Jews in the smuggling business.[44]

For some fifty years, smuggling remained a beneficial multiethnic enterprise. Near Zhvanets, for example, four mounted Cossacks saw a group of Jews riding on wagons loaded with contraband. On seeing the Cossacks, the smugglers chose to drop their stock and run into the forest. While the Cossacks were collecting the merchandise, a mounted patrol attacked them and captured the goods and the Cossacks' horses.[45]

In another case, several Jews tried to bring merchandise into Russia not far from Satanov. A Russian financial inspector, Zvontsov, stopped them, confiscated their goods, and brought the loot to Kamenets to hide. A Pole, Surowecki, spotted Zvontsov, stole the merchandise, and brought it to his own village of Verkhovets. Meanwhile, the border control clerk went to the village of Verkhovets, searched the entire village, and found the twice-stolen goods covered with straw in Surowecki's barn.[46]

Economic interests brought together Jews and Christians in the shtetl. The capricious state clerks came down on both Christians and Jews—and both Jews and Christians had to seek a way out under duress. Let us take a look at Kozlov, the customs house clerk in Radzivilov, a nasty and brutal official convinced that nobody could penalize him.

Just appointed a customs clerk, he turned to stealing from merchants who duly paid their duties. In 1797, one Leyb Elievich moved fox furs across the border and paid all his taxes to the customhouse. When Kozlov took one fox fur for himself, Leyb came to Kozlov's house for payment. Kozlov paid him a couple of złoty, hardly a tenth of the price, and kicked the confused merchant out of his house. The shtetl dwellers saw him hitting other Jewish merchants in the face.

It took months before the complaints of Leyb Elievich and others arrived in St. Petersburg. Meanwhile, Kozlov used a unit of Cossacks to terrify the surrounding shtetls. Witnesses reported that he regularly incited peasants against Jews. He also turned to confiscating Hungarian wine from Christians in villages and shtetls. On top of that, he demolished a Jewish brewery that provided jobs and fed the local population and built a bathhouse for himself in its place.

The elders of the Austrian town of Brody dealt regularly with Radzivilov customs but could not reconcile with Kozlov's humiliation of venerable merchants. Brody elders such as Landau, Berenstein, Schorr, and Trachtenberg, all very wealthy and well connected, complained to the chamber of commerce and gave a damning portrayal of Kozlov. Radzivilov Christians joined the Jews in their complaints against Kozlov.

The chamber summoned Kozlov. He went to the capital and returned home prouder than ever, spreading a rumor that he would soon be promoted. Eventually, owing to the joint efforts of Jews and Christians, Kozlov was removed. This did not help Christians and Jews establish the rule of law in the shtetl, but it did help them understand their shared values and taught them how to cooperate in the midst of complete lawlessness.[47]

Both Christian and Jewish townsfolk deeply disliked informers, who ruined their cross-border trade. One Jewish community in Volhynia had an informer, Shvarts-Apel, arrested and sent to the Kremenets prison under a bogus pretext, but in fact for "exposing contraband."[48] The kahal elders in Berdichev did whatever was in their power to kick out from the town some eleven Jews who regularly reported smuggled goods to the authorities.[49]

Many Jewish communities regularly had their troublemakers and informers either sentenced for arson or, after 1827, drafted into the army.

Yet another Jewish community managed to stop the destructive denunciator Shaya Rabonovich, who bragged in the courtroom of how many Jews he had ruined with his denunciations. His self-serving remarks did not help. The judge had him flogged and sent to Siberia for allegedly setting fire to a Jewish house.[50]

No Christian or Jew in the shtetl of Radzivilov knew where Leyba Tabiovich obtained his tasty port. Perhaps in Dubno, which was legal, or perhaps in Brody, which was not. But everyone in town was shocked when the local mailman, Sokolovsky, purchased a couple of bottles of port from Tabiovich, found the drink suspiciously good, and suspected the port to be Austrian contraband. He returned to the Tabioviches', rushed into their house under the pretext of a contraband search, went downstairs to the cellar, and found another fifty-two bottles of port.

Scared to death, Mrs. Tabiovich failed to convince Sokolovsky that her husband had purchased the port in Dubno. Sokolovsky sealed the basement and proceeded to write a letter to the governor. In it, he denounced the local customs for allowing contraband of medicine, wines, beers, and letters across the Austrian border. An underpaid mailman, Sokolovsky sought empowerment: he was ready to act as the state watchdog in the defense of the interests of the treasury, for a modest monthly remuneration, naturally.

At that point, the multiethnic shtetl clashed with the state administration. Port drinkers rallied around Tabiovich in their rejection of the informer. A trustworthy tavernkeeper was a commodity, and the shtetl dwellers were not ready to leave him to the mercy of his fate. Local clerks, the chief of the customhouse included, were in no rush to initiate an investigation against Tabiovich. The town dwellers, Eastern Orthodox, Jews, Polish Catholics, guild merchants, and court officials declared war on Sokolovsky. The mailman Sokolovsky was bewildered and dismayed when he realized that Radzivilov customs would not allow him to bring in a barrel of mineral water from Austria that he needed for health reasons! Sokolovsky complained to the local court, then to the district court, and later to the provincial court, but to no avail. The authorities found no infringement of the law in Tobiovich's transactions and soon returned the sealed port to him.[51] One can imagine what kind of "lehayim" Jews, Russians, and Poles drank afterward in Tabiovich's tavern to celebrate the defeat of the informer.

RABBINIC FEEDBACK

There are many other testimonies bearing witness to the productive cooperation of individuals of various ethnic and religious backgrounds in the risky and lucrative contraband business. However, the predominance of Jews in trade made them only too visible among the smugglers. Jewish communal and spiritual leaders regularly heard Russian administrators referring to contraband as the Jewish evil. Complaints of the Russian administration about what was called Jewish smuggling affected the orders received from St. Petersburg, the parlance of the governors, and articles in the Russian press. Some rabbis realized that smuggling was detrimental to the Jewish reputation in the eyes of the administration. Of course, they could have passed over this issue in silence, as they too benefited from smuggling: Jewish international merchants routinely sent their tithes to support communal philanthropies. But the rabbis did not sit idle. The stakes were too high.

In 1817, the Volhynia rabbis turned to action. They petitioned the provincial authorities to allow them a meeting in Zhitomir of all Jewish communal elders. They planned to discuss the "evil of contraband," declare it shameful, and perhaps design a ban of excommunication for it. The governors, in most cases pragmatic and well informed, welcomed the petition, yet the St. Petersburg central administration declined it. Their pretext was that the meeting of the leading rabbis would require additional expenses, which they did not want to impose on the impoverished Jewish communities.[52]

The reluctance of the central administration cooled down the Jewish leaders, but they did not abandon their efforts. One of them, Rabbi Isaac Mikhal from Radzivilov, himself of Galician descent, was indignant to find in a Russian commercial newspaper a call for the entire Jewish people to "get rid of contraband." How could one accuse an entire nation of lawlessness when only a few Jews were engaged in contraband, exclaimed

Rabbi Isaac Mikhal. He turned for help to Kankrin. His letter showed a high degree of Russian-Jewish self-awareness, patriotic responsibility, and aversion to foul play where the law was concerned.

The rabbi sought to convince the Russian government that most traditional Jews were rational people with good intentions. Jews, he said, had always been loyal subjects of the state were they lived. There was ample proof of this in Jewish lore. "My son, fear the Lord, and the king: and avoid the renegades," quoted he from the book of Proverbs (24:21). The Talmud, too, noted the Rabbi, urged Jews to pray for the welfare of the government. He quoted, "Pray for the welfare of the ruling power, since but for the fear of it, men would swallow each other alive" (*Avot* 3:2). The rabbi expressed indignation with the smugglers. He referred to the classical Judaic legal codex, *Shulkhan Arukh*, which identified those who conceal state taxes as violators of the biblical commandment "thou shall not steal" (*Hoshen Mishpat*, 369). Only very few representatives of our people, lamented the rabbi, "from the rabble," "invent ways to bring contraband into Russia through their swindling." Certainly, those few damaged the reputation of the Jewish people.

Rabbi Isaac Mikhal asked the authorities for permission to impose an oath on the Jews in three provinces. The oath would forbid Jews from smuggling under threat of excommunication, and would demand that they inform on smugglers. Would this frighten them, we might wonder? Most likely, yes. An excommunicated Jew was not allowed in the synagogue, butchers would not sell him kosher meat, his wife could not use the ritual bath and was sexually unavailable to her husband. Rejected by local families, their children would be outcasts on a shtetl street. Converting to Christianity would be the only way out for them—and not an easy one. Eastern Orthodox and Catholic shtetl dwellers together with their priests by no means welcomed converts. *Zhid kreshchenyi—chto vor proshchenyi*, "A baptized Jew is nothing but a pardoned thief," ran the popular Slavic proverb. The threat of excommunication was probably quite effective, since no traditional Jew would want to end up beyond the communal and cultural boundaries.

Now the situation changed. Kankrin found the proposed oath a sound measure and sent it back with his endorsement to Prince Vassili Levashov, the governor of Kiev, Podolia, and Volhynia provinces. Kankrin particularly liked the fact that other respected communal leaders—Motl of Chernobyl, Israel of Ruzhin, and Moshe of Savran—agreed to join Isaac Mikhal. Since all three were charismatic Hasidic leaders with enormous popularity and mass following, Kankrin was quite right to assume that the suggested oath would be almost universally accepted as binding. Unlike Kankrin, Levashov was sour about the measure. The intention was good, but excommunication, he wrote back to Kankrin, reflected Jewish doubletalk and would hardly be effective. Kankrin made his decision: postpone the measure until a new regulation concerning the Jews was issued.[53]

We can only stipulate why Levashov evaded telling the truth by referring to what he considered inherent Jewish dishonesty, and why Kankrin decided to pass on that proposal. Most likely, with all his good intentions to eradicate smuggling, Levashov refrained from putting his true thoughts on paper. And not without reason. If three or four rabbis could establish a procedure capable of stopping what the government had been trying to check for thirty years, this signified that they, the Jewish rabbis, and—even worse—the Hasidic *rebbes* were the genuine power in the Russian borderlands, not the ministers of His Majesty, the Senate, and not the provincial administration. This was exactly what the governor and the minister of finance were reluctant to put on paper.

REGENERATION OF SMUGGLING

Radical measures aimed at eradicating smuggling could not entirely stop what had become for many Jews and Gentiles a profitable business. But the new regulations did increase the risks, which a regular merchant could not afford to take. Some of the few guild merchants capable of winning over Russian clerks transformed contraband into a multiethnic cross-border enterprise. Since these wholesale smugglers controlled the contraband market under protection, they did not make it into the police reports. On the contrary, in the police reports of the 1840s small-scale smugglers—petty traders, retailers, and above all women—appear, proving that the great era of contraband trade had entered into decline. By the 1850s the shtetl was no more a center of trade in French, Prussian, and Austrian goods. Odessa, a rapidly growing *porto franco* on the Black Sea coast, had replaced them all.

Shtetl contraband was no longer on a grand scale. A good example would be Etl Shtulbeimanova, the daughter of a Berdichev third-guild merchant. In the 1840s she lost first her father and then her husband. Etl and her mother still owned a brick house in Berdichev, but the death of their providers left them in dire straights. Local Jews knew Etl as a pious woman of valor. To help herself and her mother, Etl traded retail in the Berdichev market and visited nearby towns to sell what was left over. One day she had to go to the shtetl of Lipovets, where a local policeman stopped her. The policeman saw a helpless Jewish widow before him and ordered her to take out her goods. Etl showed him her shawls, bright red small kerchiefs, some cotton goods, several bolts of cotton, percale, and calico, ninety-six mending devices for stockings, bronze-colored wool, and one decanter with five small wine glasses. How the eyes of the policeman must have sparkled!

Although some of her textile items had no stamps, it was quite clear that all her merchandise was Russian-made except for the last item. The policeman did not care. He had all of Etl's merchandise confiscated and stockpiled in the Lipovets police station. He disregarded the fact that the local Jewish community was ready to stand by Etl and that some Berdichev Jews would testify in her favor. He stated in court that if Etl could prove that she had bought those things for herself, he would allow the goods to be returned to her. For unknown reasons, Etl did not show up either for the town court or for the rabbinic court hearings. But it is crystal clear that the volume of Etl's trade would have had zero impact on Russia's internal trade. Etl traded in what ordinary people needed in order to help her make ends meet—and still, the authorities were now cracking down even on small-scale criminals.[54]

What happened to Etl hardly seems extraordinary. By the late 1830s, petty traders were obligated to have even the most insignificant items stamped or else risk legal consequences. Thus, the head of Radzivilov customs, Zabelin, in his report to the governor proudly stated that he had confiscated from one Hayka Rabonova some five cuts of calico, two prayer shawls, and two new pillowcases.[55] Similarly, a Vinnitsa policeman bragged

2.3. A Jew selling fruits, 1834.
Watercolor by J. Głogowski. BHT 87.121.8. Courtesy of LNB and the Beit Hatfutsot exhibition "Treasures of Jewish Galicia—Judaica from the Museum of Ethnography in Lviv, Ukraine," Photo Archive, Tel Aviv.

of how he had taken several white pillowcases and some black- and bronze-colored cloth from a Jewish widow engaged in petty trade; the woman's goods had no stamps.[56]

As the scale of contraband diminished, Jews hid illegal items under their overcoats: thus, several Jews were caught in the town of Kruptsy with five cuts of calico and six calico aprons. The police of the town of Kremenets trumpeted their confiscation of a bolt of foreign fabric for one overcoat, a white nightgown, and two pairs of white suspenders.[57]

The customs officer who stopped two Berdichev Jewesses, Maria Berkova and Shifra Chervonskaia, and confiscated dozens of unstamped kerchiefs and pieces of cotton banned for import had good reason to do so. The detention of one Sura Haimova with forty-nine boxes of needles and 250 pieces of woolen braids allegedly purchased in Ostrog but in fact smuggled across the border is also understandable.[58] But why would the Radzivilov customs clerks arrest third-guild merchant Reisa Goldzhtein and confiscate her thirty-three lemons and six pounds of rhubarb?[59]

The regime did its best to disrupt the links between Jewish merchants and local clerks and resubmit the latter to rigid central control. These measures strengthened the bureaucracy but did not contribute to the establishment of the rule of law. Few large-scale international merchants survived and moved from the shtetl to Odessa, where the contraband moved, too, but most of trading townsfolk were out of contraband business and were forced to turn to alternative means of existence.

THE POSTHUMOUS LIFE OF CONTRABAND

By the late 1830s, Jewish merchants were still active in cross-border trade, but the exchange between Central Europe and the shtetl markets had faded. The number of Jewish merchants passing through customs between Russian and Austria had dropped to about 12 percent of what it had been in the 1790s, although Jews were still visible as international traders.[60]

Their economic future was far from being predictable. In 1839, two merchants from Berdichev, three from Starokonstantinov, and six from Proskurov crossed into Austria through the Gusiatin customs. All of them were traveling to Brody to purchase merchandise brought there from Leipzig. All were relatively young, from twenty-five to thirty-nine years old. And all of them found themselves under close surveillance of the customs clerks and numerous voluntary stool pigeons. The police received a denunciation that one of these Jews was staying with a person known to the police as the head of a contraband gang. Following the denunciation, Kankrin personally ordered the immediate detention of the Jews implicated in suspicious activities.[61] It became increasingly difficult, if possible at all, to continue cross-border trade.

Besides, the Russian authorities chose to abandon their protectionist principles. They radically reduced the duties for 622 items of import and cancelled duties for some 32, although they left some 300 articles of trade unchanged. It was a decisive step toward free trade, and in 1851, only 25 of some 90 types of merchandise previously forbidden for import remained.

Now Russia began importing goods on its own, endorsing import controlled by high-ranking state clerks and repressing local individual initiative. From then on, the extraordinary role of Jews as agents of international trade had diminished and what the authorities called Jewish contraband came to be delegated to small-scale petty traders, women, and losers. Once Odessa emerged as a major trading and smuggling center on the Black Sea, the trade route via Brody became obsolete, and the establishment of the railway network changed the economic balance in the region.

The old-fashioned contrabandist moved from the provincial Glupsk of Mendele Moykher Sforim to the cosmopolitan Odessa of Isaak Babel and Sholem Aleichem, where he would smuggle contraband commodities from the foreign steamships into the Odessa catacombs or sell contraband French postcards to the visitors of the Fankoni Café. The new Jewish smuggler entered the Purimshpiels, amateurish comic performances on the holiday of Purim, as a good-for-nothing petty trader, broke, father of a destitute family, whose lucid puns, sharp jokes, and desperate humor made little impression on the unwitting Russian policemen and failed to keep him from being arrested.[62]

Before what Russian bureaucrats called "Jewish contraband" came to an end in the shtetls, the contrabandists had bedeviled the Russian administrators, and not only the minister of finance or local governors. On his deathbed, Baron Kampenhausen, who was the state treasurer and the minister of the interior, imagined himself persecuting and shooting Jewish contrabandists. Despite the tragic circumstances, his personal doctor could hardly contain his laughter on hearing his agonizing client act out his chase, shooting, and victory over the contrabandists.[63] Naturally, Jewish contrabandists were the nightmares of Russian administrators—yet they became the fighters for freedom for the ordinary Jews and Slavs.

While Russia was responsible for turning international trade into contraband, contraband could be claimed responsible for a good deal of Russian cultural production. For Russian culture at large, the hunt against what came to be known as Jewish smuggling had unexpected results. Middle-class fashion was a source of pride for Jewish and Christian women, and household commodities came to be associated with a new word: *kontrabanda*, smuggled goods, contraband. The fashionable, the beautiful, the utilitarian, and the positive became forbidden and illegal and had to be smuggled.

If one wanted to look good, feel well in one's clothes, and use convenient household items, one had to break the law. Convenience and lawlessness merged in the minds of ordinary people. Russian popular culture associated fashion and commodities with illegality. Jewish smugglers came to be seen as indispensable providers of such commodities: the more indispensable they were to everyday life, the more illegal.

Babel, who smuggled Italian, Ukrainian, French, and Yiddish elements into his literary Russian, did not hesitate to celebrate lawlessness in trade, which he saw as useful, democratic, and beautiful. What he called "the noblest part of our contraband" was a luminary presence at Odessa's popular celebrations: "the noblest part of our contraband, the glory of the land from end to end, performed on that starry, blue night its ruinous, seductive business. The black cook from the 'Plutarch', which had arrived three days before from Port-Said, brought beyond the customs area the plump bottles of Jamaican rum, greasy Madera, cigars from Pierpont Morgan's plantations and oranges from the outskirts of Jerusalem. This is what the foamy tide of the Odessa sea brings ashore."[64]

Eduard Bagritsky celebrated contraband (in his case, carried on by the Greeks and based on Russia's Black Sea coast) as the utmost example of free will, liberating anarchist rebellion, and absolute freedom. It opposed officialdom and provided ordinary people with necessary commodities. Contraband was for him a "useful thing, a good thing."[65]

Not only did the suspense of contraband dazzle the Russian Jewish imagination, so also did the heroic qualities of the smuggler. This East European Robin Hood became the epitome of freedom. For example, Ostap Bender, the protagonist of the most famous Russian twentieth-century novel, *The Golden Calf*: a charming and industrious fellow who combined the courage of a Ukrainian Ostap and the entrepreneurship of a Jewish Bender, still failed to smuggle his jewelry across the Soviet border.

Or we may think of Osip Mandelstam, who believed that real freedom is something stolen and that a genuine poet, like François Villon, is a "thieving angel."[66] As the twentieth-century philosopher Merab Mamardashvili observed, smuggling became one of the forms of existence of Russian culture, its unique positive value.

This happened because the shtetl brought together people of different religious backgrounds and social status eager to have a modicum of free trade. Even those ordered to fight it contributed to the shtetl's illegal freedom. Why was it so important? Because everybody, Jews in particular, wanted to add fresh blood to the main artery of the shtetl: its marketplace.

CHAPTER THREE

FAIR TRADE

overnor General Ivan Funduklei was uneasy about the shtetls that belonged to Polish magnates, were situated on the Russian land, and were economically dependent on the Jews. Rumors of suspicious activities of Jews and Poles reached his receptive ears and left him deeply concerned. He had heard that Jews and Poles were stockpiling arms, trading wholesale in horses to help reestablish the Polish cavalry units, and using the annual fairs as a cover for Polish conspiratorial meetings.

Funduklei wondered whether the government's outlawing of the wholesale export of horses to prevent the enemy from purchasing this means of warfare had been in vain.[1] And what was the point of capturing new western lands for the Russian Empire if the towns' profits still went to the magnates? Funduklei could sense the latent unrest and ordered envoys sent out on special assignments to investigate what the Poles and Jews were up to during the fairs.

Thus, Gendarme Corps Major von Gildebrandt received a note stating that a secret society called the *balagolas*, made up of about sixteen individuals, was roaming about between Kiev and Volhynia provinces. The major was to travel as an undercover agent and try to identify these people. His colleague, Major Gaivoronsky, had to move secretly to Balta and engage in conversation with Poles coming to the St. Onufry fair. His task was to listen to rumors and find out what the incoming Poles were talking about.

Colonel Radishchev, from the same cohort, received instructions to go to the biggest annual fair in Berdichev "and secretly find out the political expectations of the Polish gentry, especially whether there are emissaries among them under aliases." Radishchev was to arrest anybody selling or distributing suspicious objects such as "rings with a Polish eagle, Lithuanian horseman, or iron signets in the form of a chain" symbolizing the greatness of the Polish-Lithuanian Commonwealth, which no longer existed. The instructions were to the point: "many Polish gentry get together at the Berdichev fair, collect money for Polish exiles, and spread all sorts of rumors."[2] This was a familiar task for the gendarmes: four years earlier Colonel Bek from the same corps had gone on a similar mission.[3]

Thus, in late spring 1840, three secret Russian agents went on the road. Eventually they wrote detailed accounts of the shtetl fairs, where they spied on the Poles. What they actually found was the marketplace, its burgeoning life, and the Jewish trade, which had transformed the shtetl into a civilization in and of itself. Too independent and robust, it was destined to clash with the Russian authorities, who attempted and failed to control it.

FIGURING OUT TRADE

Like the Russian envoys on special assignments, the Russian thinker and ethnographer Ivan Aksakov also visited the Ukrainian markets and observed that "Jews added to trade a particularly febrile agitation—they ran, hustled and bustled, accompanying each word with quick gesticulations; everywhere one hears their swift guttural talk, on each and every step they stop a visitor and offer him merchandise."[4]

These agitated and ubiquitous Jewish middlemen, called *faktors*, also fascinated Pavel Shpilevsky, a Belorussian ethnographer, who observed that the factor would "fulfill all your wishes, however difficult they might

3.1. A Jew from Galicia, 1834.
Watercolor by J. Głogowski. BHT 87.121.13. Courtesy of LNB and the Beit Hatfutsot exhibition "Treasurer of Jewish Galicia—Judaica from the Museum of Ethnography in Lviv, Ukraine," Photo Archive, Tel Aviv.

be" and would spend the entire day "doing chores for as cheap as half a ruble."[5] Andrei Glagolev, in his picturesque notes, portrayed Jewish men in wide hats, smoking pipes and "living at the marketplace from morning till night." Trade was life and the marketplace was the heart of the shtetl.

The shtetl at its height was able to satisfy any demand because it drew everybody into its spiral: in addition to merchants, 77 percent of all townsfolk and 18 percent of artisans also engaged in trade.[6] Jews were overrepresented in the marketplace. In Podolia, the privileged Jewish guild merchants numbered 858, while Christians numbered only 80. The Jewish population exceeded Christians fivefold (140,000 against 29,000), while

Jewish merchants exceeded Christians tenfold. In Kamenets-Podolsk district alone, Russian clerks identified 62 Jewish and no Christian guild merchants.[7] In the first third of the nineteenth century, the number of Jewish merchants in Volhynia grew fivefold, while the number of Christian merchants remained unchanged. Overall, Christians and Jews among guild merchants constituted 21 and 79 percent, respectively, in 1797, and 4 and 96 percent, respectively, in 1832.[8]

The Jews had reason to be proud. In fifty years, Jewish merchants grew twenty-fold in number and more than threefold percentage-wise. In Kiev province, for example, 168 Jewish guild merchants constituted 27 percent of the total in 1797, whereas by 1845 they constituted 84 percent, numbering 3,281 male and 3,102 female merchants.[9] The situation in Berdichev worsened for the Jews toward the mid-nineteenth century, but even in the 1850s Countess Radziwiłł still emphasized the tenfold Jewish predominance in local trade.[10] This situation so embarrassed a state clerk that in his report to Nicholas I he crossed out Jewish and Christian ethnic diversification and put both groups of merchants together in order to create an ethnically neutral aggregated figure.[11]

With this clumsy gesture the state clerk attempted to conceal the fact that Jews were a major mediator between the town and the village. Peasants received permission to trade only later in the century, but from the 1790s to the 1820s Jews were first and foremost intermediaries between urban and rural areas in central Ukraine, "the richest in grain among not only all the Russian, but also among all the Polish provinces."[12] Due to their trade activities, the golden age shtetl did not have "piles of corn as big as houses, enough to feed all Europe" that in the 1770s had been left rotting in Podolia and Volhynia.[13]

Moreover, before the 1861 abolition of serfdom brought thousands of peasants to the marketplace, the Jews brought the market to the village. For example, in the shtetl of Makhnovka, near Berdichev, Jews travelled to the surrounding villages and purchased geese, hens, cattle, veal, fish, and ducks from the peasants. In 1820 alone they bought about seven hundred head of cattle and moved the livestock to the nearby Berdichev marketplace for retail.[14] In exchange, Jews brought iron tools, tar, haberdashery, and a variety of multicolored textiles to the villages. Not for nothing did

Gogol make one of his folklore figures a Jew selling a devilish red shirt at the Sorochinsky fair in his *Evenings on a Farm near Dikanka.*

The more Jews participated in trade in a certain locality, the lower the prices and the faster the turnover. A major nineteenth-century Ukrainian ethnographer, Pavlo Chubynskyi, observed that prices in Jewish stores were for the most part fair and that Jews were equally trustworthy when dealing with both Christian and Jewish merchants.[15] It was not Jewish trade but the ugly mercantile attempts to control it that prevented faster economic growth and ruined free trade. In cases where the Russian governmental measures were effective, as for example in the town of Kremenets, instead of a flourishing Christian trade, the town slipped into an irreversible commercial decline.[16] This was also true elsewhere: the shtetls prospered as long as the Jews were involved in trade.

The Jews had to survive in the economic niche that the magnates had carved for them, or perish. Trade was demanding, yet one could survive. The intensity of trade accounted for some fascinating developments. Economists show that density of population and intensity of trade go hand in hand. In the first half of the nineteenth century, the population of Ukraine grew by 55 percent (46 percent in European Russia). Although there was a constant southeastward relocating of the population, Kiev and Podolia provinces still had the highest population density in Russia, excluding Moscow province. In addition, no other region in the Pale of Settlement had such a considerable Jewish population as Volhynia, Podolia, or Kiev provinces.[17]

Epidemics of contagious diseases notwithstanding, this region had the lowest death rate in the empire, and Volhynia and Podolia were not affected by the terrible murrain elsewhere in Russia in the 1820s. Peasants from the northern Russian provinces, particularly the Belorussian ones, escaped to Volhynia and Kiev provinces during the years of famine, according to the annual reports of the ministry of the interior.[18]

Some Jews also escaped there. Reinbarg, a tailor from Kobrin, knew that the Ukrainian shtetls were more prosperous than his native Belorussian shtetl. He considered this opportunity when in the early 1830s famine struck the Kobrin district, potatoes became expensive, and bread became a luxury. Nobody had old clothes mended or new ones made anymore.

Struggling to survive, Reinbarg felt that he had reached bottom. He bought a passport that allowed him to move through the Pale and went to Ukraine in search of job opportunities. For several years he worked as a tailor throughout Kiev and Volhynia provinces. He was caught as a vagrant in Berdichev and drafted into the army, spent a year as a private in Łomża, then deserted and went back to Kiev province.

There he met Iankel Pinhasovich, a miller from Belaia Tserkov, who gave Reinbarg shelter and offered him a partnership. For several years the two men sold grain, flour, and groats. At the end of the second year, Reinbarg bought out his part of business for the sum of 50 rubles and moved on to trading apples with another Jew. After half a year he had enough money not only to provide for himself, but also to pay 30 rubles to the Belaia Tserkov kahal, asking them to legalize him and inscribe him in the communal register. He might not have been a successful tailor, but he certainly was ready to go into any kind of trade—and the shtetl marketplace needed just that: jacks of all trades.[19]

DENIZENS OF THE MARKETPLACE

Jews were extraordinarily active economically, though, as we shall see, trade was not in their genes, and Jews bowed down neither to Mammon nor to Mercury. Being double-taxed, Jews found their way by creating an exchange of unparalleled intensity. The economic niche that the Polish and Russian regime created for them shaped the Jewish predisposition to trade in the same manner that the medieval laws of Catholic Europe made them prone to money-lending.

The shtetl was a town invented for trade, and trade was an occupation ascribed to the shtetl. The trading stalls, an architectural element "that distinguished the shtetl from the surrounding villages," was its defining locus.[20] Catherine II encouraged shtetl trade by granting the shtetl dwellers the privilege to establish trading stalls, home-based stores, and hangars.[21] The annual fairs, the Sunday bazaars and the weekly trade rallied around these stalls. Usually built of stone in the form of an arcade imitating European marketplace galleries, they combined a number of back-to-back and shoulder-to-shoulder stores under one roof and were the embodiment of the indefatigable shtetl trade.

Almost all, if not all, the stores in the shtetl marketplaces belonged to Jewish merchants. In the late 1790s, Russian clerks registered four stone and six wooden stores in the center of the marketplace in Nemirov, sixteen stone and fifty-five wooden stores in Tulchin, and thirty stone and sixty-five wooden stores in Trostianets. In Satanov, they observed, thirteen Jews had their stores sheltered under one shingled roof. In Felshtin, the marketplace arcade encompassed twenty-two stone stores, and the central trading square in such shtetls as Dunaevtsy, Kitaigorod, Chernyi Ostrov, and Iarmolintsy had a similar number of trading stalls either leased or owned by Jews.[22] Since the shtetls had no residential segregation, Jews sought to live closer to the place of trade: they occupied 60 to 85 percent of the houses lining the marketplace.[23] Seeking to transform the area surrounding the marketplace into one uninterrupted trading arcade, Jews established stores right next to churches.[24]

The dizzying array of available goods offered by Jews suggests that it was a *super*market, not just a market*place*. Jews exhibited on the counters of their trading stalls the entire gamut of local Ukrainian and imported Oriental textiles: rolls of silk, thin and demi-cotton, multicolored tulle and soft sari, velvet and batiste and calico, taffeta and satin fabric, as well as wool, yarn, and thread. Among stockpiled goods were haberdashery items, including pillowcases, kerchiefs, gloves, stockings, and socks. Next to them the Jews placed the delicacies—Russian caviar, sugar, coffee, Chinese pekoe tea, chocolate, dates, peaches, figs, oranges, Turkish beans, almonds, and raisins.

Behind the counter were sacks and barrels: the Jews always had salt and fish, perhaps the items most in demand in the shtetl daily trade. The upper shelves of the marketplace stores were packed with leather goods such as boots and belts. For female customers, Jewish traders had earrings and hairpins. And, of course, Catholic and Eastern Orthodox would find items that made them particularly happy: tobacco, tobacco boxes, and pipes.[25]

Ordinary townsfolk also came to trade at the marketplace, either from rented stalls or from their wagons. For that, they needed a permit. To obtain one, a Jewish townsman had to pay a half ruble duty to the state treasury and bring a special ticket from the communal elders. "Itsko

Chervonyi pays his dues and taxes on time and can go in for trade," read one of them in Hebrew. Moshko Ratmanovsky "has paid his taxes on time, does not have any arrears, and is allowed to trade," read another, also in Hebrew. These were formulaic and widely used statements. In 1825, sixty Jews and ten Christians applied to the Vasilkov town hall for trading permits.[26] Permits were granted, and they rushed to sell whatever they had in stock or to act as middlemen with no stock, as a *mishures* or a *faktor*, making money on commission for bringing an incoming merchant directly to a storeowner.

Each marketplace offered "everything one's heart desires," as the nineteenth-century Russian counting rhyme put it. The Vinnitsa marketplace with its one stone, twenty-four wooden, and thirty-nine mobile stalls on wheels traded in textiles, spices, wax, and candles, and varieties of smoked fish and caviar from the internal Russian provinces.[27] Tulchin and Nemirov offered colonial sugar, coffee, tea, chocolate, dates, and oranges. Trostianets boasted of calico from a local factory and beer from a local brewery, both items bought there wholesale and resold in marketplaces as far away as Berdichev. Uman lost its fairs after the town was confiscated by the state, the Potockis remaining out of big business, yet because of the presence of the military, the town boasted two hundred trading stores and traded mostly in local wheat, mead, candles, tobacco, and bricks.[28]

Not only the Polish szlachta, who constituted an exceptionally high 10 percent of the prepartitioned Polish-Lithuanian Commonwealth (Rzecz Pospolita), but also other Jews, Eastern Orthodox, and peasants were among the regular customers. A Russian cultural historian noticed that regular townsfolk and peasants "observing the lifestyle of the elite, dreamt of possessing luxury goods, which ranged from small items such as ribbons, mirrors, and combs to more expensive items such as clothing, china and furniture."[29] Generally, besides grain, salt, textiles, vodka, and fish, Jews offered practically any commodity—and did it with gusto.

Rabbi Moshe Haim Luzzatto did not write his ethical treatise *Mesilat yesharim* (Path of the Just; Amsterdam, 1740) for East European Jews alone, yet his book became especially popular with them, perhaps because Luzzato's key concept of *zrizut* (alacrity) fit in very well with the commercial excitement and dexterity of the shtetl dwellers.[30] When a certain Rabbi Isaac met a certain Rabbi Nathan in the marketplace, he saw precisely this "great alacrity so typical of him."[31] This alacrity could help transform the shtetl into the Russian Amsterdam or Hamburg, should the Russian authorities be willing to endorse and encourage it. But they didn't.

Investing large sums into one type of merchandise incurred risks that Jews could not afford. A monopoly of wholesale stock of a certain type of commodity fit in the slow and cumbersome magnates' businesses—or those of the guild merchants. For a Jew to specialize in a certain type of product meant to build a monopoly from the bottom up and become too vulnerable. It seems that Jewish merchants heeded the Talmudic warning *tafasta meruba—lo tafasta*, "if you grab too much, you have grabbed nothing."[32] They seem to have resorted in their daily activities to the Talmudic principle *bari shema, bari adif*—between "for sure" or "maybe," "for sure" is preferable. Applied to financial options, this principle implied that certainty overrode potentiality. Selling less "for sure" was always better for a Jewish trader than "maybe" selling more.[33] Or, if we are willing to use the colloquial language of the marketplace, *az men ken nit kakn, iz a forts alayn oykh gut*—"if one is not able to shit, a fart is also good."[34]

Jewish trade was as impressive as it was funny. Today we would find someone simultaneously trading in shoelaces, sausages, and computers neither efficient nor smart, but the Jews in the shtetl would find it to be both. Iankel Gershkovich from Belaia Tserkov, an indefatigable wholesale merchant who crossed the Russian border several times a year, would be a good and representative example. First he declared 1,700 feet of white cloth, 420 feet of wool, and twelve harnesses. The next time he brought 1,700 feet of cloth, 100 pounds of potassium alum (as an effective blood coagulator), and thirty woolen hats.

Abram Yankelevich from Fastov brought 100 pounds of each of the following: candles, ginger, sandalwood, pepper, and coffee, five packages of paper, and 100 spools of thread. Volko Mordekhaevich, also from Fastov, brought 2,000 feet of tick fabric, 300 feet of cloth, 1,000 feet of calico, another 1,000 feet of various textile goods, 200 packages of paper, 100 pounds of potassium alum, 60 pounds of sandal, and another 60 pounds of ginger.[35] The volatile market made Jews masters of all brands and commercially omnivorous. As such, they worked harder than any Christian wholesaler: no wonder they monopolized the market!

Jews offered a wide variety, but in limited quantities. These are exactly the products one could find, for example, in Letichev, which specialized not only in locally produced lard, wax, soap, incense, clay and wooden utensils, and powdered amber (used as laxative) but also in multicolored ribbons and female adornments. This relatively insignificant shtetl could offer something gourmet, too, for example German wines from Gdansk and Leipzig, English beer, and French cognacs and champagne.

At the same time at the Medzhibozh marketplace, far more advanced than that of nearby Letichev, Jews traded in Oriental textiles, particularly colored cashmere, paisley, batiste, and footwear from Mogilev and Nemirov, as well as Shwabian, Prussian, and Ivanovo textiles and brocade, in high demand among Polish nobility.[36] Here one would also find olive oil from Provence; Turkish tobacco; and Dutch, Swiss, and Parmesan cheese, olives, and cigarettes. For all of these items, Medzhibozh or Letichev merchants did not need to go as far as Nizhnii Novgorod or Leipzig. They could purchase most of these as well as other items wholesale during the "great meetings" of foreign merchants, as a Russian report portrayed the Berdichev annual fairs.[37]

Shtetl trade prefigured all-in-one department stores, while specialized trade was not Jewish trade, as Jews working for Christian merchants demonstrate. The Christian merchant Grigory Chistovsky from Kremenets and his three Jewish assistants traveled from the east to transport twenty-one wagons of salt. One Pole, three Jews, and one Eastern Orthodox, all agents of the Polish magnate Knieski, brought twenty wagons of flour to a Jewish factor in Zhvanets, Podolia.[38]

This type of wholesale specialization was good for the rich, well-protected, and slow Christian monopolists, something ordinary Jews or even well-to-do merchants could not allow themselves. Although the margin of income would be quite substantial, the risks were too high. Besides, the income was never certain—it was always a "maybe" income. Therefore such endeavors were not the shtetl Jews' type of business.

Jews had to make do with less, move faster, and obtain their return quicker—only to reinvest it again and again. They undertook projects that their Christian counterparts rejected as unprofitable. In Uman, for example, after the 1830 Polish rebellion, the Russian government confiscated the Potocki estate. The Russian treasury obtained not only the town but also its liquid possessions, including 7,000 *spustov* (44,000 gallons) of vodka. The Ministry of Finance did not accept preliminary offers, chose to auction the stock, and invited the wealthiest merchants to participate. The Christian first-guild merchant Panfil Abakumov bid 2.95 silver rubles per measure but then realized that the authorities would not sell him the entire stock, got angry, and withdrew from the bidding. All or nothing, was his logic. As a result, the stock was divided unevenly between the bidders, various parts of it ending up in the hands of Jewish merchants. They were satisfied with a low margin of profit, eager for a quick turnover.[39]

If there was anything for which Jewish trading was rightly (and wrongly) known as Jewish, it was this readiness to be satisfied with a not-so-beneficial financial arrangement. These merchants could repeat to themselves a biblical proverb well known in the traditional Jewish community: "Better a little with the fear of Lord than great wealth with turmoil."[40] They could also think of the *dayenu* principle from the famous Passover song: "It would have sufficed for us!"

Because Jews sought to turn any item into marketable merchandise, shtetl trade was not always innocent. Some Jewish traders, along with the smugglers, dealt in merchandise that could not but alarm the authorities. Take, for example, Moshko Poliak from Makhnovka, who purveyed victuals and commodities for the army. Local police accused him of selling three hundred rifles to the local gentry. A search proved that he had stored about thirty swords, twenty bayonets, and fifty rifle chargers in his attic. This was not the first time that Jews had purchased wholesale and resold the ammunition of the relocated troops, including bullets, small shot, and powder.[41] Did this imply that the governor general Funduklei was right, and that Jews were secretly supplying arms for the rebellious Polish szlachta?

Poliak, whose quite suspicious real last name was Warshavsky ("from Warsaw"), his nickname meant "the Pole," managed to convince the police that the commander of the Ekaterinburg regiment had left all that ammunition with him for reselling. When Poliak pulled out not only several valid permits signed by the military but also a certificate of his 500-ruble government award for blameless service, the authorities returned everything they had confiscated.[42] It was precisely this kind of trade that made Jewish trade suspicious in the eyes of the regime. The more versatile the shtetl trade, the more the regime wanted to control it.

ALL ROADS LEAD TO BERDICHEV

Controlling the shtetl marketplace was like regulating the Polish economy while on Russian soil. Long before the Polish partitions, in order to accommodate their Jewish subjects, who were to bolster trade, the Polish magnates petitioned the king, obtained the corresponding privileges, and established annual fairs in their towns as early as the sixteenth century. After the partitions, things changed little. While before they had turned to the crown asking to establish fairs, now the magnates turned to the Russian minister of finance. Prince Radziwiłł, the governor of Przemyśl and a distant relative of the Berdichev Radziwiłłs, put it clearly in a private letter: towns needed fairs in order to compete.[43]

Seeking profit for the imperial treasury, the Russian governors carefully monitored the fairs, counted the customers, and made sure no contraband merchandise was on sale. They approved the town halls' or magnates' requests for new fairs, and sometimes initiated requests themselves. Thus, Volhynia, Kiev, and Podolia provinces became dotted with fairs. By the 1840s, central Ukraine boasted two thousand fairs—accounting for half of all the fairs held in Russia, and far exceeding the number in any other provinces in the Pale.

The town-owners used popular religiosity to boost the fairs. They requested that fairs be established on saints' days, when peasants went en masse to the towns to worship in the churches, light candles for saints, and kiss the icons. Even underdeveloped shtetls such as Letichev had five annual fairs, all falling on Eastern Orthodox holidays: one during Holy Week, the second on the feast of St. Nicholas the Miracle-Maker in December, the third on the feast of the Deposition, the fourth on the feast of Virgin Holy Shrouds, and the fifth on St. Nicholas of the Spring day, in May. Fairs lasted from Sunday through Thursday and almost never coincided with Jewish religious holidays—otherwise, who would work the fair?[44]

These fairs were a whir of never-ending activity. Like the Polish crown earlier, the Russian authorities now sought to create internal turnover, realizing that "the entire well-being of a shtetl depended on fairs."[45] Once a fair in one town ended, another fair started somewhere else, usually a day's ride away. Those merchants who did not manage to sell their wares in one shtetl could continue their business in the next.[46]

On the last page of the calendars, whose circulation was in the dozens of thousands—in Polish, Russian, and Hebrew—a merchant could find a list of annual fairs, indicating their locations and length, and the distance between the towns.[47] Because of this schedule, the fairs in Ukraine never ended. It was the same situation on the eastern side of the Dnieper River. The December Kharkov fair followed the November fair in Sumy, the Romny fair followed Kharkov's, and then the trade moved to Poltava and Krolevets. Ivan Aksakov, who closely observed this phenomenon, called it a "mobile marketplace."[48]

Fairs in different towns seemed similar, but each fair specialized in certain products. What Braudel described as the process of specialization of the markets did not affect the Jewish commercial modus operandi but did affect the shtetl fairs.[49] Dubno and Rovno offered hop, seeds, and pigs, with Jews dealing in all of the above. Balta and Nemirov became famous for livestock trade. Two of the fastest-growing shtetls in Volhynia, Polon-noe and Shepetovka, provided textiles, boots, fur coats, and locally brewed wines and vodkas.

The Kiev Contract fair (*Kontraktovaia*), not that of a shtetl, functioned as a stock exchange, yet Jews there were still offering wholesale sugar, grain, alcohol, coal, salt, and lumber. The Balta and Berdichev fairs had less turnover than such famous fairs as the one in Kiev or Nizhnii Novgorod. Still, Nizhnii was unique, far from any other fair at a huge distance of hundreds of miles, whereas the network of the "mobile marketplace" in Volhynia, Kiev, and Podolia provinces with their one hundred to two hundred annual fairs had no rivals in the empire. Rabbi Nachman of

Bratslav claimed that it would be better for a Jew to become a merchant and go in for trade than to become a teacher—if only he could go to the marketplace and scorn it in his heart.[50]

Let us pay a visit to the Trinity fair in Balta. Despite its dirty roads and narrow bridges over the Kodyma River, Balta welcomed about ten thousand people annually. They traded in mead, grain, oil, tar, glass, wooden and clay utensils, hides, leather goods, fish, fresh and dry fruits, but most important, salt and cattle. Merchants brought some nine thousand horses from the Don River steppes and the southern districts, some of them unique breeds. Wholesalers shipped cattle from the Kherson and Bessarabia regions and paper and silk from Russia.

When a Russian police envoy inspected Balta in 1840, he did not find the fair particularly impressive. Horses were sold for 250,000 rubles total, manufacture for 50,000, and haberdashery for 20,000 rubles in banknotes.

3.2. Marketplace in Kolomyia, eastern Galicia, ca. 1930, a hundred years after the shtetl's golden age.
Photo Alter Kacyzne. BHT 87.111.2. Courtesy of YIVO and the Beit Hatfutsot exhibition
"Treasures of Jewish Galicia—Judaica from the Museum of Ethnography in Lviv, Ukraine," Photo
Archive, Tel Aviv.

Retail customers spent about 10,000 rubles on their purchases, and overall the turnover that year was about 330,000 rubles.[51] To quote the police report, the merchants "did not manage to sell their entire stock, as people did not have enough money." Reports of the Ministry of Interior also lamented the low efficiency of such fairs, caused by high prices and years of famine.[52] In fact, comparatively speaking these sums were quite extraordinary: one Balta fair exceeded the income of the ten major fairs in Belorussian shtetls combined.[53]

Lacking almost any manufacture and totally dependent on trade, the Balta fair was the heart, nerve, and sinew of the town. Because of its seasonal trade and the opportunity to lease the houses and storage spaces to incoming merchants, Balta remained the economic center of Podolia for more than a century. The southwestern Russian press recognized godforsaken Balta as the core of the province's grain, cattle, and livestock market. Clients not only from the Russian Empire but also from Austria, Prussia, and Poland came to Balta to trade. Incredibly, they bought horses at the Balta Trinity market even for export to America.[54]

The Balta fair, like perhaps any Ukrainian fair, also impressed its visitors visually, although not everyone could express this impression in words or images. Though it did not have its own Gogol, the fair's sheer beauty fascinated two national Polish painters, Józef Brandt (1841–1915) and Józef Marian Chełmoński (1849–1914), who immortalized it on their canvases, *The Fair in Balta* (ca. 1870) and *The Horse Fair in Balta* (1879). These late Romantic artists captured not only the untamed and unbridled nature of the wild horses sold at the fair but also a deeply disturbing feeling: look what we lost and who we could have been, had Balta remained Polish!

No fair in the Pale could compete with that of Berdichev. After the partitions, Matvei Radziwiłł, the Polish owner of the town, hurried to make sure that his main source of income would retain the same privileges as before. He wrote an ingratiating letter to Paul I of Russia, saying that in 1765 the Polish king had confirmed that the town of Berdichev would have ten annual fairs, creating extremely beneficial circumstances for all the townsfolk. Radziwiłł appended a copy of the Polish kings' privilege in Russian translation and humbly requested its renewal.[55] Hence

Berdichev kept its annual fairs and eventually became the most important trading center of right bank Ukraine.

Because of its annual fairs, Berdichev grew with unprecedented speed. About three local Jews a year declared their newly acquired capital and became guild merchants. In 1829, with a population of 34,000, Berdichev boasted 335 third-guild, nine second-guild, and two first-guild merchants. At that time, 95 percent of those merchants were Jews, all of whom owned stalls and stores in the Berdichev Old Market. Ten years later, the number had grown to 477 third-guild, twenty-four second-guild, and seven first-guild merchants—ten times more than in the nearby provincial center of Zhitomir.[56]

The most important reason for the town's growth, however, claimed an anonymous Russian expert, was the enormous influx of people, who came, as we already know, to the local annual fairs. We can only sympathize with the parents of Nosson Sternhartz, whose son became the scribe of Rabbi Nachman in the small shtetl of Bratslav instead of establishing his family business in Berdichev: they were bewildered by what they considered his crazy choice.[57]

The Berdichev fairs competed with the largest trading centers outside the Pale of Settlement. In 1812, for example, one out of ten Berdichev fairs attracted 4.5–5 million rubles' worth of merchandise, bringing an income of four to eleven percent to the trading merchants. Although Berdichev's St. Onufry fair could hardly compete with the Romny, Kharkov, or Kursk fairs with their turnover of 13 million, 10 million, and 14 million rubles, respectively, one must take into account the intensity and density of the fairs in Ukraine in general and in Berdichev in particular.[58]

In the 1830s, several Berdichev fairs enjoyed the same turnover as the Contract fair in Kiev. Merchants brought some 1,700,000 rubles' worth of Russian goods to the Berdichev St. Onufry fair, 190,000 rubles' worth of paper items and textiles, 130,000 rubles' worth of refined sugar, 361,225 rubles' worth of various types of comestibles and tobacco, 26,000 rubles' worth of spices and tinctures, 370,000 of European and 164,000 rubles' worth of Asian goods. The Uspensky fair in Berdichev was no less impressive, with its 1,030,000 rubles' worth of Russian goods, 196,000 rubles' worth of European goods, and 79,000 rubles' worth of Asian goods.[59]

Why was Berdichev so popular? There was no other town in the province offering the benefits of Berdichev. In state-owned towns such as nearby Zhitomir, merchants had to pay a duty of 180 rubles in banknotes, whereas in Berdichev, a private town, the duty was only 100 rubles. With all its urban trade, Berdichev remained a cheap, semirural place with unpaved streets, an easily affordable cost of living, and relatively cheap real estate. A house on the outskirts of Berdichev cost between 5 and 14 złoty, and ten new Jewish families settled there annually late in the eighteenth century.[60] As a shtetl with its own regulations, Berdichev was hard to compete with, particularly since the town also offered a bonus not always available elsewhere—entertainment.

The Ukrainian fairs epitomized adventure, entertainment, unexpected fun, and unheard-of miracles. In Berdichev, a local theater offered Polish plays. A retired clerk ran a casino in his house and welcomed gamblers to join the card games. Three traveling Dutch showmen displayed wax figures and a *cosmorama* with a sophisticated system of mirrors and lenses through which spectators could see various world landmarks. The Russian secret envoy reported that one of the Dutchmen "fed his anaconda snake chickens, rabbits, and doves in public." An Italian who called himself Dominicani entertained the public with a cast of rare animals.

The town authorities also organized horse races, if mediocre ones, but even they were a thrill for the people coming from the backwoods of Volhynia and Podolia. Trapeze artists demonstrated all sorts of vertiginous tricks under a circus tent. One Yiddish memoirist, without providing a date for the event, tells the story of a traveling circus that brought an elephant to a Berdichev fair. The elephant ran away and walked straight into the Gnilopiat River, from which nobody, including the owners, could convince it to come out until the entire fire brigade had arrived.[61] Perhaps at a similar fair, Rabbi Pinhas of Korets watched a tightrope walker balancing on the rope and observed that everybody needed to find his own individual way of serving God.[62]

Berdichev also offered something of spiritual value, connecting secular trade and religious pilgrimage. Poles came here to look at the miraculous icon of the Virgin Mary, whose healing capacities and miracle-working reputation attracted hundreds of Catholic believers to the chapel

3.3. A synagogue in Uman.
IA, f. 9, spr. 73, ark. 83. Courtesy of the Institute of Archaeology of the National Academy of Sciences of Ukraine.

of the local Roman Catholic church. Russians and Ukrainians flocked to the wooden eighteenth-century Eastern Orthodox church with its famous medieval icon of St. Nicholas the Miracle-Maker. For the Jews, the town was the gravesite of Levy Isaac of Berdichev, one of the illustrious Hasidic masters and a living legend of Jewish folklore. Like worshipping the icon of the Virgin Mary or kissing the icon of St. Nicholas, praying at the grave of Levy Isaac was believed to be healing, comforting, and invigorating, a remedy for all diseases and a blessing for any endeavor.

The fairs, including those of Berdichev, were impressive for anyone except the adepts of a well-managed state, that is, governmental clerks of all ranks, who left detailed accounts. No doubt, chaos reigned at the fairs, and the trading was crazy and disorganized. Jews sold goods from their stalls and traded from the windows of the houses at the marketplace as well as from the streets, which led from the marketplace in different directions. Peasants sold produce from wagons parked all over the marketplace. Trade agents pulled at the sleeves of potential customers, offering them the best deals. Jews, recalled Aksakov, "grabbed their goods and took them in all different directions, brought them to villages and hamlets, to the lazy gentry, to the stay-at-home Cossacks, to flamboyant male peasants, to chic female peasants."[63]

The density of trade was indescribable, to the great joy of pickpockets and swindlers. The street leading through Balta was one long trading stall, packed with wagons and merchandise. Makhnovka Street in Berdichev had wagons lining both sides, and the houses on the street overflowed with customers and salesmen. One could easily be crushed by the multitude of horses and people and could inadvertently bump into someone while pulling out money. Customers and salesmen eagerly exchanged Yiddish and Slavic obscenities.

No consideration was given to either sanitary or fire safety. In fact, among the many hundred trading stalls in Berdichev's Old Market, ninety-two were very old, overcrowded, and falling apart; several of them used as outhouses. If a fire broke out, there would be no way to save anybody, warned the cautious police observers. It would be much better, suggested the police, to relocate the fairs, as was done in Russian towns proper, to lands beyond the territory of the town.[64]

The fairs, however, were too well embedded in the architectonics of the shtetl. Relocating them would change what the shtetl was all about. Instead, Governor General Bibikov sought to establish more fairs—for example, in Uman.[65] His logic was not only to develop internal trade but also to make good use of the key players at the fair, the Jews. Thus he made an attempt to establish annual fairs in Belaia Tserkov. In his request, Bibikov underscored that this town, still in the possession of Count Władisław Branicki, stood right on a strategically important road connecting Kiev and Odessa, and in the proximity of Skvira and Vasilkov. Bibikov emphasized that "trade had previously moved to the borders of the empire but now there is drastic need to establish centers of trade in the interior of the empire." He suggested establishing three fairs, each one week long: St. Nicholas, in May; the Savior, in August; and St. Luke, in October. Belaia Tserkov, observed Bibikov, had 7,043 Jews, the backbone of the town's trading capacities. Its 6,120 peasants were still serfs and could not take charge of the trade, nor could the shtetl's 475 Poles, 68 Christian townsfolk, or 411 members of the gentry. On the other hand, the Jews already had one first-guild, one second-guild, and thirteen third-guild merchants in town. "Only Jews," claimed the governor, "go in for trade and manufacture." The fair would not only be profitable for the state treasury, it would help "local Jews pay their debts."[66]

Kankrin grudgingly agreed, with all sorts of caveats, although he wanted to see more fairs outside the shtetls and under Russian, not Polish magnate, control—in Poltava, Kharkov, Kremenchug, and Zhitomir, towns with a smaller Jewish presence.[67] While local authorities contributed to the blossoming of the shtetl trade, the central administration sought to undermine it. The shtetl found itself in the center of a Polish-Russian economic and political rivalry, but also in the focus of Russia's version of the Enlightenment, with its aversion to trade, considered by the leading liberal-minded East European officials as something antithetical to the genuine economy.

DOWN WITH BERDICHEV!

The Russian authorities realized that the annual fairs made some towns prosperous while towns without fairs slowly declined.[68] The key role of Berdichev in Ukrainian trade and the absolute predominance of Jews in this trade triggered deep anxiety. Leading figures of the Russian state, beginning with the minister of finance, were confident that it was manufacture and agriculture rather than trade that created a stable economy. Followers of the Prussian enlightened thinkers, they viewed trade as suspicious, uncontrollable, and volatile. To their sheer dismay, in the western borderlands it was also Jewish-driven. Since Jews came to be associated with trade, leveling the towns economically meant fortifying some towns at the expense of others and suppressing what contemporaries called Jewish trade.

Enlightenment ideas accommodated the growing xenophobia. The governor general spoke directly to ethnic prejudice when the central authorities asked him why certain towns were not prospering. "The most important reason," he emphasized, "is that trade belongs predominantly to Jews, a cunning and greedy people, who under various pretexts almost always and everywhere manage to keep the turnover of capital entirely in their hands." He added significantly that "the concentration of trade in Berdichev ruins other towns, such as Kremenets."[69]

Like him, the government also decided that Berdichev had become too powerful and out of control. Although it was economically flourishing, it was still a town in private possession, while merchants from the nearby state-owned town of Zhitomir suffered. In the 1830s the government decided to undertake a number of steps to subdue Berdichev, one of which proved to be successful: playing one town against the other.

Nicholas I had heard enough about Berdichev to realize that this economic center was Polish and Jewish, hardly Russian at all. What could be done to diminish its impact and buttress the development of the state-owned, and therefore in his eyes, Russian towns? Establish the Contract fair in Kiev to compete with Berdichev, advised Nicholas. Allow Jews to trade at the fair, although they were banished from the town in the 1830s, and let them contribute multi-thousand duties to the treasury.[70] Do not allow the Volhynia Jewish bankers to make their credit available for the Kiev Contract fair wholesalers, lest it again benefit Berdichev.[71] And do not allow more kosher canteens in the Kiev marketplace than the absolute minimum.[72] After all, the idea was to offset Berdichev, not to benefit the Jews.

But that was not enough. Following Nicholas's advice, the authorities chose another town, state-owned Zhitomir, as Berdichev's competitor. Hearing the rumors from the capital, the Zhitomir elites concocted a petition to meet Nicholas halfway. They requested that Zhitomir be granted all sorts of privileges to help them attract Russian merchants, and, to put Berdichev down, establish two fairs in Zhitomir right before the fairs in Berdichev, which would then have to make do with the leftovers. They also took precautions to prevent Berdichev from establishing its own town hall, independent from Zhitomir. This was an economic and political step with barely any anti-Jewish overtones. After all, fifteen Jews, most of them third-guild merchants, signed the anti-Berdichev petition, in addition to the head of the Zhitomir town hall and the two wealthiest Christian merchants.[73] However, it was definitely an anti-shtetl step: the gold of Berdichev sparkled too much.

The Russian authorities decided to try and upset the shtetl economies by establishing new district centers in state-owned towns so that the shtetls would then legally report to them. The government-orchestrated fight between Berdichev and Zhitomir was not unique: other towns and shtetls were drawn into its devastating whirl. For example, the authorities provoked a conflict between the prosperous Medzhibozh and the nearby impoverished Letichev, which was underpopulated, in shambles, and without manufacture, a pharmacy, or even a mill.[74] Instead of transferring the administrative center to Medzhibozh, too Jewish for their taste, the authorities chose to stimulate the development of Letichev with its Russian administrative offices and state archive.[75]

In neighboring Belorussia, the two shtetls of Pinsk and Karlin also entered into bitter rivalry when the emerging Karlin tried to become administratively independent from nearby Pinsk.[76] Although these intertown conflicts had different origins (such as the distribution of the tax burden), they were not unknown in the Polish-Lithuanian Commonwealth with its ongoing rivalry between Kremenets and Vladimir-Volynsk, on the one side, and Ostrog and Lutsk on the other.[77]

Neither Christians nor Jews knew that the authorities were playing the towns one against the other. An impressive cohort of Berdichev Jews tried to justify their cause. They convinced their attorney to help them construct an appeal to the Kiev provincial military general governor Levashov. Well-known local tycoon Mordko Guberman signed the petition first, which outlined the inconveniences of Berdichev submitting to the Zhitomir town hall. The merchants of Berdichev had to travel forty miles to Zhitomir each time they needed a certificate issued or a tax payment arranged, he explained.

If one believes the complaint, about *ten thousand* Jewish traders had to obtain required documents in Zhitomir. Round trip by wagon cost 10 rubles, and then there were food and living expenses while the Berdichev Jews negotiated their way through the red tape in Zhitomir. Furthermore, such a trip disrupted local business. Berdichev townsfolk were wasting tens of thousands of rubles without any benefit for the town. Of course, more reasonable would be to establish the town hall in Berdichev and once and for all put an end to its underdog position.

3.4. A town hall in Slavuta.
IA, f. 9, spr. 42, ark. 5. Courtesy of the Institute of Archaeology of the National Academy of Sciences of Ukraine.

The Zhitomir Jewish elders and several Jewish traders immediately reacted. Their response to Levashov contained a vociferous and well-substantiated bluff. Those Berdichev Jews seeking to move the magistrate from Zhitomir to Berdichev were just a bunch of corrupt opportunists. The Berdichev Jews had to go from one town to another for documents once in three years. Should they establish their magistrate in Berdichev, local Zhitomir merchants were likely to lose their privileged businesses. The entire town would suffer, since Zhitomir merchants brought more than 120,000 rubles to the town treasury per year, they argued.

Levashov found the appeal of Berdichev Jews undeserving and harked to the pleas of the merchants of Zhitomir. Civil Governor Rimsky-Korsakov agreed with him: Berdichev Jews were engaging in all sorts of wrongdoing to damage Zhitomir Jewish society; I will not issue any passports for them; they will not be able to go to St. Petersburg and complain.[78]

The battle between the two towns had just begun. It lasted for more than a decade and involved some insidious doings and backdoor arrangements on both sides. The Zhitomir merchants bent over backward to find fault with their Berdichev colleagues and prevent them from establishing an urban self-governing institution of their own. In turn, the Berdichev merchants pointed out their several thousand trading townsfolk, including ten first-guild, eleven second-guild, and five hundred third-guild merchants. They emphasized that the town provided 10,000 silver rubles in taxes to the state, more than enough to establish a local magistrate. Prince Radziviłł himself asked the government to reclassify Berdichev as a town in the Makhnovka district, noting how inconvenient it was to make transactions in Berdichev and legalize them in Zhitomir. He also realized that this was about Russia being against the shtetl with its Jewish trade and a Polish town-owner, not only about Zhitomir versus Berdichev.

The case reached the ministers, the Senate, and the tsar, who supported a broader political agenda: bend the szlachta-owned shtetls down to the state-owned towns, subjugate the residue of Old Poland to the Russian Empire, and suppress the uncontrolled prosperity of the shtetls. Government bureaucrats vacillated, suggesting either that Berdichev be reclassified in Kiev province or suppressed altogether. The opponents of Berdichev emphasized that it was a powerful and lawless town. Its fairs attracted suspicious Poles from Galicia, Poznań, and the Kingdom of Poland. These gatherings were reminiscent of the violent and disordered Polish Sejm. Poles came together "to play cards, talk, sin, and dream of the reconstruction of the Polish republic."

Most notoriously, they argued, Berdichev had turned into a center of Jewish fanaticism. When a rabbi arrived in town (most likely when Rabbi Israel of Ruzhin arrived in town for his betrothal to the daughter of Moshe Halevi Efrati), they unharnessed his horses and carried him through the town on their shoulders with unheard-of religious enthusiasm.[79] No state bureaucrats were capable of suppressing these outrageous deeds. Jewish trade and Judaism had become a threat.

The overplayed critique of Berdichev by Zhitomir supporters made Nicholas reclassify the town in Kiev province and ascribe its dwellers to a nearby Makhnovka magistrate.[80] In the late 1850s the authorities transferred the police and fire station to Berdichev, endorsed the establishment of the town's artisan guilds, and established the town offices in Berdichev proper.[81] In the 1850s, after multiple attempts to suppress Berdichev, the governor of Kiev, Volhynia, and Podolia provinces reported that trade on his territory "was concentrated in Kiev and Berdichev." He mentioned that these two towns—one of them under imperial control, the other still a shtetl in the private ownership of the magnate's family—traded in grain products, cattle, horses, sheep, leather, tar, iron and wooden utensils, salt, fish, cloth, wood, and textiles, amounting altogether to about 2,000,000 silver rubles' turnover.[82]

Berdichev was diminished but not defeated. The local fairs continued to buttress the town economy, but it already resembled the clumsy fictional Kasrilovke of Mendele Moykher Sforim rather than the shtetl in its glory.[83] At mid-century, the banking house of the Galperins almost collapsed, while the banks of the Trachtenbergs and the Efrussis (Efratis) already had one foot in Odessa, which came to replace Berdichev as the center of Russia's southwestern trade.

Elsewhere in Volhynia, Podolia, and Kiev provinces, the confiscation of the towns from the Polish magnates, together with the resettlement of thousands of midranking landlords and the subsequent impoverishment of all those who remained, contributed to the deterioration of trade in the shtetl. "All those Jews who had dealt exclusively with the landed gentry remained altogether without any means of making a living," insightfully observed Yekhezkel Kotik, pondering the fate of his own Belorussian shtetl Kamenets.[84]

Furthermore, Russia did its best to erode the strong Catholic presence in the western provinces. Dozens of monasteries were closed, thousands of Catholics of non-Polish ethnicity joined the Eastern Orthodox Church, and so did the Uniates, Eastern Orthodox who reported to the pope, once Nicholas legally banned them in 1839. The monastic treasuries, from which the Jews had always borrowed money for trading purposes, now became educational funds. These newly established funds demanded from the Jews the principal the Jews had borrowed, even though the arrangement was that Jews would pay only the interest over a long unidentified period.[85] Relatives of the borrowers who had been dead for years,

3.5. The old palace of the Sanguszko magnates in Slavuta.
IA, f. 9, spr. 42, ark. 4. Courtesy of the Institute of Archaeology of the National Academy of Sciences of Ukraine.

the synagogues, the kahal members, and even entire communities were deemed responsible for the debts.

Not only did Jews lose their permanent source of liquid funds for transactions, they now found themselves deeply in debt.[86] The triangle of power—the Russian administration, the Jewish economy, and the Polish owners—which greatly benefited the Jews was replaced by a dual model in which only the Jews and the Russians remained. And the Russian authorities had a very peculiar attitude to the trading towns, free retail trade, and economic competition.

THE PEOPLE OF THE *GESHEFT*

When all was said and done, Russian police envoys traveling to Balta and Berdichev found almost no suspicious activity at the fairs they visited. Gaivoronsky discovered that the Poles viewed Russian policy in the western borderlands as attempts to further humiliate the glorious Polish people. Radishchev established that the Poles spent most of their time in the inns, cursing Russia, but were not scheming anything subversive. And von Gildebrant most likely had nothing to report, once he found out that *balagola* was the Yiddish for cabman, and that most cabmen were simpletons engaged into all sorts of gossip about Jews, Poles, and Russians while driving their customers around.[87] The only two significant ramifications of the envoys' trips were their detailed reports about the fair trade.

Trade transformed the shtetl into a fascinating economic center and propelled the exchange not only of commodities and money but also of words. The shtetl enriched the languages of its merchants as much as it enriched the merchants themselves. If we dig into Yiddish and Ukrainian vocabulary as an archaeologist digs through cultural layers, we encounter intense linguistic exchange between Jews and Slavs. In the Dubno region, Ukrainians used the Yiddish word *balagola* for a cabman. The Ukrainian for "it is not really so great" and the Yiddish for "a bargain" came together in their popular expression *to ne velyka metsiya*.[88] Ukrainians routinely used the Yiddish *handel* for "trade"—and owing to such writers as Oleksandr Zderkovskyi and Olha Kobylianska, this word entered the Ukrainian vocabulary. Jews, on the other hand, used the Ukrainian *keshene* (pocket and wallet, Ukr: *kyshenia*), *holoble* (yoke, Ukr.: *holoblia*), *halme* (brake: *halma)*, and *skrynie* (trousseau, Ukr.: *skrynia*), which became indispensable in Yiddish everyday usage.

Together with the produce they bought from peasants, Jews also appropriated Slavic expressions concerning trade. They wed Slavic verbs and Yiddish numerals to convey a profoundly Jewish meaning: *kupil fuftsiker, prodal za fertsiker, abi svezhi grosh*: "I bought it for fifty, sold it for forty, just to have fresh money"—or to stay in business. They took the verb *yarmarkuvaty*, Ukrainian for trading at the fair, and copied it into the Yiddish verb *yarideven*. And exactly like the surrounding Slavs, the Jews mocked those who were trying to *zayn mit ayin tukhes af tsveyn yaridn*—"to sit on one backside at two fairs."[89]

Russian officialdom did not like the shtetl trade, and instead of helping it become the cornerstone of the borderland economy, the new Russian Hamburg or Breslau, it chose to suppress it. And with the shtetl trade, the regime denigrated trade in general. Russia continued to develop, and quite successfully, both its internal and especially its state-controlled wholesale trade, particularly along the Volga River in the interior Russian provinces. As far as the western provinces and the market town trade was concerned, however, the Russian administration was adamant and chose ideology over profit. The regime endorsed the opinions such as that of Prince Repnin, scandalized by Jews who "sell cheaper than the [Russian] merchants."[90]

The Russian regime did support, reform, and accommodate its guild merchants engaged in wholesale trade.[91] Yet simultaneously the regime adopted the anticapitalist and xenophobic myth of Jews as a people of commerce, lovers of *gandel* and *gesheft*, hence cunning, dishonest, swindling, untrustworthy, and unreliable. Pavlo Chubynskyi, sympathetic to the Jewish traders, still allowed himself the following observation: "*Gandel* for the Jew is his most cherished occupation from childhood to the grave."[92]

As a result of the tireless efforts of Russian soil-bound writers with their anti-Western phobias, this Jewish *gesheft* came to signify what was alien and despicable about the immoral Jews, associated with the shtetl— a threat to Russian statehood. The more palpable was the fall of real wages in Russia the 1860s to 1880s, the more vociferous became the Russian xenophobes eager to blame the entrepreneurial profit-oriented Jew.[93]

The xenophobic writer and journalist Vsevolod Krestovsky put the word *gesheft* into wide circulation, using it in his diatribes against Jewish emancipation. He argued that a Jew could be neither a Russian officer nor a Russian patriot since Jews thought only about their *gesheft* and bowed down to the opportunities of the *gandel*, not to the holy task of defending their motherland.[94]

Under the prolific pens of the Russian xenophobes, some of them famous writers, *gesheft* turned into an essential Jewish ethnic feature. Nikolai Leskov claimed that any little Yid, if he had half a brain, could get a substantial amount of money through a safe *gesheft*, a sign of disgustingly low morality.[95] For Dostoevsky, the Jews and sleazy *gesheft* were synonymous. When his Christian Orthodox Grushenka, lover of Fedor Karamazov, engaged in a questionable business that Dostoevsky calls *gesheft*, people start to consider her "a genuine female Yid."[96] Chekhov considered *gesheft* as something despised, akin to the deception of one's brethren and to promiscuity.[97]

At the turn of the nineteenth century, negative ethics became negative politics. The rejection of the Jew morphed into a rejection of the capitalist way of life. With Lenin, *gesheft* acquired the antibourgeois semantics of class hatred, not without some moderate antisemitic overtones. Lenin cursed his opponents not only for being "skeptics" but also for being treacherous bourgeois—*gesheft*-makers, as he put it.[98]

The Soviet imagination amalgamated "Jews," "business," "trade," and "treason" into one nasty concept. Valentin Pikul, the author of popular pseudohistorical novels, discussed in one of them the 1911 assassination of Prime Minister Stolypin as a successful *gesheft* of the murderer Bogrov, who happened to be of Jewish origin.[99]

Russian dictionaries introduced this word often, without indicating its Yiddish origin but almost always pointing out its negative meaning. One dictionary defines *gesheft* as meaning "salary" or "business," which Russians use either ironically or "regarding the Jews."[100]

Most recently, this myth informed a reductionist and essentialist vision of the Jews as a tribe of service nomads, the people of Mercury, thus reenacting Russian anti-Judaic myths of Jews as a clan and a tribe whose God dwells in the spirit of exchange.[101]

Once the vision of the Jew as a sleazy *gesheft*-maker dominated Russian discourse and the government was seeking out the best ways to undermine what it saw as Jewish trade, instead of liberating and benefiting from it, the era of the golden age shtetl came to a halt, and with it the great promise of the Russian Jewish encounter. The shtetl marketplace emptied, and a premonition of bloodshed permeated the air.

CHAPTER FOUR

THE RIGHT TO DRINK

Meilakh Goldfeld, while driving his wagon, reveled in his recent deal. He was bringing three barrels of fruit wine and two barrels of absinthe to the inn he ran from the cellar of his house. Avrum Khodorkovsky, one of the top Cherkas tavernkeepers, had sold it to him dirt cheap. The wine was beautifully balanced, with a bittersweet finish. Meilakh would no longer have to sell the sour wine of that blockhead, Kvitnitsky. Meilakh smacked his lips. He was proud of himself, of his negotiating skills, and of his barrels.

He had no idea that he had become a pawn in a game involving all the bigshots in town: the Cherkas governor; two leaseholders of the liquor trade, Lubarsky and Khodorkovsky; and liquor sales monopolist Fishel Kvitnitsky. Fishel had paid the Russian state treasury up front and obtained a liquor monopoly license. Now only Fishel was allowed to sell wines locally. All tavernkeepers had to buy from him, and no one else could import wine or vodka.[1]

The liquor monopoly was a tasty business in need of surveillance. One day in 1821, Fishel intercepted Meilakh Goldfeld, who was bringing wine to his inn. Where is your wine from? Khodorkovsky? How dare you! If everyone purchased outside alcohol, Fishel's monopoly would become obsolete, and he would not be able make back what he had paid the treasury. Fishel turned to the governor: Khodorkovsky and others were undermining his state-supported business!

There was little the governor could do. Khorodkovsky and Lubarsky had purchased a privilege from the Polish magnate Prince Sanguszko to lease the town taverns. The shtetl was split in half: one Jewish leaseholder reported to the Russian state treasury; the other two reported to the Polish magnate. Jews traded in liquor; liquor reeked of politics.

If the tavernkeepers purchased Kvitnitsky's alcohol, they would have had to raise their prices, would have lost clientele, and would not have been able to pay their dues to Sanguszko. They would have been out of business. Nobody could bring together two incompatible laws, one protecting the privileges of the gentry and the other protecting the state treasury. While the Russian regime and the Polish gentry stayed above the fray, the competing Jews decided to destroy the competition.

And destroy the competition they did. Khodorkovsky arranged for the illegal sale of alcohol through a number of innkeepers, Meilakh Goldfeld included. Fishel's trade shrank, and he started losing money. His petitions to the governor fell on deaf ears. Nobody could force Khodorkovsky to purchase from Kvitnitsky. The local gentry, government clerks, officers, and the provincial governor general all visited Khodorkovsky's cozy establishment, described in documents as "the best tavern in town," enjoyed his services, and did not care about the source of his liquor. The enraged Kvitnitsky then filed an accusation with the district prosecutor. Khodorkovsky's attorneys counterattacked: Kvitnitsky, they explained, was a liquor monopolist in control of wholesale trade, not of tavern-based retail trade, and thus their patrons could not be accused of undermining his business.[2]

Meilakh's absinthe was flammable and could have sparked a vodka war between Sanguszko, who still owned part of Cherkas, and the Russian authorities, who managed the other part. Smoldering in Cherkas, the conflict exploded elsewhere. It turned into an exhausting vodka war in which everyone had a stake: the Russian authorities, liquor monopolists, tavernkeepers, Polish landlords, and especially ordinary Jews, who were pivotal to the liquor trade and tavernkeeping in the shtetl.

LIQUID HARD CURRENCY

"Jews are fools," goes a Ukrainian proverb. "They have vodka and they sell it." This centuries-old piece of Slavic wisdom might not be accurate anthropologically, but historically it is, particularly the second part. Some Jews drank vodka, yet a disproportionately large number of them dealt in the liquor trade. This marriage of convenience between Jews and alcohol goes back to the early sixteenth-century manorial economy. To secure their well-being, the magnates granted Jews the privilege to produce and sell liquor, called a *propinacja*. Peasants on the magnate's estate could purchase liquor only in the local taverns and inns.

Since the manorial economy drew on serf labor, grain was cheap and stable, but vodka increased in price.[3] While annual fairs attracted trade to the towns, vodka helped convert grain surplus into local assets. People came to the fair, traded, and went to the taverns to celebrate their deals. Vodka became for the magnate economy what the Polish *złoty* was for the crown treasury: currency. The magnates deemed Poles capable of producing but incapable of selling vodka, and Ukrainian peasants incapable of either. Somebody else had to help them translate grain into money. They leased their privilege to the Jews.

The Russian clerks in charge of shtetl inventories referred to inns, bars, and pubs as "Jewish taverns." This was also true in the Old Poland, where Jews dominated the liquor trade. Around the 1750s, 55 percent of the taxpaying Jews in Podolia were engaged in the liquor trade.[4] By 1795, about 85 percent of Jews permanently residing in rural areas of Eastern Poland (outside the shtetls) were in this or that manner involved in tavernkeeping: practically all the rural Jews. By the time of the partitions of Poland, the liquor trade had become the Jewish occupation par excellence. For the founders of Slavic Romanticism such as Nikolai Gogol, Adam Mickiewicz, and Taras Shevchenko, the quintessential Jew was a tavernkeeper.

4.1. A Jewish innkeeper, 19th century.
Oil painting by J. Maszkowski. BHT 87.T.125.17-19. Courtesy of LKhG and the Beit Hatfutsot exhibition "Treasures of Jewish Galicia—Judaica from the Museum of Ethnography in Lviv, Ukraine," Photo Archive, Tel Aviv.

After the partitions, the Jewish tavern found itself under the Russian Empire. Catherine II introduced the liquor monopoly system in 1767, extended it to the newly acquired territories in 1795, and created the liquor trade monopolies. Make your best bid: receive a liquor monopoly and collect all the income from liquor trade in a certain locality. Following the Polish experience, Catherine was sure that this arrangement would be profitable. Liquor monopolists, she knew, relied on state protection, and repaid the state with higher bids for the local monopolies. Direct income from selling liquor monopoly licenses increased from 7 million to 10 million rubles in the 1780s, to 28 million in 1807, to 72 million by 1827, to 92 million in 1839, and to 297 million by 1894.[5] At the height of Russia's industrialization, liquor trade revenues yielded 25 percent of the country's annual budget.

The Russian authorities were very curious about this situation. They tried to look into the gentry ledgers, forcing some information out of the magnates. Sanguszko, for example, shared the shtetl Cherkas (population around 1,370) with the Russian state treasury. The treasury received 1,765 rubles in taxes from town dwellers and merchants, while Sanguszko obtained an income of 15,874 złoty from the liquor brewers and tavern-keepers. Cherkas was in the southeast, and the situation in other parts of Ukraine was similar. Taverns along the Austrian border in the Dubno district belonged to Count Miączyński, who received a handsome 18,000 złoty income annually.[6] Boguslav, belonging to Count Poniatowski, boasted 406 houses, which brought 1,263 złoty in taxes, whereas the beer brewery made him 3,000 złoty and the sale of liquor another 5,500.

The shtetl of Mezhirich, confiscated from a Polish magnate, had 1,514 inhabitants and yielded an income of 4,298 rubles, of which the income from Jewish breweries and taverns—3,300 rubles—constituted 78 percent. In Starokonstantinov, the possession of Countess Rzewuska, about fifty inns and taverns, yielded 67 percent of the town revenues.[7] The situation was similar in shtetls belonging to such Polish landlords as Ganski, Branicki, and Radziwiłł. Let us take a look at the Polish landlord Jabłunowski, owner of Chigirin, a small town of 694 souls. These 694 townsfolk paid 6,926 rubles to the state treasury and 2,429 złoty (about 600 rubles) in taxes to the town-owner. However, the mere thirty-two Jews in charge of local tavernkeeping provided Jabłunowski with an income of 9,000 złoty (2,250 rubles)!

In the mid-nineteenth century, the entire Kiev province made 3,482,906 rubles in taxes, of which 494,028 came from breweries and 1,065,300 from excise taxes—that is, 45 percent.[8] Compare these numbers with the amounts of money the landowners received from their serfs: 10 percent of their entire income at best. Even if the Jewish population in some shtetls was small, the Jewish liquor trade yielded 65 to 80 percent of the magnates' income.[9]

The more economically attractive the shtetl, the more liquor it sold, and the more it sold, the more economically attractive it became. Taverns hit their highest sales rates during fairs. Jews, Russians, and Poles measured liquor in barrels holding forty buckets (160 gallons) each, in buckets holding 12 liters (four gallons) each, and in *shtofs*, bottles holding about 0.6 liters or five ounces each. Small towns and villages with no fairs but with a *shinek*, a low-key pub, sold 200 to 600 buckets of vodka annually. The shtetls with established fairs, however, sold as much as 1,200 buckets every two weeks. Kamenka and Makhnovka, with inns on the roads leading from Berdichev to Odessa, sold 1,800 and 2,500 buckets monthly, while Chernobyl sold 2,000 buckets biweekly during fairs.

The Boguslav district boasted 116 annual fairs and sold 43,000 buckets. In the Uman district there were 189 taverns and 22 roadside inns, which sold about 64,000 buckets of wine and vodka annually. The Lipovets district with its 238 urban taverns and 287 rural inns sold 65,000 buckets annually, 3,500 of which were sold in the shtetl of Lipovets alone. Of course, most consumers came from elsewhere in the province to trade at the marketplace. Still, according to the figures, every dweller in the Uman district drank on average one bucket of vodka per year, and in Lipovets three.[10]

The shtetl was as much a market town as it was a liquor town. In this way, shtetls differed radically from villages, which sometimes had an inn or a pub, but often no inn at all. Several dozen villages around the Kagarlyk district southwest of Kiev—together with all the roadside inns between villages—sold about 5,000 buckets of wine per year. The shtetls, however, in the mid-1820s in Kiev province belonging to Countess Branicka, Bishop Czyżewski, and landlord Rulikowski, boasted twenty-two wine cellars, eight hotels, seventy-one restaurants, one coffee house, twenty-four roadside inns, six canteens, and 738 taverns. Kiev province had 264 taverns selling 49,000 buckets annually, a figure most likely underreported.[11] For this reason, the Polish landlords sought to transform their villages into a *mestechko*. They were very well aware of what that implied economically and did not need all the data. Yet the data was eloquent. The Radomyshl district, for example, with its 275 taverns and fifteen inns, sold only 13,500 buckets. No fairs, no business.

Jews had to pay upfront to lease a tavern. From 1807 to 1811 in Ushitsa, Zelman Abramovich leased a tavern for 53 rubles in banknotes per year; Gershko Iosiovich in Gaisin and Itsko Srulevich in Vinnitsa, for 33 rubles each, and in Letichev, Leiba Aronovich paid 53 banknotes, equal to one quarter of the price of a decent shtetl house.[12] Gedalia from Brailov leased a Medzhibozh roadside tavern for 15 silver rubles per year.[13] The Uman Jewess Perla Peiarovskaia leased her tavern for 150 rubles a year. When the Russian authorities arrested Michal Głębocki and confiscated his estate, including a house and a winery and inn, only Iankel Karpman made a bid on it, readily putting down 109 rubles in banknotes.[14] The maintenance of their taverns cost the landlords very little: labor was cheap, and revenues were astonishingly high.

Tavernkeeping was much more profitable than serfdom, the cornerstone of Russia's rural economy. The liquor business shaped the shtetl industry, trade, and finance. Vodka became the shtetl's source of energy. Its steady flow was responsible for most of the town's economic well-being. Whoever controlled the liquor trade controlled the shtetl.

The Russian authorities sought to impose the principles of an absolutist economy on the liquor trade and found themselves in a trap. Trade for them was harmful, and the vodka trade was a social ill. Senator Derzhavin visited famine-stricken Belorussia and claimed that Jewish leaseholders and taverners had ruined the peasants. Enlightened Polish thinkers such as Stanisław Staszicz and Hugo Kołłontaj vociferously argued against Jewish tavernkeeping.[15]

However, Alexander I and Nicholas I realized that their enlightened zeal was at odds with their sober economic management. The laws reflected the domineering autocratic ideology, whereas the economic realities reflected its mercantilist goals. As long as the Russian regime maintained this paradox, the shtetl enjoyed its privileges, revenues, and a good drink.

Russia's concern for the peasants, disapproval of the arbitrary landlords, and desire to make Jews productive brought this period to an end. Under the influence of Derzhavin, Alexander I in his 1804 Statute on the Jews outlawed Jewish tavernkeeping in rural areas. He planned to move Jews to urban centers and thus prevent the ruin of the Russian peasant, so prone to drunkenness. With the same enlightened goal in mind, the Senate in 1807 ordered the eviction of all Jews from rural areas in Volhynia and Podolia, particularly emphasizing the ban on Jewish rural tavernkeeping.[16] In its special 1808 regulation, the Senate again forbade brewery, innkeeping, the liquor trade, and the lease of those trades in rural areas. None of

4.2. The 1818 brewery in Slavuta.
IA, f. 9, spr. 11A, ark. 1. Courtesy of the Institute of Archaeology of the National Academy of Sciences of Ukraine.

these orders took effect since, as one historian stated, the magnates "struggled to preserve life as it had been."[17]

The minister of finance also realized that removing Jews from the liquor trade was counterproductive: Russia could not afford it.[18] The Senate remained pragmatic and went so far as to allow about a hundred Jews to manage, although not own, breweries and produce wheat vodka outside the Pale of Settlement, "until Russian artisans appear there to take over this trade."[19] Nicholas I permitted Jewish tavernkeeping in towns and within two miles around the towns. By "permitting," Nicholas merely left things the way they were. Vodka won—but not forever.

THE REVEALER OF SECRETS

The tavern was as important for ordinary Jews as the synagogue. What Jews could not discuss freely in the synagogue they could easily chat about in the tavern. Despite its unhealthy environment, ordinary Jews liked their taverns. Jews gave them proper names—feminine, tender, diminutive, almost erotic: "The Little She-Dove" (Golubka), "Vydumka" (Fantasy), "Chubataia" (With a Forelock).

For shtetl dwellers, the tavern became the nexus of all secular networks, social, psychological, economic, financial, and informational. The tavern functioned as a psychiatrist's office, a want-ads page, a club, and a pub all in one. In taverns, Jews discussed business, looked for and found jobs, cut deals, compared commissions, traded in commodities, purchased groceries and haberdashery, engaged in matchmaking, changed and fed horses, repaired wagons, lent and borrowed money, spent the night on their way to a fair, shared news, hired servants or peasants as part-timers, played billiards or cards, listened to the Russian officers and Polish gentry gossip about politics, observed gentile fashion and Christian wedding celebrations, sang songs, and listened to music, and, yes, they also ate, drank, smoked, and danced.[20]

From the brief notes of travelers, one can glimpse what could be obtained, seen, or heard at the tavern. Grand Duke Nicholas, the future Nicholas I, had coffee in a Jewish tavern in Lithuania and borrowed a wagon with horses to continue on. The Decembrist Lorer, one of the participants in the 1825 rebellion, learned top-secret information from Jews in a tavern about the arrest of his accomplices.[21] Poles spent their time in the inns and taverns during annual fairs: they played cards, bet on horse races, and spoke Polish among themselves.[22] The Pole Jankowski from Vasilkov parish, a renowned klezmer musician, participated in a Purimshpil performance at a Jewish tavern.[23] The story of Mordko Portnoy from Zvenigorodka makes clear that the tavern also served as the local source of classified job ads: Mordko went to Kiev in search of part-time employment and stayed at the Rzhishchev inn, where traveling Jews told him that there was nothing to be gained in Kiev and he should not go there.[24]

Taverns were many, so tavernkeepers had to be inventive in order to attract clients. Some installed billiard tables and clavichords. Many tavernkeepers sold barrels, half barrels, and shtofs—rectangular heavy glass bottles with the Russian tsars' insignia. Some taverns provided breakfast or dinner, others a bed without meals, but they all offered a wide variety of drink. In some cutting-edge taverns one could sample sherry and French vodka, rum, absinthe, local and imported fruit and grape wines, fashionable coffees and chocolate, pekoe tea, and tobacco. In some fancy centrally located taverns the authorities forbade selling cheap drinks: root beer (*kvas*), brandy, beer, and mead. For that one had to go around the corner to a regular pub or buy a glass from a private winery in a shtetl house cellar.[25]

Taverns provided relief for the repressed libido of the shtetl. Russians, Poles, and Jews sought an escape in the tavern from all sorts of religious, social, and cultural prohibitions. Hasidic masters, the spiritual authorities for many shtetl Jews, understood the enormous psychological power of the tavern. They could have legitimately argued that immersing oneself in the blatant physicality of the tavern was incompatible with Judaic piety, but instead they chose to uplift and spiritualize its pleasures. They even claimed that what Jews did in the taverns could bring them closer to God. Rabbi Pinhas of Korets considered drinking a positive and even a mystical experience. Jews, he said, came from a world of *ahdus*, unity: this was their main secret, and the secret comes out when wine goes in, to quote a well-known Jewish proverb. Therefore, when Jews drink, the secret becomes apparent—and the sense of unity and fraternal love brings them closer to one another.[26]

Rabbi Nachman of Bratslav encouraged dancing and singing. Joy, he claimed, is an expression of gratitude before the Almighty. Dancing and singing from joy sweetens the divine punishment of the Jews.[27] Apparently, the endorsement of drinking and dancing in the court of a Hasidic master was an effective way to compete with the attractions of the tavern—and a way to transform its irresistible corporeal fun into a spiritual quest.

Let us enter the tavern. If it had massive iron-coated gates on the ground floor or a fenced-in adjacent yard with thatched stalls, a traveler could drive through. There, members of the tavernkeeper's family would

4.3. A shtetl drive-in tavern, Iaroshev, Podolia.
Binyamin Lukin's private collection. Courtesy of Binyamin Lukin.

unharness the horses and unload the wagon. This was a drive-in tavern. A non-drive-in tavern was smaller and less profitable. The former served as a hotel for travelers, envoys, clerks, and merchants. The latter had a more modest function, providing drinks and snacks.

The shtetl Khodorkov, for example, boasted at least twelve drive-in and thirteen non-drive-in taverns. Taverns also served as homes. Just one door separated the tavernkeeper's bedroom from the guest dining room. Privacy was as problematic for the guests as for the tavernkeeper's family.[28] The blurring of public and private space was the everyday reality of the tavern, making secrets impossible.

Beirish Kova's tavern in the shtetl of Poritsk in Volhynia was also his home and a hotel. This tavern was nothing unusual, neither better nor worse than hundreds of others. Kova's tavern was a large building, about seventy feet long and thirty feet wide. To get in, one had to pass between two wooden poles supporting an old shingled roof, go through the iron-coated gates, and traverse the tavern entryway with its shabby stone ceiling. Here one could leave the carriage. On the left side of the entryway were two guest rooms for visitors. The ceiling was wooden and stucco-covered, the wood floor unpainted.

The rooms had four doors leading in all directions, four windows, and, quite impressively, two stoves, one Dutch for heat and one Russian for cooking. Some of the rooms of the tavern didn't match—it had been smaller, but Beirish had enlarged it with what materials were available, not matching the initial design. The second guest room had a stone ceiling, old wooden floor, one door, two windows, and a heating stove. At the back of this room was a small storage room, four feet long and two feet wide, where traveling merchants could store their belongings. On the right side of the entryway was a store, with a stone ceiling and walls, wood floor, and one window. It was not particularly impressive, but functional.

Beirish Kova could not make a living just by selling liquor; he was also a storekeeper. Behind his store was another room, eleven feet long, with a plastered wooden ceiling, a heating stove, and a trapdoor on the floor covering the entrance to the basement. Down the ladder was a huge stone cellar as wide as the entire house. This is where the food was kept—herring, cabbage, potatoes, and pickles, but also barrels of grape wine and rye vodka. The Kovas resided in the attic. Behind the house were stalls for horses, made of stone, with roofs. The house and stalls needed considerable repair. Poritsk had half-dozen taverns like this one.[29]

Beirish's tavern was the Hermitage Museum compared to Kvitnitsky's tavern in Uman from earlier in this chapter. The only good piece of furniture he had was his billiard table. The rest was shabby: a rotted-out floor, rickety chairs, broken windows and shutters, flaking plaster, spiderwebs in the corners, a crude stove, and gloomy walls, as noted by a commission of inspection. Kvitnitsky served his drinks in eleven pieces of glazed earthenware, which was all he had. His stock was mediocre: sixteen bottles of rum, eighty-one bottles of regular grape wine and twenty-right of sour red, and twelve bottles of brandy. The members of the commission took a bottle of brandy with them "for inspection" and ordered Kvitnitsky to quit selling his low-quality red wine.[30]

Still, the shtetl taverns were better than the roadside inns. In his story "The Steppe," Anton Chekhov has his travelers go to a Jewish roadside tavern—dirty, with a suffocating heavy sour smell, warped chairs, holes in the floor, a dirty oilcloth on the table, and fly-specked pictures on the walls. The flowers on the velvet jacket of the innkeeper, reminiscent of huge bedbugs, eloquently round out this caricature.[31] The Ukrainian realist writer Hanna Barvinok (pseudonym; real name—Oleksandra Bilozers'ka-Kulish) also portrayed the Jewish roadside inn as a cold, reeking, unwelcoming, and strikingly poor place.[32] These fictional portrayals are echoed by the real observations of a contemporary inspector: "There is nothing on earth worse than a roadside inn in the backwoods of Lithuania and Polish Volhynia—yet the inns of the Ukrainian steppe are no better when it comes to dirt and bad construction."[33]

The travelers of Chekhov and Hanna Barvinok expected to find in a roadside inn the coziness of a hotel in town. They were asking the impossible. The inn near Belaia Tserkov, on the road from Kiev to Uman, had a straw roof, a chimney and a stove, four small windows, an unplastered wooden ceiling, and wooden doors. A cellar and a granary dug in a nearby hill and covered with earth show that this had definitely been a peasant hut. Like the Belaia Tserkov inn, the Dobranskaia roadside inn on the road connecting Kiev and Berdichev was also in a former peasant hut.

The tavernkeeper made most of his income from the various food items he sold to travelers and from the pastures belonging to the inn. He charged for food and for grazing. So did the leaseholder of the Tseberman road inn, which had a big cistern with water for cattle and a pasture for the bulls and horses of the Ukrainian *chumaks*, who traded in salt between the Crimea and Kiev province.[34] Unlike shtetl taverns, roadside inns kept a low profile.

The inhabitants of the shtetl liked the taverns precisely because of the blurred line between home privacy and public exposure. For one night, a traveler became a member of the household, and the Jewish family listened to the conversations of the visitors and become part of the larger world of politics. A place where wine went in and secrets came out, the tavern was what in the Judaic mystical tradition is called a revealer of secrets. Jews needed neither yellow press nor mystery novels; they had the tavern. They had no desire to part with it, although envy and xenophobia led some to spread calumny against Jewish tavernkeepers.

TASTING JEWISH VODKA

Accusations against tavernkeepers selling low-quality liquor made the business unrewarding. Russian contemporaries bemoaned the low quality of vodka of the liquor monopolists, who were interested above all in a quick return. They were notorious for diluting vodka, not distilling it properly, and destroying the market for cheaper port and beers. While this happened mostly outside the Pale of Settlement, the wholesalers in the shtetls were not much better. In the shtetls, however, some minimal quality had to be maintained because of the competition—the lease-holder of the landlord's tavern. The constant threat from the much better protected wholesalers left the private tavernkeepers with only one option, to sell a quality product. Good vodka helped outdo the calumnies.

The case of Moshka Telezhinetsky, a tavernkeeper from Shepetovka, is revealing in a number of ways. In 1836, Doctor Kirichenko of Zaslav accused Moshka of poisoning the peasants, and the clerks on the Volhynia provincial commission rigorously investigated the charges, which were serious: homicide. The investigation found that the deacon of a village church in the outskirts of Shepetovka decided to drink in honor of his deceased relatives. He came to Telezhinetsky and purchased seven buckets of vodka (twenty gallons). The next day he invited the clergy and peasants from his parish to join him. They started around 10 a.m. and stayed until after 3 p.m., finishing two buckets of alcohol. Mikhail Andreev, a peasant prone to drunkenness, liked free vodka. He barely made it home. A few hours later he was not feeling well, and by evening his condition worsened. The next day he was dead.

Doctor Kirichenko of Zaslav managed to see Andreev still alive and later came to testify to his death. Kirichenko wrote a diagnosis, along with some nasty xenophobic comments, and dispatched it to Zhitomir. Peasant Mikhail Andreev, he wrote, "died from vodka bought in Shepetovka from a local Jewish tavern belonging to Moshka Telezhinetsky." Provincial authorities jumped on the case: too many peasants had been at the party. Besides, a few years before a Jew had been suspected of ritual murder in nearby Zaslav. If Telezhinetsky was guilty, they would have an excellent explanation for the peasants' mortality rate other than serfdom.

The Zhitomir police sent orders to Shepetovka: arrest the tavernkeeper and conduct a search of the tavern.

The police discovered four things that seemed suspicious. They opened a chest and found some strange white powder. In the kitchen, they spotted some herbs of unknown provenance. From Telezhinetsky's purse they pulled a strange note with Jewish inscriptions, which they identified as kabbalistic. And finally, the vodka: thee barrels sealed by the leaseholder's stamp. They filled a bottle of vodka from one of the barrels and sent all four items—vodka, herbs, the note, and the powder—to Zhitomir for investigation. The case seemed promising: this Moshka was obviously a necromancer out to poison the Eastern Orthodox clergy and peasants.

The Volhynia provincial commission contacted local chemists, who tested Telezhinetsky's vodka and, to the commission's dismay, discovered no "narcotic, mineral or metallic ingredients." They not only found it "absolutely harmless" but added that it was of good quality. The result: the police released Telezhinetsky and accused the doctor of "poor care and

4.4. A tavern in Telezhyntsi, Shepetovka district.
IA, f. 9, spr. 43, ark. 20. Courtesy of the Institute of Archaeology of the National Academy of Sciences of Ukraine.

behavior."[35] Unfortunately, Doctor Kirichenko was not the only one making such accusations.

BELLIGERENT PARTIES

No matter what the quality, vodka prices were low, but the tensions they triggered were very high. Take Istkovich and Leibovich, who leased state treasury taverns in Rzhishchev. Three other Jews leased taverns in the part of town belonging to landlord Berezowski. Naturally, the two parts of town, "Russian" and "Polish," competed for clientele. Itsko Nemirovsky from Vinnitsa found himself in a similar situation. He saw how his neighbors, not burdened by special state taxes, sold cheaper cherry and grape wines by the glass. He complained that he had been betrayed by landlord Jozef Lubiszczewski, but his appeal was useless.[36] Itskovich and Leibovich also accused the landlord of ruining their state-supported business, also in vain.[37]

Unlike the treasury tavernkeepers, the gentry tavern leaseholders didn't have to make special duty payments; furthermore, the landlords allowed other shtetl dwellers to retail liquor from their cellars. In towns shared by the Russian state treasury and the Polish gentry, the Russian liquor monopoly clashed with the Polish leaseholding.[38]

This clash was deep-rooted. Polish magnates retained their monopoly on the liquor trade, whereas the new Russian liquor monopolists were also seeking profits: after all, their investments yielded on average a 300 percent return! Among the 216 liquor monopolists across Russia, twenty-nine managed liquor trade on the state lands of the Pale of Settlement.[39] Only out for themselves, the liquor monopolists brutally suppressed individual brewers and aggressively took over their assets. Like Jewish liquor leaseholders, the liquor monopolists introduced fixed prices, and fixed meant high. With a monopoly of the market, the liquor monopolists cared little about the quality of their wine and vodka; their only concern was quantity.

Tens of millions of rubles in state revenues were at stake. The tsars mobilized state institutions to protect the monopolists from interlopers. Alexander I and Nicholas I allowed the liquor monopolists to use the army to protect their trade. Clandestine bartenders, brewers, and taverners undermining the local monopoly were brutally suppressed. Armed guards prevented residents and travelers from bringing liquor purchased elsewhere into the towns. Outside the Pale of Settlement, the guards protected entire cities from vodka smugglers, while inside the Pale they controlled the entrances to shtetls and villages.[40]

The disparity in prices turned competition between the state liquor monopolists and the magnates' tavernkeepers into a vodka war. Jews involved in the liquor business found themselves in two belligerent camps. The vodka wars involved everybody—Polish magnates, governors, ministries, the Senate, the tsar, and ordinary Jews. With varying intensity, this war played out almost in every shtetl.

In 1824, merchant Leiba Barsky signed a contract with the state treasury to be a liquor monopolist in the district of Zvenigorodka. He promised to pay the state about 12,000 silver rubles per year, established fixed prices, and expected to make a lot of money. We can imagine his annoyance when he realized that Countess Branicka, the owner of lands nearby, had leased out four small inns only two miles from the taverns that he controlled. Formally, that was her land. To Barsky's dismay, the liquor in her inns was cheaper than in his taverns. Naturally, the peasants and townsfolk flocked to Branicka's inns and brought bottled liquor back home.

Business in Barsky's taverns dropped precipitously. Facing bankruptcy, Barsky pleaded with the minister of finance for help, but Kankrin could do nothing: the state department of crown assets had no jurisdiction over Branicka. "Send your people to prevent anyone from buying from those inns," was the advice. "The local guards would help you." Perhaps they would have, but ordinary shtetl dwellers gathered in gangs, beat up Barsky's guards, and continued to frequent Branicka's inns.[41]

Barsky was not alone in his frustration. Before him, Berko Gedaliovich from Bershad had a similar problem with wine retailers in Zvenigorodka in 1803 and failed to pay his monopoly duties.[42] In the late 1820s yet another monopolist, Froim Zaslavsky, competing with Branicka's taverns, found himself in the same predicament. As a second-guild merchant, Zaslavsky was extremely wealthy. He purchased a liquor monopoly license for the entire Tarashcha district and planned to collect duties from dozens of local tavernkeepers. Naturally, he locked in prices for all the taverns under his control.

The inventive Branicka pursued her own profit. She ordered the establishment of inns between villages, on the trade roads, and in farming areas. Zaslavsky considered this illegal. Landlords could have their inns only in the villages and hamlets, not in between. His monopoly benefited the state treasury, and he pleaded with the state to protect him. The court found itself in a legal quandary. As in Barsky's case, the judge recommended that Zaslavsky appoint "mounted inspectors and guards to make sure no wine from elsewhere is brought to town."[43] That is to say, since we cannot enforce legislation, you must resort to violence.

The shtetl dwellers disliked fixed prices, particularly on alcohol. Drinking was a moment of freedom, although very few used this word, forbidden in early nineteenth-century Russia. At their secret parties, Alexander Pushkin and his school friends would raise their glasses "to her." Likewise, the shtetl dwellers could not pronounce the word "freedom," but they could raise their glasses. Now they could not afford even that. Locking in prices restricted the freedom to drink, turning ordinary Jews into rebels.

In Uman, the Jews succeeded in nearly bringing down the business of Grosman and Berenshtein. These two liquor monopolists controlled sales of vodka and rum, paying about 2,000 rubles to the state treasury. They also owned a pub in the cellar of the town prison. To control their monopoly, they established guarded checkpoints at the entrances to the town. As in Troianov, Kremenets, and Berdichev, guards stopped and checked anyone entering the town on foot or by wagon, and their baggage was inspected to make sure they had no liquor on them. Meanwhile, Uman tavernkeepers paid the monopolists 0.45 rubles in taxes for a bucket of rum and 0.15 rubles for a bucket of vodka. Town prices on liquor rose sharply, the guards detained retail smugglers, and the situation became increasingly tense.

In the 1830s, however, Uman was no longer a private town: the state had purchased it from the Potockis and turned it into a military training center. The authorities did not like the volatile situation in town; they agreed with the protesting Jews and abolished the checkpoints. By doing so they de facto introduced free trade in liquor. Berenshtein and Grosman could not pay their arrears, and petitioned Kankrin to release them from payments. Ordinary Uman dwellers rejoiced: they had got what they wanted—the freedom to drink a cheap shot.[44]

Unlike Uman, Troianov had no military to help the Jews out. And Berliand, a local leaseholder of the liquor trade reporting to Count Belinski, was no better than the monopolists in Uman. He ordered his guards to attack a competing tavern, physically humiliate its leaseholder, and search the houses of local townspeople suspected of purchasing vodka elsewhere. The court and police preferred to keep out of it: after all, Berliand served the landlord. His guards, the court acknowledged, were "illegal but efficient." For ordinary shtetl dwellers, purchasing outside the leaseholder's jurisdiction was an act of defiance.[45] Other shtetls moved from defiance to outright rebellion.

NEWS FROM THE FRONT

Berdichev Jews started their rebellion with the *herem*, Hebrew for the ban of excommunication. It appeared on the doors of the Great Synagogue and outlawed alcohol "made in Berdichev." The names of Rabbenu Gershom and Yehoshua bin Nun, invoked in the ban, left no doubt: to drink Berdichev-produced vodka meant being banished from the Jewish community forever.

Berdichev townsfolk could hardly survive Shabbat without a shot of brandy. They found it excruciating to have to refuse liquor available in any local pub, and needed an extraordinary incentive to make the boycott work.

The entire Jewish population took part. Nobody wanted to pay an exorbitant sum for a bottle of wine or a *shtof* of vodka. In addition to economics, religious arguments also played a role: Rubinshtein, the leaseholder of the local liquor trade, had converted to Christianity. As a Christian supervisor of the production of Jewish liquor, he dismissed Judaic dietary stringency, not always applicable to brandy but obligatory for wine made from grapes. For this and other reasons, the Jews of Berdichev committed themselves to the ban. They allowed themselves the dispensation of consuming outside vodka if they could get it out of town and bring it in.

Rubinshtein could not contain his anger. In a short period of time he lost 10,000 silver rubles in duties. He complained to everyone—the Senate, the governor general in Kiev, the police chief in Zhitomir, and the town-owner of Berdichev. He convinced Prince Radziwiłł to make a complaint too. Radziwiłł appealed to the bias of Russian statesmen: Jews, he said, had used their religious laws to harm the loyal owner of the town.

Radziwiłł's claims might have touched on a sensitive issue, yet Rubinshtein knew that the Russian government was often unable to exercise its power. The only power that could crack down on Jewish resistance, Rubinshtein decided, was that of religion. An apostate himself, he turned to Mordekhai Twersky, a Hasidic master of enormous clout, and pleaded with him to persuade the Jews to cancel the ban. We have the police to thank for recording that these two had a meeting—most likely a very brief one.

Berdichev was too important a town for the Russian authorities to feign neutrality. Grudgingly, they had to intervene. They decided that the town tavernkeepers should recompense Rubinshtein 15,000 rubles, which the tavernkeepers, the first victims of the boycott, could not afford under any circumstances. Then the authorities ordered an investigation and arrested the alleged group who had set the ban. Three respectable town merchants, Abram Brodetsky, Sheftel Berlinblug, and Moshko Varshavsky, were thrown into a detention cell. The detainees dispatched a protest from prison to the investigator, insisting that they knew nothing about the boycott. Puzzled, a government detective turned to people in the streets.

Local vodka, they replied, was "much too expensive." In violation of state regulatory politics, Rubinshtein had shamelessly raised prices. In addition, he sold vodka by the Polish quart, which was smaller than the Russian quart, but priced it higher than the Russian measure. Russians reported that Jews threatened to stop drinking vodka for one year, unless it cost 20 kopeks a quart. Catholics claimed to have heard Jews saying they would never drink the vodka of the vile convert Rubinshtein, whatever the price. But these were just rumors; the Zhitomir magistrate could not prove the guilt of the detained Jews and transferred the case to the Volhynia court, then to the Senate.[46] Meanwhile, the flow of vodka in Berdichev miraculously stopped.

Rubinshtein realized that the Senate could rule in favor of the towns-folk and against the Polish magnate, which he needed to prevent at all costs. Rubinshtein harnessed his horses and rushed to St. Petersburg. There he shoved bribes at several statesmen and made sure they would approve a decision favoring him and not the town dwellers. He succeeded, and on his return tripled his grip on liquor sales. Still, he acquiesced to popular protest and fixed the price in the amount of 20 kopeks per quart of wine.

Rubinshtein also made some harsh decisions. Since all taverns in town belonged to Radziwiłł, he ordered Radziwiłł's insignia placed on the doors. The Volhynia civil governor asked him to take them down—why should there be a reminder of the Polish szlachta in a Russian town?—but Rubinshtein disobeyed. He had his mounted guards controlling check-points and road boom-barriers: do whatever you deem necessary, but protect my monopoly. Berdichev turned into what a contemporary called a "serf town." Radziwiłł was the alcohol king, Rubinshtein his liquor min-ister, and ordinary townsfolk were liquor serfs.

Witnesses observed how the mounted guards would surround any-one coming through Berdichev on a wagon and shout, "Do you have any vodka?" They even had the nerve to stop a retired Russian officer in a coach, found several bottles on him, and demanded excise payments. As the officer had no money on him, they took his horse as collateral and put him under arrest until he paid. The townsfolk voiced protests and the governor sent inspectors to check out the situation on the ground, but Rubinshtein swiftly dismantled the checkpoints. Once the inspectors went back to Zhitomir, the guards were back in place.

The guards went so far as to stop a governmental envoy carrying mail through Berdichev. The mailman resisted. The guards pulled swords to make him obey and check his mailbags. It is no surprise that the mounted guards with szlachta insignia were also Jews. Except for the town-owner, almost everyone involved on either side was Jewish. What is surprising, however, is that the guards had good reason to detain the mailman. It turned out that two Jews, Borul Raiker and Shlioma Parshchik, had in-vented a way to punish Rubinshtein's greed and obstinacy. You deny us an affordable shot of vodka? We will smuggle.

Borukh and Shlioma were extraordinarily resourceful. They purchased special government mailbags, commissioned uniforms, and hired Leibko Prilutsky to be in charge of mail transfer. They looked like normal Jews leasing Russian post services and driving express mail through Berdichev. The difference between them and genuine Jewish postmasters was in the quality of their mail. It was liquid and measured in buckets. They could carry about eight hundred buckets of express mail at a time.

Rubinshtein himself beat up Prilutsky when he discovered the fraud, and he had the authorities forbid the smuggling of vodka under penalty of law. Popular protest, however, continued for years. Jews would leave Berdichev before sunset for out-of-town taverns and come back at night with a bottle of vodka sticking out of every pocket.[47] Some went individually, trying to circumvent the checkpoints on the way back; others returned in crowds to confront the guards and break through.[48]

Berdichev set a precedent replicated elsewhere. As in Berdichev, one day in the mid-1830s the Kremenets dwellers found a *herem* in the form of Yiddish handwritten leaflets on the doors of the town synagogues: under threat of excommunication, nobody should drink local vodka. Russian town clerks called these leaflets "sheets with horrible oaths" in the "Jewish language."

Everybody knew what the ban meant. The ordinary Jews of Kremenets had declared war on Pinkas Bronshtein, a wealthy liquor monopolist. Just like Rubinshtein, he had singlehandedly fixed high prices on vodka and had closed the town to any outside liquor. Before his stool pigeons could scratch the leaflets from the doors of synagogues, dozens of people managed to read them.

In the oral culture of East Europe, news traveled fast. By midday, the entire town knew what was going on. Jews enlisted the support of the Christian population. The taverns were empty. The town became sober. Bronshtein, facing ruin, filed a report with the governor. The boycott undermined his calculations with the state treasury and was a "harmful action directed against state interests."

While the authorities were considering what action to take, Bronshtein and his associate Iosel Gintsburg went to see the rabbi of the town and tried to intimidate him. Without his signature or approval, the rabbi mentioned, the ban was just a piece of paper. Still, he murmured the classical Talmudic *dina de malkuta-dina* (the law of the state is the law for the Jew) and promised to make an announcement in the synagogue over Shabbat. However, on Shabbat he made no mention of the matter. Bronshtein assumed that his competitors had conspired against him, and he rushed to Zhitomir.

As a guild merchant, Bronshtein was confident that the Volhynia governor would meet with him; as a monopolist, he also knew that he had many enemies. In Zhitomir he discovered that Aizik Brodsky and Gershko Goldenberg, high-profile tavernkeepers in town, had already filed charges against him. Bronshtein returned to Kremenets and changed his tactics. He filed another complaint with criminal charges, in which he accused Goldenberg and Brodsky of being responsible for the boycott. Those who had rebelled, he argued, did so against an obedient servant of the Russian tsar, second-guild merchant Pinkhas Bronshtein.

As a trustworthy person in his own eyes, Bronshtein promised to bring witnesses to court to testify against the enemies of his business and of the state treasury. He also requested rabbinic court hearings. The accused responded that this was fine, provided that the witnesses were not Bronshtein's relatives. The rabbi agreed, as this was the accepted practice of Judaic law: relatives were not acceptable witnesses. Then Bronshtein requested that the witnesses testify in the synagogue without taking an oath. Goldenberg and Brodsky refused. During this exchange, Bronshtein's income plunged to a ten-year low.

The authorities finally came to the rescue. The governor ordered that Goldenberg and Brodsky explain themselves. The two admitted that they had a grudge against Bronshtein since he refused to sell them high-quality vodka, preferring to sell it just through his taverns and offering them only half-distilled vodka. It was not a stretch for Bronshtein to suspect them, honest taverners, of masterminding the boycott. But what boycott, the two asked, was Bronshtein talking about? A certain Grinberg had bought two buckets of vodka for a wedding; Berenshtein and Fishman had purchased two buckets for circumcision ceremonies; they themselves had also purchased and sold ten buckets. There was no ban in effect![49]

Yet there was a ban, of course: the liquor monopolist used to sell about three hundred buckets per week. The two taverners cleverly misguided the investigation. The ten to fifteen buckets now sold weekly represented a 90 percent loss: Goldenberg's and Brodsky's explanations were laughable. Furthermore, we do not know if the figures that they gave in order to distance themselves from the boycott were even accurate. It was very clear, however, that the entire town, Christians and Jews, was ready to protect its modicum of freedom: inexpensive vodka. Bronshtein either had to revoke his fixed prices and give in to his ordinary but rebellious brethren or face bankruptcy. The Jews had won their right to drink.

"MAKING RUSSIAN PEASANTS DRUNK"

The regime considered the vodka conflict an anomaly and sought to resolve it. The best bet was to make the Polish gentry surrender and keep them from infringing on Russia's treasury revenues. The landlords' inns in the proximity of state-owned taverns were an affront. A list of subversive taverns lay on the desk of the minister of finance. Kankrin looked into the matter and realized that the problematic taverns were new, not mentioned in inheritance papers, lay far beyond the landlords' inhabited areas, undermined state trade, and should be liquidated.

The landlords protested. Tyszkiewicz, Krasnicki, Kruszelnicki, and others sent back the paperwork with counterarguments. Their taverns were old, inherited mostly from the Potockis; there were no other inns in close proximity to their taverns and the state-owned lands were at a distance of six to seven miles. They had inherited from the Potockis the right to deal with their new possessions as they deemed necessary. The inns served travelers on the trade routes; it would be pointless to shut them down.[50]

The Russian administration discovered that the taverns in question were in fact in a strategically favorable position. Located on the roads connecting the key market towns, they allowed purchasing cheaper vodka. The ministerial commission ordered that the distance be measured from the landowners' possessions to their taverns and from their taverns to the state-owned territories and inns. The result was shocking: to cover that distance one sometimes had to walk a mere fifty steps!

This was an outrage, but it would be difficult to lay blame on the gentry. The head of the Kiev provincial economy department helped the administration find a scapegoat. The rising Russian nationalism praised the "official nationality" at the expence of all others. Hence Russians could not be responsible, but the religiously alien Jews could. "The Jews lease taverns from the gentry and the gentry established these taverns close to state land leased to liquor monopolists," he claimed. These Jews "sell alcohol and beverages much cheaper than in the state-controlled estates." And finally: "this undermines state trade."[51]

Bound by their commitment to the landlords, the Russian authorities looked into the monopoly problem, and made several discoveries: Jews thought "only of their own benefit" and had no desire "to follow the will of the government." They sold vodka cheaper than the established price and provided free fish and salt, attracted Christian peasants, make them purchase on credit, and ruined them. Christian peasants flocked to Jewish inns because "in many districts they cannot buy lower than the established state price." Finally, the authorities stated that removing Jews from the taverns would undermine the income of the gentry.[52]

Since the town-owners in the Pale were mostly Polish, undermining their income was tantamount to reducing their political significance. The impoverished gentry would not have money to purchase horses, organize cavalry, and rebel against Russia. Instead, they would have to beg the state for help—which they would receive in exchange for loyalty. It was not necessary to ruin the gentry completely, but merely to remove one of their main sources of income: the Jewish tavernkeeper.

Instead of introducing a free liquor trade, the Russian regime sought to make the liquor trade free of Jews. Nicholas undertook a number of decisive steps to banish Jews from this business. He attempted but failed entirely to remove the Jews from the area within fifty miles of the border with Austria. It turned out that Podolia province alone had more than 170 taverns within fifty miles of the border. The state was unable to compensate all those who would lose their taverns. In the 1840s the government did succeed in evicting those Jews who lived in rural areas. The state also nullified the peasants' debts to Jewish tavernkeepers and forbade Jews from selling on credit.

4.5. An old shtetl innkeeper with his wife, Western Ukraine.
Binyamin Lukin's private collection. Courtesy of Binyamin Lukin.

This eviction resulted in the rapid expansion of the shtetl population and the worsening of its economy. Thousands of former innkeepers and their family members, now unemployed Jews, made their way back to the shtetls and established dozens of new prayer houses, but also contributed to the subsequent unemployment in and impoverishment of the shtetl. Simultaneously, the regime endorsed the notion that Jews forced the Russian peasant to drink, which became one of the key points of late nineteenth-century anti-Jewish propaganda. The later antisemitic image of the overcrowded shtetl and the Jew destroying the Christian peasantry were among the consequences of the campaign of the Russian regime against the Polish gentry. The shtetl and its Jews became the immediate victims of this campaign.

Much later, the Jews were removed entirely from the liquor trade in Russia. The state abolished serfdom in 1861, launched rapid industrialization in the 1880s, and introduced a state monopoly on the liquor trade in 1894. The claim of biased ethnographers that Jews made the Russian peasants drunk prompted a final governmental decision.[53] All liquor trade was now a state monopoly; the Jews were out. Although tavern-keeping was a risky profession riddled with economic and psychological conflict, Jews and Slavs benefited from it over several centuries.

The removal of Jews had dreadful consequences for everybody. The introduction of a state monopoly made several hundreds of thousands of Jewish families destitute overnight. One Russian historian observed that at that time, some "200,000 Jews were deprived of the scanty livelihood they had derived from the taverns."[54] Several years later, antisemitic propaganda used the liberalization period in the wake of the 1905 Russian Revolution to incite peasants (and soldiers of peasant stock) against the Jews, who allegedly corrupted Russian peasants. The Jews filed for foreign passports and started packing.

State prices on alcohol, now without any competition, only caused people to drink more, not less. The credulous population was easily incited against the eternally guilty Jewish innkeepers, which preserved the shaky balance of social stability. Although the regime won the war against an affordable drink, destroyed the Polish magnates' liquor economy and Jewish tavernkeeping, the shtetl dwellers—Ukrainians, Russians, Poles, and Jews—still had the last laugh. They immortalized the freedom to drink in East European popular culture across the religious, linguistic, political, and ethnic divide.

BOTTLED FREEDOM

Samuil Marshak, a leading Russian children's poet, wrote an adult epigram on drinking: "Here are some reasons to get drunk: a divorce, a funeral, a wedding, a departure, a success, an award, a promotion—and simply getting drunk for no reason." Drinking for its own sake takes Slavs away from the controlled realm of officialdom with its imposed festivals and ideology.

It also frees them from poverty and distress. A Ukrainian female peasant song praises vodka, as nourishing as porridge: "*Hey, horilka, bila-bila, ia b tebe lozhkoiu iila*"—"Hey, vodka, very white, I would eat you with a spoon!" A Ukrainian folksong has its rebel peasants calling for "pouring vodka over the rim," so that "life in the world will be better."[55]

Aleck the Mechanic, a tailor from a short story by Sholem Aleichem, stayed sober all year round since he could not afford brandy. But on Simkhat Torah, the day when the annual cycle of Torah reading is completed, he would reward himself for his enforced sobriety. Sholem Aleichem wondered "how such a small man can pour so much liquor into himself."[56]

Drinking "for the sake of rejoicing" became so widespread at the Hasidic courts that Solomon Schechter in his Vienna years concocted a Hebrew parody: his Hasidim cannot tell *tikkun*, soul-improving, from a bottle of brandy. His main character, a novice, spends days learning how to drink without measure "for its own sake" and feels it incumbent "to drink with every effort I can make until I fall down wherever I sit— so that no one, God forbid, suspects me of not being an accomplished Hasid."[57]

Adam Mickiewicz's Poles went to relax after Mass to a Jewish tavern: "z kaplicy, że była niedziela, Zabawić się i wypić przyszli do Jankiela": "after church, since it was Sunday, they went to have fun and drink at Yankel's." They had fun in the Jewish tavern—of course, they had little if any fun in church![58]

Drinking as a path toward personal freedom permeated East European culture from the top down. Though drinking contributed to the state treasury, it also challenged state ideology. "Open the cellars—the mob is having fun today!" wrote Alexander Blok about the inebriated 1917 Russian Revolution.[59] To drink whatever one wants and wherever one wants became an act of defiance. "We could drink no more," a Russian poet ironically swears, "But we could drink no less."

The revolutionary Vladimir Mayakovsky described the netherworld with the scornful word, "temperance."[60] In his canonic poem, "A Confession," Czesław Miłosz ironically questioned his status as a prophetic figure since he indulged in the only-too-human "well-chilled vodka, herring in olive oil."[61]

The main character in one of the most subversive Russian novels, *Moscow to the End of the Line,* by Venedikt Erofeev, drinks rosé wine, lotion, eau de toilette, and cologne, and in complete delirium derides communism, the Slavic soul, and Russian chauvinism. Ready to drink his glass straight down, he pronounces, "Share with me my repast, Lord."[62]

Russian satirist Igor Guberman, exclaimed, "A tavern, a brothel, a pub, a bar—may our feast be blessed amid the fumes of divine grace."[63] However, East European tradition joined together not only drinking and freedom, but drinking and creativity. Bulat Okudzhava, the famous Russian bard, placed a red rose, the symbol of poetry, in a dark glass bottle of imported beer. It makes perfect sense that Mikhail Bakhtin, a leading Russian twentieth-century thinker, saw Rabelaisian excessive drunkenness through the East European lens, as a popular expression of freedom. The Russian proverb puts it best: "Have a drink in the morning and you will be free all day."

Of course the drinking shtetl, though "free all day," could be pretty violent.

CHAPTER FIVE

A VIOLENT DIGNITY

Gershko Kapeliushnik the hatmaker had dealings with Christians, listened to their derogatory remarks about his Judaism, and paid them back in kind. He had about six Christian apprentices in his shop in Ilintsy. In 1828, Kazimierz Zozulinski joined Tomasz and Piotr Kozlowski, all three of them Catholic apprentices, in their complaint against their master. They lamented that although Gershko was a qualified artisan, he criticized Christianity in their presence, fed veal to them on fast days, and made acrimonious remarks that expressed doubt about the truths of Christianity. When they warned Gershko that God would punish them for listening to his obscenities, he replied with words that were "tempting and blasphemous for Christians." Their reluctance to provide details implies that Gershko enticed them with the common Judaic invectives against Christian theology: Jesus was a poor bastard and the immaculate conception was obstetrical nonsense.[1]

Gershko's behavior was not exceptional. Jews and Christians routinely exchanged insulting remarks about each other's religions. Verbal and other forms of violence were as endemic among ordinary shtetl Jews as among gentiles. The shtetl was profoundly politically incorrect. More important, this kind of behavior was a positive affirmation of one's identity—through deprecating the identity of the other.

Gershko found a way to reinforce his Jewish identity by speaking aloud against domineering Christianity, the state religion firmly embedded in the shtetl reality. This was an outward affront—and an act of self-assertion, an unusual way to rejoice in his Judaism. Gershko would not have been able to do so had he not been confident in his own security, power, importance, and independence.

The shtetl in its splendor did not have a monopoly on violence. Slavs and Jews alike conceived of violence as an acceptable means of communication. Abuse—physical, rhetorical, and verbal—was a daily occurrence. Violence was one of the indispensable languages of the shtetl, an environment in which outbursts of brutality were as normal as Sunday bazaars.

5.1. "Jews Preparing to Attack," a satirical pencil drawing by W. Rossdorfer. *BHT 87.212.4. Courtesy of BN and the Beit Hatfutsot exhibition "Treasures of Jewish Galicia—Judaica from the Museum of Ethnography in Lviv, Ukraine," Photo Archive, Tel Aviv.*

It was a sine qua non for the Jews, who sought to affirm their Judaism before Christians; for the Eastern Orthodox, eager to prove themselves and put Jews and Catholics down; and for the Catholic Poles, unhappy with their lot and seeking to uplift themselves at the expense of Judaism. Mastery of this violent language was an issue of survival. Jews excelled in using this language until the Russian regime decided to monopolize it entirely, a decision that had a far greater impact on the Jews than did the monopolization of liquor production.

THE JEWISH SHARE

Like the liquor trade, violence in the shtetl was on lease; unlike the liquor trade, Catholics, Eastern Orthodox, and Jews all sought to make violence their own. The shtetl in its glory was bathed in political incorrectness precisely because its dwellers had little other means of protecting themselves. The intensity of the shtetl economy made legal means of conflict resolution ineffective. Since the courts were corrupt and slow, Jews saw violence as a much more effective tool in settling financial disputes. Your debtor cannot pay? Not a problem; our guys will help.

This measure meant physical enforcement. In Korostyshev, Berko Kholodenko and Avrum Usherenko quarreled with Moshko Rabinovich over money. They did not have time to settle the matter through the rabbinic or local Russian court. Hence Rabinovich's hostile takeover: he used his men to seize Avrum's and Berko's belongings.[2] In Berdichev, the Jewish bakers were also unwilling to resolve their conflict peacefully with Duvid Shekhtman, who dared enter the baking business without paying his dues to the guild. The guild members went to his house, seized his money, and beat him mercilessly for violating their monopoly.[3] No one was allowed to defy the independence and dignity of the bakers' guild!

But why beat your brethren if you can delegate this privilege to the Russian police, thought Moshko Stavinsky from Boguslav. Stavinsky quarreled with Mikhel Portnoy, a local tailor, and intended to trap him. When Portnoy decided to become a cab driver and came home with newly purchased horses, Stavinsky convinced the town police that the horses had been stolen. Despite the testimony of the seller, who confirmed that the deal was legitimate, the police arrested Portnoy and sent him to the conscription post as punishment for the purported horse theft.[4]

Everyday violence was an effective means of communication: if it did not solve matters, it sent a clear message. Menashe Burshtein had many good reasons to hate merchant Berko Abramovich, his neighbor in Radomyshl and competitor. Abramovich was an influential person and could have offenders penalized. In 1824 he had Shmuil Tsesarik and Shaya Shkolnik sentenced to corporal punishment for blackmailing him.[5] The situation turned against Abramovich when he and Burshtein crossed paths. Abramovich was unable to pay his debts to several lenders, Burshtein included. The indignant Burshtein took his son-in-law with him and went to the Radomyshl town magistrate.

They found Abramovich already there, sitting in the waiting room. Without further ado, they started kicking him. The presence of the Russian clerks next door did not bother them in the least; Radomyshl was their territory. For Burshtein there was nothing wrong with this way of settling accounts, but he probably felt otherwise when the violence he had unleashed came back around to him. He wrote a dramatic complaint while under house arrest with a policeman on guard in his dining room day and night during the investigation of his assault.[6] He was ready to infringe on somebody else's territory but did not like assaults on his own.

Burshtein was not a particularly violent person. Unlike him, Tenenboim, the owner of an illegal restaurant, was a nasty bully. A newcomer to Vasilkov, he would do whatever it took to assert himself—by humiliating others. He and his wife ruined and beat widow Aksenfeld, a competitive innkeeper. The court found the Tenenboims guilty, and they had to spend two weeks in prison and recompense Aksenfeld monetarily. Now the Tenenboims hired Mimrenkova, a Christian peasant, to help them in their restaurant, although Russian law forbade Jews from having Christian servants.

Half a year later, Mimrenkova asked for two rubles in advance of her annual salary. In response, Tenenboim's mother-in-law hit her and refused to give her any pay. Then Mimrenkova bumped into Tenenboim himself, drunk and rowdy. He slapped her across the face and hit her in the head. Mimrenkova burst into tears and yelled that she would complain to Lieutenant Coronel Iankovich, head of the town administration. As she walked out the door, Tenenboim shouted after her, "I am not afraid of him!"

He was too drunk to be afraid. His neighbor, a Catholic, reported that Tenenboim ran out of his house and walked to the nearby post office, yelling, "The town head wants my money but I won't give him anything— I am a poor man!" Tenenboim also attempted to break into Iankovich's house and assault him. His neighbor saw that Tenenboim was intoxicated, couldn't keep his balance, and was getting into trouble. "Bring him back home!" he shrieked to Tenenboim's wife. "How can I?" she replied. "He is crazy!"[7]

No, he was not. A mean person in private, Tenenboim was out to crush and kick and punch in public. The forgiving town head understood what had happened and did not take Tenenboim to court. But Mimrenkova did. The court found Tenenboim guilty of beating a female peasant, but four well-to-do Jews bailed him out. Few people in Vasilkov considered the case a big deal. The Polish neighbor, the Russian administrator, and the four Jews shared the sense of the normality of this verbal and physical abuse: Tenenboim did not deviate very much from the norm. This was an aggressive yet acceptable way to prove that one was a master.

The Christian peasant Mimrenkova was better off than the Jewish teenager Iudko Zatulovsky, who worked for Srul Rashkovsky, an orphan and a newcomer and the owner of a granary in Vasilkov. Srul sold groats and farina and employed Iudko full-time for 29 silver rubles a year. On the eve of Passover, Iudko came to Srul and asked for a three-ruble advance. Srul shook his head. Iudko began bargaining, and quickly lost his temper. In a heated verbal exchange, the aggravated Srul kicked Iudko down, grabbed a knife, cut Iudko's throat, and ran away. Iudko made it to a local doctor, who treated what he diagnosed as a "freshly inflicted and deep wound." When Iudko recovered, he sued Srul. In the courtroom, however, Srul denied the charges and was let go, though he remained under serious suspicion. A deep scar remained on Iudko's neck until the end of his life—a reminder of Srul's insecurity.[8]

Yiddish writers support the evidence we find in the Russian documents. In the imaginary shtetl of Dubrovichi, the invention of Dovid Bergelson, local butchers clash with the nasty Elisha, the kosher meat tax

5.2. Torah shield of the society of butchers "Zovhei tsedek."
Zhitomir, 1848. MIK 125. Courtesy of MIK and the Center for Jewish Art at Hebrew University, Jerusalem.

collector. The butchers beat up two men who supported his monopoly—and then punch and kick Elisha, who barely survives the fight. In Opatoshu's novel *In Poylishe velder* (In Polish Woods) Mordko and his father Avrum, from a family of woodcutters, would hit any challenger with a big wooden stick.

The Jews in the shtetl of Sholem Ash's novels settled all issues through physical violence. Leyb, a shoemaker's apprentice, hit his master, tortured his bride, who had tried to blind him, beat her after they were married, and knocked out his son Motke before the vengeful Nosson the Robber came and crushed him. These imaginary Jews also resorted to violence when defending their competitive economic territory, their dignity, their independence, and their small modicum of power.

DEFYING THE POWER

Although in 1797 the Russian regime rescinded the right of the communal elders to decide on legal matters, the kahal still retained substantial power in the Jewish world. The elections of communal elders and treasurers were all fraught with fighting—even though local policemen stood guard supervising the procedure. Quite often, elections began with disagreements and swiftly moved from verbal violence to a skirmish. Punches were more eloquent than rhetoric. Self-confident and self-important, the Jews were not afraid to use their fists, particularly when shtetl power was at stake.

Power in the shtetl was circumscribed by the borders of the town, was of limited value beyond it, and provided questionable return. But limited power did not mean no power at all. Power implied certain communal privileges and freedoms, independence and self-respect, and the more heterogeneous the community, the more tension surrounded their distribution. Relations between the wardens of the self-governing communal institutions—the *kahal* and *havurot*—and their members could flare up at any moment. Ordinary Jews would not easily give up their right to make decisions and say their piece.

In 1800, on the Shabbat before Purim, the chief Uman policeman, Balagopulo, came to the synagogue and requested that the Jews elect the *parnasim*, communal supervisors. He also suggested that those with more capital have a more decisive vote. Yankel Gershunovich and Zevel Kravets did not like this arrangement. "Why should the wealthy be privileged?" Gershunovich cried in indignation. "Everybody should have an equal vote." Balagopulo tried to appease the two, but they continued to protest against the voting privileges and managed to disrupt the elections. Balagopulo failed to establish order and left. The next day he had Gershunovich and Kravets arrested for saying "brazen words" in public.[9]

To prevent fighters for equality from speaking up, the burial societies, the most powerful social institutions in the shtetl, routinely used rhetorical violence as a means of inhibition. The Letichev Burial Society warned all shtetl dwellers that if they failed to inscribe themselves and their children into the society register and pay their dues, "no sacred or clean place" would be allocated to them, that is to say, they would not get a proper burial.[10] This was more than just a threat. When in nearby Slavuta a man named Barakh spoke out against the influential printers Shmuel Aba and Pinhas Shapira, they beat him, accused him of attempted arson, had the police imprison him, and, when he died, had him buried outside the Jewish cemetery, next to the outcasts and suicides.[11]

The Jews could sometimes be violent, but they were not without dignity; they would not let an affront go unpunished. Jews used not only their fists but also their tongues, making verbal abuse one of the best possible responses to coercion. *Havurah* or *hevrah*, the Jewish voluntary society in charge of philanthropy, mutual aid, and other acts of charity, means "confraternity"; speaking against it undermined its purpose. For this reason, the *havurot* prohibited their members from "speaking ill" of the society, threatening them with fines or cancellation of privileges or both. The frequency with which this paragraph appeared in the communal Hebrew registers suggests that slanderous talk was common not only among ordinary Jews but also among the pious groups in the shtetl.

The Burial Society of Miropol included in its statute a reminder of the punishment for anyone who "opened his mouth" or used "bad language," either in the home of the dying or at the cemetery.[12] In Miastkovka, one Yaakov ben Avraam Aba "spoke out against" both the burial society and the Righteous Workers Society and was banned from any post of significance in either society for three years. Avraam ben Aharon, from the same community, gave an even more caustic critique, since the wardens banned him for three years and added, "no *aliyot*"—they would not call Avraam to readings of the Torah, whatever the family or personal occasion.[13]

There was a better way of keeping the unruly under control. Virtually every Jewish confraternity threatened to erase the names of potential offenders from the pinkas. The erased or crossed-out names in a pinkas served as a silent reminder of those Jews whom the wardens had penalized. Since in the popular imagination the pinkas was the holy Book of Memory and Book of Life of the Jewish community, one wanted to be inscribed in this book, not erased from it. Erasing a name was a painful punishment. But even that threat would not stop Jews from courageously speaking up against an abuse of power.

When they didn't find justice among their communal leaders, ordinary Jews turned to the Russian courts. Perhaps the sluggish yet more objective Russian justice would work better than the quick yet capricious kahal, and we will see in the next chapter whether it was really the case. Russian court documents recorded sad stories. The Mogilev kahal elders in Belorussia physically abused Abram Gershkovich's father, seized his property, triggered his sudden death, and falsified his death certificate.[14] The elders of the Lipovets community found out that a certain Abramovich had traded in yeast without paying a special duty. They came to his house, beat his wife, pushed down his little son sitting on the family trunk, and confiscated the trunk, worth about 50 silver rubles. Eight days later the child died.[15] The Moshensk kahal made registered members pay an exorbitant tax of 175 rubles each, and when a certain Mordkovich could not pay, the kahal elders quartered Cossacks in his dwelling and incited them against him. The Cossacks pulled all the sheets off the beds and poured water on them—an innocuous act compared to what the Jewish elders did in Mogilev and Lipovets.[16]

Squeezed from power by the Russian administration, the kahal elders disliked when ordinary Jews displayed their independence and disobeyed the kahal's decisions. Elia Grach, a kahal elder in Belaia Tserkov, was deeply upset when Danilo Bondarenko, an ordinary local Jew, chose to defy the kahal. Bondarenko dared to sympathize with one Akiva Gofman, a victim of the kahal arbitrariness, and Bondarenko convinced a local policeman to release Akiva.

When the rumors reached Elia Grach, he went to punish Bondarenko personally, and had the police arrest him, fine him, put him in gallows, and send him to the Vasilkov prison.[17] Like Grach, Rabbi Reuven Vaksman from Balta was also a community elder. In 1842 the brothers Itsko and Iankel Kopyta spoke out against his reelection as one of the kahal elders. When he lost the election, Vaksman did not hesitate to go and assault each of the brothers.[18]

While some Jews succumbed to intimidation and complied, others remained defiant. In 1816, Kalonimus Zalman "acted out against" the Letichev Burial Society and "offended the warden." This was nothing compared to a group offense in the same community. One Mordekhai, nicknamed Tonky Nohy ("Thin-Legged"), and his accomplices came to the synagogue and in protest against the existing system of privileges pushed the burial society elders from their bench—even though, the scribe noted, "the bench belonged to the society elders."

The burial society warden immediately ordered that the bench of the "youths," as they called the offenders, be painted with tar. Most likely the warden used other methods to compel Mordekhai and his friends to ask forgiveness before the burial society, because they actually did.[19] These young men acted brazenly because they had no other way to seek social justice. They demanded communal equality here and now and had no desire to compromise their modicum of communal dignity.

Not all were truth-seekers. Avrum Grinberg, a paramedic from Belaia Tserkov, proves that some Jews were real pests.[20] With his barber's certificate allowing him to perform minor operations, Grinberg scandalized and hurt a number of his clients. When somebody rebuked him for professional negligence, Grinberg beat that person in a dark street. In several other instances, he insulted people publicly. When Jews complained to the elders, Grinberg could not control himself and attacked members of the kahal. Belaia Tserkov Jews brought criminal accusations against him to court, but the court let him go.

Krakovsky, a kahal elder, petitioned the authorities to expel Grinberg to Siberia "for his quarrelsome disposition" without any "court procedure." To support his request, Krakovsky secured some 130 signatures of town dwellers. When the town magistrate refused to do so, the kahal made its last argument reminiscent of Grinberg's own wanton conduct: it accused Grinberg of stealing bricks from the old synagogue and jeopardizing the reputation of the entire community, and suggested auctioning his expensive and prestigious fur hat, *shtreyml,* and distributing the money to the poor.[21] For this Jew the *shtreyml* embodied a sense of piety and dignity—but the community had no other way out to curb his wanton conduct but to expropriate it.

Wealthy merchants, not just ordinary Jews, also used violence to assert themselves. Bitman from Vakhnovka was a tycoon who had the Christian peasants and petty Polish szlachta at his service. On a whim, Bitman "cursed his servants and slapped their faces." Bitman had plans to add communal power to his economic status. He joined the local Jews at the communal elections, which, he envisioned, would add communal respect and power to his monetary worth.

The town Jews had either to elect him as an elder or to appoint his puppet Jews. Neither of the two happened. The congregants listed the candidates, from which Bitman and his supporters were absent. One Moshe Litvak took the list from the desk and was about to begin the voting procedure when Bitman rushed to him, grabbed the list from his hands, and tore it into pieces. A local policeman observing the incident recorded that Bitman was cursing the congregants, shouting "obscenities and wanton words." When the police took Bitman outside, he was offended and shrieked, "Arrest all of us!"[22]

Unlike the brazen Bitman, well-to-do Berko Rabinovich from Zvenigorodka realized that popular support should come first and arbitrary conduct second. He bribed several dozen of the shtetl poor, organized them into his group of supporters, and fed them for a week before the magistrate elections. When the townsfolk finally elected him as the magistrate counselor, he demonstrated his great talents as a crook. He treated his gentile colleagues at the magistrate with disdain and dismissed the opinions and concerns of people who might vote against him in the next elections. He appointed a swindler as his scribe, bribed false witnesses, and said derogatory things out loud about other members of the magistrate. Jews and Christians joined efforts to compose a plea to the governor asking him to rid them of Berko.[23]

There were cases when the protests of ordinary Jews against the kahal really took the form of what the Russian authorities would call a rebellion. Incidents happened in Minsk and Podolia provinces involving violent attacks by ordinary Jews on the kahal authorities.[24] Others incidents became known as the vodka wars, discussed in chapter 4. Yet another incident took place in Starokonstantinov, Volhynia province, just after Nicholas I made the decision to begin drafting Jews into the Russian army and signed the harsh 1827 Statute on Conscription Duty, requiring a twenty-five-year period of service from Jewish boys and men.

As elsewhere in the Pale of Settlement, the Jews of Starokonstantinov had been involved in secret fundraising: they needed money to support the Jewish deputies in St. Petersburg, bribe Russian ministers, and prevent the inclusion of Jews in the conscription pool. By hook or by crook they needed to disrupt what the Russian government considered an attempt to integrate the Jews and what the Jews took for an attack on Judaism.

On September 21, 1827, policeman Krukovsky came to the kahal elders, four guild merchants and a communal rabbi. Krukovsky informed them that the tsar had approved the *ukaze* on army service and that they should prepare the conscription lists. When ordinary Starokonstantinov Jews realized that their efforts to prevent the new reform had failed, they blamed their own kahal elders, turned against them, and attacked their houses. They were poor but they were not nobodies, and they readily resorted to violence to protect themselves from the violence of the state and the kahal. The local police had to summon an additional army unit to suppress the outburst.[25]

If their independence and dignity were at stake, Jews did not differentiate between types of power. The authorities are against us? We will reply in kind. Gershko Plotnitsky, summoned to the office of Juror Nikolenkov, a Christian vested with some power, and when he appeared, the juror ordered his assistant, also a Christian, to hold Gershko down while Nikolenkov beat him. Furious, Gerhsko could not control himself. He pushed the assistant away and rushed out of Nikolenkov's office. On his way out, he dealt a hard blow to one Esinsky, a Christian clerk, punched another Russian clerk in the chest, and ran away, yelling "abominable obscenities" in Russian. No one could detain, restrain, or appease him: Plotnitsky kept shouting that he had been beaten.[26]

The unruly Plotnitsky used violence, disputing the authorities' alleged monopoly on violence. If violence was a common language of the Russian Empire, the Jews mastered it before they discovered Pushkin and Gogol. We have seen Jewish guards in Berdichev assault Russian travelers, merchants, clerks, and the military, whom the guards suspected of carrying foreign liquor on them. We have also seen Jewish contrabandists violently opposing Russian customs clerks' attempts to stop them from smuggling.

Abram Meerovich from Ekaterinopol fought the Uman guards, who on a sunny day in 1797 tried to detain him for purported stealing.[27] The 1800 case of Letichev town-dweller Abramovich presents him as a bold man who publicly offended the town head.[28] Thus it is not an anomaly that Aharon-Leyzer Kotik, the town tax collector, slapped the Russian government inspector across the face.[29] In 1830, a certain Umansky from Boguslav morally offended and apparently physically abused the Russian titular chancellor Kudrevichev.[30] Jews responded to violence with violence, as this was their only way to reify themselves in a violent society.

Mordukh was one of these "measure for measure" Jews. An experienced shtetl barber-doctor who knew, among other things, how to treat venereal diseases, he relied on the free domestic help of those whom he cured for free, including Anna, a Christian lady. In 1824, local policeman Kravchenko came to Mordukh to fetch her—why should a Christian work for a Christ killer? The law forbade Jews from employing Christians in their homes. The irate Mordukh first cursed the policeman with such brutal words that, according to Kravchenko's statement, "he could hardly stand on his own two feet." Then Mordukh hit Kravchenko, grabbed and lifted him up, and threw him into the street. When several policemen came to arrest him, Mordukh refused to go to a detention cell—and the policemen had to "carry him in their arms."[31]

Compared to Mordukh, an anonymous Jewish merchant from Berdichev was a paragon of civilized manners, but even he asserted his dignity as a merchant in an insulting manner. He came to the town offices for a passport and had to stand in a long line to get his papers accepted. Irritated by the long wait, he exclaimed that the state clerks should treat Jews better and not call them names. Why? Because the Jews paid them. The clerks replied that in fact, they were paid directly from the state treasury. To this, the Jewish merchant retorted that the tsar did not pay them sufficiently, whereas the Jews did. His offense seems to have been nothing out of the ordinary and was left unpunished.[32]

Meek and unassuming in nostalgic memoirs, Jews emerge unabashed from the archival documents. Jews boldly settled accounts when it came to getting even and protecting their independence. Violence put Jews on an equal footing with Christians long before any civil rights did, precisely because Jews in the shtetl were adamant about defending their own cultural space, independence, and dignity.

This kind of physical and verbal violence of Jews against their own Jewish authorities was not uncommon. Ordinary shtetl Jews were as politically correct as the neighboring Eastern Orthodox peasants, Russian army soldiers quartered in the shtetls, and the impoverished and embittered Polish gentry. Shtetl Jews were learning what it would take to be Russian Jews.

Before they mastered the Slavic language, they mastered the shared language of the Slavic culture. They used this language not only in their dealings with other Jews or Christians in power but also in their dealings with Christianity, the official religion of the state. Their "political incorrectness" shows that Jews resorted to violence to prove their Jewish identity, like Gershko Kapeliushnik, mentioned at the beginning of this chapter, who publicly challenged the domineering Christian beliefs to reaffirm his Jewishness.

POLITICALLY INCORRECT JEWS

In the nineteenth-century Ukrainian shtetl we find very few, if any, cases of what Gavin Langmuir calls "psychopatological violence" stemming from popular religious zeal, "motivated and explicitly justified by the irrational fantasies of paranoid people whose internal frontiers of faith were threatened by doubts they did not admit."[33] The blood libel trials of the eighteenth century remained part of the Polish past, or occurred in Lithuania (Velizh) or in the Russian interior (Saratov), and the only one occurring in the village of Bilokrynychky, near Zaslav in Volhynia province, was expediently dismissed by the Senate as baseless.[34] The 1911 Beilis case, with its Catholic "expert" on the Talmud and Russian racist far-right accusers, was still in the distant future.

However, early in the nineteenth century Russian statesmen considered any non-Eastern Orthodox religion harmful, including Catholicism and Lutheranism, and Judaism was for them "one of the most harmful religions." Orthodox hierarchs maintained that the true religion had to be universal within the borders of Holy Russia, and Eastern Orthodox was the only one. After a brief flirtation in the 1810s between the mystical-minded Alexander I and English evangelical missionaries, the Russian authorities abandoned the idea of mass conversion of the Jews.[35] In the best tradition of enlightened thought, they were ready to tolerate individual Jews but felt aversion toward Judaism. The shtetl Christians treated the Jews they dealt with as good Jews; the rest were evil Yids. Popular Slavic wisdom wrapped this feeling in a rhyming proverb: "Trusting a Yid is measuring water with a sieve."

To prove the validity of Judaism, Jews threw this rhetoric back at those who used it: they mistrusted the gentiles, *goyim*, and would spit on the ground when passing by a church. They also spat on the floor of synagogue while reciting the line in the everyday concluding prayer *Aleynu* about those "who pray to the emptiness and void and bow down to the god who does not save." Although censors had long crossed this line out and had forbidden Jews to reprint it in prayer books, it nonetheless remained in the oral culture as it contained a hidden response to continuous Christian oppression and drew on homophonic puns.

Rik, Hebrew for "void," also was associated with Hebrew for "spit" (*rok*), while "god who does not save" could also mean "God is not Jesus." Jews spat on the floor when they mentioned those who bow down to the void and emphasized that Jesus was not God.[36] Jewish enlightened thinkers complained that Jews spat in the synagogue during prayers and that it was deplorable—but they cautiously avoided a detailed explanation.

While many Jews disrespected Christianity, only some of them dared to treat Christianity as the Church treated Judaism. These few Jews made such daring statements that the bedazzled Russian clerks could not allow themselves to write down exact quotes from the offensive speeches. Consider several examples. The teenaged carpet-makers Duvid and Rakmiel from Tomashpol did not know how to keep their mouths shut. In 1801, they received a commission to do a tapestry in a village in Bessarabia. They worked next to the "red corner" of the hut with its gamut of Christian icons. To entertain themselves, Duvid and Rakhmiel exchanged some indecent comments on the substance of Christian iconography and the veneration thereof, resorting to Slavic foul language. The peasants heard their outrageous statements and denounced the two.[37]

Like these carpet-makers, the Jewish lady Finkelstein from Zhitomir could not restrain herself when it came to the Judeo-Christian divide, particularly when she had litigation against Moshko Blank from Starokonstantinov. Finkelstein knew Blank as a dishonest businessman who sucked up to Russian Christianity and ingratiated himself with the Russian administration. She also knew that Moshko's sons, inspired by their father, had converted to Eastern Orthodoxy. Finkelstein decided to utilize the courtroom to curse Moshko and his sons in public—thus emphasizing the superiority of Judaism. She told Blank what she knew about the manner of dying and the posthumous condition of converts from Judaism. Finkelstein was clever enough to say these things in Yiddish.[38]

If not for their extraordinary strength and centrality to the shtetl life and economy, Jews would not be able to rejoice in their Judaism—publicly, with pomp, sometimes challenging their Christian neighbors with outright mockery of Christianity. Jews reaffirmed their religion by putting Christianity down, reversing what was regularly done to them by Christians. Celebrating Judaism in the public domain scandalized Christians; Christians complained of such Jewish audacity.

Thus, for example, in Lithuania, several Jews spent Hanukah putting on an amateur performance with a Jew performing as Jesus on stage. In Belorussia, following protests of the Christians, the police grumbled that Jews were also extremely noisy during Passover, arranging fireworks and shooting their rifles in celebration of their redemption from Egyptian bondage. Here, too, Christians felt insulted. Also in Belorussia, several Jews got exuberantly drunk on Purim, dug out a wooden effigy of Jesus from a road chapel, and carried it on their shoulders around the shtetl, singing and mocking a church procession.[39] Elsewhere Jews went out on Christian holidays, particularly to the church processions, and engaged in clashes with Christians.

In the early nineteenth century, we hardly find victimized Jews hiding themselves in their attics from the chastising sword and missionary word of the Christian Church. The contrary was closer to the truth: the shtetl at its height was afraid of nothing. Its Jews were people with self-respect, although a peculiar kind. The manner in which Uman Jews treated two clerics from a local church is particularly instructive.

Communal attorney Berenshtein complained to the governor general, pointing out two men who were guilty of theft and sacrilege yet were unpunished members of the Uman Cathedral clergy: Zarusky, the sacristan, and Starodubski, the deacon. During the high holidays of 1821, the two allegedly sneaked into a Jewish study house and stole silverware, candles, and a wooden table. The Jews complained, but no action was taken. The frustrated Jewish community commissioned Berenshtein to file charges against the church, the Uman town head, and the police. The town officials were soon forced to apologize; the governor general demanded immediate action and a report.

The Jewish version of the story portrayed two men in cassocks with large crosses on their chests carrying a heavy oak table out of the study house at night. In the Christian version of the story, the Jews for some reason suspected the sacristan and the deacon, assaulted them, tied them up, kept them under surveillance the whole night, and the next day took them around town, exposing the two to public disgrace. Thus, explained the town authorities, even if the two men had stolen something, they had already been punished. Moreover, the town authorities seriously doubted that the clergymen could have stolen anything, as the robbery had occurred on Yom Kippur. And on Yom Kippur, explained a well-informed policeman, the Jews spend day and night in the synagogue.[40]

Absolutely wrong, replied the Jews. The deacon and the sacristan could have known that Jews spent the Yom Kippur services in the prayer house (synagogue) but did not go to the study house (bet midrash), which usually had a separate entrance or was a separate building. The Jews caught the two suspects immediately afterward and had them prosecuted according to Jewish mob law. The noninterference of the police on either side suggests that the authorities knew the Jews had a good reason to act this way and considered it safer not to get involved. This would also explain their reluctance to investigate the robbery: they probably considered the guilty party punished and the case resolved. At any rate, the Jews emerge from this story as a community to be reckoned with, while the church appears passive and silent, unprotected even by the Christian authorities.

As Christians stole from the Uman study house, Jews stole from the churches, although those involved in sacrilegious offenses were ordinary Jews, not Jewish clergy. These were Yiddish-speaking criminals stealing indiscriminately from Jews and Christians alike. One such criminal, Shmul Tsiner, and his accomplice Borukh Moshkovich, together with a number of other Jews, robbed a church near Balta. The police found in the house of Osia Portnoi a large silver cross, a silver goblet, some incense, copper candlesticks, and a number of other articles that obviously had come from the church. Shmul took a more practical trophy: a camisole, a silk gown, three Schwabian shirts, pillowcases, a red wool coat, a wedding shirt, and a special priest's apron. His colleagues took sixty-one strands of pearls.[41]

These young Jewish men were hardly unique. The head of a Rado-myshl gang of robbers stole copper cauldrons from Volko Budnitsky, two horses from a priest, and several copper utensils from a parish church.[42] The Makhnovka Jews Berkovich, Volkovich, and Rubonovich, accused of stealing church property, also demonstrate that some Jews engaged in Christian sacrosanct activities: if offenses against the religious "other" was the norm, so were offenses against religious property.[43]

The adventures of several Jews in Polonnoe top many other examples of Jewish defiance. All involved agreed that sometime around the late 1840s, eight Polonnoe Jewish merchants celebrated Sukkot (Tabernacle). The group included some wealthy people: Mordko Pronman, Motia Kramar, Gershko Lvov, Ios Melamed, and Moshko Kagan. These Jews, who grew up seeing Catholic and Christian Orthodox churches dominating the shtetl skyline, manifested what a Jewish scholar called "the transgressive craving for the cross."[44]

They also found an interesting way to rejoice in their Judaism by making fun of Christian symbolism. They gathered in the tavern of Pinhas Gurvits and indulged themselves in abundant and festive libations. The tavernkeeper's wife Miriam and her children observed the scene. The guests and the host moved from wine to vodka, and then began what the witnesses considered blatantly sacrilegious behavior, "making fun of the Holy Miracles of the Christian church."

First they undressed Beirish Stoliar to his underpants, put him in the corner of the room, and made him stretch both hands to his sides, as if he were being crucified. Then they slapped his cheeks, as a Jewish teacher would do to a bad student in the *heder*. They accompanied this ritual with some crude statements, although the participating Jews later failed to reproduce what they had said. Then Gurvits donned a gown as if he were a priest, brought in a Jewish boy, and started pretending to baptize the boy—all in front of Beirish Stoliar as Christ. Once the "conversion" was over, the show continued with a mock Christian wedding, the same boy now playing the groom.

Two local Poles, Teteriukowski and Rembertowski, observed this performance through the window. Scandalized, they rushed to write a detailed description of what had happened. Jews, they said, had been insolent enough to "crucify the Savior." During the performance, they maintained, "all the Jews were bareheaded." For the figure of Jesus, the Jews chose a Russian peasant—perhaps Beirish Stoliar was a corpulent *stoliar* (carpenter) and did not look like a feeble Jew. They claimed that when the mock Jesus stretched out his hands, one of the Jews said in Russian, "In the name of the Father, the Son, and the Holy Ghost"—and spat on the floor.

At the height of the blasphemy, Mordko Pronman, an already tipsy late arrival, appeared at the door. Motia Kramer grabbed him and yelled, "Cross yourself, you fucker, don't you see who is standing there?" and pointed to Beirish, with his hands outstretched and his bare torso. Pronman touched his fingers to his head and stomach but did not reach to the right and left shoulders. During the interrogations, the Poles acknowledged that they invented the last episode, yet one of the participating Jews attested that Kramer had asked Mariia Gurvits, not Mordko, to cross herself before the Living Savior.

Had this incident happened under Polish rule before the partitions, the eight Jews would have been brought in chains to a public trial. Sixty years later, with Russian nationalist parties and state-sponsored antisemitism on the rise, the Polonnoe offense would have eclipsed the 1911 Beilis blood libel case, when a Kiev-based brick-plant clerk was accused of killing a Christian boy and using his blood to bake Passover matzo.

In the first half of the nineteenth century, however, the authorities had much more common sense and the Jews had much more influence. The chief of police read the denunciation and immediately arrested all the Jews involved. A bribe of about 1,000 rubles quickly went into his pocket. One detention cell for all, please. The bribe worked. Sitting sober together in one cell, the protagonists and directors of the show produced an explanatory note, which, probably greased with another handsome sum, convinced the police to let them go.

The two Catholic accusers considered the leniency of the investigation a joke. They realized that one of the Jewish offenders was in good relations with the governor and that sending a complaint to Kiev would be useless. Therefore they sent a second denunciation to the St. Petersburg headquarters of the Russian secret police. The Polonnoe Christians, they maintained, were indignant at the inefficiency of the authorities. Jews had behaved sacrilegiously, had offended the Russian Christian Orthodox Church, Christianity, and the Savior. The Jews were Christ-hating people. The local Catholic priest, the denunciation added, had parish members—three women—who had met one Perl Iglovaia and told her about the terrible behavior of her Jewish brethren. Perl had allegedly replied, "We have stepped, we are stepping, and we will be stepping on your creed."

The secret police called for a new investigation, compelling the governor to conduct it with due rigor. The new detective agreed that the authorities had not been serious about the case. Apparently the Russian administrators who dealt with this case could not stop laughing while reading the reports. They laughed at the naïve Catholic townsfolk who discovered that Jews had crucified Jesus Christ—of course they had! They grinned at the testimonies of the cunning Jews, who claimed they had been "so drunk" that they "could not remember anything." They found it hilarious that the Jewess Perl had humiliated Catholicism—they also understood that most likely this improbable statement had been forged by the outraged Catholic ladies. They laughed when they discovered that the previous investigation had found the performance funny and the accusation laughable. They were so amused they could not even appropriately punish the offenders. Perhaps they understood that they were dealing with Jews eager to appropriate rather than reject Christianity. Paternalistically, they warned the Jews that "such cases would no longer be tolerated."

As a penalty, they exiled Pronman and Gurvits outside the Pale of Settlement: not to Siberia but to the nearby Chernigov province, under police surveillance. Two years later, Promnan and Gurvits asked for permission to come back home and were unofficially allowed to do so.[45] Their participation in what a Jewish historian called "reckless rites" proves that Jews appropriated the shared language of violence and used it as they found fit. Fifty years later, with the shtetl in decline, they would think twice before engaging in anything similar as they, and the Russian administration along with them, had become different.

ANTHROPOLOGY OF VIOLENCE

Jews in the shtetl were quite the opposite of those meek, short, narrow-shouldered, nearsighted, hunched over, physically inept images we find in memoirs and travelogues and prose narratives. Priest Morachevych, who travelled to Novograd-Volynsk and observed the "hunched and awkward, weak and inept" Jews, was as inaccurate in his portrayal of the Jews as the first Jewish ethnographer of the shtetl, Shloyme Ansky, who argued that Jews abhor physical strength.[46]

The well-fed and able-bodied Jews of early nineteenth-century Ukraine combined the mental qualities of urban dwellers and the corporeal capabilities of peasants. Srul Rashkovsky from Belaia Tserkov, who cut the throat of his employee Iudko, could carry the heavy millstone from his granary. Gershko the hatmaker had big hands, not only a big mouth. Portnoy, accused of stealing horses, wanted to become a cabman—a profession that required lifting a loaded wagon if the roads were impassable and dealing with horses, a physically demanding business. Mordekhai Tonky Nohy, despite his nickname, "thin legs," was most likely tall and robust if he managed to push the plump burial society elders off their bench. The Jews of Uman were able to overpower a sacristan and a deacon, and Morduck the paramedic had to have been to be quite large in order to throw a policeman out of his house. They did not hesitate to use their physical strength to defend their independence or professional dignity or defy those in power.

Shtetl business made its dwellers physically fit. Several Jews from near Brody participated in the activities of a local gang controlling illegal cross-border trade. These Jews were able to handle a lance to intimidate the mounted border patrol; a sword if they had to engage the guards in a fight, and pistols to protect their booty from the Cossack guards. Described by the intimidated Russian clerks as "brazen," they moved on horseback from place to place with their entire arsenal, including four pistols per person.[47]

Customs inspectors near Orynin encountered Jewish smugglers who had mounted guards on the border. When Cossacks challenged them, they resisted with wooden sticks, and the Cossacks had to retreat empty-handed. A certain Mordke Piramud rode through the woods near Kremenets on his stallion loaded with black pekoe and floral tea and several rolls of Morocco leather—altogether 345 pounds' worth of goods.[48] A rabbi from the shtetl Kravets was riding his horse through the forest near Dubno when several moujiks attacked him—but the rabbi managed his horse better than the attackers handled their pitchforks.[49] Jews had to know how to handle weaponry and overpower border guards in order to rescue their accomplices in case of arrest and confinement.[50] To survive

5.3. The shtetl smiths, Polonnoe.
Binyamin Lukin's private collection. Courtesy of Binyamin Lukin.

in the competitive world of peasants and Cossacks, Jews had to match them in physical strength.

The professional occupations of Jews also required average and above-average physical skills. Jews dealt with cattle, worked trading grain, carried around barrels of liquor, lifted and transported produce and goods, chopped and transported wood, toiled in the artisan shops, and engaged in various kinds of hard and demanding physical labor. Jews were able to share in the everyday shtetl violence because they were physically capable of doing so.

The Jews' central position in economy and trade inspired their self-confidence. Their perfect knowledge of "horrible obscenities" and "brazen words" that could knock a policeman off his feet also facilitated their successful participation in the various forms of shtetl violence. In the golden age shtetl, Jews were able to stand up for their religious identity, personal independence, and professional dignity—and the shtetl remained a stronghold of Judaism as long as Jews continued to do so.

The Russian authorities, however, were uncomfortable with the shtetl dwellers' equal share in what they sought to claim as their own prerogative. The regime put many of its ethnic minorities down in order to homogenize the country, and the Jews would be no exception.

THE STATE MONOPOLY ON VIOLENCE

In 1768, a bloody peasant rebellion called the *Koliivshchyna* decimated several Jewish communities in Ukraine, most notoriously that of Uman. The scar these events left on the Jewish collective memory was so deep that forty years later, Rabbi Nachman moved from Bratslav to Uman to pray for, bring to perfection, and uplift the souls of those Jews who had perished in the Uman massacre. More than a hundred years after the rebellion, in the early 1880s, the first full-scale pogroms hit the cities and towns of the southeastern Pale of Settlement, destroying 100,000 Jewish businesses, ruining 60,000 families, leaving 20,000 homeless, causing about 10 million rubles' worth of damage, and leaving up to several dozen Jews and gentiles dead and wounded.[51]

Between the Koliivshchyna and the anti-Jewish atrocities, deportations, mass migrations, state-instigated violence against ethnic minorities, and radicalization of the Jew of the early 1900s, the golden age of the shtetl was a time of relative peace. For more than half a century, the Jews of the Pale knew neither mass nor organized anti-Jewish violence. The Russian authorities went to great lengths to check any organized violence against their newly appropriated ethnic minorities, Jews included.[52] Even during the 1881–1882 pogroms, contrary to common opinion, the government took pains to suppress the riots and check the assaults against the Jews. Remarkably, the shtetls in Podolia and Volhynia (with the exception of Balta) knew very little, if any, pogromist activities—unlike the new economic centers in the southeast of Ukraine.

Yet Jewish life in the shtetl was far from a bucolic paradise. Although the shtetl did not have any cataclysmic violence, its dwellers of different social status and ethnic origin had to deal with "everyday functional violence" on a regular basis.[53] Christians and Jews participated in "a daily 'dialogue of violence' within the Russian Empire."[54] Violence became part of the shtetl's quotidian praxis, for Jews along with everybody else. But the regime soon intervened, thus radically changing the physical profile of the shtetl.

The Russian regime applied violence just as did the landlords, who humiliated Christian Orthodox serfs, peasants, and Jews. "If flogging male and female peasants, young and old, was a matter of no importance," asked Yekhezkel Kotik in his memoir, "then why should beating a little Jew be an exception?"[55] The magnates ritualized Jewish discrimination in the ritual of *majufes*: every year in May, a Jewish leaseholder would come to the manor of the Polish landlord to perform a humiliating dance and an ingratiating song, thus submitting himself to the landlord, who would condescendingly pull the Jew by his sidelocks.[56]

Some Polish landlords, acting as judges, victimized entire Jewish communities, while others meted out punishment to individual leaseholders. The Berdichev Jewish elites regularly complained of the arbitrariness of the owner of Berdichev, Matvei Radziwiłł, who indiscriminately humiliated members of the town elite since, he explained, they failed to abide by their leasing contracts and provide him with a befitting sustenance.[57] In nearby Makhnovka, the landlord Ivan Miączyński had the entire family of his leaseholder beaten and ruined.[58] Landlord Straszinski summoned a certain Itsik Kurlabkin from Skvira and had him whipped and put in the gallows for three days.[59] Of course, Jews were free townsfolk, not serfs, yet the memoirist Kotik was right: the landlord ignored this difference when it came to penalizing.

The town-owners gladly delegated the privilege of using violence to their economy managers. Landlord Dulski, for example, having promised a new fur coat to someone in Berdichev, called for his economy manager and ordered him to get a new fur coat by the next Monday. The manager summoned several Jewish tailors and furriers, brought them to the house of a local Pole, and ordered them to start making a new fur coat immediately. The Jews refused, explaining that they had other commissions and also that it was almost Shabbat. The enraged manager hit one of the tailors, cut the beards and sidelocks of others, punched them, locked them in, and left. He forced them to work from Friday through Sunday, day and night, violating the sanctity of Shabbat, and underpaid them when they were finished.[60]

The Fastov economy manager Novoselski was no better: he summoned Ios Kagan, had him whipped, watched as he was given twenty lashes, and then switched from physical to moral humiliation, ordering a local Jewish barber to cut off Kagan's sidelocks.[61] In Makarov, the town-owner and his manager mercilessly beat the elders of the local Jewish community, Dutgarts and Naroditsky. The two Jews went to the local doctor, who examined them and found their "buttocks and bellies covered with cuts and bruises."[62]

In Rtishchev, Shmelik Kagansky went to estate manager Beliavsky and asked for wood to warm the house for the Jäger regiment privates, billeted locally. Beliavsky blew up: you are responsible for the soldiers—go get your own wood! He hit Kagansky with his huge fists, then pulled out his whip and whipped him, if we believe Kagansky's deposition.[63] In many cases, the magnates applied callous measures to penalize Jews, appropriated Jewish belongings, and left Jews in dire straits. The magnates did not ruin the Jews entirely, however: after all, the Jews were their livelihood, their geese who laid golden eggs.

When a shtetl went from being a Polish private town to Russian regime ownership, the use of violence became the prerogative of the Russian *gradonachalnik,* head of the town council, and the *politsmeister,* chief of town police. The Ukrainian Romantic poet Taras Shevchenko in his fantasy "Son" (Dream) depicted cruelty permeating all levels of Russian society. "I saw the tsar approaching his senior clerk ... and punching him hard in the mouth. The poor creature licked himself and hit the lower clerk in the belly, with a thud; and that one whacked a lower boss on his back, and that lower one smacked someone of yet lower rank, who in turn hit one of the lowest clerks, and these, already outside, rushed through the streets and began beating the unbeaten Eastern Orthodox, who yelled: 'Our father the tsar is having fun!'"[64]

The Russian police were exactly within this chain of command. Major Rezunov, chief of police in the shtetl of Bar, behaved as if he were a townowner. Only he had the right to use violence. Unhappy with his meager state salary, he summoned the local Polish gentry and Eastern Orthodox magistrates and reprimanded them for several hours, then gathered Polish and Jewish guild artisans in the town square and publicly cursed them. Furthermore, he sequestered wheat and other goods from Jewish merchants and made the town elite pay for his personal expenses. In order to extract every kopek that he could in taxes, he kicked, punched, and flogged ordinary townsfolk, including pious Old Believers. The Eastern Orthodox elders, although they were at odds with the Christian sectarian Old Believers, could not abide this behavior and joined Jewish communal elders in defense of the townsfolk.[65]

In Balta, for another example, the town police chief Sakhnovsky learned that the Jews had buried a fourteen-year old Jewish boy who had died the same day. The Jews informed Sakhnovsky about their legal rule of burying the dead preferably before the next day. Sakhnovsky, suspecting foul play, gathered the Jewish elders and the members of the burial society, forty people in all, and demanded that they exhume the body. The Jews refused. The enraged Sakhnovsky called them rebels, took his stick, and started beating left and right, trying to force the Jews to follow his orders. Failing to do so, he put all forty Jews under temporary arrest.[66]

The more Russian officials entrenched themselves in the shtetl, the more they became confident of their impunity—and so did the troops. Billeted in the shtetl, the soldiers protected Jews against outsiders, but also exposed them to their wild behavior. Always respectful of Russian power, Grigorii Bogrov depicted the lower ranks quartered in a Jewish house as unruly, vulgar, and offensive.[67]

In Ruzhin, the locally billeted regiment decided to establish a temporary military hospital in the home of Shlioma and Khaia Ekhtman. For this purpose, the quartermasters entered Ekhtman's house, inspected it, and found his pregnant wife Khaia, lying in bed in a room allocated for the hospital. Without further ado, they dragged Khaia from her bed. Later her husband complained that she soon "gave birth to a stillborn baby."[68] According to a doctor's report, Abram Dantsig and Leizor Shulman were on their way home from the Cherniakhov fair when a group of twelve soldiers attacked, beat them, stole their hard-earned money, and left them with the "traces of the beating on their bodies."[69]

As long as Jews were the masters of the marketplace, they were able to pay back the Poles' and Russians' violent behavior in the same currency: nobody prevented them from doing so. During the cataclysmic violence of the 1880s—the pogroms—Jews organized patrols and had groups of up to 300 people armed with clubs in Berdichev, Volochisk, Rovno, and Balta, ready to defend themselves against the assaulting mob.[70] Yet in the last quarter of the century, things started to change rapidly, and economy played no lesser role than ideology. The modernization of the empire introduced new industrial manufactories, which made the Jewish artisans in the shtetl obsolete.

The backbone of the shtetl, the Jewish artisans now left for big cities and joined hired workers. The railroads and new centers of commerce such as Odessa, Kiev, and Kharkov attracted the trade previously centered in the shtetl, and the shtetl marketplace lost its allure. Finally, although the authorities applied deadly army force to neutralize the riots, they forbade Jews from organizing any self-defense—considered in the turbulent 1880s and revolutionary 1900s as an affront or provocation or both.

The regime introduced an exclusive monopoly on violence. Jews were ordered to keep their hands to themselves. Those who disagreed moved to the cities and joined the red-shirted class struggle. The shtetl with its undertrained and inefficient police was left unprotected and ruined by the iron age of Russian industrialization. No more the backbone of the local economy, the Jews in the shtetl lost their strong sense of Jewish dignity.

Wooing the peasants to neutralize growing unrest in the village, the regime chose to disown the Jews, blame them for all the Russian economic failures, present them as the exploiters of the peasantry, outlaw self-defense as revolutionary subversion, and leave Jews defenseless before the vengeful mob. Previously protected by the regime, the Jews appeared in the late nineteenth-century conservative media as aliens who, together with Poles, sought to smuggle in socialism and destroy Mother Russia. The authorities quickly realized they could manipulate this hideous myth to further their political goals.

Undermined by ill-conceived social reforms, industrialization, restrictive regulations, and public vilification, the Jews were no longer masters of the situation. They could do little when the regime incited the xenophobic mob and the brainwashed troops against them, trying to redirect social unrest during the 1905 Russian revolution against an internal enemy. Nonetheless, Jews retained a peculiar East European mode of asserting their dignity, defending themselves, and using the languages of violence they had learned so well.

A VIOLENT HERITAGE

In the functioning of shtetl violence, Jews dealt with Christians as they dealt with other Jews and as Christians dealt with them: individually. The golden age shtetl had no pogroms for over a century. In the second half of the nineteenth century, however, the incomplete Russian abolition of serfdom and the clumsy reform of the peasants turned thousands of them into a volatile social group seeking employment in urban areas. Instead of rectifying its mistakes, the regime presented itself as the protector of the impoverished Christian peasantry and chose to blame the Jews, alleged bloodsuckers and exploiters and subservient helpers of the Polish landlords, for the deteriorating situation of the Russian peasant. In addition, the administration hypocritically endorsed the conservative public discourse that equated the growing unrest in the society with the impact of the rebellious Poles, separatist Ukrainians, and suspicious Jews.

At the first opportune moment, the assassination of Alexander II, the former peasants who had not yet adopted urban identities moved in from the suburbs and nearby villages and ruined the Jewish urban economy. The army, no longer in the towns, the understaffed, underpaid, and undertrained police, and the Jews themselves were caught by surprise. Dealing with a strong, aggressive mob armed with axes was very different from dealing with an individual policeman, town clerk, or business partner. No one was prepared for events to take this course, the Jews no less than anyone else. Now the peasants on one side and the army and police on the other entered into fierce competition for the monopoly on violence. In the early twentieth century, the rising proletarians, revolutionary groups, and armed units of the regime's combatant xenophobes entered the pool of competitors. It took the Jews some time to come to grips with the rapidly changing social environment and adapt themselves to it.

But before the pogroms radically changed the balance of power, shtetl violence belonged to everybody and to nobody. Historians have forgotten this aspect of the shtetl reality, but the Yiddish language has preserved it. Most Yiddish curses reveal their unquestionable Slavic origin. *Azoy a paskudnyak*, "what a scoundrel," they say, using the Germanic for "what a" and Slavic for "scoundrel." The adaptation of Slavic obscenities for Jewish usage testifies to the Jewish share in East European verbal violence. "Skot," a Russian peasant would say scornfully about a perfidious person, "a piece of cattle." "Shkots," a shtetl Jew would say to curse his unreliable partner by fusing the Hebrew *shekets* (rodent) and the Slavic *skot*. "Triastsia vashii materi, daite dorogi"—"shake your mother, let us pass!"— shout Ukrainian peasants in Ukrainian to two Jews in Mendele Moykher Sforim's novel, Mendele and Alter, who block the road. Of course, Mendele's Jews understood this shared language of verbal violence.[71]

To reify their identity as clever and reasonable people, Jews repeated and learned through reiteration by peppering modern languages with Slavic obscene idioms. A brief tour through the pages of Michael Wex's book on modern Yiddish introduces a rich variety of evildoers, blockheads, and morons of Slavic descent. We meet here a wide variety of idiots and loosers, such as a *kaleke*, a *shlak*, a *parshivets*, a *bolvan*, a *yolep*, a *pentiukh*, a *propn*, a *zhlob* and a *khlop*, quite at home in their North Ameri-can environment.[72] Sociolinguists add to this list the indispensable *kurve*, a misogynist curse of Ukrainian or Polish origin.[73] These words all moved into Yiddish from the realm of the Slavs.

Protecting personal dignity required returning the favors of the sur-rounding culture. Samson the Nazarene from Jabotinsky's novel of the same name explains how to respond to violence: "When they beat you with a bat, grab a real bat, not a reed one."[74] Everyday shtetl reality taught Jews to respond to violence in kind. Jews took this lesson from the shtetl into modern politics. The governor of Vilna, Victor Von Vahl, ordered twenty-six participants in the 1902 May Day demonstration flogged, and in response, Hirsh Lekert, a shtetl shoemaker, shot and wounded him.[75] Jabotinsky was instrumental in organizing the first self-defense units dur-ing the 1905 pogroms—an undertaking that eventually inspired some 1,100 young Jews to join the "fighting units," or voluntary militia.[76]

Following their example, Mikhael Halpern organized Jewish self-defense groups in Nes-Siona, and Moshe Smiliansky did so in Rishon Le-Tsion. Dozens of Jews left the shtetls, moved to Palestine, joined the kibbutz movement, and established self-defense units.[77] Eliyahu Golomb from Vylkovysk became one of the founders of the Jewish Legion, Haga-nah and Palmach. Sow the fields, instructed the legendary Joseph Trumpel-dor, under the protection of guards. Interrupt prayers, echoed Yehoshua Stampfer, one of the founders of Petakh-Tikvah, if you need to resist at-tacking tribes.

To claim that solely Orthodox or ultra-religious Jews used violence for economic, religious, or political purpose seems like an undeserved compli-ment to the representatives of Judaic Orthodoxy.[78] Jews, any Jews, obser-vant or not too observant, on a par with their gentile neighbors, did not restrain themselves from using violence. To defend their dignity and inde-pendence, Jews needed to master the vernacular languages, including the languages of violence. Shtetl Jews assimilated certain salient aspects of sur-rounding society long before enlightened thinkers urged them to do so. The political incorrectness of modern Jews of East European descent is part and parcel of their shtetl—and broader East European—heritage, a means to assert their Jewish identity and give expression to their national dignity.

CHAPTER SIX

CRIME, PUNISHMENT, AND A PROMISE OF JUSTICE

One summer day in 1824, the parents of twelve-year-old Itsik Leibovich from Belaia Tserkov did not send him to *heder*. Itsik was
hanging out in the street, watching a unit of Russian soldiers
march by. Itsik admired their insignia and uniforms, their white straps
and gallant moustaches, glittering copper buttons, and their rifles, real
rifles. Ah, how Itsik wanted to be a soldier and hold a real gun! Just imagine, Itsik the Warrior!

Following the unit down the road, Itsik passed by the house of the
Tulczanskis. Although the Tulczanskis were formally members of the
Polish szlachta, there was nothing left of their bygone noble status except
antique carpets, curved sabers, pistols, and a rifle hanging on the wall of
their guest room. Was anybody home? Itsik entered through the open
door. The heavy rifle hung on the wall. Itsik cautiously took it down and
rushed out. The soldiers were still passing by. Now Itsik would join the

battle! The rifle was heavy. Itsik slowly lifted it, jokingly aimed at a passing soldier, pressed the trigger, and shouted with bravado: paff-paff!

The rifle fired. The small-shot discharge hit Riazhkov, a private in the Jäger regiment. Shocked and scared to death, Itsik dropped the rifle. He had no idea it was loaded. Minutes later, he was caught, arrested, and thrown in a detention cell. Days later, his case was dispatched to the Kiev main court for urgent consideration. In prison, Itsik learned that fortunately, because he had not been able to lift the rifle high enough, he had only slightly wounded Riazhkov in leg. The private would have to spend some time in the hospital but his life was not in danger. However, these circumstances did not mean that Itsik was innocent.

The court brought criminal charges against him: a Jewish boy had made an attempt on the life of a Russian soldier! The charges were so serious that the court reported to the Head of His Majesty's Main Staff, who in turn informed the tsar. Known for his warm disposition toward children, Alexander I forbade punishing the boy with anything more than exhortation. He dismissed the prescribed physical punishment and ordered the case closed. The tsar was convinced that whatever crime Itsik had committed, he had done it "for fun and without intent." Alexander reiterated in a special note to the war minister that absolutely no punishment should be given to the boy. But who then was to blame? Alexander advised rebuking Tulczanski for having left a loaded weapon unattended and making him pay three years' salary to the temporarily disabled soldier.[1]

Jewish underage boys obviously did not raise arms regularly against Russian soldiers, nor did Russian tsars pardon Jews on a daily basis for assaulting the troops. Yet this case stands for many in that it illuminates the counterintuitive relations between Russians, Poles, and Jews in the Pale of Settlement. Itsik's story proves that there was a certain level of rapport between Jews and Poles in the shtetl. A Jewish boy was passionate about becoming a soldier rather than a rabbi. Despite Itsik's outward offense against the army, the pillar of Russia, the tsar displayed mercy, understanding, and forgiveness. Following the tsar's decision, the court pardoned the guilty Jewish boy and punished the innocent Catholic member of petty gentry.

The archives tell us many stories about the rudimentary objectivity rather than inherent prejudicial attitudes of the Russian courts, about shared and unique parameters of Jewish criminality, and about a relatively benevolent attitude of the Russian regime toward the Jews, apprehensive of the Ukrainian peasants and highly suspicious of the Poles. Before Russia introduced racial profiling of the Jews, considering them aliens as bad and as disloyal as Polish Catholics, it treated Jews as the equals of, if not better than, many other borderland ethnic groups. What transpired in Russia's treatment of the Jewish criminals is precisely this sense of a new legality and promise, different both from the Old Polish times and from the prejudiced justice in Late Imperial Russia. For over half a century, Jews walked into the Russian courtroom expecting that their voice would be heard and their interests protected. This promise of legality inspired Jewish hopes, which vanished altogether with the end of the golden age shtetl.

JEWISH PLIGHT, RUSSIAN JUSTICE

The Russian penitentiary system was remarkably inefficient. The interrogation process was a formality, confessions took the place of proof, and the executive branch was often unable to carry out verdicts. Convicts in early nineteenth-century Russia were rarely sentenced to severe punishments, and the regime seemed more liberal toward criminals because the country was, in Jonathan Daly's words, "in a far weaker position to discipline and control the society than its Western European counterparts."[2] Russia had a lower effectiveness of the legislative systems, not a lower crime rate.

Nikolai Dubrovin compared the Russian court system to "legal chaos." Bribes, the "poison of the courts," rather than the discretion of the judge determined the final decision. A plaintiff could never approach a clerk without making a donation. Ordinary people brought "a towel, a jar of honey, a large gingerbread, and sometimes a loaf of bread" to have their case favorably adjudicated.[3] Boris Mironov observed a decrease in the crime rate in the first half of the nineteenth century, identifying a tendency to "release detainees," and proving that more than half of those indicted were exonerated. For that reason, he concluded, in early nineteenth-century Russia the crime rate was four times lower than in France and eight times lower than in England.[4]

Yet the Russian courts did not project a judicial bias on the Jews. Of course, a Jewish litigator always needed to make extra efforts to get justice, but in the end justice usually was meted out. Beinish Finkelshtein, a jeweler from Zlatopolie, lost diamond and pearl jewelry worth 18,000 rubles to a dozen robbers, who thoroughly ransacked his house. The police arrested several of the robbers and found some of his stolen belongings in Odessa, but he spent three years trying to get the court to bring all those involved to justice.[5]

Abram Fridliand, an army purveyor of good standing, filed a complaint against his partners, who had sold him livestock and did not deliver. He also used personal connections to get the governor to intervene—and only then did his frightened partners return the stock.[6] Duvid and Rakhmiel, two Jewish carpet-makers accused of blasphemy, had their case considered in the Mogilev-Podolsk court, which released them and gave them passports and money to get home.[7] The lenient decision regarding the Jews from Polonnoe and the story of Itsik the Warrior both show that the Russian court not only arrived at a favorable decision but also did not consider Jews innate criminals, and was unwilling to increase the prison population at their expense.

Jews found the Russian court a better option precisely because it seemed like a third constituency, equidistant from the internal Judaic and external Polish legal systems, and by virtue of that position, it promised justice. Before the Polish partitions, internal communal conflicts among Jews were adjudicated by the rabbinical court (*bezdn*), the magistrate courts, and, in the shtetl, by the Polish town-owner, who acted as the local supreme judge. Before the partitions, Jews throughout the Polish-Lithuanian Commonwealth, not only in Ukraine, did their best to avoid Jewish jurisdiction: the magnate's justice was biased but perhaps less biased than the rabbinic court.[8] After the partitions, the Russian regime, in European fashion, required that Jews go to the local municipal courts, corrupt but less biased than the magnate's court, and forbade the kahal elders from judging legal cases.

Yet things did not change overnight. For some twenty years the scribes of the Russian courts were Poles, and their records were in Polish. Seeking to squeeze the Polish influence out of its legal system, Russian administrators promoted local, non-Catholic urban dwellers to positions of clerks, scribes, and judges. The new regime sought the sympathy of the urban population, accused the previous regime of arbitrariness, and changed the legal balance in favor of the non-Catholic townsfolk, among whom Jews were overrepresented.

The Catholic Tulczanski had good reason to protest the tsar's verdict penalizing him for leaving his rifle unattended, but he would have been blowing against the wind. In 1800 the Kiev district court considered dozens of cases between Poles and Jews and decided in favor of the Jews. The court dismissed a lawsuit between the Herszkowicz brothers and Jan Hański, an ensign from Kiev, refusing to take sides. Berko Ovsherovich, the leaseholder of a village, convinced the court that two Polish innkeepers should pay him 1,250 rubles. Moshko Brodsky from Cherkas sued Count Alexander Samnyłów, who owed him about 200 rubles and never paid; the court sided with Moshko. The court also sided with Hershko and Abramko Iankelevich against Ignacij Goliowski, who lost his appeal to reverse previous court decisions. Two kahal elders representing the entire Jewish population of Boguslav sued Count Potocki himself, and insisted that the case be transferred from Kiev to their local district court. Feeling his power slipping between fingers, Potocki exclaimed, "They never used to have this right!"[9]

Apparently they had gained it—together with expectations that the Russian court would be an objective mediator between Jews and gentiles. The Russian courts had a vested interest in the result of the trials: Poles were respected Christian members of the landlord estate, while Jews were merely infidel Christ-killers and no more than sleazy merchants. Yet resentment toward the Polish szlachta, associated with disloyalty, eclipsed anti-Judaic bias and brought about a more nuanced attitude toward the Jews, sometimes giving the impression of objectivity, if not sympathy, toward them. Jews could have misunderstood the geopolitics behind this attitude, but they rightly perceived it as a promise of justice. They were not afraid of the Russian court and had good reasons to trust it. However slow and corrupt, the judges used their common sense and the Russian law, not the racial discourse and conspiracy theories they would use later in the nineteenth century.[10]

The golden age shtetl dwellers believed that justice was possible and achievable and that Russia would treat them objectively, as useful and loyal townsfolk, not as daydreaming Catholic Poles or rebellious Ukrainian peasants. Compared to the eighteenth century, Jews found that their legal situation had changed for the better.[11] Notka Mordukhovich from Radomyshl lent 100 rubles to the Catholic Church metropolitan Smogorzewski, future archbishop of Ukraine, who never repaid the debt. Notka took him to court and received Smogorzewski's house in compensation for the unpaid debt.[12] Gatsberg took Makhnovka landlord Jan Moczínski to court for beating him and his family members and stealing their belongings, and the court ruled against the Polish shtetl owner.[13]

Kagan from Fastov, whom we met in the previous chapter, used his excellent knowledge of Russian law to bring economic manager Novoselski to justice for beating him in public. Novoselski sent a countercomplaint, threatening Kagan and demanding that he justify his case before him, as would have been done in the old times. "Why should I?" exclaimed Kagan, "Novoselski is not a Russian state clerk, and I do not need to justify myself before him." He insisted on a court hearing, and the administration subpoenaed Novoselski.[14]

Jews sought and found justice in the Russian courts. Iudka Eliovich, the leaseholder of a village, resorted to the Cherkas court when his debtor, Gunka the peasant, failed to provide tar that Iudka had commissioned from him and paid for in advance.[15] Finkelstein from Zlatopolie complained that the district police chief had stolen diamonds from him during a search of his house. The court ruled to bring the clerk to justice.[16]

For years, Meer Kats of Skvira leased stores from Lubov Uvarova, the owner of Pavoloch, and was her trusted contractor. He made his cash revenues readily available to her and members of her family—until one day Uvarova refused to repay him an 850 ruble debt. Kats believed in the Russian court, which eventually decided in his favor and forced Uvarova to pay. Kats also realized that the involvement of the state would eliminate possible conflicts: he was ready to sign new contracts with Uvarova only in the presence of a local administrator, he stated.[17] Likewise, the Jewish community in Berdichev litigated for years in the St. Petersburg courts with Prince Radziwiłł, in hopes that the Russian justice system would mitigate the magnate's old-style rapacious exploitation.

The Jews' new trust in Russian jurisprudence paralleled the growing skepticism of the rabbinic courts, which were unable to implement their own decisions, particularly because the power of the Jewish elders was steadily declining. Tsal Rozenfeld, a butcher, went to Rabbi Ber Kagan, the head of the Kiev rabbinic court, to complain about a certain Jewish butcher who had taken kosher meat worth 250 rubles from Rozenfeld and never paid. The rabbi's decisions were most likely good but inconsequential. Rozenfeld realized this and filed a complaint with the district court.[18] When Maria Berenshtein from Kamenets-Podolsk did not return the 6,000 rubles she had borrowed from Haim Gorenshtein from Kiev, the latter did not even bother to turn to the same Rabbi Kagan but took his complaint directly to the Russian court and then to the central administration, which eventually helped him get his money back.[19]

The case of Rivka Balakleisky, the widow of a tavernkeeper, proves that Jews preferred rabbinic to Russian courts only when the matter was heavily charged ethically. Rivka cared little that her recently deceased husband had been on trial for five cases of robbery, larceny, and sheltering gangsters. After his death, she was concerned only with her dressing gown and mattresses, which her husband's two guarantors, Berko and Gershon, had confiscated from her house in lieu of payment.

Rivka rushed to a local scribe and had him write a complaint to the district court, but could not justify it. The court was unable to settle the matter, and "requested that the magistrate allow a rabbi to solve this case in a tertiary court." Rivka agreed, since she reckoned that Jews "did not dare engage in falsehoods before their spiritual leaders."[20] We should note here that it was the Russian court that endorsed the procedure and delegated power as the only source of justice.

As Mironov emphasized, "law and justice were not empty words either in pre- or in post-reform Russia."[21] The economic stability of the shtetl relied on the mitigating factor of Russian legalism, which in turn for a good part of the nineteenth century abstained from employing religious bias in the decision-making process. It is particularly fascinating that the Russian criminal taxonomy significantly contributed to this sense of justice.

ANTHROPOLOGY OF CRIMINALITY

After the partitions of Poland, the Russian regime issued internal documents describing those traversing the Pale. The police, however, never mastered the vocabulary needed to portray the Jews properly. Criminals of Jewish origin could easily manipulate their identity, not because many did not really look like stereotypical Jews but because the Russian police for more than half a century did not practice ethnic profiling. For Jews, this administrative negligence meant tolerance.

In the era preceding photo IDs, the police measured Jews by the Slavic yardstick. If the police records said average height, dark-skinned, and fair hair, they meant Russian average height, a tan complexion, and Slavic hair color. Because of the Slavic frame of reference, Jews seldom looked Jewish in the police descriptions or as described in their internal passports. On the contrary, more often than not they were described as genuine Slavs.

Of course, the police portrayals were not befitting of Gogol or Turgenev. We may even wonder whether the Jews thus described by the police owed their Slavic looks to the clichés of the Russian clerks or to certain anthropological characteristics stemming from a similarity of housing, diet, occupation, and natural environment. Perhaps the limited bureaucratic vocabulary of the police accounts for the too Slavic-sounding depictions of the Jews. Be that as it may, one point is clear: the police clerks portrayed Jews as ordinary human beings, with the same types of features as everyone else. Jews were described as fair-haired and shaven or bearded, yet almost always without sidelocks or large, hooked noses.

Thirty-five-year-old Gitsik traded in rings and signets: his passport described him as being of average height, black-haired, and clean-shaven.[22] Shtromvaser, from somewhere near Ruzhin, was a thirty-one-year-old Jew, 164 cm tall, with blond eyebrows and beard, gray eyes, regular mouth and nose, clean-shaven face, and a birthmark under the right eyebrow, according to the police description.[23] Thirty-eight-year-old Itsik Vinogradov from Boguslav was six feet tall, fair-haired, and bearded, with a thick moustache and brows, gray eyes, dark complexion, and a medium-sized nose. Forty-six-year-old Kiev-dweller Yaakov Liplir was of average height, with a pleasant, elongated face, medium-sized nose, gray eyes, and dirty-blond hair.

The police preferred plain universalistic language to depict Jews. Of course, the passports of the Jews had their Jewish names and creed there, yet to determine someone's ethnic origin only by a passport description of facial features was next to impossible. Belaia Tserkov-dweller Shimon Veksler was thirty-five: he had a clean-shaven face, dirty-blond hair, regular nose, and gray eyes, a description that sounds like that of a Slav. Forty-year-old Hirsh Vol from Orynin was of above-average height, with fair hair and a small beard with visible gray hair, a plain dark face, and a regular mouth and nose; over his right knee he had a scar from a horse-kick. If not for his sidelocks, mentioned in the description, he would have sounded like an average Slav.[24] Markus Shteltser from Austrian Brody was described as short, with fair hair, oval face, gray eyes, and a medium-sized nose.[25] Shirko Averbukh from Vasilkov was of average height, with a long wrinkled nose and face, gray-brown eyes, and dark blond hair, with a reddish beard and moustache.[26]

These were ordinary Jewish townsfolk. To aid recognition, runaway prisoners, wanted criminals, and gangsters had much more detailed portraits in the police wanted circulars. But even in these cases, distinctive marks singled such individuals out as criminals rather than as Jews. Of course, the criminals themselves cut off their sidelocks, shaved their beards, and changed their attire to look less recognizable. However, the normative Slavic vocabulary used by the police in their documentary descriptions was not insulting toward Jews.

The tavernkeeper Hershko Leibovich, exiled to Siberia, was described as slim and tall, with gray eyes and a sharp nose.[27] Yankel Raisfeld, a runaway prisoner from Siberia, travelled with a false passport containing, however, a true description of his physical appearance: he was taller than average and had a very dark, pimply complexion, black hair, dark eyes, and large, wide nose. Iosel Lubarsky, another runaway Siberian prisoner, was slim and of average height, with a short beard, black hair, and one mangled eye. Forty-year-old Iosef Kanevsky from Zolotonosha was short, red-haired, and of strong build. Ilia Shapir, 170 cm tall, had a pockmarked face, dark blond hair, and a light moustache and beard, and was missing two upper teeth. Thirty-year-old Nusen Slobodetsky was taller than average and black-haired. To avoid suspicion, outwit the police, and pass for a pious Jew, Slobodetsky, clean-shaven in prison, had false sidelocks sewn to his skullcap. He would remove them together with his skullcap when committing a burglary.[28]

Many Jewish criminals had "regular" or "moderate" noses, Slavic-looking gray eyes, and fair hair. Jewish gangsters could easily manipulate their identity—altering sidelocks, clothing, or beards—and their documents, according to the circumstances. These items gave them flexibility of identity. Nothing was further from the truth for these Jewish criminals than the stereotypical image of a short, hunchbacked, and weak Jew. Perhaps such a Jew, to be found, no doubt, in the shtetl, was capable of forging counterfeit coins, but not of harnessing a horse or handling a rifle. The police want ads, unable to tell a Jew from a Slav, facilitated the freedom of action for the Jewish criminals.

A CRIMINAL MINORITY

The Russian geopolitical agenda after the Polish partitions put Poles in a situation of preferential prejudice and Jews in one of preferential objectivity. In addition, the absence of anti-Judaic sensibilities embedded in police and court practices placed Jews in a favorable legal situation, fertilized by bribes or reinforced by bailouts of successful marketplace merchants. As a result, Jews found themselves in an absolute minority behind bars.

Although shtetl dwellers participated in various activities that bordered on criminal, Jews did not have a large presence in the prisons. In 1820, the Kiev prison housed 178 inmates, fifteen of them Jews. Later in the year the ratio of convicted or detained Jews to the general population of the largest district prison was even lower.[29] In 1825, out of twenty-five inmates of the Lipovets prison, three were Jewish.[30] In 1824 the Makhnovka district prison had one Jew among thirty-eight detainees, and a year later it had four Jews out of thirty-four detainees. Four years later this prison had two Jewish inmates out of twenty-eight.[31]

Geography did not change the Jewish crime rate. In 1825, four Jews were incarcerated in the Tarashcha prison with twenty-one other inmates. The Skvira prison had two Jews out of thirty-seven prisoners, while the prisons of Cherkas and Chigirin had no Jews among dozens of Christian inmates, Zvenigorodka had six Jews out of fifty-five detainees, Lipovets, one out of six, Makhnovka, three out of 34, and Uman one out of 47. With a minor margin of error, Jews constituted an average of about 5 to 10 percent among detainees and convicts—significantly lower than their ratio in the general population in Kiev province.[32]

Although Podolia had a far greater Jewish population and a higher ratio of Jews to gentiles, the underworld of the district prisons included very few Jews. The Kamenets ordinance house had two Jewish inmates out of forty. In the Gaisin, Litin, Balta, and Mogilev prisons, most of the detainees were Polish Catholics, and none was Jewish. The Olgopol prison housed seven Jews, most of them on trial and not yet convicted.[33] Logically, there should have been a higher number of arrested Jews, since Jews were very involved in the competitive economy.[34]

A marketplace without a pickpocket or swindler was not a marketplace, and those who visited the Berdichev annual fairs did not fail to notice the abundance of petty thieves. Particularly if we remind ourselves of the high ratio of Jews to the general population—50 percent in most shtetls—the figures of arrested or sentenced Jews appear disproportionately low. It is hard to believe that Jews were as ethically impeccable as they appear in the Jewish communal hagiographies. The point is that the Russian regime did not consider them a priori as criminals or as rebels, but this attitude would change with the advance of industrialization and the revolutionary era.

Most Jews committed crimes predicated on their status as an economically dynamic ethnic group. Nine of the fifteen Jews detained in the Kiev district prison in 1820, including Duvid Sholiovich, his wife Rukhlia, and his daughter Fredia, were vagrants without documents. Of the remaining six, one Jew had allegedly been recasting copper coins, one supposedly had participated in the murder of a Pole, one had stolen a bolt of fabric, and the other two had stolen horses. Volia Gershkovich had bought and resold copper tubes, which turned out to have been stolen.[35] Three Makhnovka Jews had stolen religious artifacts from a church. Jewish women, just as they worked at the taverns or at the marketplace stores, also played a large part in these illegal economic pursuits. For example, Maria from Skvira district was charged with felony on pawned items. Crime superseded both gender and cultural differences: consider two Lipovets Jews, David and Moshko Gendliar, who had stolen not only several horses but also 1,700 pounds of lard.[36]

Nicholas I's new regulations of the 1830s restricting internal Jewish mobility triggered an increase in the Jewish prison population but hardly changed the Jewish criminality pattern. In the 1840s, nineteen out of twenty-nine prisoners in Vasilkov were Jews, detained but not yet convicted. Most of them were roaming without documents or living illegally outside the Pale of Settlement. Several had stolen and slandered. Others had stamped illegal goods with forged stamps, falsely identified their age, employed Christian peasants as servants, undermined the state sale of alcohol, or failed to abide by a contract.[37] From a legal standpoint they had technically committed crimes, but they were hardly accomplished criminals.[38] These Jews shared cells with Christian horse thieves, rebels, murderers, vagrants, burglars, and priests who had forged birth certificates.

While robbery and vagrancy characterized both Jews and Christians, rebellion and murder stood out as predominantly non-Jewish criminal endeavors.[39] In the 1820s, Jews were called "cunning" but not "regicidal," as in the 1880s, or "revolutionary," as in the 1900s. The legal authorities treated them as normal people engaged in economic pursuits who were detained, accused, or penalized mainly for administrative misdemeanors and economic felonies.

Their uneven share in trade revenues pushed unlucky Jews into the redistribution of the means of production—in other words, stealing. Jews excelled in this endeavor: they were as skilled as the gypsies yet less aggressive than the peasants. Leizer Mailovich from Zolotonosha was charged with running horse robberies, although the police failed to prove him guilty.[40] The police were more careful in Makhnovka, where they proved that Leizer Kraizman had stolen four horses. During the Iliinskaia fair in Romny, Esel Shkolnik made good use of the agitation of the populace and stole merchandise from a Jewish merchant's house. Ios Goldman, together with his son and nephew in Berdichev and Gerts Kagan in Boguslav, also found that stealing from Jewish merchants was the best way to improve their material condition.[41]

Jews were neither rebellious like the Ukrainian peasants nor disloyal like the Polish magnates; trade alone shaped their criminality. In the mid-1820s, Jews from the Tarashcha district prison stole horses and sheepskins, and those from the Zvenigorodka district prison stole cows and animal bristle. Some of the detained Jews were caught in left bank Ukraine, imprisoned in Kiev, and sent to Zhitomir for trial—the span of their operation exceeded hundreds of miles. Others, accused of vagrancy and stealing, disappeared the moment the police came to their doors with a search warrant—and these Jews either were not found for years or were found much later some five hundred miles away. Economic crime required the kind of mobility matched only by the mobility of the shtetl trade itself.[42]

In Jewish popular memory, robbers were not liked, as is apparent in the Yiddish expressions *gneyvish un gezeylish hot keyn hatslokhe nisht* (stealing and robbing bring no happiness) and *beser a kasherer groshn eyder a treyfe kerbl* (an honest kopek is better than a dishonest ruble), yet the thief's métier was also called a *hokhmes-ha-yad* or a *finger-melokhe*—the art of the fingers.[43] We can determine what the shtetl Jews loved by reading the lists of items they stole. Cash staunchly occupies first place, and therefore Jewish burglars preferred either merchants' or landlords' houses, where they could potentially find cash. Only once do we find a vagabond who planned on but did not take 200 rubles in cash from the house where he was temporarily working. He knew that the lady of the house had put money aside for Rabbi Twersky, a Hasidic master, and he refused to steal from a holy man.

Horses were second only to cash. A horse was a highly mobile commodity that one could resell dozens of miles from the place of theft. Textiles immediately followed horses and cash. Thieves loved ready-made clothes: the brocaded caftans of the szlachta, silk gowns, dresses, military uniforms, fur coats, and fancy overcoats. Apprehended Jewish gangsters,

6.1. A shpanyer machine for making brocade, eastern Galicia, 19th century.
BHT 87.359.3. Courtesy of LME and the Beit Hatfutsot exhibition "Treasures of Jewish Galicia—Judaica from the Museum of Ethnography in Lviv, Ukraine," Photo Archive, Tel Aviv.

according to the police reports, wore fashionable and expensive attire. The gap that elites, according to Braudel, try to create between themselves and the masses by introducing fashion standards was exactly what these gangsters were trying to eliminate.[44] Hence their interest in textiles, preferably bolts, easy to convert to cash and hard to identify. Rivka Balakleiskaia tried but failed to convince the judges that her husband's partners had stolen "thirty feet of bed-linens, her calico dressing-gown and her husband's demi-cotton caftan." The court found that the stolen goods were no longer recognizable.

Commodities of silver and gold—watches, candlesticks, jewelry, and so on—from Jewish houses and from churches followed textiles. Although they were definitely more valuable, they were also riskier and easily identifiable. Haim Rudnikov was caught because the Jewess Gelman recognized her own pearl-adorned headband and other adornments worth 365 rubles, which Haim had stolen from her. Kitchenware was last on the list. Borukh Bukovsky, the head of the Radomyshl gangsters, stole horses wherever he could, but specialized in copperware—cauldrons, pots, kitchenware, and church items, including chalices.[45]

Far a ganev, says the Yiddish proverb, *iz keyn shloss nishto*—"for a thief, no lock is an obstacle."[46] The Jewish gangsters Tsiner, Moshkovich, Portnoi, and others cleaned out a number of houses, including the house of a priest, a church near Balta, and most likely a synagogue. Their booty included a camisole, a silk gown, three Schwabian shirts, two Schwabian sheets, regular sheets, a fur coat, and an apron. They also stole raw textiles—surplice lace, bolts of cotton towels, and blue, green, and amaranth fabric. Their large take included a silver shield (most likely a *Torah schild*), sweaters, and a brocaded priestly breastplate, several large silver and copper crosses, chalices, censers, and candlesticks. They also stole about sixty loose pearls.[47]

Items from horses and chalices to cauldrons and goblets were needed in the home—or else had to be resold, entering a topsy-turvy version of the marketplace exchange. The police and the courts fully understood what was going on and penalized Jewish criminals as thieves, not as "anti-Christian minded" Jews. Tsiner and Portnoi had nothing to complain about; there was a modicum of justice in the shtetl.

Justice existed for Jewish murderers, too. Nobody in 1830 would call them, as the antisemitic press did eighty years later, "murderous Semites" waiting "around the corner" to kill their Slavic prey. Jews were largely underrepresented among murderers, but they sometimes did kill. Let's take a look at Froim Ioskovich from Sandomierz, who drove a fancy three-horse britzka. This comfortable means of transport was very much to the taste of Haim Kalmanka, a wealthy Jewish merchant from Berdichev who was traveling home from Poland with a barrel filled with silver rubles. The barrel was later found empty on a field near Berdichev, and Kalmanka had disappeared. The police interrogated several innkeepers and their families from the nearby Jewish communities and implicated cabman Froim, who was charged with premeditated murder and larceny.[48] Another cabman, Itsko Provorny, active in and around Shpola, confessed in

6.2. Spoons.

MNK-IV-Z-1147. MNK, no. 234. Courtesy MNK and the Center for Jewish Art at Hebrew University, Jerusalem.

the Zhitomir prison that he had killed his client and stolen his horse, money, and belongings—and that two other Jews had helped him.[49]

Avram Rudy, accused of robbing and killing a Russian cabman, makes us think that cabmen—those suspicious *balagolas*—were a high-risk group.[50] For example, two cabmen, Yankel and Maiorko from Tomashpol, were involved in minor larceny and horse theft, but sometime around 1840 they starting planning another robbery, for which they needed a partner. At that time, their neighbor and colleague Abram Sapozhnik was returning from a fair on his own sleigh. He stopped at an inn in Kopaigorod, where Yankel and Maiorko made him an offer. Sapozhnik rejected their advances and threatened to denounce them. "Pay me back my three and a half rubles you owe me," he said. "Then maybe we'll talk."

Yankel and Maiorko agreed to pay him only three rubles. The half-ruble difference sealed Sapozhnik's fate. While all three were driving back home through the forest, they struck and killed Sapozhnik with a wooden stick, removed his shirt, and threw his body into an empty Tikhtiliisky well, twenty-five feet deep. They also killed Sapozhnik's horse and sold the sleigh in a nearby shtetl. Police identified and caught the murderers when Sapozhnik's wife, anxious to find her missing husband, asked the police to look in the Tikhtiliisky well. She explained that she had had a nightmare in which her husband had cried out to her from that well, "Get me out of here!"[51]

These Jewish cabmen were by and large amateur criminals and were treated as such. They constituted a minority group even within the insignificant number of Jews in prison. Envy, greed, economic inequality, and imagined impunity triggered their crimes and brought them from court to prison to Siberia. However, the shtetl also had professional criminals—the heroes and godfathers of its underworld, genuine Jewish gangsters. They unnerved the regime, particularly because many of the gangs were interethnic, including Ukrainian peasants, runaway Russian soldiers and inmates, and Jews.[52]

THE UNLUCKY ROBIN HOODS

Trade necessitated interaction between Jews, Poles, Ukrainians, and Russians, and so did crime. The symbiosis of social outcasts mirrored the fusion that informed the Jewish economy, although in the underworld Jews ceded their centrality to Slavs. Jews joined their ranks and shared their underworld. The gangs were mobile, operating simultaneously in several provinces, and relied on an impressive supporting network, interethnic in origin. Crime demonstrated that Jews were more embedded in their Slavic environment than they were distinct from it.

In Kiev province, Russian clerk Gavrila Vrublevski joined the gang of Aizik and Shai Zvegelski, specializing in robbery. Seeking to better their chances in criminal activities, two wandering Jews joined together with an undocumented and vagabond Pole. Another Jew relied on the help of a Christian for his horse-thievery dealings. The case of Volko Modny from Torgovitsa and Avrum Sheygets from Dashev proves that even crimes as unsophisticated as stealing made Jews part of a broader interethnic network.

Modny and Sheigets were relatives, the latter married to the sister of the former, and their documented last names—The Strange and The Rascal—could have been just the nicknames. The two brothers-in-law became colleagues-in-crime, carefully staged in distant districts. They disposed of their spoils across the Austrian border in order to leave no traces. The parsimonious Sheigets and Modny hid Christian deserters and runaway peasants, but not out of pure philanthropy: they could now rely on the assistance of those they had hidden. Even if the victims of the two Jews figured out who was responsible for the robbery, they kept their mouths shut, afraid of retribution.

The only person who was not scared was Kelia Volynsky, a Jewess. When her house was ransacked, she went all the way to Dashev to find Modny and Sheigets in the local synagogue and publicly accused them of having organized the robbery. Although both scoundrels threatened to take the woman's life, they soon found themselves in the Uman prison and had to face the Russian judges, who came to protect Kelia Volynsky and others against Modny and Sheigets.[53]

These two men were low-key gangsters unable to compete with other Jewish gangs, which became so dangerously popular that Russian senators gave them the nicknames Kinsky and Pikovsky. Early in the 1810s, the police found out that there were a number of gangs operating in Kiev, Zhitomir, and Berdichev districts, and that they were, apparently, "composed mostly of Jews." The police were particularly confused by multiple links between these gangs and the Ukrainian rebels, with their astounding mass following.

One Jewish gang consisted of three Russian soldiers and Meer Hersh from Berdichev. Another included two Eastern Orthodox soldiers, two serfs of Ukrainian origin, two Christian Kiev dwellers serving as moles, and Leiba Itskovich, mentioned in the documents as the "rabbi's grandson." This gang specialized in stealing goods and reselling them through their network of shtetl second-hand dealers. The gangsters dealt in uniforms: they received about 30 rubles for a stolen piece, and the dealers resold it for a handsome 80 rubles.[54]

These inventive gangsters did not discriminate among their subjects or their objects. They ransacked the house of a priest, robbed the office of the city chancellery, and stole from a wealthy Jewish merchant. They resold the loot and shared the booty. Dozens of people profited from their business. Their success inspired their next adventure: the gangsters learned from their informants when Captain Zadorozhny would be away from his Kiev apartment, broke in, and stole a substantial 11,000 rubles' worth of goods. Had they been able to resell the entire spoils, they could have earned about 25,000 rubles in total, but the enraged Zadorozhny thwarted their plans.

Angered by the loss of his chique uniforms, he became a self-styled Sherlock Holmes and took two Kiev-based Jewish retailers by surprise. Frightened by his fury, they helped Zadorozhny find two Boguslav Jews, who in turn pointed out three Zhitomir Jewish second-hand dealers in charge of disposing of the stolen items, including Zadorozhny's uniforms. The intimidated dealers denounced the gangsters, who were swiftly apprehended and sentenced, among and on a par with other Christian criminals.[55]

Jewish gangs were a gender-neutral shtetl family business. Take Feiga, who cooperated with Jewish gangsters Shliomo Kruchko and Berko Galperin. They specialized in large-scale robberies, allegedly killing a clerk, taking his horse, and hiding their booty in a forest inn, killing the innkeeper as well, to be on the safe side. But they did not serve their whole prison term—Feiga organized their escape, although she herself ended up being arrested.[56] Krintsia Bernstein covered for a Jewish gang that specialized in robbing houses and stored their stolen goods in her house. When the gang members were detained, Krintsia went on the lam, and the police spent over nine years trying to find and arrest her.[57]

Jewish gangsters were former inmates and deserters, highly qualified underworld professionals. Yankel Raisfeld, already sentenced, escaped from confinement in Siberia. *Mit vemen havert zikh a ganev,* asks a Yiddish proverb, and answers, *mit zayns glaykhn.* "Whom does a thief associate with?—With his own kind!"[58] Raisfeld formed a gang with other Jews like him: Yosel Lubarsky, another runaway Siberian inmate; Iosef Kanev-sky, an escapee from the Zolotonosha prison; Nusen Slobodetsky, an escapee from a Romny cell; and Ilia Sapir, whose lack of upper teeth and Cossack-style moustache testified to his turbulent past. Through connections to the Odessa-based ambassador, Lubarsky obtained Austrian passports for the entire group. All five were about forty years of age, robust, and with the exception of Kanevsky taller than average. In disguise, they could pass for Christians, Tartars, or Armenians.

The gang made good use of two fancy britzkas in which they criss-crossed central Ukraine in all four directions, and relied on an efficient network of supporters. Those who benefited indirectly from their endeavors—retail merchants, corrupt police, and innkeepers—numbered in the hundreds. The gang attacked Mennonites, Jews, Catholics, and Orthodox Christians going to or from the fairs. When these gangsters stole money, their spoils reached amounts of several thousand rubles; if they robbed merchants, they preferred refined fabric; if their victims resisted, the gang killed them. If they were detained by a Cossack patrol or the police, they bribed their way out and asked to be delivered to the nearest Jewish community, which would subsequently post their bail. Arresting and incriminating these skillful men was far from simple.[59]

The police arrested and sentenced Reisfeld and several other men, but Lubarsky managed to get away. He realized that he needed a much better network of potential supporters, women included. He preferred that entire families join the gang—the Reviches and the Bukhbinders, among others. The nucleus of shtetl market entrepreneurship, the family turned into the nucleus of the shtetl underworld economy as well. The son (or a brother) of Lubarsky, and his wife, joined the family business. The gang also took in a certain Basya, who had converted to Christianity and later decided to return to Judaism. Since the Russian regime considered "splitting off from Eastern Orthodoxy" the most serious of offenses, Basya became a permanent outcast by doing so. In the gang, her job was to bury the corpses.

The Lubarsky gangsters were fierce and fearless. They committed several audacious robberies before scaring the Russian police out of their wits. In 1825 they moved from Vinnitsa to a nearby village and attacked the house of retired colonel Vassili Shkurin. They sneaked inside the house, tied up the servants, and stole several thousand rubles from Shkurin's desk. Most likely the colonel confronted them, and paid with his life. This assassination brought about a united police front across Ukraine. The police arrested some seventy people in connection with the gang. Only eight of those ended up whipped and sent to Siberia, whereas forty-five were sent back home, and twenty were declared wanted and not found.[60]

Lubarsky's men raised arms against Russian officers with a criminal intent, unlike the underage Itsik Leibovich who had accidently fired a rifle. Nevertheless, the regime treated the gangsters as common delinquents, not as vicious Jews. Those Jewish gangsters knew they would be accountable for their criminal activities—and for those only. Even in such outrageous cases as theirs, the court applied justice rather than a collective incrimination, although Lubarsky's gangsters shared the territory, know-how, social provenance, modus operandi, and even the fate of their Ukrainian colleagues, the Karmaniuk gang.

Born around 1786 to a family of serfs, Ustym Karman was baptized at birth as Sebastian Karmaniuk. Ukrainian popular legend changed his name to Karmeliuk, as his real name meant common pickpocket. The Russian government chose to call him Ustym, since Sebastian was only too suggestive in the context of Christian martyrology. A professional gangster of fascinating stamina, Karmaniuk entered the Ukrainian imagination as a freedom-loving Ukrainian serf, gifted both physically and spiritually.[61]

Karmaniuk was taller than average, heavyset, strong, and spoke at least four languages fluently, including Yiddish, which he had learned at the marketplace and from his Jewish fellow criminals. In 1812 he had a fight with his landlord, who had Karmaniuk drafted into the Russian army. To explain what had actually happened, popular legend turned Karmaniuk into the biblical Joseph by claiming that he had merely rejected the advances of the landlady. Be that as it may, Karmaniuk deserted, returned to his home in Letichev district, formed a gang, and began his career as the Ukrainian Robin Hood.

Karmaniuk's gang participated in about a thousand attacks against imperial clerks, landlords, guild merchants, and wealthy peasants. Ukrainian serfs considered him their savior. The police captured Karmaniuk four times, led him through the gauntlet, chained him, and sentenced him—and four times he ran away. He escaped from the Kamenets-Podolsk, Viatka, Ialutorovsk, and Tobolsk prisons, making his way back home to Podolia, covering tens of thousands of miles on foot or in the wagon of a credulous and welcoming peasant. His reputation as a charismatic leader preceded him: once he returned, he swiftly reestablished his infrastructure and launched new attacks.[62]

His activities as a rebel involved several hundred people, among them Jews from all walks of life. Karmaniuk repeatedly attacked roadside taverns but apparently never harmed shtetl Jews, and only once in Staraia Seniawa he reportedly stole three barrels of honey from a Jewish home. At least a dozen Jewish tavernkeepers and others hid Karmaniuk during round-ups, not always out of their own good will.

In 1827 Aron Viniar sheltered him in Novokonstantinov. Another group of Jews, including Leiba and Beila Vainboim and Hirsh-Leib Spivak, helped Karmaniuk dispose of the stolen goods and warned him of police action. Vasilli Dobrovolsky, Karmaniuk's right-hand man, a convert from Judaism Christianized in 1820, married a Catholic woman, then left her and joined the gang. In all, 205 to 305 Jews and about 400 peasants were brought to trial in various capacities once the police managed to deceive and murder Karmaniuk and suppress the rebel gangsters.

The impoverished shtetl of Derazhnia functioned as Karmaniuk's headquarters—and also served as a pool from which he recruited his gangsters. Forty-eight of the seventy-nine Jews immediately arrested after the death of Karmaniuk were from Derazhnia, and because of them the entire Jewish community of the town eventually had to pay a heavy price. Unlike previous peasant rebellions in Ukraine, Karmaniuk's rebels did not consider the Jews to be their staunch enemies. With the advent of the Russian regime, it became clear even to the Slavic underworld that the shtetl Jews were subjugated by the Polish town-owners just as the peasants were.

The Jews joint the rebels by the dozens—something that had never happened before. Shortly before he was betrayed and shot point-blank, Karmaniuk ransacked the estate of landlady Paplinskaia in the village of

Novoselski. A special Senate commission investigating organized crime in Ukraine reported that five Jews (four from Derazhnia), alongside Karmaniuk, took part in the attack on the Paplinskaia estate. In addition, thirty Jews joined Karmaniuk's combatant forces, took care of logistics, hid the pillaged goods, and sold them on the market.

The commission proved direct Jewish involvement and calculated the damage to Paplinskaia at 4,000 rubles in banknotes, 400 silver and 1,600 golden rubles, and 11,000 rubles' worth of stolen goods. For the first time, the authorities penalized the entire Jewish community, demanding that the Jews of Derazhnia recompense the losses, since "all of Derazhnia was a town of criminals and deserters." To help out their brethren, Jews from several provinces contributed about 3 to 6 rubles each toward the Paplinskaia's compensation.[63]

The links between Karmaniuk and the Jews seriously troubled the regime, but common sense prevented the authorities from calling all Jews "criminals and deserters," as would happen fifty years later, when the previously palpable anti-Jewish bias became the official line of the regime. The courts avoided generalizations and used common sense and the rule of law even when dealing with a particularly "Jewish" crime: counterfeiting.

MONEYMAKERS

Integrated into the East European underworld, Jewish underdogs carved out a niche of criminality for themselves that they shared with no one: secret artisanal counterfeiting shops.

In the 1830s and 1840s, the Russian minister of finance regularly reported on large-scale counterfeiting activities in the northern and central parts of the country. False banknotes worried the authorities, particularly since they frequently appeared in the tax collections. The clerks of the Ministry of Finance could not grasp how the fake money could reach as far as Tobolsk—six or seven thousand miles to the east from the western border of Russia. Were the Russians forging money themselves? The government clerks shook their heads: impossible! Most likely, the West was trying to harm Mother Russia.

The governor of Volhynia had no doubt that this was the case. He informed his clerks about a manufacturer in London who specialized in producing false banknotes. Naturally, he reckoned, Russia's enemies were seeking to undermine Russia's finances. But how had this money reached East Europe? Suspicion fell on traveling merchants, many of whom were Jews.

The evidence against them was thin. In one case, a traveling merchant named Goldblat from Slonim came under suspicion. He moved through Poland and visited a certain Jewish coppersmith, who had some forged coins in his possession.[64] In another case the police apprehended Shaya, who resided in Berdichev: he traveled between London, Riga, Kazan, and Nizhnii Novgorod with substantial sums of cash, purchasing goods from various foreign trading houses and marketing them in Russia. The authorities did not find any forged banknotes among his 6,500 rubles, yet they were suspicious of the fact that Shaya shaved his beard when going abroad. If one could falsify one's identity, one was likely to falsify money, they suspected.[65]

Of course, counterfeiting in Russia was done by local talent. Although the police regularly reported that most false banknotes circulated far beyond the Pale, the Jews in these central Ukrainian provinces firmly established themselves in the minor-key counterfeiting business. One case in Zhitomir began in the late 1830s as a fun game with several teenagers as protagonists, even more imaginative than Itsik Leibovich the Warrior. First, Avram Pliukh, a young man, decided to launch a counterfeiting business. He talked a certain Tarnopolsky, an adult, into this endeavor, and convinced him to rent a small house, supposedly for young Jewish boys to study grammar.

The study of grammar required several strange tools, with which the boys soon stocked the rented hut on Rybnaia Street. They then convinced a certain Finkelstein, the son of a watchmaker, and his friend Mytnik, to lend them a mold for making coins from a Jewish silversmith. They also sent Finkelstein to purchase a certain amount of tin, as well as soldiers' buttons, which they eventually melted into raw material for coins. When everything was in place, Shmul Leiba, a goldsmith's apprentice, joined them, and they began their counterfeiting business with Galker, a qualified coppersmith, who trained them.

6.3. Handwashing utensils, eastern Galicia, eighteenth to nineteenth century. *Copper. BHT 87.348.4. Courtesy of LME and the Beit Hatfutsot exhibition "Treasures of Jewish Galicia—Judaica from the Museum of Ethnography in Lviv, Ukraine," Photo Archive, Tel Aviv.*

While their fathers were repairing watches, fixing horseshoes, and forging scythes, the sons were playing a risky game. They specialized in silver rubles and 25- and 10-kopek coins. Once they had produced a good amount of coins, these young men approached another teenager, Itsko Kholodenko, asking him to help them dispose of the forged coins at the nearby markets. Naturally, the participants were paid: Tarnopolsky was the first to receive his portion of false money for providing the boys with a cover. The messengers, also teenagers, delivered money as far as Kiev. We do not know how much money they managed to exchange, but once they were caught, they bribed a policeman with a false ruble and were released.

Zhitomir Jews knew what was going on in the small hut on Rybnaia Street. One young man approached the boys and requested some false coins: he had given someone his complete Hebrew Bible as collateral and needed money to redeem his book. Another Jew denounced the boys to the authorities. The Zhitomir police colonel found a letter written in clumsy Russian on his doorstep: Jews make money from soldiers' buttons! He conducted swift searches of several houses but found nothing, even though he was very keen on catching a big fish. Yet another Jew threatened to inform the police about the clandestine operation of the boys; one of the fathers had to buy his silence. Perhaps the same was done with other potential informers, who all came into possession of the freshly minted coins.

It took the police several months to detain the counterfeiters, but by then the boys had managed to bury the evidence. The police were dumbfounded: all the criminals were teenaged boys—sons, relatives, and apprentices of respected Zhitomir artisans! As with Itsik the Warrior in Belaia Tserkov, nobody ended up in prison in Zhitomir either. The police condescendingly returned all the participants to their places of residence, left them "under serious suspicion," and placed them "under police surveillance."[66]

These teenaged Zhitomir Jews had found an unusual way to become masters of their fathers' professions. Local policemen considered what the Jewish boys had done a dangerous game, not a serious crime, and chose to admonish rather than punish them. Adult Jewish counterfeiters played a very different game, much more advanced and harmful.

Several such counterfeiters gathered in the house of Menia Shaikha, a widow from around Shpola, a woman with formidable managerial skills. Shaikha had a special trunk where she kept several metal pegs to cut coins and special wooden bars with holes for minting coins. Her second-in-command was Duvid Goldman, a silversmith and neighbor. He kept hundreds of unprocessed coins in a drawer of his work table, together with instruments for minting and polishing. Shaikha got other Jews involved, for example Ios Lebarsky, a literate twenty-five-year-old man who could read both Russian and Yiddish and was known as a talented fiddler, yet who could not find his purpose in life. He sold his house and came with his young wife to reside under the aegis of Shaikha. Iankel and Itsko Golberman, a father and son from Khodorkov, also left their shtetl and came to live with her.

Shaikha's business would have run for years if not for her inept male colleagues. They behaved themselves when in a silversmith shop but lost self-control at the marketplace. Unlike the artisan business, trade required very different skills. The counterfeiters thought they could do both—and

6.4. A trunk in Skvira Synagogue.
CAHJP, P166, G17. Courtesy of the Central Archives for the History of the Jewish People.

failed. Goldman arrived at the marketplace in the lower district of Kiev, paid for small goods with false money, and was detained. They found 123 20-kopek and seventy-one 25-kopek false coins on him—more than 50 silver rubles in cash! Where was the money from?

Goldman said he had just received the sum as change in Pechersk, the upper part of Kiev. Goldman's cabman was not ready to help his customer out and told the police that they had not visited other parts of Kiev at all. The flustered Goldman was immediately arrested. Another member of the group, Mordko Brodianskii from Zvenigorodka, was caught with eighteen 25-kopek and five 20-kopek coins, all counterfeit, and provided no explanation for how he had obtained them.

Perhaps Iankel Perchukov, another member of the gang, thought he would have more luck. He went from shtetl to shtetl trading in lemons, wax, and donuts, and bought textiles. He had two rolls of coins handy, one with old, worn-out coins that were real and another one with shiny new coins that were fake. When paying, he gave people real money first: they did not like worn-out coins. Then he offered fake money; the new shiny coins were very much to people's liking. The trick worked perfectly—

until he arrived at the Ekaterinopol fair with fake 25-kopek coins he had obtained from Shaikha. Unfortunately for him, he chose to purchase oranges from Kondrat, a peasant. Iankel gave him four 25-kopek coins and asked for change. Kondrat tried the money between his teeth, did not like it, and had other people try the coins. They shook their heads: fake! The frightened Iankel tried to flee the scene but was caught on the spot. The police found about fifty 20-kopek coins on him—and Iankel gave up Shaikha.[67]

Once Governor General Levashov learned of the case, he ordered a secret and swift investigation. A search of Goldman and Sheikha's house yielded immediate results: their trunks contained more than one hundred 20- and 25-kopek finished coins. The entire group was brought to trial. Still, the police treated them not as common criminals but as "skilled yet misled" artisans. The reports to the governor went as far as to discuss the "art" of Goldman and his accomplices.

Although the police found other networks of Jewish counterfeiters, the administration was aware that Jews played a very minor role in the world of Russian forged money.[68] Jews worked on coins, whereas most large-scale counterfeiters were producing banknotes. Jewish counterfeiting was the realm of the Jewish artisan turned upside down. The police did not know that Jewish counterfeiters and artisans were not the only ones who dreamed of coins. Even Efraim of Sudilkov, the righteous grandson of the legendary founder of Hasidism and himself a tsadik, saw coins in his dreams—coins of half and a quarter ruble, worn and sparking, old and new.[69]

The Russian police treated the Jewish counterfeiters as useful townsfolk with bad intentions: there were much more dangerous crimes to investigate. The threat of the latent Polish rebellion in the wake of the 1831 revolt and the rise of Ukrainian nationalism in the 1840s eclipsed any minor Jewish misdemeanor. Jewish economic criminality did not imply disloyalty therefore the courts did not discriminate against them. Plus, while the shtetl was economically capable, its Jews always had funds to bail out their relatives. Jewish women, comfortable at the marketplace and familiar with the family ledgers, were much better equipped to argue for their detained husbands in courts. Jews could rely on the commonsensical unbiased attitude of the Russian courts—and enjoyed the shtetl golden age as long a Russian jurisprudence, with all the shortcomings of the court system, did not single them out as Jews.

Jews were the proud dwellers of prosperous market towns no longer when in the last quarter of the nineteenth century the regime began singling them out as outrageous, impertinent, and rapacious people. In the wake of racial antisemitism, Russian court clerks more often than not used the *Book of the Kahal*, the viciously anti-Judaic concoction of a convert and informer, Yakov Brafman, that prefigured the *Protocols of the Elders of Zion*, as their main source on the Jews. Now, while presiding over cases involving the Jews, the courts looked for an international kahal masterminding Jewish criminality and seeking to destroy Eastern Orthodoxy and bring down Mother Russia, instead of applying the rule of law.

Later in the nineteenth century the new Russian passport system made the racial differences of the Jews a key feature of their identification. Racial profiling of the Jews became a trope in the Russian literary sources and in popular newspaper cartoons. The image of a Jewish criminal, with his earlocks, uncombed beard, and yarmulke, armed with a dagger and threatening the viewer point-blank with a revolver, appeared in the antisemitic press as the image of the quintessential revolutionary. This radical turn to the acknowledgment of Judaic inerasable difference was nurtured by the ideas of West European racial thinkers and had been inconceivable earlier in the century. While the reasons behind the conceptualization of Jews as aliens and Jewish revolutionaries as criminals remain far beyond the scope of this book, it is worthwhile mentioning that the xenophobic regime of Late Imperial Russia chose to single out Jews *and* Poles, and also Ukrainians, as the objects of social and legal segregation.[70]

The more biased the Russian court system became, the more Jews found themselves behind bars, the quicker vanished their loyalty and the more they joined parties and groups seeking to bring down the regime. In the 1900s, our Itsik the Warrior would have spent a term in prison, then moved to the city, joined the Jewish workers' movement, and initiated a revolutionary combat unit.

A DISPROPORTIONATE CONTRIBUTION

In a famous story about the Ba'al Shem Tov, a group of Jewish gangsters offer to take him through a secret cave in the Carpathian Mountains directly to the land of Israel. Whatever the meaning of the story, it makes one point clear: Jewish gangsters appear as guardians of secrets.[71]

Although not numerous in the Russian penitentiary institutions, Jews introduced Yiddish as a secret language into the realm of the Russian underground. Slavic criminals immediately appreciated the advantage of the secret language, a hermetic argot that others did not understand, and began consistently borrowing Yiddish terms to enrich their professional language.

If we remove the Yiddish words from the slang of Russian thieves, they would not have words to express where they slept, whom they befriended, or how they differentiated accomplices from enemies, classified types of criminal activities, and decided what to drink. Most of these words entered Russian in the nineteenth century from spoken Yiddish and retained their specific, often mocking Yiddish usage and their idiosyncratic pronunciation, referred to as the Volhynian Yiddish.

The Yiddish word for "collaboration," *shutvis,* came to mean in Slavic slang a small unit of professional thieves. *Hevre,* which for any shtetl dweller meant a voluntary philanthropic or study society, became the appellation for a group of criminals. The Yiddish for "gun" became the Slavic criminal *shpayer,* and the Yiddish for "writing," *ksiva,* came to mean identification papers for any Slav. The Yiddish for "informer," *muser* or *moyser,* turned into *musor,* the Russian derogatory term for a policeman.

The Hebrew word *pleitah,* "refugees," well known from Judaic liturgy, entered several European languages and also turned into the Slavic verb *pleitovat',* to run away from forced labor camps, as Karmaniuk managed to do several times. The Yiddish for "accomplished," "finished," or "perfect," *gmuro,* became the slang word for the most beloved drink of gangsters, pure alcohol.[72] There is little doubt that all Russian criminals would have adopted Yiddish as their own language if Jewish criminals had been able to spend more time in the Russian prisons.

Naturally, this cultural impact of Jewish underdogs far exceeded the modest Jewish contribution to nineteenth-century Russian criminality. In the 1800s, Ukrainian artisans and, quite unexpectedly, turban performers all drew from Yiddish to build their respective slangs. A Ukrainian sociolinguist found twelve different groups of borrowed Yiddish terms that enriched Ukrainian professional argots, ranging from groceries and comestibles, to money, technical terms, family relations, numerals, and curses.[73] When Slavs cry for help or warn of danger—*hvalt* in Ukrainian or *gwałt* in Polish—they echo the Jewish shtetl dwellers who opened their welcoming doors to unexpected violent visitors from the underworld.

But of course, the impact of Yiddish on the imagination of Slavic criminals far exceeded the share of the Jews in everyday shtetl criminality, which in the best days of the shtetl remained disproportionately low.

As legend has it, the Ba'al Shem Tov once identified a thief and made him repent. The thief, astonished that the Besht could envision and reveal the crime, asked him, "Why do you bother with such mean things? It would be better to look at good things."[74] We shall now move from the underworld to good things—the shtetl house and the family.

CHAPTER SEVEN

FAMILY MATTERS

S hlioma Shir knew that in order to destroy a competitor in the shtetl, all he had to do was accuse him of a sexual offense. In the late 1820s, Shlioma worked for a certain Lazebnik, quarreled with him, and then quit, but later schemed to entrap him. To this end, Shir chose Marina Kulchitsky, a fourteen-year-old Catholic girl from an impoverished Polish family who had also worked for Lazebnik. Shir envisaged that Marina would accuse Lazebnik of being an adulterer, and Lazebnik would be ruined as a Jew and a businessman. Shir's target, Lazebnik, was a twenty-seven-year-old Jew, married with two daughters. A taxpayer of good standing, Lazebnik had no clue that his reputation and family life were on the line.

Convinced or bribed, Marina went to the local Jewish ritual bath, sat down next to it, and started to cry. A woman passing by saw Marina. "What's wrong?" "That Jew, Lazebnik, had sex with me, and now I didn't get my period," explained Marina, sobbing. "Use cherry-tree bark," advised the lady. But the gossip soon spread in town. Marina herself bragged that

Lazebnik had had sex with her twice—and had promised her two cows if they had children.

This was too much not only for Lazebnik but also for his wife, Dobrisha. Her husband would never have had sex with a gentile girl, and would never trade cows for sex. Dobrisha could not let her family be destroyed in the blink of an eye. On hearing the rumors, she grabbed her husband by the hand and dragged him straight to the Kulchitskys' house. "What is going on?" she demanded. The frightened mother mumbled that Marina had told her everything about Lazebnik and the promised cows. Dobrisha was definitely not convinced. Of course, she spent some time instructing her husband to be more scrupulous when hiring part-timers, but she also filed a complaint with the court.

When the case reached the Vasilkov court, the communal elders, supported by ten Jewish witnesses, testified to Lazebnik's good character and provided him with a certificate of good behavior. Standing before the judges, Lazebnik pleaded not guilty. In turn, Marina testified that she was a virgin and had had no relations with Lazebnik. Yet, she admitted that a year earlier, when she had needed some cash, she had worked for Lazebnik at a per diem rate, and at that time a Jew she did not know quarreled with Lazebnik and then asked her to help him destroy her employer. The court found Lazebnik not guilty, confirmed that he had been falsely accused, and, after a thorough investigation, returned him to his family.[1] This case is remarkable in that four women share with us a wide range of their views on family relations.

Marina, a Polish child of divorce, took for granted that she could have sex and children at her young age and out of wedlock. The compensation of two cows she treated as a legitimate and sufficient reward for producing illegitimate children. So did her Christian mother, who saw nothing extraordinary in the arrangement, and so did the anonymous Christian female passerby, who was not surprised that a married Jew could have sex with an underage Christian girl. She simply offered what she thought was a valid natural medical measure, cherry-tree bark, believed to cause spontaneous abortion.

Lazebnik's wife emerges from this story as a true woman of valor, steadfast in the defense of her family. For Dobrisha, family was her stronghold: what had allegedly happened could never have happened. Illicit sex might have taken place elsewhere, but not by the Lazebniks. When her beliefs were challenged, Dobrisha courageously confronted the gossiping shtetl dwellers. She trusted her husband. As far as sexual life was concerned, the family realm was the only realm.

It was Dobrisha who took on herself the task of getting the calumny dismissed. Marina—or the masterminding Shir behind her back—knew well that resentment was something to be expected from other Jewish women, hence chose to give her performance right next to the Jewish ritual bath. The Kulchitskys (and Shir) lost the case in the local Russian court more to Dobrisha, the redeemer of her own family, than to Shlioma Lazebnik.

Dobrisha's case is unique, but her understanding of basic Jewish family values was common. Jewish family was about a husband and a wife sharing responsibilities for children and business. Sexual relations were inconceivable out of wedlock, particularly with gentiles. Shtetl townsfolk considered promiscuity among the most horrendous crimes and meted out severe punishments to perpetrators, something Dobrisha did not want to see happen. The wife was the first to stand firm defending the honor and the well-being of her family. Peasant gentiles or the Russian authorities—it did not matter; she was ready to do anything to save her family, the guarantor of her security, pride, and independence. As long as the Jews were able to withstand the internal and external challenges undermining the family, the shtetl would enjoy its golden age.

In turn, the shtetl created a protective environment for the Jewish family, not necessarily available elsewhere. The moment Jews moved out to bigger towns and cities, which lacked a critical mass of observant Jews, their dietary laws, endogamy, ritual purity, clothing, and many other traditional elements of shtetl society vanished. The shtetl family was not a homogeneous, conflict-free, pietistic, and utopian entity; it was quite dynamic, picturesque, vulnerable to inside and outside conflicts, and enduring.[2] Shtetl Judaism prevailed as long as ordinary Jews enacted it in their families—and as long as the shtetl economy fostered this reenactment. The decline of the family ushered in the demise of the shtetl.

FAMILY PATTERNS

The Jewish family was shaped by economy no less than by Judaism. Jews sought a spouse of the same age or nearly the same age: trade required equal participation, shared experience, and joint responsibility. The liquor dealers, merchants, artisans, and innkeepers were one to three years older than their wives, and sometimes the same age.[3] Ios Anshelev, a guild merchant from Bar in his mid-twenties, lived with his wife, who was one year younger, and had three children with her. His brother, Gershon, forty-one, also a guild merchant from the same shtetl, had a thirty-nine-year-old wife and four children. Gershon's neighbor, guild merchant Aron Trachtenberg, twenty-nine, lived with his wife, also twenty-nine, and their three children. A communal rabbi from the same region lived with his wife, who was eleven years younger—but rabbis are always an exception.[4]

Business and love played themselves out unevenly in family life: the wealthier could afford to house the entire extended family together and had more prearranged marriages. The wealthier the family, the earlier the children married. Sixteen and even younger was a normal age for a daughter from a wealthy Jewish family to be a bride. The parents would arrange a formal wedding and then have the couple living under their aegis. This tradition of providing the son-in-law with room and board was known as *kest*, the Yiddish not only for "to keep" but also for "caste."

The father of the bride sought to strengthen his caste—his pedigree—and committed himself to reinforcing his daughter's family with the provenance and financial power, whereas his inlaws contributed the *torah*, the groom's Judaic sophistication.[5] The wealthy Ios Volkovich from Ushitsa lived with his wife, their eighteen-year-old son and the son's wife Sura, nineteen; their second son, Zelik, twelve, and Zelik's wife Hava—eleven years old. There were two other families in Ushitsa with husbands and wives from eight to ten years old. In this way the elite ensured that its wealth would stay in the family and children would follow the parents' will in matrimonial questions.[6]

Early marriages among elite Jewish families in Russia were no different from those made while they were under the Polish-Lithuanian Commonwealth. Solomon Maimon, the illustrious Jewish thinker, was taken in the 1760s as an eleven-year-old into his wife's family and became a father at barely the age of fourteen.[7] In the 1820s, Skvira, Tulchin, and Nemirov merchants almost all had kest arrangements with their sons and daughters-in-law.[8]

One Jewish guild merchant from Nemirov in his late fifties lost his wife, remarried, and settled with his second, twenty-nine year-old wife and their seven-year-old son and eleven-year-old daughter. His other daughter, eighteen, and her husband, twenty, and their one-and-a-half-year-old son also lived in the same house. So did his son from his first marriage, also married, with his wife and their seven-year-old daughter. On top of that, they welcomed the parents of the merchant's wife, with their three children—thirteen people altogether.[9] They also had servants residing with them, sometimes Christian, but more often Jewish. As one document outlines, "servant Elie, servant Bluma, servant Leia."[10]

Such households of the economic elite were ubiquitous. A wealthy family in the shtetl of Kamenets-Litovsk, in Belorussia, also had three generations with all their offspring living under the same roof in the house of one Kotik, a leaseholder, tax-farmer, and communal elder. And this kind of arrangement was not limited to the wealthiest. In Nemirov, a tavern-keeper and even a shoemaker had their sons-in-law living with them. They knew that by supporting a Talmudic scholar-in-residence, they would uplift their own reputation in the eyes of the community.

In smaller shtetls the situation was no different. A guild merchant in his mid-forties from Pavoloch lived with his wife, three years younger, their twenty-two-year-old daughter, her twenty-one-year-old husband, and the young couple's three-year-old daughter.[11] Most likely this merchant, like many others, supported his son-in-law, expecting him eventually to join the family business, and he did this not only out of appreciation of Jewish learning but with his eye on strengthening his economic condition, too.

Unlike the merchants, ordinary Jews married when they could secure their family's financial independence. The Berdichev economic elite sought spouses in Brody, but ordinary Jews married locally and needed neither a matchmaker nor an arranged marriage.[12] They had nothing to lose in terms of established businesses and could afford to marry for love, which would be blasphemy for the mercantile elite. Ordinary Jews, the absolute majority in the shtetl, stayed in their own houses, uncontrolled by their in-laws. Most artisans' families did not have children before the age of twenty. They took pains to avoid registering their children for tax purposes, which makes it impossible for us to know what was actually happening in their households, but we do know that among Jews, "merchants had a tendency to live with their extended family while regular townsfolk preferred small families."[13]

In Nemirov, with its 378 male and 397 female Jews residing in 237 houses, roughly 3.3 per house, we can see how the economy framed family patterns. The upper class and middle class could afford large households. A sixty-one-year-old vodka seller lived with his fifty-nine-year-old wife, their daughter, twenty-six, their son-in-law, twenty-eight, and a granddaughter, nine. A fifty-year-old shoemaker lived with his forty-four-year-old wife, two daughters, and the daughters' husbands. Before the industrial era with its big footware factories, this shoemaker could eke out a decent living, particularly if he worked on commission for the troops.

One step lower, we encounter people who lived one family per house. A thirty-two-year-old barber lived with his two children; a hatmaker with his wife and one daughter; a tailor, also with one daughter. A melamed, thirty-three, who lived with his wife, thirty, of lower economic status, and a water carrier, who was also married, most likely kept their children to themselves, without registering them, although they unquestionably lived one family per household.[14]

Tavernkeepers' families differed from everybody else's. They rented living quarters with their siblings' families, sharing the dwelling and business responsibilities. One Podolia tavernkeeper lived with his wife and their four-year-old son; his elder brother with his wife and their one-year-old son also lived in the same inn. The household of Pavoloch, a liquor dealer, was the largest of 119 Jewish houses, with enough room for the forty-five-year-old liquor dealer himself, his forty-year-old wife, and his elder son, twenty-five, his son's wife, twenty, and their six-year-old twins; his second son, twenty, with his wife, eighteen, and their one-year-old daughter; and his third son, eighteen, with his sixteen-year-old wife.[15]

There was enough work for all the extended family, enjoying shares in the family business.

Most Jews lived in the shtetl one family per house and as married couples. The data on migration into the shtetls show that Jews arrived as families rather than as single individuals.[16]

Although socially stratified and financially uneven, the shtetl Jewish family was a proud and self-contained institution before the urbanization processes, economic downfall, and outward migrations shattered its stability and threw the shtetl down from its heights. And throughout the nineteenth century, the Jewish family had one member who merited special care, the housewife.

BEAUTIFYING A HOUSEWIFE

"I never called my wife 'my wife,' rather I called her 'my house,'" says Rabbi Yosi, a rabbinic scholar from the Talmud.[17] Not every shtetl dweller knew this metaphor, yet everybody knew that the husband was the head of the household while the wife was its chief manager. Like the surrounding Slavs, Jewish men were in power, but unlike the Slavs, it was the Jewish wife who administered it.

The Jewish family was a social nucleus run by a duumvirate. Women, the key decision makers, assumed responsibility for bartending and cooking, protecting and renovating their real estate, litigating in courts, and trading in the marketplace and from home stores. Besides, while male Jews spent their time pitching their merchandise elsewhere, Jewish women were raising the children, keeping the house in order and Judaism alive, feeding the animals, retailing groceries and liquor, selling rolls of fabric, fighting with neighbors over clientele, and distributing charity. All these functions made Jewish women much more independent than their Slavic counterparts. The Jewish family was patriarchal in men's imaginations only. The golden age shtetl was entirely matriarchal.

Jewish wives had quite a presence in the family, both visually and aurally. Many, if not most of them, resembled Toibe-Sosye from Mendele's autobiographical novel—a corpulent woman with a shrieking voice who, like Dobrisha Lazebnik from the beginning of this chapter, could be heard as she walked.[18] Unlike the feeble Jewish female characters of later urbanized literature, the shtetl wife had to be strong, powerful, shrewd, corpulent, imposing, and vociferous. Physical work at home, trade in the shtetl store or at the marketplace and dealings with peasants informed the Jewish woman's outlook. Jews, however, very rarely called their wives "baba," as the surrounding Slavs did: we find only one such case for a Jewish divorcee.[19] Jews called their wives in Yiddish "do you hear this?" ("Hersdu?") inviting their participation in every occurrence, but even so, the husband also made his wife feel that she was a real asset to the family.

The most unsympathetic gentiles could not help admiring the way Jewish women in the shtetl looked. Olimpiada Shishkina dedicated her travelogue to Nicholas I; she had no desire to praise the Jews and added derogatory phrases to dismiss the little praise for the Jews that she allowed herself. Once she observed Jewish women, however, she changed her tone. Shishkina travelled through Belaia Tserkov and Vasilkov and noticed that Jewish women wore silk head coverings festooned with large and small pearls and crystals, and, if they were well-to-do, diamond pendants. They sold retail goods in shabby stores that greatly contrasted with their expensive head covers, something Shishkina found particularly amusing. Even the poorest Jewish women put on simple calico kerchiefs covered by muslin, but all of them, following some strange custom, "had on their heads some sort of a tongue, made out of a bonnet and silk stripe." This shtetl haute couture did not forgo the modesty required in their dress code: Jewish women also wore on their bosom a two-inch-wide stripe of brocade or silk, "without which no married woman can go anywhere."[20]

Passing through the same towns fifteen years earlier, an English traveler had also noticed that Jewish women, the only trading females in the shtetl marketplace, were well dressed and "distinguished themselves by their white linen head-covers, with a loop of red ribbon or cloth placed in front."[21] These women differed not only from those in the northern but also from those in the western areas of the Pale: Yekhezkel Kotik, a careful observer, claimed that in his native Kamenets the Jewish women would try to hide themselves on market days—but they strutted around on Shabbat or during wedding ceremonies.[22] On the contrary, in the Ukrainian shtetls women dressed up even on regular market days.

7.1. A Hasidic wedding, Galicia, early 20th century.
Oil painting by J. S. Kruszewski. BHT 87.123.4. Courtesy of LKhG and the Beit Hatfutsot exhibition "Treasures of Jewish Galicia—Judaica from the Museum of Ethnography in Lviv, Ukraine," Photo Archive, Tel Aviv.

Shtetl Jews had a taste for fine, colorful clothes. Observing them, a British medical doctor and a diplomat compared them to the portraits by Raphael, Leonardo da Vinci, Carlo Dolci and other Italian painters.[23] Polish writer Kraszewski found many Jews similar to the images of Rembrandt.[24] Mikhail Kolmanovich, for example, was an innkeeper who leased a tavern, where he lived with his mother, his wife, and his brother. He felt entitled to dress like a Polish magnate. He sported a silk *kuntusz*—a long robe of fine fabric with brocade and loose, unbuttoned sleeves. Beneath it he wore a very expensive blue cotton shirt, also with gilded embroidery.[25] Most likely he also had the prescribed *tsitsit* sewn to the corners of his garment, thus Judaizing his fancy Polish attire.[26]

Kolmanovich's wife looked more modest: she wore red skirts with cloth underskirts and a warm blue velvet vest with laces. Her mother was dressed in a leather fur-trimmed *zhupan*, a fashionable short women's jacket with colored laces, with a velvet apron over it. Both women shared several multicolored head kerchiefs. If we add to this outfit a pair of women's blue-and-white leather shoes, we get quite a colorful and picturesque vision of shtetl attire—very different from the shabby rags, ranging from dirty white to worn-out gray, featured in early twentieth-century ethnographic photographs.[27]

For Shabbat and festive occasions, the wife of a merchant had haute couture items: several calico and percale dresses, a variety of multicolored ribbons, different kerchiefs, dark cherry sashes, cotton stockings, and one or two fur coats, often dyed in blue. At home she would wear a silk dressing gown. The wife of a tavernkeeper wore brocaded red and blue skirts, several underskirts, and a blue velvet vest with gilded laces. She wore a velvet or cotton apron while attending to the family dinner, and a sheepskin wool jacket, in most cases blue, to go out in winter.[28] The main colors of women's clothing were dark blue and dark red—perhaps these colors of shtetl women's clothing defined the warm and happy blue-red palette of Marc Chagall. The attire of the Jewish family shows that the shtetl at its height was a joyous and multicolored place, not black-and-white and gloomy.[29]

While rich families possessed diamonds and other fancy jewelry, a wife in a mid-ranking family of trading townsfolk could boast of a *namysto*—beads with silver coins and coral strung on silk lace, a fashion shared by Polish landladies and wealthy female peasants.[30] The educated Leah Horowitz from eighteenth-century Bolechów complained that women in the synagogue saw the jewelry of other women, became envious, and went home to argue with their husbands about new purchases.[31]

Jewish women almost never visited a shtetl prayer house, the male domain, and only infrequently attended synagogue, where they were restricted to a special women's area, separated from the main prayer hall by a wall. In early modern times, more women were willing to attend services. Following the increase in their attendance, they witnessed a steady process of inclusion. The narrow visors in the thick stone walls allowing women to follow the service turned into windows with shutters. Then the shutters disappeared, the windows became wider, and women found themselves visually exposed and more fully involved in what was happening in the men's section.[32] By the early nineteenth century, most synagogues

7.2. Wedding ring, 18th century, with the inscription "May your house be like the house of Peretz" (Ruth 4:12).
MNK-IV-Z-321, no. 113. Courtesy of MNK and the Center for Jewish Art at Hebrew University, Jerusalem.

in Ukrainian shtetls had galleries around and above the perimeter of the main hall, exposing Jewish women fully to the services. Women now could see and be seen, not only hear.

Male Jews took their wives' desire to participate in religious rites seriously. The trouble caused by an old wooden synagogue in a Volhynia shtetl near Lutsk is instructive. The local women felt uneasy in their section, built so low in the clumsy edifice that they could barely follow services. Local dwellers decided to move the women's section to a newly constructed balcony above the prayer hall, and for this purpose planned to demolish one of the synagogue's walls. Destroying a wall of the synagogue was considered sacrilege, but accommodating women was a vital necessity. The shtetl dwellers stood firmly in favor of the renovation, yet they did not want to offend tradition. Rabbi Arye Leib Bolechover of

Zaslav understood how sensitive the issue was and endorsed the reconstruction and circumventing of the ban. The shtetl dwellers needed the renovations for the sake of the synagogue itself, which was to be understood not just as a building but as a place where Jews, male and female, engaged in collective prayers, he explained.[33]

Fancy gifts, fine clothes, and synagogue comfort meant a lot for Jewish women, but what was not seen was also significant, and provided no less joy and happiness in the shtetl family.

HOLY SEX

What Shmuli Boteach calls kosher sex was as important for the shtetl as was kosher worship. Unless a Jewish wife immersed herself in the ritual bath after her monthly period, her husband could not be intimate with her. The ritual bath blessed sex, spiritualized intercourse, and transformed the carnal into the spiritual in order to produce Jewish children. Caring for a woman's body was as much about fulfilling the mitzvah as it was about a sexual relationship. Unlike the surrounding Catholics, Jews saw nothing sinful in sex, and unlike the surrounding Eastern Orthodox, they had a rather strict practice of modesty and separation of sexes. Judaic tradition sanctified sex that led to procreation. Urbanization and acculturation later in the century almost entirely destroyed this interplay of the spiritual and the carnal, but the shtetl in the early nineteenth century cherished it.

To avoid procreation for any reason was sinful. A bachelor was considered by shtetl Jews to be wretched—he could not and was not supposed to have sex. Unmarried men were readily suspected of promiscuity or, even worse, *keri*, spilling semen in vain (also masturbation), a sin that according to shtetl dwellers brought forth evil spirits who turned against the sinner. An unmarried woman or a barren daughter was also considered shameful, and a good reason to go with a donation to a Hasidic master for a blessing and a cure.

Single Jews were rare in the shtetl. One finds some single women in Russian inventories, usually widows, but very few single men. To be single was outside the shtetl norm. The worst situation for a shtetl woman was to become an abandoned wife, an *agunah*, a person in limbo. An agunah was legally married but had no real husband, who had either died while away from home with no witnesses or had simply disappeared without sending his wife a valid divorce document. As a newly single but sexually experienced female, an *agunah* and a widow attracted suspicious glances from married women and the lascivious looks of men.

Their situation was abnormal from many perspectives, and single women sought to correct it the only way they could: an *agunah* by securing the divorce document and remarrying, a widow by remarrying. And remarry they did, since marriage not only justified sexual relations but also provided them with dignity and shelter, radically diminishing threats of harassment. By remarrying, Jews could have legitimate sex, avoid becoming a burden to their children, and restore normalcy through the family.[34] Hence Jews tended to dissolve their marriages in late summer—with an eye on the early fall fairs and subsequent late fall weddings. Shtetl Jews knew that divorce implied the loss of prescribed normalcy, and hence they sought ways to reconstitute it.

Infertility was no less shameful for a man than for a woman, and while it was usually blamed on women, male Jews were not immune. A Jew from Klevan had a genital defect: his orifice was located on the wrong part of his penis, while the natural one was closed. He urinated through that other orifice. His parents discovered this dysfunction when he was only several weeks old and for whatever reason undertook no measures. He could not impregnate a woman, and went to consult Rabbi Haim Rappaport of Ostrog.[35]

Who was this unfortunate Jew: a person with a sexual defect, a legitimate member of the community, or a legally infertile Jew, a *petsua daka'*, whom Jewish law banishes from the congregation? Could he undergo an operation to allow his sperm get out, as he put it, through the "normal door"? While we do not know what happened to him, we can almost hear his voice as noted in the rabbinic responsum, trembling with humiliation yet full of hope—it speaks volumes about the meaning of family for the shtetl Jew. The man worried about his sex being functional and productive, not just about pleasure in and of itself.[36]

Women also sought to make sure their sex was productive, and for this reason they were concerned about their ritual purity. They did a regular

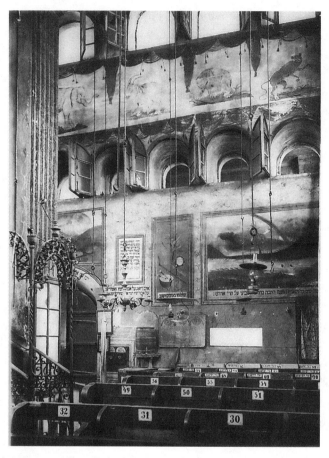

7.3. The Western wall in the late 18-century synagogue of Peremyshliany, Eastern Galicia.
BHT EXH 87.159.3. Courtesy of LNM and the Beit Hatfutsot exhibition "Treasures of Jewish Galicia—Judaica from the Museum of Ethnography in Lviv, Ukraine," Photo Archive, Tel Aviv.

check using pieces of cloth, counted the days before and after their monthly period, and consulted men of authority when they saw an irregular bloody discharge. One such woman from Berdichev saw blood while urinating, checked herself afterward, and did not find blood or feel cramps indicating the beginning of her menstrual cycle. Was she ritually impure? She went to consult the communal elders, who allowed her to have intercourse with her husband. At that point, one Aaron, a rabbinic scholar from a nearby shtetl, learned about the case, disagreed with the decision of the elders, and wrote a request to Rabbi Yosef Landa in Litin.[37] Yes, answered the latter, the elders were right, although a woman who sees no blood but does feel cramps should be deemed impure, hence prohibited from having sex.[38]

Kosher sex was about being "fruitful and multiplying," hence Jewish men assumed responsibility for the ritual bath and put aside communal moneys for a beadle and for wood. A functional ritual bath was a big deal: it provided the shtetl with its happy moments of intimacy. In 1778 the Zaslav *mikveh* burned down and women had to go elsewhere to immerse themselves. The burial society then set down in the communal record book that the society would use its funds to renovate the *mikveh* "lest women go to another place."[39] In 1787 the Letichev Burial Society firmly instructed the leaseholder of the ritual bath that every day following afternoon prayers he had to prepare "hot water for women without saving on heating."[40]

Somewhere around Zaslav, Jewish men built a bath for themselves but not for women, and a scandalized rabbi in unusually strong language urged the men to have another ritual bath for women established immediately. In the shtetl of Kalinovka, a beadle reported that the ritual bath did not have the required amount of water, and the local rabbi preferred to believe the local women, who claimed they had purified themselves in the proper way, and to distrust the male witness, the beadle, who insisted that the ablution was invalid.[41]

Contemporary Russian documents confirm the importance of the Jewish ritual bath in the shtetl. The Gusiatin *mikveh*, for example, was a shabby one-floor hut with a straw roof, yet unlike many local Jewish houses it was made of stone. It had about seven rooms inside with three separate doors, and an effective system of natural water supply.[42] When the Gaisin Jewish community needed to reconstruct its old *mikveh*, the administration issued permission, provided Jews with a blueprint of the façade to follow, and endorsed the renovation.[43]

Once married Jewish women emerged from the bath after the ritual ablutions, the shtetl could engage in kosher sex. This type of sex began with marriage. The popular Hasidic song "I will sing the Praise" (*Azamer bi-shvakhin*) celebrates a groom who embraces his bride and causes her physical pleasure—surprisingly explicit eroticism juxtaposed with a deep mystical message.

Because of their better treatment and better sanitary conditions, Jewish women delivered new babies twice as fast as Christian women (five or six versus eleven hours). Jewish child mortality was 50 percent of that of Christians, and Jewish women's post-partum disease rate was 25 percent less than that of Christians. Children born out of wedlock were almost unheard of among Jews. In the early 1870s, out of every hundred newborn children, 4 percent of Catholic babies were born out of wedlock, 3.4 percent of Protestant newborns, and 3 percent of Eastern Orthodox newborns, whereas Jewish newborns out of wedlock did not exceed 0.4 percent.[44]

This sense of normalized intimacy was almost completely lost to the new sexual mores once Jews reestablished themselves in big cities. The numbers of Jewish illegitimate children and vagabond orphans skyrocketed, and promiscuity became a new cultural norm.

PROTECTING THE FAMILY

Cases of promiscuity were not tolerated in the shtetl. Transgressing sexual norms ruined not only families but also family businesses, increasing the number of individuals in need of the communal social relief fund. Protecting the family was as much an economic as an ethical imperative. Transgressors became objects of communal ostracism, public disdain and derision, and verbal and physical violence. For a Jew charged with promiscuity, proving his or her innocence was a matter of survival. Nobody wanted to be known as a libertine: who would buy from or trade with such a person? Dobrisha Lazebnik was well aware what she was doing when defending the honor of her husband.

Like Dobrisha, one Perl Pearovskaya went to all lengths to convince the authorities that her husband was innocent. An Uman innkeeper, he got himself into trouble by taking in a Jew who had arrived in town just before Passover. The Jew asked to stay in their inn through the holiday, and the Pearovskys consented. In the evening, they agreed that Pearovsky would go to synagogue while his guest would wait for him back at the inn, and they would bless the wine together.

While Pearovsky was thanking the Almighty for deliverance from Egyptian bondage, his guest decided to relieve his urges. Uman Jews saw him with a prostitute, apprehended him, and turned him over to the police. The police then arrested and beat Pearovsky as well, as if the innkeeper was to blame for the conduct of his guest.[45] Uman Jews were disgusted by the unnamed guest-in-the-night who had chosen Passover as an opportunity for sexual adventure. Religious sensibilities fueled their anger, and they took it out on Pearovsky, inadvertently involved in a promiscuity case.

As in the case of Dobrisha, it was Pearovsky's wife who saved her husband from disgrace and proved that their family had no relation to the promiscuous guest. The matriarch of the family, she knew that not only honor but also the reputation of her business were at stake. However, not every housewife in the shtetl was as brave as Madam Pearovsky or Madam Lazebnik. Pesya Lober from Radzivilov failed to protect her recalcitrant husband, a tavernkeeper, falsely accused by the communal elders of adultery, an accusation that dealt a severe blow to the family and to the family business.[46]

Family stability meant the religious and economic stability of the community. Helping families stay together was one of the responsibilities of the communal rabbis and elders, who precisely for religious and economic reasons assumed responsibility for protecting wives from abusive husbands and keeping families from falling apart.

The punishments meted out by the communal elders were public and often relied on the support of the police. In Slavuta, the Shapira brothers attempted to restrain a certain Protagain, a drunkard, who regularly abused his wife, a relative of the Shapiras. The brothers brought Protagain to the synagogue, beat him, and led him through the shtetl as a public disgrace.[47] In Uman, a certain Berko Iudkovich beat the wife of one Naftulovich; on learning of the assault and seeing his wife covered with bruises, Naftulovich badly beat Iudkovich, who in turn had the nerve to go and complain to the Russian police. The town policeman took the side of the married couple and put the disruptive Berko Iudkovich under arrest.[48]

Again in Uman, Jewish and non-Jewish authorities came together to bring down the stingy and violent Lazar Geleliovich. Lazar suffered from epilepsy and would have deserved pity if not for his constant mistreatment of his wife. Banished from Tulchin for promiscuity, Geleliovich settled in Uman and turned to domestic violence. One day, when her husband had indulged in schnapps, his wife took a piece of herring off the plate and put it aside for a relative. This piece of herring infuriated Geleliovich. He jumped to his feet and punched his wife, giving her a black eye; when she tried to run, he grabbed an ax and cut her leg.

Although the local head of police was sympathetic to Geleliovich, he had to agree with the decision of the elders when Geleliovich's wife came and showed her cuts and bruises to the kahal. The head of police put Geleliovich in prison to prevent him from beating his wife while the local rabbinic court was considering the divorce.[49] By protecting the wife—and even contradicting the notoriously corrupt town head of police himself—the kahal sent a clear message: although the husband was officially the breadwinner, he still had no right to mistreat his wife, his partner in life and business, and the wife had every right to get separated from him.

The husband also had to assume full responsibility for his wife and had no right to shirk it. For example, the Zaslav Burial Society penalized its warden, forbidding him to collect donations before the high holidays or to perform other communal functions for having "left his wife and children without money."[50] Supporting one's wife was an unavoidable obligation even in extreme cases, such as the one of a Jew from Hotin, who complained that his father-in-law had cheated him into marriage by concealing his daughter's insanity. The man had no choice but to live with his wife, who was not able to produce a child or control herself and whom he sought to divorce. Not only did he have to collect one hundred signatures of rabbis allowing him to do so—as the law required—he also had to continue supporting his sick wife after their formal divorce.[51]

Rabbis knew that the breakup of a family would trigger a domino effect in the community: whatever could be done should be done to help families reunite and avoid semi-orphaned children or abandoned wives forced to go begging. Saving Jewish families implied protecting communal economic well-being. Rabbi Naftali Hirsh of Slavuta had a passionate and crazy Jewish couple to deal with. The husband, a well-educated Jew of priestly descent, had quarreled with his wife. Their fight sparked a reckless exchange of accusations and threats. The husband shrieked that he would divorce his wife, and the wife reciprocated. Bewildered, the husband pulled out an inkpot, took a piece of parchment, and wrote a divorce document befitting the strictest scribal standards.

When her husband was about to drop the rolled parchment into her hands, the wife remembered that a woman who is being divorced had to be seated. She grabbed a chair, sat down, stretched out her hands, and mockingly accepted the divorce document. Both sides spoke the corresponding ritual words to be expected in this situation. When they calmed down, however, and admitted that they would like to reconcile, they now presented a big problem for their rabbi, who knew that a Jew of priestly descent could not legally marry a divorcee—even if the woman had been his own wife. The Slavuta rabbi looked into the case, intending to disprove the validity of the rash homemade divorce.[52] He had to navigate between intricacies of the law in order to keep the family together, precisely because he knew that the family was the nucleus of Jewish life. For the shtetl to survive and Judaism to prevail, there was nothing more important than a strong family.

And it was this family's responsibility to ensure traditionalism and procreation, even if the two came into conflict, as happened to one family residing in a shtetl not far from Rabbi Arye Leib Bolechover of Zaslav.[53] The problem arose when a Jewish family gave birth to healthy twins and, sometime later, to another pair. The first two boys were fine; the second two after their circumcision became sick and died soon after. Rabbi Bolechover did not have the medical knowledge to diagnose a blood coagulation dysfunction, yet he correctly suggested a genetic predisposition in the family. He took into consideration the Talmudic case of a woman "who circumcised two of her sons and they died," which discusses whether she should or should not circumcise her next boys.[54] The rabbi explained to the parents that they had a medical issue and that the law forbade circumcising their boys.

7.4. Seal of the rabbinical court, belonged to Rabbi Yehoshua Halberstam.
MB-Hi3863. MNB, no.14. Courtesy of MNB and the Center for Jewish Art at Hebrew University, Jerusalem.

Sometime later, the family had another baby boy, and the rabbi categorically ruled against circumcision. If a fatality was likely, then causing it would be tantamount to murder. It was better to have an uncircumcised baby boy than to bury a circumcised one.

Several months passed and the boy showed signs of good health, but the family was concerned. How would their son answer the question of whether he was Jewish or not, once his difference from other boys became obvious? Would he be able to celebrate his bar mitzvah? The relentless rabbi, thought the parents, was concerned with his books, not with their own embarrassment. It was up to the family to make Judaism a living tradition. The family members made up their mind to perform the circumcision at home, in secret. They invited ten men for a minyan (prayer quorum), brought in a different *mohel* unaware of the family issues, circumcised the boy, and made arrangements for a feast. To their deepest dismay, the boy died.

The rabbi learned about the incident and became furious. "Who is to blame?!" he asked rhetorically. Everybody, he answered: the parents, the *mohel*, and the guests, everyone should impose penance on themselves. The entire family was responsible.[55]

By violating the rabbinic prescription, the unnamed family in Zaslav revealed what shtetl Jews cherished most. Family had to be traditional, women fertile, children brought up as Jews. In turn, the rabbi emphasized the collective responsibility of the Jewish family, which he, the rabbi, had to protect from a perverse understanding of Judaism.[56] What can be understood from his responsum is that a divine commandment could not mean dying for it. The shtetl family was about life and life only. Without this commonsense Judaism, it is difficult to explain, even considering the improvements of the general sanitary conditions in East Europe, why and how the Jewish community grew from one million to five million in a century.

FAMILY UNDER ASSAULT

The shtetl economy upset the family as well as enforced it. Trade depended on mobility, which increased the revenues of the family but decreased its stability. Jewish society was predominantly oral. Long-distance communications were poor, letters sent via post were expensive, and the Jewish pantofle mail (sending letters with an occasional traveler) was irregular. Traveling merchants were left to their own devices for weeks. Their travels exposed them to all sorts of encounters, including erotic, which led Rabbi Nachman from Bratslav to observe that "because of a brief quarter-of-an-hour of fun, people lose their portion in this world and in the world to come."[57]

Trade was gender-neutral: women also went on the road. Their husbands tolerated this situation as long as they were left to their books in the local study house. We can only imagine how the absence of a housewife challenged family life. One Azriel, a rabbinic scholar from Tulchin, inquired whether a husband could perform candle lighting and thus fulfill one of three time-based commandments incumbent on women while his wife was elsewhere engaged in business.[58]

A husband might be able to light candles by himself, but he could not always protect his wife while she was away. The mobility of trade exposed women as much as men to undesirable contacts. Rabbi Haim Rapaport dealt with the case of a married woman who traveled with her retail merchandise and her seven-year-old daughter. Her husband, a God-fearing but not particularly entrepreneurial individual, warned his wife against traveling on her own and to avoid being alone with a cabman. One day, the mother and daughter looked for and could not find a fellow traveler to join them. As a result, they had to drive through the woods in complete darkness, a fact that greatly displeased the God-fearing but not particularly entrepreneurial husband, who had the nerve to suspect his wife of adultery and turned to Rabbi Rapaport for advice.[59]

Shtetl dwellers of both sexes believed that Jewish women became particularly vulnerable when left unprotected. The *dybbuk* was known as ghostly evildoer who entered the body of a Jewish young woman on the eve of her wedding, precisely when she was no longer protected by her father and not yet protected by their husband. More often than not, this *dybbuk* was actually a real male, Jew or Christian, seeking an affair, whom the community preferred to call a *dybbuk,* the otherworld alien, to conceal public shame.[60] Here is the 1826 case of a Berdichev-born woman, married for ten years with no children, whom her husband—because of the childless situation—decided to send back home, yet without a formal divorce. While the wife remained for four years in Berdichev, her absentee husband became a successful brewer and after four years of separation decided to bring his wife back.

She agreed, and then five months later gave birth to a baby girl. She first swore that it was a miracle. Later, however, she confessed that she had been the victim of sexual advances from a Jew in Berdichev, although she had managed to defend herself and the intercourse had not been consummated. To protect the family from public disgrace—but most likely, following the rabbinic regulation that a five-month old baby should not be suspect as an out-of-wedlock offspring—the Ostrog rabbi announced the child kosher and the woman innocent.[61]

However, it was next to impossible to save another family in a scandalous situation involving a pregnant bride. A Jew married a widow who had lost her husband about half a year earlier and was in a hurry to remarry. The ceremony was conducted under a bridal canopy, the marriage agreement was read and the feast enjoyed, after which the bride went into a separate room where, screaming and moaning because of the onset of sudden labor, she gave birth to a healthy child. The rabbi elaborately discussed in his responsum whether the child could or could not have been conceived during the previous marriage, but the rabbi would never be able to bring back the lady's husband: the latter had ran away from his family disgrace as far as he could.[62]

For Jewish women, keeping silent about sexual harassment, let alone rape, was the best variant of self-defense. They chose to preserve their family over justice. When circumstances forced them to speak up, it turned out that sexual assaults often happened at home to married Jewish women. For example, a Volhynia woman married a Jew of priestly descent and five months after the wedding gave birth to a child. Once the case reached the rabbinic court, she confessed that she had spent time with her sister's husband, a tavernkeeper, who had many Jews from nearby Dubno and Olyka coming to the village fair. When the lights were turned out and the tavern was dark, one of the Jews "came to her in the evening and took advantage of her." The woman could identify the rapist, since he was the only guest who had stubble instead of a beard, which she felt while trying to fight him off.[63]

This and other cases prove that the Jews—male and female, merchants and rabbis—would get together to penalize the rapist. They resorted to the entire gamut of measures available to them, from mob violence to state and rabbinic courts. A Brody case involved men on the move, away from their families, and provides lurid detail. Three traveling merchants arrived at in Brody, a frontier Galician town, and stayed at an inn. In the evening, the wife of the innkeeper went to bed behind a screen, and her husband made do on a bench.

At night, one of the guests crawled behind the curtain and lay down next to the innkeeper's sleeping wife. The man embraced and kissed her, became aroused, and attempted to have sex with her. The report describes that his member was fully erect and that he even ejaculated, but at that point the woman had woken, shouting and waking the entire household. Although later the rapist was beaten and put on trial, Rabbi Landau had to deal with the question of whether the wife had or had not been defiled and whether she was still allowed to her husband, who was of priestly descent.[64] For the rabbi as for the wife, the status of the family was more important than justice. Whatever happened had happened; now the question was how the family could be preserved intact.

The rabbis, in charge of their community or communities, could not protect all Jews whose mobility triggered encounters disruptive for their families. Psychologically, it was easier to divorce one's wife from afar. The disloyal husbands simply disappeared, conveniently forgetting about their legal obligations toward their abandoned wives. There are many cases of husbands sending them a *get* (a divorce document) from distant places where they had gone for business.[65] This is where the empire comes in, with its intent to move commercial centers from the western areas to interior Russia.

The more intensely the Russian regime tried to move trade outside the shtetls and into the bigger towns—Romny, Kharkov, Kiev, Sumy, Poltava, Krolevets—the more trading Jews had to spend time outside their cozy shtetl environment. The head of the rabbinic court in Nemirov and Vinnitsa, Rabbi Isser, regularly dealt with the cases of abandoned wives whose husbands had died or disappeared while on business trips.[66] He and other rabbis often had to secure valid identification of those who died hundreds of miles away from their families.[67] A certain Ze'ev Wolf met a Christian lady, settled with her, converted to Christianity, and left his wife in Litin completely unaware of what had happened to her husband until twenty-three years later she finally learned about the whole situation after her husband had died.[68] These cases were not new: Rabbi Landau of Prague, while still in Yampol, also had to look into the situation of abandoned wives.[69] Back in the late eighteenth century, he also ruled on a case in which a woman from Nemirov sent her husband, a wine dealer, to Wallachia for Bessarabian wines, had no news from him for four years, and had to bribe a traveling merchant to make him appear and testify before the rabbinic court that her husband was definitely dead.[70] However, the difference was palpable: in the mid-nineteenth century, such cases triples and quadrupled.

While scandals among townsfolk were ubiquitous, attempts to protect wives from domestic violence or irresponsible husbands and women from sexual harassment put the Jewish authorities in a unique situation. The case of a wealthy and well-educated leaseholder who was having continuous sexual relations with a breastfeeding widow stands for many. The knowledgeable scoundrel knew that according to Judaic law a nursing widow had two full years for herself and a child and could not get married over this period. Approaching her sexually was considered an offense. To conceal his wrongdoing, the leaseholder wanted to marry the widow secretly, and received a harsh scolding from the Ostrog rabbi, who sought to protect the woman.[71] In a different case, one *agunah*, an abandoned wife, became the victim of her neighbor, who decided to take advantage of her unresolved situation and began aggressively harassing her. The local Jewish elders strongly admonished him and demanded that he move out.[72] In the golden age shtetl the communal elders were still able to enforce their decisions.

The abolition of the kahal in 1844 transformed the former elders into clerks in charge of communal duties before the state, and their ability to control internal family conflicts deteriorated. The introduction of state-paid rabbis (*kazennye*), in charge of vital statistics, helped monitor the family situation and birth rate but not strengthen the family. The number of Jewish divorces began to rise slowly. Reasons for divorce varied, but one circumstance they had in common, in a wider Slavic context, was the comparative independence of the Jewish woman.

Had her husband been rude to her, a woman such as Dobrisha Lazebnik would have been strong enough to protect herself from abuse. If abused and mistreated, Jewish wives did not hesitate to file for divorce and demand a *get* from their husbands. They learned trade, gained experience in the marketplace, were at home with the Russian authorities, and felt more independent than their Slavic peers. The economic decline of the shtetl combined with the gender parity in the domestic economy could have prompted a Jewish wife to choose justice over family during internal family dramas. The necessity for husbands to get police permission and spend weeks on out-of-the-Pale business trips exacerbated the situation. In the mid-1840s, the ratio of divorces to marriages among Jews in the central Ukraine grew to one in four, although in burgeoning Berdichev it was higher: 153 divorces to 320 marriages, or almost a 50 percent divorce rate.[73]

This pattern was commonplace. Twenty-eight percent of married couples in Zhitomir got divorced, as also in three of the towns in Zhitomir district. In Starokonstantinov there was a 16 percent divorce rate; in Zaslav, 8 percent; in Rovno, 10 percent. Bigger towns had several times more divorces than the shtetls. Thus, 47 percent of marriages were dissolved in Kamenets-Podolsk but only 6 percent in the district of Kamenets-Podolsk, in the dozens of surrounding shtetls; 47 percent in Letichev but only 2 percent in the surrounding shtetls. Divorces destroyed 35 percent of marriages in Volhynia, 24 percent in Podolia, and 25 percent in Kiev province in 1841, with big towns accounting for most of them.[74]

Perhaps there were many more divorces in the bigger towns than in the shtetls because people went from the shtetls to the provincial center towns to register their divorces. Yet this reason still only proves the rule: the shtetl was firmly associated with the family, whereas moving from the shtetl meant a family in crisis. Grigorii Goldenberg, a future revolutionary, related that his observant, well-to-do, and enlightened Jewish family kept a kosher kitchen, which was gone once they moved from Berdichev to Kiev. Likewise, Polina Wengeroff told how her husband allegedly forced her to give up the kosher dietary laws once the family moved to St. Petersburg.[75] While traditional Jewish life remained the prerogative of the shtetl communities through the twentieth century, those who sought to challenge the imposing communal or family power would challenge it precisely by moving out of the shtetl and going beyond traditional mores. For many young Jews later in the nineteenth century, the rejection of tradition started exactly with this type of conduct—abrogation of communal values and adoration of promiscuity, sex out of wedlock, and civic marriage, everything antithetical to the shtetl family.[76]

The urbanization of the second half of the nineteenth century brought hundreds of thousands of Jews to bigger towns and cities. Preserving a traditional Jewish family in the new industrial centers with their two or three shifts per day, proletarian barracks, and seven-day workweek was next to impossible. Moreover, during the great wave of East European emigration, when about two million Jews were on the move, the question of abandoned wives and ruined families became one of the most pressing themes of the rabbinic responsa. Despite these developments, which had a devastating effect on the Jews, East European popular memory preserved very different images of the Jewish family.

FAMILY LEGEND

To the Jewish popular imagination, the greatest threat was imminent danger to the family brought on by a folkloric evil power—a *mazik, shed, ruah*, Na'amah, Lilith, or dybbuk, the most dangerous of whom directly attacked the Jewish family.[77] It is not accidental that the most popular Jewish play of the twentieth century was S. Ansky's drama *The Dybbuk*, with its shtetl family destroyed by demons of revolutionary mysticism and class struggle.[78] Yehuda Pen, Chagall's mentor, was haunted by his favorite motif of an elderly couple at the Sabbath table, with no one else who could carry on the tradition.[79]

Shtetl Jews respected family, advocated moderation, and endorsed sex within wedlock as a commendable activity. *A shtub darf hobn a man un a man darf hobn a vayb*, the Yiddish saying goes (A house needs a man and a man needs a wife). To emphasize that family really matters, Yiddish proverbs reinforce the importance of figuring out the sexual urges of one's wife and meeting them halfway, especially those of a young wife, who in Yiddish is described as a devotee of *di groyse kishke*—which in this case does not refer to the traditional Sabbath meal. The shtetl constantly equates religious obligations with matrimonial ones. A God-fearing Jew combined the spiritual and the sexual by "kissing the fringes of his prayer shawl in the morning and his wife's breasts at night": *an erlekhe yid in der fri kusht er tsitsis, bay nakht kusht er tsitskis.*

The menstrual period, during which Judaism prohibits any intimacy, is a tragedy for a husband: *az dem vayb iz a nide, hot der man a bide*, "when a wife has her period, her husband is in trouble." On the contrary, the moment the wife goes into the ritual bath to do her purifying ablutions is the husband's moment of great expectation: *az dem vayb geyt in mikve arayn, kukt der man funem fenster aroys*, "when the wife goes into the mikveh, the husband looks out the window." Out-of-wedlock relations place an individual outside ethnic and familial borders: *a ganev iz keyn brider, a kurve iz keyn shvester*—"a thief is no brother, a whore is no sister." And, of course, since sex is about family and procreation, and since *pirya ve-rivya iz di beste mitzve*—"be fruitful and multiply"—is the best commandment, one should consistently and selflessly dedicate oneself to its implementation. *A mes iz potur fin pirya ve-rivya*: "only the dead are exempt from this mitzvah."[80]

This emphasis on the family as an absolute positive constant among Jews had a significant and longlasting impact on Slavic society. East European literati ignored the internal mobility of the Jewish family, its high rate of divorce and remarriage, and its domestic violence. For many writers, the traditional Jewish family was the most characteristic feature of the shtetl, serving as a synecdoche for the entire people of Israel—and for happiness, which according to Braudel, "whether in business or private life, leaves little trace in history."[81]

The first Russian Jewish writer, Odessa-based Osip Rabinovich, portrayed Jewish soldiers as either proudly serving in the Russian navy as a happy family or removed from the family and exiled into the army, hence deeply distressed.[82]

Aleksandr Kuprin, a key Russian democratic-minded writer, depicted a Jewish wife as the epitome of integrity. In one of his stories, a Russian doctor and a policeman discuss how futile and hopeless it would be to try and tempt a beautiful married Jewish woman whom they both knew.[83]

As a cohesive and indivisible ethnic nucleus, the Jewish family intimidated Vassili Rozanov, a gifted Russian thinker, who viewed the Jewish family as so well built and durable that it threatened, he thought, the decaying Russian family and served as a secret weapon with which the Jews were destined to defeat the Slavs.[84]

Russian folklore preserved a plethora of Jewish jokes about the strength of the Jewish family and respect for Jewish women. In one of those jokes, a policeman comes to a certain Yonkel and asks whether he has any hidden gold. Yonkel replies that he has in his possession almost two hundred pounds of pure gold, and asks his wife Sarah to step out and meet the visitor. In another joke, a neighbor asks an old Jew about his never-married young daughter recently seen nursing a baby. The old man replies, "Well, if a Jewish girl has a little bit of free time and a little bit of free milk, why can't she feed a baby?"

East European literati could not part with the legend of the Jewish family, seeking to perpetuate or question it, bemoan its loss or deconstruct it. In his "Gimpel the Fool," Isaac Bashevis Singer depicts a shtetl idiot—and even he is married and strongly attached to what he considers his family, even if his wife has affairs with other Jews and bears their children.

Closely observing families of East European immigrants coming to Prague from Galicia, Franz Kafka idealized and bemoaned the traditional family. In his letters to his beloved Czech Milena, he wrote that he wanted but could not have a family, did not deserve it, could never merit it.[85] Shmuel Yosef Czaczkes shared a similar feeling of estrangement that separated him, an Israeli Hebrew writer, from the national-messianic fervor of his own people. To emphasize this impossible separation, Czaczkes adopted the pseudonym Agnon, which was a male version of the abandoned Jewish wife, *agunah*.[86]

Ultimately, the Jewish family epitomized the beginnings and the ends of Judaism. In one of the episodes of Vassili Grossman's *Life and Fate*, Jewish spinster Sofia Leventon finds herself on a cattle wagon being shipped to Treblinka. As she is being deported from Ukraine, she meets and takes care of Davidka, an orphaned Jewish minor. They go to the gas chamber together, and so that Davidka will not suffer too long from the Zyklon B, Sofia presses him to her body. She is no Dobrisha Lazebnik, but she does the maximum what she can do to protect her imaginary family. At that very moment she feels that she "became a mother."[87]

CHAPTER EIGHT

OPEN HOUSE

The golden age shtetl was neither a town nor a village but a unique combination of the two. Urban and rural came together in the shtetl home—a unique locus of East European Jewish civilization, with Tevye the Milkman as the head of the household.

The imaginary Tevye in Sholem Aleichem's Anatevka is a unique character, a village philosopher, a man of nature comfortable with the local Slavs, an aficionado of introspections and confessions, a Rashi in the barn and a Rousseau in a yarmulke—and, most important, a Jew with a cow. The documents prove, however, that in the early nineteenth-century shtetl Tevye was not actually that one-of-a-kind. This comes as a surprise given that the shtetl, even understood as a small, very small town, was after all an urban space.

In the 1840s, at least four Jewish families in the shtetl of Brailov could compete with Sholem Aleichem's literary hero. Mendel Shtramband had an old white cow and Duvid Fuks had an old gray cow. Shlomo Skalt, a wealthier Jew, could boast of a mule and two stallions.[1] Like these Brailov

Jews, Duvid Nemerovsky, an innkeeper from Zhornitsa, had four cows and two calves.[2] Also, Mendel Blekher, an innkeeper from the shtetl of Pikov, owned a valuable cow worth ten rubles.[3]

These men were ordinary shtetl Jews. A Ukrainian historian shrewdly observed that Ukrainian towns resembled villages, with the townsfolk farming within the urban area and pigs walking freely in the streets.[4] Take, for example, Yuzvin, a shtetl near Vinnitsa. Each of the fifty-six Yuzvin Jewish families owned cows and goats: Tsapi Livshits had a farrow cow worth four rubles; Itsko Shapenzon had a better cow worth six. Moshko Haimovich had a cow of unknown quality, and also two goats worth 0.75 rubles each. Motel Sukonny had a cow worth six rubles and two goats worth 1.50 rubles each. Aizik Meir Nus, Itsko Beidor, and many other Jewish families in town had either a cow or a goat or both, as well as some cows of different colors, in good shape and as expensive as seven rubles per head.[5] Goats were easily affordable: one could be had for just three buckets of vodka, whereas a cow cost as much as a good fur coat.

Unlike bigger towns and cities, the shtetl was a unique realm without separation between the natural rural life cycle and the economic schedule of urban civilization. Many shtetl Jews, engaged in the most urbanized of businesses, still depended on domestic animals. Cows and goats provided milk, cream, butter, and cheese for the entire family and also for sale. In the Belorussian shtetls, for example Krasnopolie, 524 Jewish families had among them 256 cows, 70 horses, and 29 goats.[6] Jews were already involved in peasant occupations long before the Russian regime wanted to move them to rural land and turn them into agricultural colonists.

Shtetl dwellers kept cattle and hired sheperds, who were in most cases Jews. One of them, Motia Dardik from Belaia Tserkov, was both a salesman in the store of Ios Glushchanski and a shepherd supervising cattle in the fields of Countess Branicka.[7] Seeking to tax anything they could, Russian authorities in many localities imposed a special annual tax on Jewish animals: for a horse, a cow, or an ox, 0.2 rubles, for a goat, 0.05 rubles per head.[8] When taking inventory of the shtetl Jews of Olshan, unable to pay back their communal debt, a Russian clerk wrote that these Jews "[are] so poor that they have no cattle in their possession"—yet another proof that the norm for Jews in the shtetl was to keep cows.[9]

8.1. A shtetl house with dens and stores.
Binyamin Lukin's private collection. Courtesy of Binyamin Lukin.

In Mezhirov, the entire Jewish community protested against Severin Orłowski, the Polish town-owner, who imposed an additional one-ruble tax on Jews bringing their cows to his pasture. Better to resettle than pay an exorbitant tax, thought many. Perhaps this was one of the reasons for the subsequent decline of Mezhirov: only thirty out of 480 families remained. The rest moved their cattle and belongings to settlements with cheaper or free pastures.[10] If Jews were not allowed to be both urban and rural simultaneously, the shtetl lost its uniqueness and was abandoned.

Many shtetl Jews lived under the same roof with their cows and goats, like members of the extended family. The she-goat in the Jewish hut became omnipresent for Isaac Bashevis Singer or Shmuel Yosef Agnon, as well as for Marc Chagall. Even a strictly "kosher" modern book of papercuts teaching its readers that everybody in the shtetl was an Orthodox God-fearing Jew includes not only a Jew in a black yarmulke but also a hen, a cow, and a horse—a dream of a lost civilization that retained its contact with the rural environment.[11]

The shtetl brought together the urban ethos of a market town and the rural ambiance of a farming settlement. Shtetl Jews bought and sold, repaired watches, roofed houses with shingles—but they also milked their cows, shod horses, pastured their goats, and curdled their cheese. This unique blend of activities could not withstand the impact of urbanization. The brick era changed the architectural style of the shtetl, and the influx of Jews resettled from villages caused overcrowding and rendered cattle breeding in town impossible. Jewish Tevyes were banished by the regime from smaller shtetls. Before these changes occurred later in the nineteenth century, however, the shtetl house united under one roof the symbiotic peasant hut and an urban construction.

BETWEEN URBAN AND RURAL

The Jewish dwelling in the shtetl was architecturally unique. It included some features of a peasant hut and an urban house, yet differed from both.[12] Wealthy Jewish dwellings of course more resembled a big urban house, while poor ones looked more like small village huts. However, shared economic life and traditional ethics mattered more than any difference in size. We can immediately identify a shtetl house, rich or poor, as Jewish because of its shape.

The finest houses in Nemirov, Berdichev, Ostrog, or Uman belonged to the Jewish mercantile elite. Let's take a look at the mansion of the Goldembergs. They were not the richest Jews in Kamenets-Podolsk but their dwelling was representative, resembling the houses of Pinkas Gorvits or Leib Fiterman, also local merchants. Although all three families lived in a town, not in a shtetl, we may consider these for the sake of comparison, keeping in mind that in the shtetl one could successfully affirm one's visibility, wealth, and power even with a less pompous edifice.

The Goldembergs lived in a large, two-and-a-half floor house with fourteen iron-roofed small trading stores attached to its façade. A heavy iron-coated door with a massive lock protected each of the stores. Each store had its own wooden cellar to keep produce and dry goods. Inside the house, a corridor on the ground floor led to two living rooms, each with a window and a wood-burning stove for heat. Both rooms were regularly leased out to incoming merchants. The corridor ended at a room for servants (*liudskaia*), with one window, one large cooking stove, and a separate exit to the street. Everything was made to facilitate trade, and the servants attended to those trading in the ground-floor stores. Wooden stairs led to the second floor, where the owners resided.

That part of the house had no fewer than ten rooms, eleven doors, seventeen windows, and seven Dutch-type wood-burning stoves. One room had a door that opened onto an iron balcony overlooking a major trading street. A set of stairs led from the corridor to the attic with its three rooms, five windows, and four doors. There, under the roof, the Goldembergs established yet another servants' room with a cooking stove. Back on the ground floor, the stone steps at the back of the house led down to the basements. Then, with the *kest* in mind, the Goldembergs attached to their main building a three-story stone wing, with five rooms and three wood-burning stoves. Both the wing and the house were covered by an iron roof with four brick chimneys—quite an impressive building, with little room for cows and goats, yet retaining the indelible scent of a grocery store facing the marketplace.[13]

Compare the house of this Kamenets merchant to the dwelling of Israel Fridman, a second-guild merchant from the shtetl of Ruzhin—the famous Ruzhiner Rebbe before he escaped from Russia and established his pompous court in Sadigora, near the Austrian city of Czernowitz. His mansion in Ruzhin, in which he lived for about thirty years, had more than ten rooms, nineteen doors with fine handles and elaborate locks, seven stoves, eleven windows, several Lombard tables, finished dressers, and varnished beds.[14]

There were unusual people even among the unusual guild merchants: producers of liquor and monopolists of excise tax. Let's enter a house belonging to Yankel Hirsh Lokerman from Kamenets, representative of its kind as a multipurpose dwelling which served as a residence, a brewery, a wholesale liquor store, and a warehouse. It was spacious, boasting seven rooms, fourteen doors, and seventeen windows, but the most important part was the brewery wing, consisting of four stoves for heating and five heavy copper cauldrons for distilling vodka. The cauldrons were firmly fixed over the four stone stoves. Big wooden pipes connected the cauldrons to curved metal hoops from which alcohol seeped into buckets. In addition, Lokerman had in his possession about twelve distilling mechanisms, also kept in this wing of the house. This was the main part of

Lokerman's building, yet curiosity takes us downstairs into the cellar, an innkeeper's and brewer's Holy of Holies.

Two heavy wooden doors with two massive iron locks protected the basement, the depository for Lokerman's most valuable stock. When unlocked with a heavy, foot-long key, the uneven stone steps led down into the cellar, cold and uninviting. There, an enormous array of liquor containers was lined up: ten huge wooden barrels holding two hundred buckets each, thirty-seven smaller barrels for thirty-six buckets, and twenty smaller barrels for twenty-three buckets each. Next to the barrels, right on the cold stone floor, stood bottles and glass utensils of various sizes.

In addition to the barrels there was also bottled vodka, about two hundred buckets. There were various sugar vodkas, some fruit vodkas, and Cossack vodka. Lokerman also stored about 2,560 pounds of sugar and other raw materials, which he needed to manufacture the beverages. All in all, Lokerman had in his cellar about two thousand buckets (24,000 liters) of liquor, brandy, and vodka ready to go. His brewery brought him more than several thousand silver rubles' raw income annually. One could purchase up to a dozen houses in the shtetl with this sum of money.

Several merchants left descriptions of their real estate, others of their movable property. One of them, Marcus Steltser from Brody, arrived in Russia to trade, and married a woman named Libe Brodziner. Before being accused of smuggling, he stayed temporarily with his wife in Kremenets. Marcus and Libe used silver cutlery—tablespoons and teaspoons, knives and forks, and large silver and several small goblets for holidays and Shabbat ritual libations. When traveling, they drank wine or brandy from fine silver flasks. They owned two large silver candelabra and a silver pocket watch. In the kitchen they had copper utensils: wash basins, mugs, a samovar, a small hand mill, a mortar for spices, and copper frying-pans. Most likely the twenty-four feet of silk fabric, twenty-six cotton shirts, nine cotton vests, twelve cotton handkerchiefs, twelve cotton nightcaps, and fifteen silk collars, as well as 560 large-size pearls and 1,039 small-size pearls, they planned to sell retail.[15]

Smugglers could successfully compete with the financial elites, though caution led them to keep a low profile and appear less urban. Take Ios Volferzon, a contrabandist, who lived in a house worth 200 rubles in the remote shtetl of Slobodkovets in Podolia. His house seemed modest indeed, with only four rooms, a separate kitchen, and a stone cellar. He had a straw roof, not a shingled one, which shows he was parsimonious: even the kahal would not have known that he had extra funds to invest in his home if he had wanted to.

His house looked like a village dwelling from the outside, but inside Volferzon was a genuine urban dweller. He had plastered ceilings and wooden floors, and also nice furniture: a canapé, several wooden chairs, one wooden table, an imposing wardrobe with glass doors, and a small polished redwood table. Before leaving his house, he could look into an elegant round mirror with a one-candle candelabrum. Mirrors of this kind became so popular that, according to Hasidic stories, Rabbi Israel Fridman himself purchased two large ones for his house in Ruzhin—and was reported to have said that in these mirrors one could see one's inner self.[16]

Volferzon does not seem to have been interested in books, but he had a taste for the lavish: four landscape paintings under glass in black wooden frames adorned his walls.[17] These pictures were not unusual: surviving evidence suggests that shtetl Jews enjoyed the visual arts. Iosif Zaslavsky from the shtetl of Smela in Cherkas district brought from abroad ninety-nine micrographic etchings, verses from the book of Exodus making the image of Moses, which he was planning to retail to his brethren.[18] Portraits were rare in the Jewish home, but ethnographers tell us that a paper cut *mizrakh* containing traditional Jewish symbols was common—as we shall see in the next chapter. They were brightly colored, accurately framed, and placed on the eastern wall of a room.[19]

Livshits from Lipets was an ordinary shtetl dweller, neither a guild merchant nor a smuggler, but his occupation as a manufacturer helped him build a decent home. He slept on regular pillows with cotton pillowcases and fine percale sheets over new mattresses. In the corridor, he had an expensive framed mirror worth 2.5 rubles—the price of two goats! He stored sixteen pounds of candles and forty-five feet of textile in his closet for sale. In his cellar, he had half a dozen barrels of pickled cucumbers, beets, and cabbage for the family's consumption during winter. In his courtyard he kept six wagons' worth of straw and four wagons' worth of wood. He was a shtetl middleman trading with peasants, he was much more urban than his Slavic partners: he had at least three relatively expensive Hebrew books.[20]

Unlike the houses of the Jewish mercantile elite, those of regular shtetl dwellers were smaller, albeit larger in overall size than the houses of local Christians. The Ukrainian peasants or townsfolk lived on the outskirts in straw-roofed huts with a small roofed porch, small windows, a large corridor where a trunk usually stood, and one or two rooms, often without flooring or ceiling plaster. They used their only stove for cooking, heating, and sleeping, and had a large wooden table and solid benches on which they ate, sat, and slept. They stored utensils, food, and cattle in a number of small freestanding sheds in back of the hut.

Like peasants, ordinary Jews also dwelled in huts, *mazanki* with stone foundations, clay and straw walls, and a small orchard in the back of the house, with animals roaming freely through the streets. Unlike peasants' huts, however, Jewish homes did not have a small garden in front but galleries and stores attached to the façade and lined along the central streets, attracting those walking and driving by. The front room on the ground floor of a Jewish house served as a drive-through inn, store, or artisan's shop. *Di Yiddishe gas*—the Jewish street—was a drive-through trading store, an inn and an artisan shop turned inside out toward the customer. Shtetl architecture adapted itself to the multifunctional purposes of the townsfolk.[21]

Precisely these occupations shaped the appearance of the Jewish home: Jews not only lived in their dwellings but also stocked produce for immediate retail, hosted travelers, welcomed customers, sold groceries and liquor, cooked and baked goods, leased out space to incoming merchants, brewed beer and mead, mended clothes, and produced woodwork—and retailed everything they produced or stored. In addition, some Jewish dwellings also served as prayer houses. Moving through Medzhibozh, Russian cartographers noticed that "Jews were allowed to worship and perform their rituals in private at home."[22]

Ultimately, Jewish houses were bigger and capable of accommodating more people than Christian houses in the shtetl: in Berdichev, for example, 85 percent of the Jewish population owned 73 percent of the Jewish-owned houses.[23] This does not mean that Jewish houses were overcrowded, makeshift, or unadorned. Historical evidence suggests that Jews loved bright colors and painted their synagogues.[24] They also adorned their porches and façades with wooden decorations and painted their houses as a means to attract customers. Thus Ben Zion Dinur, the Ukraine-born Jewish historian, recalled his first childhood memory: the *blue* roof and *orange* walls of his father's house![25]

While the upper part of the Jewish house looked like an urban store, the lower part concealed its rural features. Like a peasant hut in a village, many Jewish houses had stone cellars—a kind of a year-round refrigerator in which to preserve grain, groats, potatoes and cabbage, sour cream and butter, salted meat and wine. In Zhvanets, Gersh Shimfer lived in a shingled one-story house with three rooms and an impressively cold cellar. In Gusiatin, Abrasha Latsuter's typical one-story straw-roofed house was also made of stone, with foor rooms, two pantries, eleven windows, one stone cellar, and stalls, which Latsuter apparently leased from the town-owner.[26]

The somewhat larger stone shingled house of Iankel Zamo, also in Gusiatin, had five rooms, a separate kitchen and pantry, and a double cellar with ample storage space. Like many other Jews either trading from or manufacturing inside their houses, Zamo used his home as a candle factory, producing from 400 to 500 puds of candles a year—about 15,000 pounds—yielding a stable income.[27] Moshko Syrkis's house in Satanov had a built-in straw-covered pantry and five rooms with the same dual function of an urban store and a peasant storage. The house had three stone basements and one stone store built as a wing in front. These wings and stores were unique among other huts of similar size but the basements made the house similar to peasant dwellings.

Economy shaped the configuration of the Jewish house as much as it shaped the family. Shargorod is today one of the very few Podolian shtetls with well-preserved golden age architecture. Most if not all the houses on its central market street were owned by Jews. These houses had an elevated porch, a hallway serving as a storeroom, three or four adjoining rooms inside, at least two large windows looking onto the street, and a small garden behind the house. Like houses elsewhere, they were equipped with two big stoves and solid stone basements. Unlike the tiny windows of a peasant hut, the windows of the Shargorod Jewish homes were large, with a long, solid windowsill. By opening the window, the owner of the house transformed the hallway into a store and his own family into vendors: the windowsill became a counter and the people on the other side of the window, customers. Almost every surviving house has thick wooden shutters covering the entrance into the basements, and several houses had one indoor space with a removable roof, serving Jews as a *sukkah* during the autumn holiday of Sukkot.

What about the poorest Jews? If not significally better off than the poor Christians, they were at least different. The small dwellings of Meilakh Zutel and of the widow Reiza Heilovicheva, both from the shtetl of Felshtin, were quite shabby, plastered inside, with a straw roof. The size of Meilakh's hut was unimpressive: seven feet wide by twenty-four feet long, and ten feet high. It had one room to the left of the entrance, with a wooden ceiling and floor, four windows, and two stoves. To the left of the entrance room Meilakh had another small room, with a dirt floor, two windows, a broken stove, and a closet with a wooden ceiling.[28] One could hardly trade from such a house, let alone accommodate traveling merchants. Nor were their houses in the proximity of a marketplace, or they would have swelled with attached wings, stalls, stores, and dens.

Jews lived better than most Christian townsfolk only in absolute numbers, but not proportionately. Take Uman around the mid-1820s. Who lived in town at that time? The records show 528 male and 529 female peasants, 8,544 male and 9,019 female Jews, 648 male and 700 female Christian townsfolk, and 81 male and 90 female members of gentry. Among those 20,139 inhabitants, Jews constituted 87 percent. The entire shtetl population dwelled in houses classified in the inventories as good, satisfactory, or unsatisfactory. Jews had many more good and satisfactory houses than anybody else: a *hundred* good houses versus twenty, ten, and forty-five houses of the gentry, Christian townsfolk, and peasants, respectively. Jews also had many more satisfactory houses—*three hundred*, compared to 50 of the gentry, 25 Christian and 70 peasant houses of the same quality. At the same time, there were 220 Jewish houses in unsatisfactory condition, whereas the gentry had 25 in similar condition, Eastern Orthodox urban dwellers, 11, and peasants, 75. Thus, Jews had more good houses than the Christians, many more satisfactory houses than the Christians, and almost as many poor huts as the poor Eastern Orthodox peasants.[29]

While middle-class Jews lived under more urbanized conditions than middle-class Christians, poor Jews were as poor as the poor Christian peasants in the shtetl. Jews had proportionately more houses in unsatisfactory condition, 220, more than 50 percent of total Jewish housing, whereas among the Christians not more than one-third of all houses were in unsatisfactory condition. Yet Jews also differed from peasants, of whom 65 percent lived in unsatisfactory houses. Nurtured in the democratic tradition, East European writers concentrated on this third, poorest Jewish group, reminiscent of the destitute peasants, to argue against the xenophobic claims that Jews earned their livelihood by exploiting the local Christian population. In fact, more Jews lived decently than did Christians, whereas the Jewish poor constituted a larger part among Jewish townsfolk than poor Christians among Christian residents.

A shabby dwelling was the most characteristic living situation of at least one-third of all shtetl Jews, but it did not mean that Jews actually lived like peasants. While the peasants preferred household items that were longlasting, the Jews liked theirs to be nice-looking. Very much unlike peasants, Jews dreamed of a good piece of furniture that would make their house seem urban. They would milk a goat in the wing of the house that served as a barn but would sit on a chair, not a bench, at the dinner table. Furthermore, in a Jewish house the number of doors exceeded the number of doors in a peasant hut of similar size: Jews sought to create privacy, whereas peasants often left their doorways open, covering them with just a curtain or with no door whatsoever. Elkunovich from Zhornitsa with his cows and goats had an expensive varnished chest worth 40 rubles and ten polished chairs, about 250 rubles' worth—not something peasants with their rustic wooden benches would find practical.[30]

Even the poorest Jewish homeowners lived with an urban ethos and went to all lengths to pass for townsfolk, even though their deep poverty, their houses resembling huts, and their cattle made them unquestionably rural. Jews slept in beds rather than on benches, closed the door behind

8.2. Interior of a Jewish house in Skvira.
CAHJP, P166, D11, no. 014. Courtesy of the Central Archives for the History of the Jewish People.

them, sometimes very loudly, to remind everybody about their right to privacy, and created in their tiny environment enough room to separate the sexes, whereas peasants were quite cynical about sexual differences, had mixed views about privacy, and slept several generations together in one room or on the stove.[31] Pavlo Chubynskyi, an often biased contemporary ethnographer, noticed that the interiors of Jewish homes differed from the corresponding interiors of Russians and Ukrainians: they were more comfortable.[32]

With a goat in the backyard, Jews indoors utilized items that underscored their urban cultural loyalties. In Brailov, Borukh Borinshtein lived in a poor house, yet he still had lamps in wooden frames, a varnished bed, and a silver watch. Another Brailov dweller, Fridel Lander, preferred a new varnished bed to a stove, a canapé, and a closet with drawers to a trousseau. Volko Medzhibozhsky owned two canapés, four copper candlesticks, and a writing desk with four drawers and locks. He also had two canapés and four tables. Abram Berenshtein had red copper basins, jars and trays of red copper, a samovar, twelve chairs, a simple multicolored sofa, and a closet with a glass top.

The house of Shmuel-Itshak Chemerinsky from the Belorussian shtetl of Motele was characteristic of shtetl interiors. He owned varnished furniture, a round table and chairs.[33] Unlike Chemerinsky, however, who became a wealthy lumber merchant, the dwellers of Brailov had their urban furniture along with their cows and goats auctioned off—since they could not pay their debts to a local Jewish nouveau riche, a not very pleasant leaseholder. Yet even in their poverty and their rural-looking huts they strove to pass for urban dwellers.[34]

This unlikely utopian synthesis of rural and urban in a Jewish dwelling would soon come to naught. The shtetls that accepted the resettled rural Jews had to let go of their orchards and cowsheds. Smaller shtetls turned into villages, and with houses no longer built to serve as stores, trade moved elsewhere. For Polish gentry, too, economic downfall became imminent. Half a century later, this unique shtetl architecture was gone and its civilization was lost. Paradoxically, not only the regime but also the Jews took a most active part in this transformation.

HOME IMPROVEMENT

Seeking out the urban, Jews chose to invest money in their real estate. Not always capable of building new houses and never capable of owning land, Jews had to make do with home improvements. Their efforts resulted in an appended maze of useful wings and annexes, architectural details that singled Jewish dwellings out among those of the surrounding Slavs, peasants, and townsfolk.

A Jewish dwelling had the same basic plan as a Christian one, yet Jews expanded it outward and upward, with attics, corridors, cellars, dens, hangars, wings, stores, stalls, stairs, and galleries. Stefan Taranushchenko, a renowned Ukrainian ethnographer, noticed at the turn of the nineteenth century that peasant huts had neither all those galleries nor the added attics of Jewish huts.[35] Almost every Jewish homeowner in the shtetl sought to make good use of whatever property was available—and built additional rooms in order to lease them out. Take, for example, the house of one Belorusets from Radomyshl. It was about 30 square fathoms (*sazhen'*, or more than 6 feet), 2 in width, and 15 in length, that is, about 1,000 square feet. His full lot was, however, 11 by 15 fathoms, or about 6,000 square feet, which he used to expand his dwelling. He supported his late eighteenth-century basic house model with attached porches, stores, small stalls, cellars with separate entrances, and granaries.[36]

Requests to the urban authorities prove that shtetl Jews sought to upgrade their dwellings and to abide by the new state housing regulations. These regulations were part of the cautious reforms of Nicholas I, a great fan of uniforms and uniformity. Nicholas ordered that the towns in the Pale be brought to a homogeneous urbanized appearance in the same manner in which he ordered that the Jews in the Pale wear either German or Russian dress. While the success of the latter was dubious, the former measure had better results, above all because of the vested interests of the local administration.[37]

The local administration grew uneasy with the hybrid character of the rural-looking towns, which had grown up around a Polish magnate's manorial estate, and began seriously reconsidering their outlook. Formerly the possession of Polish landlords, the shtetls now had to fit into the new requirements of imperial town planning and bear the imprint of Russian architecture. Designed in St. Petersburg, the blueprints of the buildings, private and state, reached the municipal authorities in the Pale and did not remain on paper. When in 1833 Nahman Rechister from Bratslav wanted to build a new house, the town commission had to approve a design for his new façade and demanded that he abide by the prescribed building measurements. Three other local Jews had to do the same in order to have their houses built or rebuilt, and the police enforced the decision.[38]

The regime introduced the new position of land surveyor, responsible for supervising the renovations of the town's housing development. Nobody could add a shed or a pantry at whim; the magistrate now had to approve every home alteration. The old shabby houses that looked like huts had to go, and the government committed itself to compensating for the losses. Most shtetl dwellers followed orders, but some did not. In the middle of renovating his house, Leiba Rapoport, a wealthy dweller of the shtetl of Bar, lost his business, could not come up with the money for shingles, and decided to cover his house with straw, as in the good old days. Since his house was situated in the fancy neighborhood of St. Nicholas Church and all the other nearby houses had either shingles or tile roofs,

Policeman Iaroslavtsev demanded that Leiba remove his new straw from the house. "I will have you fired!" replied Rapoport. Instead, Iaroslavtsev had Rapoport put under arrest for three days and made him comply with the law: no straw on the roof.[39]

Despite the additional expense, Jews inundated local authorities with petitions for home improvements, which exceeded the requests of the Christian townsfolk. Skvira serves as a good example. The shtetl experienced such a real estate construction boom early in the 1800s that it caught the municipal authorities by surprise: they rushed to place a special request for a land surveyor, who then drew maps and marked the borders of the town districts.[40] Subsequently, the Skvira Jews invested in renovations. Avrum Muliarski decided to enlarge his house, while Ios Sirota needed to repair the roof, and two other Jews petitioned to establish a new house in place of one that had burned down. Ios Gamarnik requested that the municipal authorities allocate a piece of land for his brand-new dwelling. Gershko Iamplosky planned to rebuild his very old house on the same lot, yet with a newly approved façade and with a wing and stalls.[41]

Seeking to urbanize their shtetl, the Jewish economic elite pioneered such renovations. Skvira guild merchant Moshko Koretsky needed stalls in order to sell goods from home, while Leib Lozovski, another local guild merchant, decided to establish a beer brewery. What they devised was a far cry from Lokerman's mansion in Kamenets, but they certainly dreamt of something as ambitious. Following their requests, the Skvira land surveyor provided them with a drawing of the new façade and endorsed the renovations.[42] Other Jews from the same town followed suit, and women participated on a par with men. Lea Kremenarova built a granary near her house and Perl Khotonicheva built a shed with a storage space for food, while the widow Oksman had a more substantial renovation in mind and requested that the land surveyor measure the entire house and nearby installations.[43]

More urban meant more imperial, and thus home improvement could trigger the envy of those who could not afford it. The family of guild merchant Sakhnovsky from Brusilov spent about 500 silver rubles rebuilding their shabby old house into a beautiful post office for mailmen, government clerks, and court messengers. The envious local forest supervisors decided (but failed) to confiscate the house and establish it as their own office. The Sakhnovskys appealed to court and had to pay a price for their good intention to urbanize their living situation.[44]

In another case, one Skvirsky was planning to build a new house, and angered one Ilnitsky, the Tarashcha clerk, who complained, "Why doesn't Skvirsky participate in the bidding? Why is everything done under the table?" The magistrate official answered calmly that Skvirsky had lost his house during a devastating fire in Tarashcha. According to the town reconstruction plan, "he could not rebuild his house on its previous location," and hence was allotted a new one, for which he paid the treasury several thousand rubles, while Ilnitsky did not want to pay more—and should therefore mind his own business.[45] Russian bureaucratic red tape could not stop the Jews. They went to all lengths to make their houses look more urban—and their shtetl more civilized.

URBAN DEVELOPMENT

The attempt to shake off all traces of the rural shows that the shtetl suffered from an inferiority complex. Its urban infrastructure was far from well developed, and like everybody else, Jews did not like this situation, yet unlike many others, Jews initiated shtetl renovation. They knew that a better shtetl would increase trade, and better trade brought more money. Financial success turned an ordinary shtetl dweller into a respectable guild merchant, and this new social status allowed people to expand trade and manufacturing further and integrate with the town elites. Ultimately, investing in the shtetl infrastructure enhanced one's own economic if not social mobility.

The lucky owners of houses at the shtetl marketplace initiated this process. The guild merchant Srul Shapiro from Skvira, for example, acquired a house on the marketplace, then used his revenues to establish a brick plant, and finally offered to build a *labaz*, roofed trading stalls in the marketplace. Once he was granted permission, the local authorities commissioned him to collect taxes from the Jewish butchers and bakers, as well as to control the marketplace weights and measures, which alone yielded about 2,000 rubles of the town's annual income.[46]

As unchallenged merchants, Jews were often singlehandedly responsible for shtetl urbanization. There were prodigiously wealthy, city-based Jews, such as first-guild merchant Fiterman and second-guild merchant Shapira from Kamenets-Podolsk, who contributed 7,000 silver rubles to the construction of a tile-covered brick house serving a Jewish hospital for eighty people.[47] The shtetl also had its Jewish enthusiasts, who established hospitals, erected trading stalls, renovated the roads, and built new stores or schools.

Take, for example, the guild merchant Mordekhai Polkovsky, who proposed constructing a building for the state Jewish school to the Vasilkov town authorities.[48] Another good example is Khaim Borispolsky, from the same Vasilkov, who decided to rebuild a shabby bakery out of his own pocket, and who convinced the town authorities to let him do so by offering to repair the nearby stalls and continuing contributing to other causes.[49] A well-to-do Jew made improvements to his house in Makhnovka, near Berdichev, and suggested using it as the town general hospital, while another Jew from Balta proposed building a new pharmacy in town.[50] Guild merchant Shtakman from Makhnovka offered his renovated house for lease as state offices—for the town clerks, court, and police.[51] Reitershternova, a wealthy Jewish woman from Balta, offered her house to serve as the military hospital.[52] Srul Vaiman from Litin committed himself to fixing all the roads and dams in town. He promised to fill all pits and diches, establish special roadside canals for water, and cover a dangerous slope leading from the marketplace with crushed stone.[53]

These initiatives were not always and not necessarily Jewish, yet Jews became the foremost contributors, as the example of the Balta case demonstrates. The town had almost no manufacturing and heavily depended on the income from local fairs, particularly on the money that incoming merchants paid to the Balta dwellers for leasing their premises as stores. The authorities sought to invest in the town's greatest asset, the main street of the town, which served as an extended marketplace, yielding 2,200 silver rubles' worth of town income annually. The town officials decided to split the fair and move the fancier part to the left bank of the river, yet embellish the right bank part by building new stalls, a circus arena, three inns, trade booths, and even one theater booth. The town officials established a committee and invited local merchants to participate in the bidding for the contract.

Initially, the Jews were skeptical. Had they done what the authorities wanted, the best part of the market would have been moved to the other part of town, and the Balta Jews would not have been able to lease out their premises. Several dozen Jewish and a number of Christian merchants joined together to convince the authorities not to move the fair.

Enter the Jewish nouveau riche, Abram Chechelnitsky and Nison Kogan, supporters of moving the fair to the left bank. They loved the idea and promised to build sixty trading stalls on the left bank for haberdashery and other expensive goods. Fearing financial losses, the Jewish merchants of the right bank now committed to building some forty new trading stalls there along the main street. They also promised an additional 200 silver rubles to the state treasury should the main part of the market remain on the right bank. While it took the governor general time and effort to make a final decision, the town then greatly benefited from the two competing merchants' groups, eager to invest in Balta's urban development.[54]

Things did not always go as smoothly as the Jewish investors wanted. Responsible to nobody, the corrupt bureaucrats thought of themselves as landlords, interested first and foremost in their own profit, and created obstacles to block the good intentions of the Jews. The Jews then found themselves forced to grease the palms of those officials who would have benefited directly from the investments.

The sad case of wealthy Kamenets second-guild merchant Feibush Blank stands for many. Allowed to build eighteen wooden stores for butchers in the marketplace, he found himself involved in a conflict between various groups of local butchers and town representatives, and ended up losing some 2,000 rubles on construction disrupted by communal intrigues.[55] Still, his story sheds light on the differences between Kamenets and the shtetls, where the authorities were routinely short of funds, and hence much more eager to accept Jewish investments. If they did, the shtetl became more urban, and if they did not, it turned back into a village, in either case losing its charming, almost utopian combination of urban and rural.

REAL FIGHTS FOR REAL ESTATE

Deprived of other types of property, Jews valued their houses as the only property that was real to them. This property went on the market quite often. In Litin in the early 1820s, Christians occasionally sold their houses to Christians, as Vassili Oleinik did with his wooden hut, an orchard, and a garden, which he sold to Captain Belsky for 50 silver rubles. More often, however, Christians sold to Jews, as the widow Agafia Sorochinskaia did with her house near the main road, which went for 40 rubles to Leiba Brodetsky.[56]

In most cases, however, Jews traded their real estate with other Jews, seeking property in places advantageous for trade. Location was very important, if not most important: Zelik and Itsko Linger sold their house to Hune Reikher for a handsome 130 silver rubles. The house faced the marketplace, stood between two other large Jewish homes, was equipped with stalls, basements, and sheds, and exceeded 65 feet in length and 46 feet in width, a superb dwelling for the extended family of a guild merchant. In another case the three Moshkovich brothers sold their family house in Yanov, which was across from the mansion of the count, the town-owner, to two Davydovich brothers. The documents do not indicate a price, although it must have been steep, given that they paid 500 rubles in sales tax. No less valuable were the stores in the marketplace. Yankel Vilner sold his to Iska Bronshtein and his wife for 126 silver rubles, and Arie Premyshlensky sold his store in Litin to his relative Kalman for 100 silver rubles.[57]

Since houses could also serve as stores, Jews fought for them with the genuine self-abnegation of urban dwellers, whose only possession was real estate. Take Duvid Slobodiansky's estate. When he passed away, one Haim Bialik considered himself entitled to Slobodiansky's house in Uman and aggressively took it over, claiming that Slobodiansky was his relative. When Slobodiansky's son appeared and claimed his rights to the property, Bialik refused to budge. While the two litigated in court, a certain Bergerova, another relative as close to the Slobodianskys as Bialik, declared herself the legitimate heir and claimed her right to the house. Allegations and counterallegations further complicated the matter. When the court finally arrived at a decision, Bialik, Slobodiansky the Younger, and Bergerova were already all deceased.[58]

As in the case of the Slobodiansky home, Brisa Shternberg's house constituted the lion's share of her assets. In 1831, Brisa's husband had purchased this house for 650 rubles. This was an extraordinary investment for the Shternbergs. To capitalize on their success, the Shternbergs resold part of their house to one Grutman. They made money this way, but their happiness came to an end. Suddenly, Brisa's husband, the head of the family, died. Grutman took advantage of this situation. He expanded his part of the house, put on a new roof, built a new stove, attached two sheds, and moved a wall separating his part of the house from Brisa's. The widow was ready to fight to the death for her house. Her private space, her dignity as the houseowner, and the memory of her late husband were all at stake. She sued Grutman and won the case. The court found her charges legitimate and valid, and Grutman was forced to come to terms with his strong-willed widowed neighbor.[59]

Real estate became a major point of contention and corrupted—or disrupted—family ties. Srul Mezhirovsky inherited his father's house in Vinnitsa, leased the house to his sister and her husband, and went to Bessarabia to make some money. Five years later he returned and discovered that his sister had died, while one Gershon Byk, an inhabitant of Vinnitsa, had taken over his house and reregistered it under his own name![60] Zisl, also from Vinnitsa, had a much more bitter experience. She was the mother of Aizik and Nuhim and the owner of a wooden two-story house with an attached store attractively situated in a new section of the town. Zisl could not understand why her artisan sons, both carpenters who showed little desire to go into trade, leased out the store, transformed the house into an artisan shop, stocked both floors of the house with tools and workbenches, refused to support their mother financially, and banished their two sisters. Unable to come to terms with her sons, Zisl had to resort to the Russian court, which ruled that the house be sold and the money evenly divided between all co-owners.[61]

The case of Leib and Duvid Sandler, two brothers who lived with their father in Belaia Tserkov, was similar. Like many other shtetl dwellers, they leased out part of the house with its granary and sheds for produce storage. This leased-out estate yieded 25 silver rubles' income per year. Then the elder Sandler died. Duvid banished Leib from the house and a fratricidal war ensued, ending up on the desk of a Russian judge, who ordered that the brothers sell the house and divide the income.[62] The unraveling of family ties was not the only price, however, that shtetl dwellers paid for becoming urbanized.

BILLETING THE TROOPS

Ordinary Jews had better and different housing than ordinary Christian shtetl dwellers. We know that thanks to an unexpected source of information, the Russian army.

Before army barracks dotted the western borderlands of Russia in the late 1870s, shtetl townsfolk had to fulfill a special obligation called quarter duty. After their summer training, the troops moved to nearby towns, where the local population had to house troops of all ranks during the winter months. The townsfolk also bore the burden of accommodating temporary military hospitals, munition and fodder supply, and regimental archives until the following spring. While the town elders assigned the quarters, town dwellers proved their loyalty by fulfilling this duty for free. While people of all creeds deeply disliked this duty, in the long run it proved to bring unforeseeable benefits, particularly for the Jews.

The Russian military administration repeatedly acknowledged the advantages of Jewish housing. For example, the headquarters of a sapper brigade were billeted by Avrum Epelboim, a guild merchant from Vasilkov. Epelboim housed the staff, the brigade archive, the furniture for the military engineering school, and some teaching materials. When he needed to do some renovations and asked the military temporarily to move out, the staff refused; they had no desire to move into any "dark and uncozy inn"; Epelboim's house was much better![63] In Uman, many state-owned buildings were in unsatisfactory condition and the military admitted that it still needed to rely on Jewish houses for quartering the troops and storing munitions.[64] If there were no Jews around, as for example in Kiev after the expulsion of the Jews in the 1830s, the army was at a loss since there were no appropriate quarters whatsoever and the army simply had no place to billet officers, let alone generals.[65]

8.3. Jewish houses, a midrank one and a poor one, in Zaslav.
IA, f. 9, spr. 44, ark. 71. Courtesy of the Institute of Archaeology of the National Academy of Sciences of Ukraine.

While the soldiers stayed with peasants in the villages or on the out-skirts of the shtetl, the regimental commanders, staff, and the noncom-batant troops preferred Jewish housing. The military officials could not find anything better. In Uman, the adjutants of General Major Kalma, commander of an infantry division, were looking for a "special house" for their chief but could only find one belonging to a Jewish widow named Gurovicheva. Since she had already fulfilled her obligation earlier that year, they paid her 150 rubles per month, a substantial sum for the mid-1820s.[66]

In Makarov, the colonel of the artillery stayed in the only decent house in town, belonging to Itsko Kondranski.[67] Likewise, Colonel Pestel, the commander of the Viatka infantry regiment, stayed in Lipovets in the house of Froim Girshberg. He would have preferred something more be-fitting an officer but could find nothing better, and the only non-Jewish house he inspected was much less convenient.[68] We very rarely find the military, especially high-ranking commanders, staying with Christians in the shtetls—unless the local Polish gentry decided to demonstrate their loyalty and allow the officers to occupy their premises.

This happened very rarely, since the Polish landlords perceived the Russians, especially the military, as occupying forces and declared their houses unavailable. Polish magnates maintained rather dry relations with the high-ranking Russian military authorities. The Poles in Volhynia hated the Russian troops, according to Russian secret police agents in the 1830s, probably not without some self-serving exaggeration.

Prince Sanguszko, the town-owner of Zaslav, closed the gates of his castle and refused to quarter cavalry brigade officers. Landlord Jabłonowski also did not let high-ranking officers of the uhlan regiment into his estate in Ostrog.[69] In a different case, two infantry regiments arrived in Uman in early 1820. The commanders soon realized that they did not have sufficient quarters to put up the troops. They turned for help to Count Potocki, the town-owner, asking him for permission to do some quick construction work and accommodate the troops. Potocki cut their advances short: this is a private town, he claimed, and there will be no state-owned buildings on its territory.[70]

The Polish szlachta did not welcome the military, whereas the Jews did, and for the troops this meant a lot. For example, in 1822 the Seventeenth Jäger Regiment moved to Vasilkov and Belaia Tserkov, and the Chernigov regiment was billeted in Fastov. One of the colonels stayed in the house of Ios Indikter, the regimental chancellery moved into the house of Duvid Rutgaiser, the regimental carpenter moved into the house of Ovsei Cherkassky, and the regimental locksmith moved into Mekhel Pruger's home. The military band was accommodated by Tsal Rapopport, and the drummers went to live with Menashe Grach, the painters with the Jewish widow Khurshanska, the division chancellery with Zavel Velints, and Aron Bederenkes made some room in his stables for the horses of the division commander.[71] In 1832 Prince Franciszek Radziwiłł, the owner of Berdichev, had to quarter the Arkhangelsk infantry regiment, and arranged for an inventory of the houses in his town. Reading through many favorable descriptions of Jewish housing, Radziwiłł came to the conclusion that Christians were useless, whereas Jews were useful for the military because of their residential pattern.[72]

If Jews had already fulfilled their duty but were asked to quarter troops again, the military compensated them. In some cases Jews had to fight with the bureaucracy to receive the payment, as happened to Shmiel Dolin from Skvira, whose house became a branch of the military hospital and a pharmacy and who never received the 123 rubles he was promised.[73] In most cases, however, Jews did receive compensation and quite often benefited financially from the quartered troops. The Jews of Vasilkov and Fastov received about 2,500 rubles in 1823 for quartering the Chernigov infantry regiment. Lev Rogov received 90 rubles for billeting the regimental commander. Shmul Zelmanovich received 221 rubles for providing lodging for the battalion chancellery and stalls for the battalion horses, and the innkeeper Iankel Morder received 110 rubles for keeping the eighteen horses of the commander. Nuhim Kagan was paid 348 rubles for battalion carpentery and Aizik Gabovich was paid 104 rubles for the battalion tannery. By the same token, Iasnogrodka shtetl dweller Shmul Kushnir leased his house to the military hospital and was paid 150 rubles annually.[74]

Some Jewish communities that were deeply in debt had their compensation transferred directly to the state treasury in lieu of their arrears instead of receiving cash for billeting the troops, as happened, for example, in the case of the Jews of Makarov, whose remuneration was transferred to the treasury by the military, where it was applied toward their 2,200-ruble communal debt.[75]

Although Jews were getting along with the billeted troops, they sometimes suffered monetarily, too. Grigorii Bogrov wrote a heartbreaking description of a group of Russian soldiers staying in a Jewish house, humiliating the Jews and destroying the household that had welcomed them: "Are you in occupied territory?" the narrator/houseowner asks himself.[76] Besides literary sources, the complaints of ordinary townsfolk reached both the Russian authorities and the town-owners. Uman town dwellers of different social status and faith complained of the inappropriate conduct of the billeted troops. In Skvira, the town council head, himself a Christian, reported significant damages to his house, while three Jewish townsfolk bemoaned the damage to their households, which officers had turned into stalls for their horses. Yos Poliak demanded that the authorities reimburse him for 460 pieces of shingle and wood from fences and furniture stolen by the soldiers.[77]

The damage to the Jewish house was a blow to the entire family. If the military did not recompense them, the offended Jews turned to the authorities. Billeted in a Volhynia shtetl, Cossacks of the twelfth cavalry regiment allegedly stole twenty horses from town-dweller Ben Iankeliovich, ruining his business.[78] Mendel Iampolskii from Boguslav had to accommodate the cavalrymen and their horses of the dragoon regiment: for this reason he could not lease out his rooms and sheds to incoming merchants; he also experienced heavy losses.[79] Uman-dweller Rosenberg filed a complaint with the governor protesting that the military had placed the eight horses of the regimental buglers in one of his houses.[80]

Iankel Livshits from Linits complained that the Belostok infantry regiment had first used part of his house to stock food, then the Hussar regiment had billeted a sergeant major and a scribe in his house, then another two officers had moved in with their four dailies and nine horses. The Livshits family first stayed in two back rooms but then could no longer reside in their own home and had to look for shelter elsewhere.[81] Despite such cases, in most instances the Jews and the troops arrived at common terms, and the state distributed social relief funds to compensate the losses.

The billeted troops protected the Jews just by virtue of themselves becoming shtetl dwellers, even for only a short time. Any rebellious group of outcasts coming to the shtetl with anti-Jewish violence in mind would break into a Jewish house—and more often than not find there a sojourning Russian officer or a group of senior soldiers. This would dissipate any anti-Jewish sentiments.

After almost a century of troops being quartered in the shtetls, the first pogroms under the Russian regime took place in the early 1880s, precisely when the army was becoming more professionalized, having obtained barracks in the late 1870s and moved from Jewish houses to their new, specially allocated premises. This brought respite to everybody in the shtetl, including the Jews, yet now the Jews had to pay dearly for the professionalization of the army, the urbanization of the shtetl, and the loss of their symbiotic relations with the natural and social environment. The incoming mob, drunk and violent and armed with axes and clubs, now found the stores and taverns and households unprotected and were free to engage in looting and destruction.

UNIQUENESS ERASED

Before the twentieth-century upheavals destroyed it forever, the Jewish house in the shtetl suffered from a misunderstanding. Russian travelers disliked it. Since they came from the imperial cities, they looked at the Jewish houses with condescending curiosity and the idiosyncratic phobias of a passerby, while also seeking citylike comforts that the shtetl house could not offer. Nor did East European ethnographers manage to capture the unique character of the shtetl house: they saw its multipurposefulness as bizarre and its symbiotic semirural character as vulgar. For a good many observers, the shtetl house was either a peasant hut yet without rural charm or a town house but without urban conveniences. They thought that the shtetl's sanitary conditions stemmed not from its semirural character but from its essentially dirty population, the Jews.

Outsiders saw nothing but dirt in the shtetl. It is "extremely difficult to move when it is raining, impossible to move along the streets, the pits are filled with refuse," Russian clerks wrote about Medzhibozh and Vinnitsa.[82] Because of "clay and black soil," in the fall and in spring Balta becomes so dirty that one "cannot drive, let alone walk through it" and its "five paved streets" do not make much difference, reported another clerk.[83] A Russian army officer observed "that Starokonstantinov is dirty beyond any measure: but if we bother ourselves to learn the reasons for this situation, we would perhaps find out that even the Jews, whom one usually blames, have nothing to do with it.... To drive through the streets of the town is a real challenge, as there is no pavement. Stones once paving the road have long sunk into the soil. When it is raining, they do nothing but prevent movement."[84] The shtetl roads were in bad shape, with potholes and puddles often trapping the wheels of the wagons, and the dirt, particularly in spring and fall, was unbearable. Seasonal puddles prevented outside observers from seeing the shtetl and its housing pattern as a unique model of civilization.

This model was, of course, transient. With the incoming Jews banished in mid-century from the rural areas, the shtetl became overcrowded. Diminishing trade in the second half of the century decreased the importance of the multifunctional houses. Old wings and dens became obsolete and shabby. Houses functioning as taverns lost their economic status as the Russians established the state-owned taverns, wineries, and stores and disrupted the centuries-old Jewish profession of liquor producuction and dealership. Traveling Polish noblemen and Russian governmental clerks disappeared completely from the shtetl horizon, and the state-owned (no longer leased) post offices invalidated the function of the shtetl Jewish house as a horse-changing and mail post.

New textile plants, shoe and ready-made clothing factories, and steel and other heavy industries made the Jewish home-based artisanal stores redundant. The proximity of the shtetl house to the market square and the roads leading to it remained an important factor, yet the shtetl house-cum-store could offer less and less, particularly as trade moved to districts near railway stations. If there was no station, the market went elsewhere, and the shtetl house was abandoned. In a sense, Russian industrialization cast an even more decisive blow on the old-fashioned Jewish economic— and in this case, architectural—legacy than all the political repressive measures put together. Russian officers did not need Jewish houses anymore, either. By the early twentieth century Russia had disowned the shtetl, which now turned into a clumsy town surrounded by beautiful landscapes and abundant pastures with which it had little in common.

Although born there, many East European Jewish literati misrepresented the shtetl. They sought to ease Jewish entry into European civilization, argued for Jewish acculturation (then called "assimilation," and understood positively), and mocked the shtetl with its backward Jews. The ugly dwellings, dire poverty, collapsed roofs, and dreadful smells should be got rid of for good, they argued. Radical Jewish writers went even further. They knew well why the Jewish house looked as strange as it did, yet they came to disdain everything anyway: what good was there in all those innkeepers, storeowners, and bourgeois bloodsuckers? The worse and the poorer the shtetl house appeared in their writings, the better they could justify their passionate drive toward a new socialist world.

8.4. Jewish houses in the shtetl of Ozarintsy.
IA, f. 9, spr. 40, ark. 6. Note the front columns and the straw on the roof. Courtesy of the Institute of Archaeology of the National Academy of Sciences of Ukraine.

Perhaps only the writer Mendele Moykher Sforim, with his unsurpassed love of Jewish everyday life, preserved the Jewish house for us as it was. "For the children," he noted with deep irony. In 1910 Mendele described a house next to the marketplace in the native shtetl of Kopyl. The house resembled an urban apartment and at the same time a peasant hut.

Mendele shows us its large living room with a den serving as stables for domestic animals during the winter cold. He lingers on its big heating stove and its cooking oven, at the bottom of which a hen sits on her eggs. He points out several tiny yet separate bedrooms for married couples and guests on the other side of the living room. He describes the Jews' furniture: a living room candelabrum, a red round table with a checkerboard, a decorative mirror in which no one could make himself out, and a paper cut *mizrakh* with exotic beasts on the eastern wall. Mendele turned out to be more perceptive than all the ethnographers put together: he shows us that the Jewish house was a kitchen, a bedroom, a synagogue, a tavern, a social hall, a rural barn, and an urban dwelling, all rolled into one.[85]

This house stood at the intersection of urban culture and rural nature and, as it never would in years hence, felt comfortable in both. In the shtetl's golden age, the shtetl house was the locus of its bucolic idyll—an idyll marked by squeaking doors, crying children, and bleating goats. Whatever the opinions of the aristocratic snobs and social critics, the Jews still managed to live in and make good use of their homes, which smelled of the old varnished wardrobe, baked potatoes, the hot copper samovar, chicken feathers, and cow manure. It was open to both urban commercial bustle and the rural pastoral. It may not have been very comfortable by our standards, but its dwellers called it *heymish*—homey.

CHAPTER NINE

IF I FORGET THEE

We last saw Moshko Telezhinetsky in his Shepetovka inn, when the police came to confiscate his herbs, enigmatic Hebrew note, vodka, and strange white powder. During the investigation, after which he was fully exonerated, Moshko explained that he had obtained the herbs from a local witch doctor named Matriona, who had convinced Moshko that herbal inhalations would cure his sick wife. Moshko claimed to have inherited the Hebrew note—a kabbalistic amulet—from his father, although he assured the police, perhaps tongue-in-cheek, that he did not really believe in magic powers. Moshko's vodka, as we already know, was deemed excellent by the Zhitomir lab, but what was that strange white powder?

It was a bit of earth from the land of Israel. Moshko told the police that the Jews poured some earth on the heads of the deceased as a memory of where the Jew belonged.[1] We do not know how and where he obtained it. His comments during the depositions suggest that for Jews in East Europe, a bit of the Holy Land sprinkled into the grave was a key moment in the burial procedure. While the burial symbolized a reunion with the God of Israel, the added earth signified a return to the land of Israel. The ritual manifested the popular belief that the deceased Jews of the shtetl would rest in peace next to their biblical forefathers in the redeeming earth of the land of Israel, even though they were buried in the black soil of Ukraine.

This belief was not unique to East European Jews.[2] Their Jewish brethren from Muslim countries were also well familiar with it. For example, Rabbi Yosef Haim, a major figure among Iraqi Jews, brought a sack of earth back from the land of Israel to his community.[3] In the Ashkenazic milieu, this ritual acquired magical underpinnings and became particularly widespread.

Hasidic masters did not invent the ritual but provided insightful explanations. Rabbi Pinhas of Korets, the father of the famous Jewish printers, claimed that the land of Israel preserved an unparalleled sense of unity— even the soil of the Holy Land was permeated with it.[4] Rabbi Nachman of Bratslav observed that people brought "white earth from the land of Israel," which looked "exactly like earth from our lands" yet had a "much higher level of sanctity."[5] The grandson of the founder of Hasidism, Rabbi Efraim of Sudilkov, argued that the land of Israel contained all the souls of the Jews and was the source of all their souls.[6] Rabbi Moshe Tsvi of Savran went even further by claiming that a righteous person who died in exile was brought after death to the land of Israel, while an evil person, even if buried in the land of Israel, was taken from there into the lands of exile.[7]

The soil of the Holy Land had magic powers for all those who listened to the sermons of the Hasidic masters or shared their views. A man once approached Rabbi Israel of Ruzhin and told him that he wanted to move to the land of Israel. "What is your reason?" asked the tsadik. "They say," said the man, "that worms in the land of Israel do not devour human bodies after death." Although the tsadik laughed at the man's gullibility, the reference "they say" implied that at least some Jews saw the earth from the Holy Land as a protective measure against posthumous physical punishment.[8]

Diaspora Jews envisioned the land of Israel as a symbol of their distant biblical past, a sign of unification between the chosen people and God, and a reminder of the curses of exile. The ritual of pouring Holy Land earth into the grave was so great that popular demand could not be satisfied. A place and a physical substance, the land was the dream of many affordable to only a few. Yet East European Jews sought to assure themselves that the distant and unattainable land was in intimate proximity, at least for the deceased.

Reiterated in the Judaic daily prayers, the mantra of a return to the Holy Land now became reality. Jews could not return to the land of their forefathers while alive, but perhaps they could after death. The Jews made the land, along with its major symbolic sites, the Temple and Jerusalem, immediately present in the everyday reality of the shtetl. Perhaps this attachment united most Jews long before the political commitment to Zionism—and religious or socialist opposition to it—split the golden age shtetl community. Jews rallied around this symbolic land, derived their joy from it, and attached to it their hopes.

FACING THE TEMPLE

Any shtetl Jew could reach the land of Israel, go up to Jerusalem, and enter the Temple of Solomon merely by walking to the shtetl marketplace, crossing it, and entering the Great Synagogue. The shtetl preachers called it *mikdash meat*, a small temple, yet even without this metaphor the Jews in any Jewish community knew whom they were facing when stepping into the synagogue.[9]

Across the entrance, supporting the Holy Ark on both sides, two wooden pillars symbolized the Yakhin and the Boaz, the columns guarding the entrance to the Holy of Holies in the Jerusalem Temple, which the Romans destroyed in 70 C.E. The curtain of the ark separated the sacred realm of the worshippers from the most sacred realm of the divine, while the latter housed the tablets in the Temple and the Torah scroll in the synagogue. The curtain embroidery elaborately wove together the Temple ritual items, including the tablets, the head cover of the high priest, and the twelve pieces of bread placed before the altar.[10] The Ashkenazi Jews took the word *tsits*—a golden plate with the inscription "Holy to the Lord," one of the key attributes of the high priest—and used it for the sparking shield placed on the synagogue Torah scroll.[11]

9.1. Holy Ark in a Ukrainian synagogue.
CAHJP, P166, G18. Courtesy of the Central Archives for the History of the Jewish People.

Jews used Jerusalem Temple imagery to ornament their synagogues. The image of a cow or an ox, often seen on Holy Ark curtains, stood for the prophet's statement "we will replace the bullocks [of the Temple offerings] with the offerings of our lips."[12] Since prayers replaced offerings, the *bimah*, on which the Torah scroll was placed, replaced the sacrificial altar. Just as offerings had brought people closer to God, the reading of the Torah scroll now brought God closer to the people.

Unlike the Jews of Central Europe, East European Jews crowned the four-pillar *bimah* of their synagogues with a formidable canopy representing the tabernacle, the place where God revealed his glory to Aaron and Moses. This glory now radiated from the Torah scroll, while the canopy symbolized a wedding between the divine text and the Jewish people. Perhaps these Temple-centered theological metaphors allowed Moshe of Kożienice to claim that Jewish worshippers should imagine themselves "as if standing in the Temple in Jerusalem."[13] In the same vein, Yaakov Yosef of Polonnoe argued that one could use the words of the Judaic liturgy and of the Torah as stones to build oneself into a Temple.[14]

East European Jews were particularly anxious to transform their synagogues into the Jerusalem Temple by borrowing its attributes. They displayed seven-branch candelabra in their synagogues, placed the lamp for the eternal light in the upper part of the ark, and erected a wooden decalogue above the ark precisely because these objects replicated the Temple's golden *menorah*, its "eternal light" placed on both sides of the Holy of Holies, and its Ten Commandments recited daily in the Temple.[15] Jews attached small bells to the Torah crown to remind themselves of the bells and the breastplate of the high priest serving before the Almighty. They inscribed on the cornice of the ark *da' lifnei mi ata 'omed*, "remember before whom you are standing."

This cue returned the worshipper back to the times of the Temple, when Jews believed that God dwelled in the Holy of Holies—and nowhere else.[16] Furthermore, a Jew setting foot on the synagogue threshold and reciting the traditional "and I in awe will come into Your house and bow down before your Holy Temple" imagined himself entering the Temple through the Golden Gates and bowing down in front of the abode of the Most High.[17] An art historian observed that all these visual signs and texts "correlated with the concept of the Torah Ark as God's throne, since the Torah ark in the synagogue is the substitute for the Ark of the Covenant."[18]

While this Temple-centered symbolism characterized many Diaspora synagogues, the Great Synagogues of the shtetls added unique emblems, ornaments, embroidery, and inscriptions. Some of these were drawn from popular mysticism. Think about a carved or sewn crown, one of the key Holy Ark adornments: it served as a *keter*, the emblem of the King of Universe, the first and the highest among the ten *sefirot*, or divine emanations. Placed in the synagogues above symbols of government such as the Russian double-headed eagle, the crown served as an excellent Jewish reply to the ongoing dispute with the dominant Christian ideology: although the Temple had been destroyed, the crown of Israel had not fallen.[19] The ambiguity of the crown as both a symbol of the Russian monarchy and a Judaic symbol gave this message a sense of loyalty. Jews emphasized that they were pro-Russian and placed the symbol of the monarchy high, but their Jewish God was even higher.

Symbols also helped popularize Hasidism. Once the Hasidic masters introduced a new formulaic recitation of the Divine Glory, which began with the word "crown," Hasidim in their prayer houses canonized this motif, seeking to visualize their liturgical innovations. The Holy Ark covers in Hasidic prayer houses now displayed citrons, palm fronds, and the myrtle and willow branches used on Sukkot, the harvest festival. These four species symbolized the four letters of the ineffable divine name. A Jew holding together all four species brought together in a mystical way the four letters of the name of God. He thus reenacted the moment when the unified divine name once marked the presence of God in Jerusalem. By the same token, the shofar portrayed on the Holy Ark curtain now announced the messianic ingathering of the exiles and "the messianic restoration of the Temple in Jerusalem and of the resurrection."[20]

From Ostrog to Tykoczin, Jews covered the synagogue walls with the texts of prayers in order to affirm liturgical innovations, especially those of a kabbalistic nature. Mystical-minded Jewish leaders used these texts, including the sixteenth-century prayer *Lekha dodi*, recited at the beginning of the Shabbat, to popularize new forms of liturgy and emphasize their redemptive undertones.[21] Photographs by Jewish ethnographers in the 1910s captured multiple esoteric references to final redemption embedded in the symbolism of the East European synagogues.[22] What may seem esoteric now was very clear to the Jews, who most likely explained the meaning of the synagogue images to their children by resorting to the Midrash, a collection of early rabbinic tales and commentaries.

The symbols of the ornaments also functioned as words. Put together, these words formed an imaginary story that ignited the Jewish imagination. For example, the images of unicorns and lions appeared everywhere in East European Jewish visual culture, from the Torah Ark to illuminations on the voluntary societies' record books to carved tombstones. Made of wood or plaster and then gilded, these two animals were symbols and allegories, texts and commentaries, to be seen and read at the same time. The unicorn stood for Joseph (or for Menashe, the son of Joseph) and the

9.2. Torah shield donated by Avraam ben Levy Hacohen and his son, ca. 1902. *MIK, no. 114, Kiev collection. Courtesy MIK and the Center for Jewish Art at Hebrew University, Jerusalem.*

lion for Judah. Placing them together created a comforting and appeasing encounter between Judah and Joseph in the book of Genesis, but it also made for a conflicting understanding of this encounter in Judaic lore.[23]

Judah and Joseph were both kings and messianic figures, one alluding to the Messiah son of Joseph and the other to the Messiah son of David, competing for an exclusive role in the redemption of Israel.[24] Who was more important: Joseph, who saved the Jews from famine and brought them to the land of Egypt, or Judah, whose descendants brought the Jews back to the land and built the Temple?

The shtetl dwellers, including women and children, knew these tales from childhood. They saw both Judah *and* Joseph as pivotal figures for the redemption of the exiled, dispersed, and subjugated Jews. There would be no return to Jerusalem without these two patriarchs. Portrayed on the curtain covering the ark or placed above the ark, the unicorn and the lion taught worshippers that the Torah played an absolutely central role in that redemptive scenario. Following and studying the laws of the Torah led to and were themselves the redemption. East European Jews came to the Great Synagogue to look at and read their redemptive symbols, to re-imagine themselves in a Jerusalem rebuilt and a Temple restored, and to rejoice.

JERUSALEM AT HOME

Jerusalem and its Temple found their way into almost every Jewish home through the pictures, etchings, or paper cuts that Jews routinely placed on the eastern wall of the house, a reminder to turn in prayer toward Jerusalem, as the prophet Daniel did in Babylonian exile.[25] These folk-art pictures were treated as ritual objects, for they entailed not only images but also texts. *Shiviti ha-Shem negdi tamid,* "I have always placed God in front of me," states the biblical verse, the first word of which gave a name to the popular ritual object known as *shiviti*.[26] "In front of the One who Nurtures the Worlds [you] are staying," Rabbi Efraim of Sudilkov commented on this verse.[27] God appeared on the *shiviti* through his awesome name, the *tetragrammaton*, written in big letters that looked out at the worshipper from the picture. A Jew not only read but watched these words in prayer—and sensed fear and awe before the Almighty.

9.3. A *mizrakh* paper cut by David Rosengarten, eastern Galicia, ca. 1900.
BHT 87.305.1. Courtesy of LME and the Beit Hatfutsot exhibition "Treasures of Jewish Galicia—Judaica from the Museum of Ethnography in Lviv, Ukraine," Photo Archive, Tel Aviv.

Rabbi Nachman, who also prayed in front of the *shiviti*, offered a curious reading of the biblical verse "I have placed God in front of me always" inscribed on it. He stressed the second half of the verse and asked, what "always" stays before God? He answered, the land, the land of Israel. If so, then "always" from the inscription on the *shiviti* can be interpreted as "God placed in front of him the land."[28] Thus, suggested Rabbi Nachman, the Holy Land lay before a praying Jew, embedded in the verses of a homemade paper cut. Imagine the shape of the Holy Land while praying and grasp its awesome power, recommended the no less mystical Rabbi Pinhas of Korets.[29]

Like many other ritual objects, *shiviti* was a picture that Jews read and interpreted. Popular artists used to present the text of Psalm 67 on the *shiviti* as a diagram in the form of a seven-branched candelabrum. Kabbalist interpreters loved the symmetrical structure of this psalm with its three first and three last seven-word verses and its central ten-word verse. Jewish mystics perceived its form as an esoteric commentary on the Temple menorah. Capitalizing on this perception, popular artists presented the verses of the psalm as a textual seven-branch candelabrum with three branches on the left, three on the right, and one in the center.[30]

Jews used the equally visually attractive *mizrakh* to make esoteric references to the Holy Land more explicit. The *mizrakh* included an image of the Jerusalem Temple with its recognizable columns; fauna allegories reminiscent of the land and flora images referring to the flourishing sprout of redemption; apotropaic (healing) amulets composed of Hebrew letters and verses from the traditional books, from Prophets to Psalms to the Talmud. Like the *shiviti*, the *mizrakh* invited the worshipper to watch and to read, focusing on the implications of prayers. The images of the *mizrakh* provided an array of these implications. Since in nineteenth-century Jerusalem "women made paper-cuts, multi-colored pictures, ornaments for *tefillin* begs with images of the Holy Land and panoramic views of Jerusalem to be sold in the Diaspora," it is unsurprising that the shtetl *mizrakh* displayed images that connoted the land.[31]

Many of these images were visual commentaries on verses from traditional Judaic sources.[32] Cuneiform trees stood for the Temple, which, according to the biblical text, King Solomon built of Lebanese cedar logs.[33] Deer referred to the *erets tsvi*, the land of deer, an attribute of and a metaphor for the land of Israel.[34] Likened to deer skin, this land extended itself when Jews settled on it and followed the Law—and shrank when Jews abandoned the land and turned away from the Law. The eagles on the *mizrakh* had many meanings, one of which comes directly from the verse often inscribed on the same picture: "on the wings of eagles I will bring you to me."[35] Roaring lions stood for Judah and for the awakening, strength, and eternal kingship of the Jews.[36]

Animals also referred to the famous motto of Judah ben Temah, which often appears on the *mizrakh*: "Be strong as the leopard, swift as the eagle, fleet as the gazelle, and brave as the lion to do the will of your Father in Heaven."[37] Yet whatever their textual origin, on the *mizrakh* they formed a new symbolic meaning: follow the will of your Father in Heaven, and you will fly on the wings of eagles to the land flowing with milk and honey, where you will regain the might and kingship of the biblical Judah.

This was all deeply esoteric, widely popular, and full of uplifting promises. The symbols of the *mizrakh* provided ordinary Jews with the subtle meaning of everyday life and helped them bear the psychological burden of exile. Furthermore, these symbols streamlined the prayer and transformed the redemptive scenario embedded in the daily Eighteen Benedictions into a vivid visual experience.[38] The images and the prayer raised Jerusalem and the Temple from ruins. The liturgical efforts of the worshipper created a utopian space that welcomed Jerusalem into the shtetl and transported the shtetl dweller back to the land. Home and synagogue all morphed into the sacred realm of the Temple.[39]

A Jew standing in front of a *mizrakh* somewhere in Shepetovka and reciting the evening prayer could feel that he was a participant in this redemptive process. The *mizrakh* symbolically turned an individual Jew into a master of *tikkun*, the fixing of the world. Jerusalem would not be rebuilt if a Jew did not recite his prayers with the proper intent. As one scholar has observed, this was "particularly potent in the liturgical context of the *mizrakh*, for one of the main purposes of the prayer is to promote the building of Jerusalem and the Temple."[40]

The Temple was at hand even without a *mizrakh* on the wall. All a Jew needed to do was to take a Hebrew book from the shelf and open it, and the Temple would emerge in front of his eyes. Any book would suffice: the genre did not matter. What mattered was that many books displayed on their title page a vignette in the form of the Jerusalem Temple with its very recognizable columns, a triangle cornice supporting two palms spread in priestly blessing, sometimes two lions or two angels, or more often—a crown, a cornucopia, or a jar with flowers, hinting at the budding redemption from the liturgy—and an open curtain. If there was no such vignette, then the inscriptions on a rudimentary ornament made up for it. For example, Slavuta books for this purpose had on the title page a circumscribing statement claiming that "who dwells in the secret place of the Most

High will rest under the shadow of the Almighty."[41] In the context of book learning, "dwells" came to signify reading, "rest" the redemption, and "shadow" the abode of the Most High, that is, the Temple.

The title of the book, placed in the middle of such a vignette, was an invitation to come through the open curtain into the new holy of holies— the Hebrew text of the book, revealing to the reader the secrets of the Torah. The Temple also was a mobile image calling for action. It invited one to read and cleaved the worshipper to the immanent, the immediately available God, through reading. Entering the book through the Temple pillars of the title page, the reader simultaneously became a worshipper, a Levite, and a priest in the Jerusalem Temple, and the process of reading became divine service. Opening a book became a homecoming. Not only the daily liturgy but also book-based study replaced the Temple service, and was a reminder of this service by virtue of being its replacement.

9.4. Jerusalem, the Tower of David, one of six enameled cartouches decorating the Torah crown.

Żółkiew, Eastern Galicia, late 18th century. BHT 87.326.8. Courtesy of LME and the Beit Hatfutsot exhibition "Treasures of Jewish Galicia—Judaica from the Museum of Ethnography in Lviv, Ukraine," Photo Archive, Tel Aviv.

What about very poor Jews who had neither books nor paper cuts? A peddler who could never afford, unlike wealthier merchants, a silver goblet with embossed grapes of the land of Israel or a spice box in the form of the Temple tower supported by deer? Let us think of a poor widow who did not have even a paper cut *mizrakh* and could not make one of her own. Does this imply that she could never feel the beauty of the land or taste its sweetness? She could: not only by going to the synagogue, but also by going to the tsadik, the Hasidic master.

THE TEMPLE INCARNATE

At the turn of the eighteenth century, Hasidic leaders found that their arch-enemies, the Mitnagdim, were no longer persecuting them. In 1804 the Russian regime legalized separate Hasidic prayer houses, and the Hasidim built themselves up by using Temple imagery and reaching out to the masses with the use of the high priest praxis. Wherever the Hasidic masters, *tsadikim*, chose to settle, be it Kotsk, Bratslav, or Sadigora, their adherents imagined it to be the new place of the Temple. Before their tsadik, Arthur Green has insightfully observed, the enthusiastic Hasidim would burst into frenetic dancing as if imitating King David rejoicing before the Holy Ark.[42]

Rabbi Moshe Tsvi Giterman of Savran, a Hasidic leader in Podolia and Bessarabia, a tsadik, cast this transformation in a theological mold. When the Temple existed, he wrote, there was a king, and heads of the military units, and a high priest, "but now after the destruction [of the Temple] the Almighty gave us in his mercy the righteous of the generation (*tsadikei ha-dor*)."[43] He meant the Hasidic leaders, who were called "the righteous," *tsadikim*, not just any righteous Jews.

Meeting the tsadik in person thrilled ordinary Jews just as a pilgrimage to Jerusalem thrilled the Jews of ancient Israel. Believing that the tsadik was in local-call distance from the Almighty, Jews flocked to his court seeking uplift, comfort, and healing—precisely as Jews went up to the Temple. Like a priest in the Temple, the tsadik donned a long white *kittel*. In the solemn atmosphere of the third meal at the end of the Shabbat, the tsadik blessed and distributed pieces of a huge challah braided in twelve parts, reminiscent of the twelve loaves of showbread placed on the golden table right before the Temple altar.[44] Avraam Yehoshua Heschel traced a parallel between the biblical Aaron, the first high priest who had to bless all the Jews, good and bad, and the Hasidic master, who blessed the multitude. The tsadik's blessing was compulsory, as was the blessing of the high priest, responsible for all the Jews.

Like their brethren who brought offerings to the Temple in order to atone for and cleanse themselves of their sins, nineteenth-century Jews went to the tsadik with a redemptive sum of money, a *pidyon*, to improve their spiritual or physical condition. The sum more often than not corresponded to the numerical value of the Hebrew name of the person for whom the tsadik was asked to intervene for with the Almighty. The warden of the court of the tsadik accepted the sum and the tsadik received a note, a *kvittel*, containing the name of the claimant, a brief request for help, and a detailed explanation of the problem.[45]

In the solitude of prayer, the tsadik then read the note and recited the name of the claimant. Focusing on the name of a Jew with an intention to better his or her situation, the tsadik took his followers under his aegis in exchange for the financial support of his court. The tsadik did not invent this new type of apotropaic magic; rather, he reenacted an ancient custom. The *pidyon* dates back to the Temple ritual; it references the sum that the father of a newborn son gave the priest to release his son from Temple service. The pious East European Jews used the same word but altered its meaning, though the Temple-based redemptive agenda remained deeply embedded in the practice of *pidyon*.[46]

To maintain their opulent courts, Hasidic masters divided their spheres of influence into *ma'amadot*, communities that supported their tsadik through voluntary monetary contributions. These *ma'amadot* seem to have deliberately imitated the Second Temple–era *ma'amadot*, twenty-four subgroups introduced by the Pharisees in ancient Israel. The ordinary Jews of these *ma'amadot* took turns helping the priests in the Temple.

Rabbi Heschel, who spent his last years of retirement in Medzhibozh, explained why the Hasidic masters took donations—gold and silver and other necessary material things, reminiscent of God's claim, "mine is silver and mine is gold."[47] "By virtue of these donations," Heschel reasoned, "the people would be uplifted … cleaving to the tsadik of the generation"—exactly as they had been uplifted two thousand years earlier, knowing that they were personally supporting the Temple.[48] Heschel interpreted the verse of the Torah (Ex. 25:1–3) so that the *ma'amadot*, a nineteenth-century invention of the Hasidic masters, appeared as a divine commandment and the tsadik was not only a high priest but also invoked the Temple itself.

The tsadik appeared before the Jews as a high priest in his splendid white garments. He distanced himself from the masses but simultaneously made himself accessible for those who came for a blessing or healing. And like the biblical high priest who served as an intermediary between divine grace and the people of Israel, the tsadik acted as a conduit, pouring God's blessings on his followers and streamlining their prayers to their highest addressee. At his court, the tsadik prayed with a *minyan,* a prayer quorum. Yet, like the high priest who stood alone in the Sanctuary behind the curtain, the tsadik, for example Rabbi Duvidl Twersky at his Vasilkov court, was separated from rest of the minyan by a waist-high wall.

Following the Temple ritual, the tsadik distributed leftovers among his followers, although his were different from the leftovers eaten by the priests in ancient Jerusalem.[49] The former contained divine sparks that the tsadik uplifted by consuming; the latter came from the regular altar offerings designated for the Almighty. Their function was one and the same: consuming holy food facilitated cleaving to God. Rabbi Heschel explained this custom through a metaphor: the tsadik, he said, experienced divine involvement: God blessed the food on his plate; the tsadik distributed the leftovers from his plate, and the Jews consumed them, allowing the divine blessing to reach all those who cleaved to the tsadik.

Rabbi Israel of Ruzhin was confident that the tsadik embodied the Jerusalem Temple and that the customs of his court imitated the Temple service. As Jews in the past begged the Almighty residing in the Temple "do not hide your face from us," they now sought to see the face of the tsadik.[50] The Rabbi of Ruzhin did not hesitate to compare the tsadik's table to the altar in the Temple and the tsadik to the high priest himself. Furthermore, he once went as far as to refuse to deliver a sermon when his followers failed to bring him wine: no ritual wine libations, no divination of Torah riddles by a sui generis high priest.[51]

Rabbi Heschel connected these and other Hasidic customs directly to the Temple rituals. However, he did not restrict the function of a tsadik as a conduit between the upper and lower worlds to the great Hasidic masters only. He opened it up to any Jew. By cleansing and sanctifying oneself, any person deserved to become a tsadik, "one of the sons of the divine Temple." Once an individual achieved this level, the land would sing glory to the tsadik, who nurtured the world just like the God of Israel.[52]

Rabbi Levy Isaac from Berdichev put an intriguing spin on this meta-morphosis of the Temple into a tsadik. Why does the Torah state that the patriarch Jacob left Be'er Sheva and *went* to Haran, outside the land? The Torah should have said that Jacob *descended* to Haran. Levy Isaac eluci-dated: Jacob is a tsadik. Wherever a tsadik goes, the sanctity of the land moves together with him.[53] Thus the tsadik is not only the Temple but also entails the spirit of the land. According to at least one testimony, Rabbi Israel of Ruzhin also shared the belief that "any place where the tsadik stands is called Erets Yisroel" and that "one had a feeling of the land" wher-ever the tsadik resided.[54]

Nobody formulated these ideas better than Rabbi Nachman of Brat-slav, considered an eccentric by some contemporary Hasidic leaders. Rabbi Nachman famously said that wherever he was going, he was going to the Holy Land. In 1798, he undertook a dangerous and risky trip to the land of Israel. By going there, he sought to achieve the level of a mystical ascent, at which he could attain prophetic gifts, comprehend the deepest esoteric mysteries, and meet the highest embodied wisdom dressed in the venerable garb of the Jewish patriarchs. Most important, however, Rabbi Nachman took to the road in order to overcome his own physicality, his human passions and desires, to transform himself into a pure spiritual being and and to experience a *unio mystica*, a unity with God. With a verse from Isaiah in mind—"When you pass through the waters, I will be with you"—he traveled from Medvedovka in Podolia to Istanbul to Haifa to Tiberias.[55]

His brief visit to the actual Holy Land inspired him with a sense of leadership. Rabbi Nachman repeatedly and consistently resorted to the land as a thinking tool. For him, the meaning of Erets Yisroel lay in its potential—and in the human ability to explore this potential. The Holy Land embodied belief, while Jerusalem signified spiritual integrity, divine awe, and absolute faith. If one could not pray properly or was weak in one's faith, one went into exile.

On the contrary, living in the land was tantamount to acquiring God. Not "having" but "acquiring": Rabbi Nachman emphasized the dynamic and creative aspect of the spiritual quest. Rabbi Israel of Ruzhin used a different metaphor: he compared the land to a blanket. This blanket did not itself warm anyone but instead returned to the Jews the warmth of their good deeds. Without these good deeds, the mere presence of a Jew in the Holy Land made no difference. The land of Israel entered the Jewish imagination as a call for action, a deed.

The tsadik appears at the very center of this notion of good deeds. For Rabbi Nachman, the tsadik replicated the land in his actions, his appearance, and his impact on the people. The sermon of the tsadik embodied the land. Not just the tsadik's Torah but his profane actions, speeches, and even his commonplace acts (*derekh erets*) fulfilled the same function: all of them led to *Erets* Yisroel, common to all Jews. Rabbi Nachman also understood the songs of the tsadik as songs of the land (*mi-zemirat ha-arets*).

Therefore, the Jews needed a tsadik in order to be able to taste the Holy Land, argued Rabbi Nachman. The tsadik spiritually absorbed those who came to him—exactly as the land absorbed those who did good deeds and rejected those who did evil.[56] Rabbi Nachman's uncle, Efraim of Sudilkov, observed that if we cleave to the tsadik, he can cleave us to God, which is precisely what the Jerusalem Temple accomplished for the ancient Jews.[57] Half a century before Hasidic rabbis existed, Rabbi Moshe Haim Luzzatto, who died in the land, had said that the divine presence resided within the righteous ones, tsadikim, just as it resided in the Temple. However, it was the Hasidic masters, the tsadikim, who claimed this housing of the divine presence as their exclusive domain—and extended it to include Jerusalem and the Holy Land.

9.5. Ritual handwashing ewer with the messianic-era Leviathan biting his tail, formerly belonged to Itshak ben David Kepler of Kuty, 1851.
MNK-IV-M-3006. MNK, no. 106. Courtesy of MNK and the Center for Jewish Art at Hebrew University, Jerusalem.

"IT IS NOT IN HEAVEN"

In the late eighteenth century, thousands of East European Jews were drawn closer to the Holy Land. In 1777, about five hundred Jews from the northeastern part of the Polish-Lithuanian Commonwealth made *aliyah*—moved to the land of Israel—thus changing the balance of the predominantly Sephardic settlement of Israel. Unlike their Sephardic brethren, these Ashkenazi newcomers dreamed of building a religious utopian community. They focused on Torah study and on the performance of commandments centered on the Holy Land and unavailable in the Diaspora. These Jewish pietists believed that their resettlement would pave the way for the coming of the Messiah. They drew their inspiration from Rabbi Eliyahu ben Zalman, the Gaon of Vilna, doyen of European rabbinic scholars and leader of the Mitnagdim, who were the staunch opponents of the Hasidim.

With the ongoing struggle between the two factions, the leaders of the Hasidic movement realized that promoting new study groups in the land of Israel was just as important as debating with the Mitnagdim in East Europe. For Hasidim to allow their opponents to establish new kollels—study institutions for married and adult Jews—in Tiberias, Hebron, and Safed was tantamount to handing them leadership in the Holy Land.

Furthermore, if the Messiah was to come in 1840, the "round number" Jewish year 5,600, as some claimed in the name of the Gaon of Vilna, Hasidic masters should be part of the Jewish resettlement, a process that the historian Arye Morgenstern deftly captured as "hastening redemption." Bans of excommunication pronounced by the Mitnagdim against them were still in effect (they were lifted in 1802), and Hasidic masters began moving to the Holy Land for good. By doing so, they hoped not only to avoid persecution but also to secure flourishing Hasidic communities in Safed, Tiberias, Hebron, and Jerusalem, four communities that conveyed the meaning of the Holy Land for the Jews at that time.[58]

Moving to the land of Israel in those years was a feat in its own right. Travel by ship was dangerous; the price of the trip was exorbitant; the prospect of survival in the place of destination slim. In 1800 a tiny Jewish community of about 6,700 people, called the old yishuv, represented about 2 percent of the 275,000 Ottoman locals. The situation was a far cry from the flourishing time in the sixteenth century when Jews were in control of textile and dyeing industries and the spice and silk trade. In the 1800s, by contrast, Jews could survive only through charity collected by rabbinic messengers regularly visiting Jewish communities in the Diaspora. Despite these conditions, neither the extreme poverty nor the horrible sanitary conditions could prevent the rise of these new centers of Jewish life.

After two Hasidic masters, Menahem Mendel of Vitebsk and Avraam of Kalisk, moved to Tiberias in 1777, Hasidic leaders from the Ukraine followed. In 1794–1795, Yaakov Shimshon of Shepetovka, Issakhar Ber of Zaslav, and Issakhar Ber of Złoczów also settled in Tiberias. Then Zeev Wolf of Cherny Ostrov and Yehuda Arye Leyb Segal of Volochisk arrived, followed by several hundred Hasidic families.[59] By 1840, Hasidim from Volhynia had become the second largest group in the Holy Land Jewish community.[60] When the first—and perhaps only—Hasidic female leader Hannah Rochel, known as the Maiden of Ludmir (Vladimir-Volynsk), encountered tensions at home, she followed the same route, moving to the land of Israel, reestablishing herself as a female rebbe, and creating a center of piety for women in Jerusalem.[61]

The joy of return was marred for many by the horrible economic conditions. "We write this letter from the bitterness of our souls," penned one of the kollel students. "There is no bread, no water, no salary, and no clothes."[62] The resettled Hasidic families were no better off than the several hundred Jewish families of the *perushim*, disciples of the Vilna Gaon who arrived in 1808 from the Lithuanian lands. Famine, natural catastrophes, and exorbitant taxes exacerbated the situation.

To help them out, five leaders of the Holy Land Hasidic community, including Rabbi Avraam Dov from Volhynia, assumed responsibility for collecting charity. Back in Ukraine, Avraam Yehoshua Heschel, Yaakov Shimshon of Shepetovka, Yosse of Rashkov, and Israel of Ruzhin volunteered to promote and supervise the collection of funds known as *halukah* (distribution) for the Hasidic communities in the land. They provided messengers with letters of support to various communal leaders and personally promoted the collection of charity for support of the Jews in the Holy Land.[63] Rabbi Israel of Ruzhin became the central figure of this fundraising campaign: he not only dispatched messengers but also urged Jews to be pragmatic and not leave for the Holy Land unless they had enough financial resources.[64]

Meir Menahem Rotschild shrewdly observed that "now you have the established system of *halukah* for the first time supervised by people coming from East Europe, which put an end to the disorganized system of fundraising."[65] However, the fundraising issue proved to be daunting, particularly since in Ukraine, Barukh of Medzhibozh, the grandson of the founder of Hasidism, would readily support only Hasidim from Belorussia, not those from Poland. Similarly, Schneour Zalman of Liady agreed to extend his support solely on condition that the Hasidim in the Holy Land became adherents of his Habad Hasidism.[66]

Despite these internal conflicts, messengers from the Holy Land went from town to town, gave sermons in the synagogues, brought manuscripts for publication, sold books by rabbinic scholars residing in *Erets Yisroel*, and reached out to ordinary Jews. The messengers most likely inspired awe, piety, and charity—and increased the awareness of the land among shtetl dwellers. Tsvi Hirsh Segal from Tiberias went to Zaslav and Ostrog in 1789 and spoke about the life of Hasidim in the Holy Land. In 1799, Yaakov Shimshon of Shepetovka personally set out for Ukraine to collect charity. In 1803, Tsvi Hirsh Segal joined Meir from Byhov and Daniel Polisker on another fundraising trip to the Hasidic communities. Later in the 1830s, Israel Bak, a former Berdichev dweller who established the first Jewish printing press in Jerusalem, also went back home to collect funds in Volhynia. The messengers crossed the breadth and length of Ukraine, from Bar and Uman to Dubno and Radzivilov, sparking the imagination of ordinary Jews with their stories about everyday life in the land.[67]

We can guess what the messengers preached orally based on their written appeals. In the appeals, the land seemed to speak through the messengers: "the Land proclaims," "the Land wakes up," "the Land wonders," "the Land of unrivaled beauty even in its ruin."[68] These metaphors, softened by the tender feminine of the Hebrew word "land," reinforced the communal belief that the land, the Jewish people, and God were one.

The messengers emphasized *ahdut*, the unity of the Jewish people. They made no distinction between the Holy Land communities of Hasidim and Mitnagdim. Instead, they praised the dedication of students from both groups. In exile, people could fight to prove who was better, the Hasidim or Mitnagdim, the Ba'al Shem Tov or the Gaon of Vilna, but in the Holy Land this did not occur. This attempt to bridge the gap between the two camps, combined with the shared fundraising effort, helped eliminate internal communal animosity.

Several messengers told enthusiastic stories about the self-abnegation of those who settled in *Erets Yisroel* and dedicated themselves to Torah study. Others related their going up to Jerusalem, ascending to the Temple Mount, and reading the worn inscriptions on the tombs of the prophets on the Mount of Olives. Hence, hundreds of Jews in dozens of towns of the Pale of Settlement listened to those who had seen and traversed the Holy Land. Jerusalem was no longer just a myth from the prayer book: it became real and called for action.

The messengers' cri de coeur revealed the dearth of basic necessities among the Jews in the Holy Land—bread, water, oil, clothing, jobs, money.

The sharp contrast in the appeals between the beauty of the land and the destitution of its people opened the hearts and purses of many. "Is this the land flowing with milk and honey?" bemoaned Eliezer ha-Levy, who was very close to Moses Montefiore, after the earthquake of 1837 claimed the lives of several hundred Jews in Safed. Although this destruction came from above, the task of fixing the ruined communities remained in the hands of the people. The messengers reassured the congregants that whoever contributed to charity for the Jews of the land would be considered a person who performed the commandment of "settling the land."[69]

One of these messengers was Aaron Alkalai, a fifty-year-old Sephardic merchant from the Ottoman Empire who spoke German, French, and Italian, and perhaps also Ladino and Turkish, but did not speak Russian. Detained in Yampol, Alkalai told the police that he had traveled from Odessa through Balta and Uman to Ruzhin, where he met with Rabbi Israel Fridman and asked him to pray for him, Alkalai, and his family. This story was most likely a pretext, since he actually had spent about ten days at the court of the tsadik.

Alkalai was directly involved in a campaign to financially support the construction of a new synagogue in Jerusalem, which would be finished in 1867 and would become known as Beth Knesset Hurvah.[70] Among Alkalai's papers, the police found what they called "harmful letters about the coming of the Messiah": a message from one Alkalai "on behalf of the Sephardic Jews," and an appeal entitled "The Basis of the Right of the Reestablishment of the Kingdom of Zion," signed by one K. F. G. Seifert.

The authorities misunderstood and misinterpreted the contents of these letters; however, the succinct police information allows us to figure out what documents Alkalai actually had on him. One of his appeals pleaded for financial support of Jewish communities in the land of Israel and offered a new service in compensation—prayers for the donors and their families at the Cave of Mahpelah in Hebron, believed to be the gravesite of the biblical forefathers and foremothers. We should note in passing that Alkalai kept meticulous records of the people who commissioned prayers.

Most likely the second letter was signed by Rabbi Yehudah Alkalai, a Jerusalem-born Sephardic rabbinic scholar and mystic who also served as a communal leader in Serbia. Alkalai, whose prophetic imagination was later admired by the Zionists, argued that settlement in the land of Israel would facilitate the coming of the Messiah and help speed up the redemption. Perhaps this particular emphasis on the coming of the Messiah irritated the Eastern Orthodox clerks most, since for them the only messiah was Jesus and his coming was to benefit Christians, not Jews. The third appeal found on Aaron Alkalai came from a philosemitic nineteenth-century society that considered Jewish settlement in Palestine part of the Christian redemptive scenario and therefore suggested a "distribution of three classes of privileges in the future Palestine," for which the Jews in the Diaspora should pay three gulden and up.

Perhaps Rabbi Yehudah Alkalai's relative, Aaron Alkalai brought these appeals to Balta, Uman, and Ruzhin. He went all the way from Odessa north to Ruzhin because he knew that Rabbi Israel Fridman had been enthusiastic about Holy Land resettlement, had signed fundraising proclamations, and had personally supervised the activities of messengers coming to East Europe on fundraising missions. It is not surprising that the police also found among Alkalai's papers a list of communities where he was likely to get financial support, perhaps provided by Israel of Ruzhin himself. Following the list, Alkalai moved westward through Podolia and Volhynia. We know that before he was arrested and brought to Zhitomir (and later released), he was in Belaia Tserkov, Berdichev, and Yampol.[71]

This was not the first and not the last arrest among Holy Land messengers, whom the Russian authorities considered suspicious for both religious and political reasons. Shlomo Plonsky, for example, settled in the land of Israel and sent home letters with a redemptive subtext. His messianic references, augmented by a clumsy translator, seemed brazen in the eyes of the Russian police. When Plonsky came back in the early 1820s on a fundraising mission, the police detained him, found on him an appeal concerning the construction of a synagogue in Jerusalem, and imprisoned him.[72] In 1836 in Vladimir-Volynsk, one Fliterman was also arrested for having in his possession an appeal calling on East European Jews to support financially the construction of a Jerusalem synagogue. Fliterman ended up as a soldier recruited by force for a three-year term, his punishment for not handing over the appeal to the police.[73] Perhaps

Aaron Alkalai managed to avoid this fate only because as a wealthy merchant, he knew how to bribe his way out.

The secret police documents confirm that Jewish *and* Christian Palestinophiles in Western Europe were reaching out to the Jews in Eastern Europe. The idea was to galvanize their religious imagination and their messianic expectations, which one should carefully distinguish from political nationalism, even if the Russian authorities failed to do so. A Christian hiding under the alias of "Siegfried Justus I" initiated the above philosemitic messianic Christian society and presented himself as "a legitimate heir to the throne of David, King of Israel, priest in Jerusalem."

He preached the upcoming restoration of the Jewish people in Palestine, an event he viewed as a key stage in the unfolding Christian salvation. On behalf of his society, he printed and sent out a brochure in German entitled *Man as a Citizen in God's Kingdom*.[74] Siegfried Justus also published an appeal and forwarded it to Jewish communities in the Russian Empire. The police intercepted the appeal and showed it to Count Benkendorf, chief of the Russian secret police and a man of balanced opinions. He passed it to Nicholas, who read it, disliked it, and ordered all copies destroyed without being sent to the addressees. Somehow, the appeal still reached the Jews in the Pale.[75]

Attempts at separating the Jews in Russia and those in the Holy Land failed. General Governor Bibikov learned of the intercepted messages about a synagogue in Jerusalem and came to the conclusion that the Jews wanted to rebuild their destroyed Temple. He hated the idea that his subjects were raising funds, as it were, for the construction of that execrable Temple, a home for those whom he believed to have sentenced the Savior to die on the cross. Bibikov immediately dispatched a letter to Benkendorf. The Jews, he wrote, "have turned to political dreams enticed by Polish patriots." He advised "acting cautiously to uncover a secret Jewish mail network." And he asked to be kept informed regarding the "issues uncovered in the intercepted correspondence."[76]

However, the fundraising for Holy Land Jews was no longer just a matter of internal Jewish concern. It became an international issue, even before international Jewish organizations came to being. After the Safed-centered earthquake, the head of the Christian Orthodox Church Mission in Palestine also got involved. He endorsed a petition of the heads of the Jerusalem Jewish community to the Russian Ministry of Foreign Affairs and pleaded to allow fundraising among Russian Jews eager to help their wretched brethren.

The Vilna general governor disagreed, and the Ministry of the Interior supported him against Governor Vasilchikov, who sympathized with the Church Mission request. The minister retorted that not all the money collected earlier for this purpose had been sent to Palestine; this fundraising campaign would increase fanaticism among Jews and reinforce their desire to leave for Palestine, and furthermore, it would prevent them from making regular tax payments. The Vilna and Kiev governors agreed that financial support of the Jewish communities in Palestine reinforced Jewish religious separateness, precisely what they, as promoters of assimilation, were trying to avoid by all means.[77]

The new links between Jews in the Pale and those in the Holy Land also alarmed the Russian authorities, for far more important reasons. The land was geographically and politically part of the Ottoman Empire. The Russian Empire had belligerent relations with the Ottoman Turks, with five wars in fifty years in the Crimea, Bessarabia, and the Caucasus. Although the Russian Empire supported the Eastern Orthodox Church in the Ottoman Empire and increased its diplomatic presence in the Holy Land, raising funds for the Jews in Palestine (who had to pay taxes to their Ottoman authorities) was akin to helping the enemy.[78]

To the Russian eye, the desire of Jews to settle in the Holy Land did not seem innocent either. Rising Polish nationalism and several attempts to restore the political independence of vanquished Poland cast a negative shadow over the Jewish efforts to restore their presence in Palestine. Precisely in the second quarter of the nineteenth century, Russia sought to extend its geopolitical influence over the Holy Land—which in fact served a pretext for the Crimean war. Jewish fundraising juxtaposed with Russian strategic aspirations, creating a sense of competing messianisms: Russia could not allow Jews to control financially the land it sought to control politically.

There was also money at stake. The Russian authorities were reluctant to endorse any additional charities because they knew that many Jewish communities had substantial debt; allowing the Jews to do more fund-raising would prevent the timely payment of their arrears. Therefore, the government prohibited any additional communal taxes and ordered police to carefully check the data provided by informers.

This strategy was of little use, for the Jews still managed to raise funds. According to one informer, the Jews in the town of Kremenets, and perhaps in the surrounding shtetls as well, had special *kruzhki*—tin mugs or wooden charity boxes. Jews placed them on the dining tables in their homes and on the counters in stores, designating them specifically for support of the Holy Land communities. Rabbi David Tsvi Mendel Auerbach (either from Dunaevtsy or the head of the rabbinic court in Kremenets) would come secretly and collect these funds and subsequently transfer them to Palestine through rabbinic messengers.

When the Russian police conducted a search of his house, they confiscated two stamps, two wallets, and one small cloth sack containing a modest sum of 10 golden and 16 silver Russian rubles, only part of the 74 rubles the rabbi had collected according to his register. Rabbi Auerbach was cautious enough to record only the first names of the donors, and the police could not find anyone involved. Yet the police realized that he had been in this business for several years, as he was reported to come several times a year to collect money from the charity boxes.[79] If the denunciation held water, then in the Kremenets district alone Rabbi Auerbach had raised more than 200 rubles annually for social relief of the Jews in the Holy Land.

Such charity boxes could be found in each and every Jewish home. Jewish families used them for various philanthropic purposes: to assist poor children who had survived a fire, contribute to the *hekdesh* (house for itinerant beggars), support brides without dowries, and help sick Jews. While the activity was the same as it had been for centuries in any traditional Jewish community, the purpose in this case was different. Helping the Jews in the Holy Land became one of the highest priorities for East European Jews, comparable only to the commandment of ransoming prisoners.[80] Jewish women, who usually prayed at home, made this exalted purpose an intrinsic part of their ritual blessings over the candles before the Shabbat: right before the blessing, they put some money aside in the home-placed charity box. By doing so, observed Shaul Stampfer, "a woman was able to unite the two good deeds of blessing the holy Sabbath and supporting the Jews of the holy land."[81]

Despite the prohibition, Jewish communal leadership in Volhynia and Podolia imposed additional taxes for the benefit of the Holy Land Jewish communities, particularly to help establish a synagogue in Jerusalem and maintain Hasidic groups in Hebron, Safed, and Tiberias. Again in Kremenets and Vladimir-Volynsk, the rabbi commanded Jews to contribute between 4 and 20 silver kopeks from the sale of each quart of flour, while in Berdichev, Jews swore that they would put aside 20 kopeks from each quart of the sold flour in order "to build a synagogue in Jerusalem." The police intercepted a twenty-eight-page register of donors and decided to make an extra effort to intimidate the Jews by trying to stop illegal fundraising and bringing the contributors to the police post.[82]

During police interrogations, Jews in Kremenets claimed that they knew nothing about those special boxes with funds for the Jerusalem synagogue. "Ask our wives," they said. "Maybe they know." This was an excellent trick. Warned in a timely manner by their husbands, Jewish wives played the fool. For example, Eidlia Goldenberg claimed that she had a charity box at home inherited from her deceased mother, and that her clients put money in for clothing for the poor, and that she herself opened and sealed the box while handing out the money. This trick worked well: the Russian police could reconstruct neither the networks of the *halukah* nor the way Jews raised funds to help build a synagogue in Jerusalem.[83]

When the government outlawed any new communal charity boxes for special needs, the Jews persevered in raising funds unofficially, but once Tsar Nicholas was gone, they sought and found support among their financial elites, acting on an official level. Harking to popular agitation, banker Iosif Galperin from Berdichev, a significant contributor to the *halukah*, turned to General Governor Vasilchikov, asking him to endorse special fundraising in favor of the Palestinian Jews, who were suffering from famine. After all, the governments in Prussia, Austria, Italy, and England had already endorsed such a measure. Vasilchikov contacted the minister of the interior. "Let them have a special book under Galperin's supervision," was his grudging reply.[84]

In the 1810s to 1830s a new bond was formed, connecting East European Jews to the Jewish communities in Palestine and Jews in Western Europe. This bond placed the shtetl at the center of a major international social relief effort. The interaction went both ways: the messengers from the land brought along sacks of earth that were used, among other places, in Shepetovka. Cultural products from the land—along with ritual objects produced by the new settlers in Palestine—found their way into the everyday life of the shtetl.

Unpublished manuscripts by Holy Land rabbis and mystics also reached the shtetl: the Ostrog-based printer Aaron Klarfein obtained and published a mystical autobiography from Jerusalem by Haim Vital, who was personally responsible for making the Lurianic kabbalah known among mystics worldwide.[85] The brothers Shapira, Slavuta publishers, also received a number of manuscripts from Jerusalem, which they expediently put into print.[86] Books penned by messengers from the Holy Land Jewish communities, including illustrious scholars such as Haim Yosef David Azulay, became part of the repertoire of the Hebrew printing presses and were much sought-after reading.[87]

The land of Israel and the shtetl established direct theological and communal links with one another. Events such as the 1837 Galilean earthquake or the 1856–1857 famine in the Holy Land became unofficial headline news for East European Jews: what was occurring in distant Palestine hurt them, too. Helping the Jews in the Holy Land was also an act of honor and self-assertion: East European Jews knew they were emulating their West European brethren, who had long provided social relief to Jews in Palestine. The formulaic "we will merit seeing Jerusalem and the Temple restored" recorded in the minutes of the voluntary confraternities had not yet attained its political overtones but had definitely acquired a sense of geographic proximity, communal belonging, and philanthropic action.

Precisely at that time, in 1836, Polish Rabbi Tsvi Hirsch Kalisher contacted Baron de Rothschild and asked him to purchase lands in Jerusalem and sponsor the reconstruction of the Temple, so that the Jews could restart the temple-based rites. A rational thinker in the tradition of Maimonides, he was confident that such things as return, resettlement, and redemption depended on the good will of his people, not on miracles.[88]

JERUSALEM OF UKRAINE

In the 1790s, the future Russian tsar Paul I and his wife, Mariia Fedo-rovna, travelled incognito through their expanding empire from St. Petersburg to Chernigov to Brody to Vienna. In Brody, they visited a local synagogue "to satisfy their curiosity." In their letters, the couple depicted the town as "that ugly Jerusalem."[89] The comparison between the shtetl and Jerusalem found in travelogues seems metaphorical at best, but in it there was more than just metaphor.

Rabbi Shakhna Tsvi of Nemirov claimed that a Jew residing far from shtetl, the Pale of Settlement, and the Judaic cultural realm was in what he enigmatically called the *erets gzerah*, the land of calamity or the waste-land.[90] At almost the same time, Rabbi Rapaport from Ostrog also considered that a Jew sent by the decision of the government to a place beyond the Pale was sent to what the rabbi called the *erets gzerah*.[91] The Hasidic Rabbi Yehoshua Heschel Rabinovits from Uman recorded in his memoir how in the 1860s the Russian government had tried to exile his father, a Hasidic master from Linits, to Siberia, which he called the *erets gzerah*.[92]

The Bible mentions this "land of calamity" only once. On the Day of Atonement, a messenger takes a goat designated by the high priest to be thrown from a rock. The goat should be taken from the Jerusalem Temple through the wasteland, a desert, an unpredictable and unknown land of danger.[93] The biblical text seems to use "wasteland" and "land of calamity" interchangeably. This land lay outside the protected Jewish realm.

In the rabbinic imagination of the nineteenth century, perhaps shared by ordinary Jews who walk through history without leaving a trace, the land outside the shtetl was this biblical land of calamity, the non-Jewish wasteland. If the territory beyond the shtetl was the *erets gzerah*, like the territory outside Jerusalem, was the shtetl then a Jerusalem for its Jews? Why did the dwellers of Vinnitsa call the Jewish quarter of the town, perhaps its oldest part, *Ierusalimka*, the feminine diminutive of Jerusalem? And why did Russian writers from Leskov to Chekhov ironically called the Jews "the Jerusalem nobility"?

The shtetl became connected to the Holy Land in many different ways. Jews often believed that the tunnels dug under the shtetl houses led to

Jerusalem.[94] Hasidim told a story about the Baʻal Shem Tov, the founder of their movement, who unsuccessfully tried to reach the Holy Land by moving with a gang of robbers through a secret cave in the Carpathian Mountains.[95] Capitalizing on this and many other similar stories, Shmuel Yosef Agnon imagined a she-goat who found one of these secret tunnels connecting a shtetl to the land: the goat enjoyed the grass of the Holy Land and came back to her sick shtetl master with her milk tasting of honey—the taste of the land of Israel.

Yearning for Zion, the Jews illustrated their communal books with images of an ox, a Leviathan biting its own tail, and a deer; these were the mythical animals announcing the redemption from exile and the return to the Holy Land. Those who did not live to see the redemption had images of flowers—"the flourishing redemption"—and deer carved on their tombstones. Like a bit of earth from the Holy Land sprinkled into the grave, these tombstone ornaments comforted the Jews, making them believe that they were part of the redemption process and the land of Israel.

Once Jews fill their houses with wisdom, prayer, learning, and acts of loving kindness, Levy Isaac of Berdichev elaborated on *Pirke Avot* 1:44, in the messianic future their houses would go up directly to the Holy Land.[96] Waiting for this miracle to happen someday, the Jews imagined their shtetl as a Diaspora replica of Jerusalem, the Jerusalem of Volhynia or the Jerusalem of Podolia, with its holy community, its Temple in the form of a Hasidic court, its high priest, the tsadik, and its abundant visual references to the land, from synagogue adornments to homemade traditional art to tombstones.

Jews naturally preserved the image of the shtetl, bemoaned the loss of the East European Jewish town in the fires of war and revolution, and cherished the quest for its remnants, the ethnographic expeditions of the early twentieth century, because the shtetls were the Volhynia dwellings of Jacob and the Podolia tents of Israel. Although Belaia Tserkov or Shepetovka were ordinary Ukrainian towns, the presence of a Jewish "holy community" infused these towns with a sense of holiness. Every Jew from the shtetl knew that the shtetl was no Jerusalem, and yet everybody knew that there was a spark of Jerusalem in the shtetl.

The boy from Agnon's story sneaked behind the goat, traversed the secret tunnel, and reached the land. His sick father, however, neglected the note his son had sent him with the goat, slaughtered the goat, and sealed his fate: he was never able to find the entrance to the magical cave and reach the land of redemption. Like Agnon's father, the shtetl dwellers stayed where they were, in the East European copies of Jerusalem. The stronger the earthly Jerusalem posited itself as the new epicenter of modern Jewish life, the faster the shtetl lost its status as a golden Jerusalem of the Diaspora. By the early twentieth century, Jews had realized that their shtetl was no more a Jerusalem of Ukraine.

CHAPTER TEN

THE BOOKS OF THE PEOPLE

O
n June 3, 1835, Leizer Protagain, the depressive drunkard and abusive husband we briefly met in chapter 5, woke up early in the morning, went to work as a bookbinder for the Slavuta printing press, then left for morning prayers. He returned home, drank a glass of vodka, slept for two hours, and left again to wander about the marketplace. Later that day several Slavuta Jews, including the butcher Kune Reznik, the embroider Meir Shmukler, and warden Arie Tsegener, came for afternoon prayers to the Tailors' Synagogue, unlocked the door, and found Protagain's body hanging from a cross-beam.

The town clerks, police, and district doctor were immediately summoned to examine the corpse and determined that it was a suicide. Local Jews also maintained that Protagain had come to a bad end because of his depression and heavy drinking, which they had observed over several years. The commission appointed by the general governor arrived at the same conclusion.

However, this conclusion was soon overturned owing to an ambitious and dodgy Eastern Orthodox priest, a greedy and sleazy Jewish informer, and a noble envoy from St. Petersburg, who let himself be duped by the other two. Twisting the evidence to fit their vicious agenda, the priest and the Jew managed to convince the authorities, the envoy, and the tsar that Protagain had not taken his own life. Rather, the brothers Shapira, owners of the local printing press and members of a dangerous Hasidic sect, had helped him. Protagain had supposedly wanted to denounce to the authorities the malevolent antigovernmental and anti-Christian invectives in the newly printed Slavuta editions of the Talmud, the legal codex *Shulkhan Arukh*, and Hasidic books. Allegedly he had also planned to convert to Christianity. The Shapira brothers, fearing devastating governmental reprisals and trying to cover up what slanderers considered their sinister and illegal publishing, then purportedly murdered the potential informer.

This infamous event, known as the Slavuta case, brought several dozen people, including the Russian clerks who supported the commonsensical conclusion of a suicide, to the Kiev military court. The judges considered Hasidism a dangerous and subversive Judaic trend and the Hasidim a sect guilty of the most hideous antigovernmental beliefs. They deemed the confiscated Jewish printed material—in fact published with the censors' permission—as books that spread anti-Christian sentiment and undermined the stability of the regime. The judges charged Shmuel Aba and Pinhas Shapira with homicide, along with their father, Moshe Shapira, the founder of the Slavuta printing press and himself the son of the tsadik Rabbi Pinhas from Korets—all of them people of profound piety, dedication, and learning.

Although the Shapira brothers survived the trial and corporeal punishment and spent about fifteen years in semiconfinement in Moscow, not in Siberia, the case had a devastating effect on the Jewish printing industry. In 1836, Nicholas I ordered the Slavuta press as well as all the existing Jewish presses closed and instead allowed only two, one in Kiev and another in Vilna, under the strictest governmental surveillance and censorship. Thus he brought to a halt an unprecedented era of development of Jewish book printing, deeply rooted in and highly beneficial for the shtetl culture and economy. This Nicholaevan regulation had unexpected ramifications for the Jewish readers.

UNDER THE AEGIS OF ENLIGHTENMENT

The arrival of the Age of Reason in East Europe yielded paradoxical results. Enlightenment enthusiasts discovered that reading French books placed them on par with the level of the rational-minded gentry in France, Austria, and Prussia. Yet those enthusiasts of the Enlightenment among the Polish magnates and Russian authorities, above all Catherine II, also realized, on the other hand, that international trade was good but local manufacturing was better. The idea of importing in general and importing books in particular went counter to their mercantilist politics of aggressive export. If reading books could shape the century, then books should be produced locally.[1]

The magnates in prepartitioned Poland discovered that the establishment of a printing press improved their town's economic visibility, produced books for export, enlightened the town dwellers, and increased the town income. In 1790, after being granted permission by King Stanisław August, the enlightened Prince Sanguszko allowed Moshe Shapira to establish a Jewish press in Slavuta.[2] The no less rationally minded Polish town-owners Czackys and Koniecpolskis endorsed Jewish printing in their shtetl of Poryck (Poritsk).

More ambitious than his peers, Count Marchocki planned to transform his town into a Hellenistic polis with high culture, an independent court with enlightened judges, a sort of republican administration, and a Jewish printing press, expecting his shtetl of Minkovtsy to become a new Paris, if not Athens.[3] The Eastern Orthodox landlord Zorich, struck with the same enthusiasm, allowed a Jewish printing press to operate in his town of Shklov.[4] Once Russia swallowed Eastern Poland, Catherine II extended the right to free book printing throughout the western borderlands: just publish, no special resolution needed.[5]

Both East European agents of power, first Polish, then Russian, saw the establishment of Jewish printing presses as part of their own rational program of enlightening their subjects. Following their benevolent decisions, several dozen new Jewish presses dotted the East European map.

10.1. The Great Synagogue in Korets, where Rabbi Pinhas of Korets, the father of the printers Shapira, began printing Hasidic books in 1776.
CAHJP, P166, D1, no. 012. Courtesy of the Central Archives for the History of the Jewish People.

Printing presses appeared in Belaia Tserkov (Heb.: *Sde Lavan*), Belozerka, Berdichev, Boguslav, Bratslav, Dubno, Dubrovno, Korets, Medzhibozh, Mezhirich, Minkovtsy, Ostrog, Polonnoe, Poritsk, Radzivilov, Shklov, Slavuta, Sudilkov, Zaslav, and several other shtetls.[6] Compared to the two mid-eighteenth-century book-printing manufacturers operating in Poland, in Żółkiew and Vilna (Wilno), the number of Jewish printing presses grew tenfold. The golden age shtetl was as much about the marketplace as it was about independent printing presses—and books.

Jews, however, had a very different understanding of the purpose of book printing and of the ways in which to enlighten their brethren. The newly established printing presses issued the Hebrew Bible with commentaries, homilies, ethical treatises, medieval Midrash, tractates of the Talmud, Jewish legal codices, rabbinic responsa, and prayer books, yet no secular works. But they also published books on Kabbalah and Hasidism, quite disproportionately: out of the first hundred titles published by the Jewish printers in Korets, sixty-five were kabbalistic or Hasidic; in Polonnoe, thirty-one out of the first hundred; in Ostrog, twenty-five out of a hundred; in Berdichev, thirty out of ninety; in Dubno, ten out of forty; in Sudilkov, fifteen out of a hundred; in Slavuta, fourteen out of seventy.

Smaller and shorter-lived printing presses were even more determined to publish books on Kabbalah and Hasidism: in Mogilev, fourteen out of thirty books were kabbalistic; in Minkovtsy, twelve out of thirty-eight; in Bratslav, seven out of seven; in Belozerka, three out of four; in Dubrovno, three out of six; in Medzhibozh, thirteen out of twenty-four; in Mezhirich, three out of four; and in Boguslav, one out of four.[7] These and other printing presses seem to have been established exactly for that purpose: to bring mystical esoteric works to public and pave the way for the popularization of Hasidic works. Kabbalists such as the sixteenth-century Isaac Luria (known as ha-Ari) had already enjoyed the renown, respect, and admiration of East European Jews for two hundred years. Hasidic masters who drew on him and referred to him enhanced their legitimacy and contributed to their popularity.

Thus, several small printing presses were brought from elsewhere, assembled, and put into use just to get mystical treatises and prayer books published, and then once again were moved elsewhere. Books on Jewish mysticism constituted between one-fourth and one-third of all titles printed by large presses and from one-third to four-fifths printed by small presses. At least half of all titles appearing at the turn of the eighteenth century in Jewish presses in Kiev, Volhynia, and Podolia provinces fell in the category of Jewish mysticism and Hasidism, with printing presses such as the

10.2. The 1822 Slavuta edition of Mishnayot with the glossa of Levy Isaac of Berdichev.

one in Korets publishing almost exclusively writings by Kabbalah scholars and Hasidic masters for five to seven years.[8] Of course, many of these books were highly esoteric and were published in limited quantities for a very limited number of subscribers able to read and understand them. Still, even if we do not know their exact circulation, we may admire the sheer magnitude of second, third, even fifth reprintings of such books within a short period of time.

The number of what can be called Hasidic book grows exponentially if we include in their number the basic books of Judaic learning for which Hasidic masters wrote endorsements or brief glosses. Let's take a look at the publication of the Mishnah, the Slavuta reprint of a standard Amsterdam edition. It included several canonical commentaries such as Ovadia

Bartenura and Yom Tov Lipmann Heller, but also, on the initiative of the publishers, "several novelties of our great Rabbi, the luminary, the Hasid, the well-known Levy Isaac of blessed memory who was the head of the rabbinic court in the holy community of Berdichev." Any reader of this basic book was assured that Rabbi Levy Isaac belonged to the same rabbinic tradition of scholars who helped ordinary Jews make sense of the key book of the oral Torah.[9] Such additions demonstrated the absolute centrality of Hasidism to the Judaic tradition and added Hasidic flavor to the traditional books.

Take also the Medzhibozh edition of Yaakov ben Asher's *Tur* or *Turei ha-zahav* (Golden Pillars), the first Jewish legal codex. On the verso of the front page of this edition there was a rabbinic endorsement issued by Schneour Zalmad of Liady. While there were of course economic considerations for issuing any endorsement that protected the printers from potential competitors, Schneour Zalman's endorsement, just by virtue of being included in the book, emphasized that Hasidism and the Jewish legal tradition were one, that the accusations that Hasidism was sectarian or charlatan were nonsense, and that Hasidic masters fully respected traditional Jewish law. This endorsement was crucial because, in terms of circulation, the *Tur* exceeded by five- and tenfold the codex written by Schneour Zalman for his Hasidim (*Shulhan Arukh ha-rav*) and would thus be found on the shelf of any house of study in any shtetl.[10]

These books proved to the Jewish masses that Hasidism had firmly placed itself at the center of Jewish learning and that the calumny declaring the new movement to be a group of charlatans taking advantage of the gullible masses mired in superstition did not hold water. Hasidic books took the form of commentaries on Judaic tradition, on the books of the Bible, legal sources (*halakhah*), and Judaic ethics (*musar*). This kind of attention of the Hasidic masters to the basic needs of the Jewish literate population helped transform Hasidim from an egalitarian sect to communally concerned leaders.

The censors, Jewish informers, and Russian administration were scandalized by the rapid spread of mystical teachings, which they considered to be backward obscurantism. An enlightened Jew from Kremenets complained in his reports to the Russian administration that "there has not

10.3. The 1806 Medzhibozh edition of Yaakov ben Asher's "Tur" (Pillar) with the endorsement of Schneour Zalman of Liady.

remained a single book into which Hasidic rules have not been included as a special addendum."[11] Wolf Tugenhold, the doyen of Jewish censors, attached to one of his reports an explanatory note stating that in the Jewish printing presses such as those of Berdichev and Polonnoe, "not one useful book has been published." "These presses are a sort of nest of kabbalistic and mystical compositions," he lamented.[12] Count Guriev, the general governor of Kiev, Podolia, and Volhynia provinces, acknowledged that the Slavuta printing press, along with other Jewish printing presses, "served as an extraordinary catalyst for the spread of the Hasidic sect among Jews."[13]

Despite these repeated accusations, the Jewish presses in the central provinces of the Pale operated successfully. Before Nicholas I ordered the closing of all Jewish printing presses, Jewish printers enjoyed half a century of unheard-of freedom, through the late 1830s. What they published provides an unexpected glimpse into a shtetl culture not yet fully controlled, monitored, or suppressed by the Russian regime. What Jews read at that time tell us who the Jews were—or sought to be—in the golden age shtetl.

FREE PRESS

After the Polish partitions, the magnates still in control of their shtetls were not familiar with the contents of Jewish book printing, while the Russian authorities were not aware of its scope. Most Jewish printing presses operated beyond any external control. With more than a dozen Jewish presses in the Ukraine, the regime had little knowledge of their location and quantity, let alone their output. Late in the 1790s, newly appointed Jewish censors in Riga customs knew of the Jewish printing presses in Korets and Slavuta. They warned the Volhynia governor that there may have been other Jewish printing presses under his authority and that he should prohibit Jewish printers from publishing books without the censors' permission.[14] The governor seems to have had more important issues to occupy himself with, as ten years later the authorities still knew very little about Jewish printing.

This negligence created a vacuum of power. In 1811, Alexander I ordered the preparation of an aggregated report on all printing presses and bookstores in Russia. The report showed that in St. Petersburg there were twenty-two presses with 132 printing machines and forty-one bookstores. The towns of Kostroma, Kursk, Saratov, and Vitebsk each had one printing press and one bookstore. In the Ukraine the administration registered one Christian printing press in each of the following towns: Berdichev (at the Carmelite monastery), Kremenets, Lutsk, Pochaev (at the Eastern Orthodox Laura), and Zhitomir.

Only four Jewish presses were entered in the government records: one in Poritsk, with a single printing machine, owned by Brodsky; one in Slavuta, with eight printing machines, owned by the Shapiras; one in Polonnoe, with two machines, owned by Gershkovich; and one in Korets, also with two printing machines, owned by Zingelman. The owners of the four presses also acted as book distributors.[15] While the data prove that Jews were more active than Christians in book manufacturing, it is unclear where the other printers were.

The authorities were aware of these four Jewish presses because in the 1810s, Slavuta under the brothers Shapira published at least seventy titles, Polonnoe forty-six, Poritsk twenty-nine, and Korets twenty-three. The administration of the province could have missed small presses such as one in Mogilev-Podolsk, with three titles published before 1811, in Mezhirich, with four titles that appeared between 1808 and 1810, and in Medzhibozh, with one title appearing in 1811, but the regime knew nothing about such long-operating presses as Minkovtsy, with about twenty titles published by 1811, Ostrog, which had published some thirty-three titles, Berdichev, with sixty-nine, and Sudilkov, with thirty-two titles. The authorities had no idea that there were at least eight other Jewish printing presses operating in the three central provinces of the Pale.

The regime failed to establish administrative surveillance because first, the printing presses still reported to the town-owners and not to the Russian administration, and second. a printing press was what we call today a small business. The owners of this business worked from home. The printing machine occupied one room in a private house of four to five rooms. Copper molds with galleys were put on specially built shelves. Wooden boxes with heavy lead type stood on the floor. Wood-carved vignettes were carefully kept in another closet in an adjacent room. Paper was bought only for immediate use, never for stock. The owner stored unsold books in the attic. The accessories, instruments, and machinery weighed about sixteen puds (250 kilograms) yet fit inside a single room or wing of a shtetl house.[16]

Some printers used more than one machine, yet most of them had no premises specially designated as a printing shop. In Sudilkov the Blits family, representative of any printing press at the time, had three printing machines in two different houses; the Blits' son-in-law had two in his home, Maizel had three, and Madfis had another three. In Ostrog, Feivel Eisenberg worked on four machines, Abram Klarfein on four, another member of the Klarfein family on two, and Eliezer Margolis on two. The Ostrog printing manufacturer with twelve printing machines matched

ספר
שני
לוחות הברית
חלק שני
אמרות טהורות · מפנינים יקרות · הכל על שתי תורות · בכתב
ובפה מסני מסורת · עריכות וסדורות · מגבור בגבורות · איש
אלדי בוצינא קדישא מרד'ראר'ע'א דארעא דישראל · הרמה השלם בכלדורגמות
וחכמת · גלויות וסתומות · הגאון אשר שפעת יפעת אור תורתי ·
זרה בכל התפוצה · מקצה אל קצה · כבוד מהדרד ישעיה במדרד
אברהם הלוי זצל ממשפחת הורוויץ · הפטן וזמין במנותהו באתיא
קדישא · ונשמתו בנני מרחמים תחות כרסיא דעתיקא קדישא
וסיה לראש מסדרי · מוס תכדי · כן התמסי · שקף עץ אבדה הגדול בעל כנסת הסורס
בגולי לוחיסן שם החכמה והרעל וחמבה אבן הראשה אבן פנה חדשוד תעדו זאגן הגדול ממת
דרמא כמהר'ר שמואל כל ל'די אבר רם דרכך מרבא התוקל · צדי · אשר נהן כסי כם ומוספ לאבית
מפר הגבבד הוה לרשום לסאר עיני הבמים מאר היכד · יובתחסי מוכהר כמהד · מפר וקסרוס דהב
מאסיר יחוו עיני מיפרהם · כישמר איס כתי'ס הסלום ·
באוסטרהא
בשנת תקסב לפ'ג חות ממשלת
אלכמנדר פאולאוויטש
ראני האדרוזלל · שרליאוזדל יד'ת

10.4. The 1802 Ostrog edition of the kabbalistic treatise "Shnei lukhot ha-berit" (Two Tablets of Law).

Sudilkov, which had eleven, but both the Sudilkov and Ostrog printers had their machines in private houses, distributing work among them like the members of a medieval guild.

Selling books was also a small-scale operation comparable to the retailing of wine or herring. The shtetls of the early 1800s had very few regularly open Jewish bookstores.[17] Faivel Eisenberg ran his bookstore in the Ostrog marketplace. Aron Zantberg owned the only bookstore in Berdichev, which faced the marketplace and attracted hundreds of customers, especially during annual fairs.[18] Printers sold books from their printing presses to wholesale buyers and peddlers, who brought books to the shtetl fairs and retailed them there. The Sudilkov printer kept a notebook in which he meticulously recorded when and where he sold books to clients. Like many other testimonies of that time, it did not survive.[19]

Customers knew that for a retail book one had to go to a fair. They would consult pocket calendars for the dates of the fairs; these calendars were also available through the same printers. The head of the local town police was certainly aware of the small printing presses and of retail book-selling at the markets but treated such operations as private, small-scale trade not worthy of special attention. What was produced locally was legal. Unless there was book smuggling involved, the police were not concerned.

By the 1830s this free book market had undergone radical changes. The Jewish printing presses had grown into powerful industries involving hundreds of people. In the early 1840s the Romms in Vilna had at least five printing machines and their type weighed about 1,600 kilograms, whereas in Slavuta the Shapiras had seventeen printing machines and type weighing 11,200 kilograms. One can only imagine the number of people engaged in the Slavuta business if one takes into consideration that Sudilkov with its eleven printing machines, two-thirds of Slavuta's capacity, had about 130 people engaged in book manufacturing.[20]

Concealing book-printing activity became practically impossible. The fierce competition between the presses—such as between the Romms and the Shapiras concerning the printing of complete sets of the Talmud—involved not only printers but also rabbinic authorities from several countries, which made Jewish book printing even more visible.[21] This visibility triggered an open season on Hasidic books in the 1830s and stricter censorship, initiated by the regime.[22]

Despite state attempts at regulating Jewish book print, Jewish printers bent over backward to keep book production outside government control. They realized that greasing the palms of Iosif Zeiberling, an unscrupulous Kiev-based Jewish book censor in the state service, made him more lenient toward certain titles on their lists, although this measure did not work with such devoted reformers as the Vilna-based censor Wolf Tugenhold. Colonel Gets, the head of the gendarme corps, reported that Zeiberling obtained 800 silver rubles annually from the Shapira brothers in exchange for "merciful" censorship of their Jewish books—a sum that exceeded Zeiberling's annual salary.[23] If bribery did not help, books often appeared with the censor's approval yet containing everything the censor had crossed out. Feivel Eisenberg from Ostrog obtained approval for a kabbalistic prayer book and then printed the book with the back date and the name of a previous publisher, leaving intact everything the censor had ordered removed.[24]

After the 1836 ban that followed the Slavuta case, printers still had books in stock. As late as the 1840s, Jewish readers were still purchasing books from Slavuta, Ostrog, Sudilkov, Polonnoe, and Kopys (Kapust, Belorussia) owing to the resourcefulness of the Jewish printers. Shepsel Slavin in Kopys cut a deal with Lipa Hanina Shapira, son of the arrested Pinhas Shapira: he would sell the remaining Slavuta books, sometimes adding a title page of his own, "printed in Kopys" to the bulk printed in Slavuta. Slavin most likely forged the Vilna permission (not without orthographic mistakes, which betrayed him) with which he distributed and even reprinted important Hasidic books by Schneour Zalman of Liady and Dov Baer Schneersohn, books on Lurianic Kabbalah by Haim Vital, and also kabbalistic prayer books.[25]

Just as happened with forbidden foreign commodities, the book trade went from free press to internal contraband. Ios Perlin, a Sudilkov printer, continued to produce and sell books secretly. The police discovered separate folios of books in his attic as well as twenty-six custom house seals six years after the ban.[26] The informer Yaakov Lipps reported that once the governmental inspector in charge of the closure of the Slavuta press had left town, the printers returned to printing the Talmud.[27] Shaia Vaks, another printer, eight years after the ban continued republishing and selling Slavuta books such as the Hasidic and kabbalistic prayer books.[28] He seems to have still been engaged in this business in 1849, fourteen years after the closure of the press.[29]

Jewish printers resorted to legal measures as well. They asked the authorities to release confiscated printing instruments and allow them to finish printing what they already had started. Late in 1836 Count Benkendorf, head of the Russian secret police, complained that government measures meant to eliminate the ossified prejudices of the Jewish people (this is how he referred to Jewish traditionalism) were not sufficient, that the decision to shut down all the Jewish printing presses had not been implemented, and that under various pretexts, Jewish presses were working "day and night" still printing books and trying in this way to defer the implementation of the ban.[30] Apparently it was not so easy for the regime to suppress the half-century-long tradition of free Jewish printing, particularly since it was a loyal servant of at least two masters, a Polish town-owner and a Russian governor, while in fact reporting to neither.

Thus, before the government could introduce rigorous supervision of Jewish book printing, there was very little control over the production of Jewish books. When the government outlawed the existing printing presses, printers managed to operate their businesses illegally for years. In the first third of the nineteenth century, Jewish publishers brought to print whatever they chose and whatever they considered marketable. The spread of kabbalistic and Hasidic books in Russia occurred because of this relative absence of government control and supervision, and therefore what occurred in Ukraine differed markedly from what was taking place across the border in Austrian Galicia.[31] Furthermore, these mystical books were popular among the Jewish elites and were also read by the broader Jewish public. Yet the books popular among ordinary Jews were not necessarily the homiletic works of Hasidic masters, as the enlightened state clerks and ingratiating informers wanted the government to believe.

CIRCULATION: HOW MANY BOOKS?

To find out what ordinary Jews read when they were free to decide and printers were free to publish, we must reconstruct book circulation, an issue about which Jewish printers left almost no evidence. Prayer books, various editions of the Bible with commentaries, and tractates of the Talmud probably had larger circulation than homiletic tractates or Kabbalah, but this is just an intelligent guess. The contemporaries who left oblique testimonies had personal motives and can hardly be trusted. Guild merchant Daniel Gartenshtein from Volhynia pointed out to the government that in neighboring Starokonstantinov alone there were about 20,000 books, as many as 200,000 in Berdichev, and "about a million books in the province."[32] There were in fact many books, but perhaps not quite that many.

The answer comes from the new Shapira printing press established in Zhitomir in the 1940s instead of Kiev as had been previously suggested by the government. Kiev was at the time beyond the Pale of Settlement. In the mid-1840s, the sons of the Shapira brothers, the latter still imprisoned in Moscow, won a bid, reopened the press, started operating under strict surveillance, and reported all their data to the government. Before they moved the press from the shtetl of Slavuta to the district center of Zhitomir, the Shapira printers conducted lengthy negotiations with the authorities. Drafting the new contract, they noted their thirty-year experience in the printing business, knowledge of the market, the convenience of book storage and a paper factory in Slavuta, and the availability of typographic machinery. They proved that with their previous expertise they would be able to restart an efficient printing business as soon as the contract was signed. The only source of that expertise was their previous publishing experience in Slavuta.[33]

The Shapiras knew at least three aspects of the market very well. First, the government allowed only one printing press for the entire Ukraine, making Zhitomir the monopolist in this book-thirsty region. Second, certain books could be published in greater numbers and certain could not: the Shapiras applied their knowledge of the market to new circumstances. Third, the circulation of the books that they would resume publishing should make up for the loss of all previously operating presses. There was also an external aspect to count on. The Russian government clearly expressed its intent to have the Zhitomir and Vilna presses compete with one another for customers, to stabilize book prices and control competition administratively. This intent implied that Vilna and Zhitomir should not differ greatly as far as the circulation of a single title was concerned.

Vilna was the first city to start publishing according to the new regulations. In 1843, the Romms' printing press published 75,450 copies of various titles, with an average circulation of about 1,500 copies for each title. Their most sought-after titles, with between 2,000 and 3,000 copies printed, were the Passover Haggadah, daily prayer books, yearlong prayer books, special prayers for women in Hebrew and Yiddish, and the Pentateuch. The only exception to these relatively modest numbers was the calendar, of which 10,000 copies were published, and in the next year 30,000.[34]

The Shapira press in Zhitomir became highly competitive, producing 4,000 copies of the Pentateuch, 2,200 copies of any book on ethics (such as *Orhot tsadikim*, Paths of the Righteous); between 2,000 and 3,000 copies of prayer books and dirges, 3,000 to 4,000 copies of the graveyard prayers, and about 30,000 copies of the table calendar. In the following years, the circulation of Zhitomir books stabilized at around 1,000 for kabbalistic treatises, 1,500 for tractates of the Talmud, 2,000 copies for the prayer books, including those with kabbalistic underpinnings, 3,000 copies of the protective prayers and dirges, more than 15,000 copies of the table calendar, and an unsurpassed 11,500 copies of *Tsene-rene*, the Yiddish classics and favorite women's reading, a fusion of biblical text with rabbinic tales and ethical dicta.[35]

Looking at these figures, we can conservatively suggest that in the pre-1835 period, presses in Sudilkov, Polonnoe, Slavuta, and Korets could produce about 1,000 copies of a title. The smaller Jewish presses most likely published 300 to 500 copies. Tractates by the Hasidic masters, many of them prepaid and preordered, hardly exceeded 250 to 300. If the Shapiras carried into the new era the previous ratio of books of different genres, then the Slavuta press circulation for such titles as the Pentateuch, ethical tractates, and various prayer books and dirges would have been about 1,500 copies, whereas tractates on Jewish law, books by Hasidic masters, and Kabbalah varied between 400 and 600 copies.

Aware of the low distribution of Hasidic books, Rabbi Nachman repeatedly emphasized the importance of his written teachings. He argued that the stability of the world depended on the study of his printed books, and that his books enhanced spiritual reawakening, serving both as prayer books and as protective amulets. It was important to have his books on the shelf, even if they were not read. He urged his followers to purchase his books by any means possible.[36] Still, Hasidic masters knew that homilies were not hugely in demand. Yaakov Yosef of Polonnoe was reported to have realized that the production of his books was very expensive and the circulation was very small.[37] Most likely, Hasidic titles frightened the enlighteners for reasons other than popularity and circulation.

We should also take into consideration Hebrew writings imported to the shtetl from elsewhere in Europe. In 1807, for example, guild merchant Moshe Zilberman passed through Volochisk customs with about 2,000 volumes, which he had brought from the Austrian Tarnopol: 730 different prayerbooks, 270 books of Torah with Rashi, 260 Yiddish translations of the Torah (most likely *Tsene-rene*), 230 dirges, about 200 booklets with various blessings and prayers, 43 various Talmudic tractates, and other titles in lesser quantities.[38] With one significant exception, to be addressed later, he brought popular prayer books, separate prayers for various occasions, dirges for fast days, and the Pentateuch in Hebrew and Yiddish. Special kabbalistic tractates were in the absolute minority: he brought these books for the elite, not for ordinary Jews. Only after the Slavuta case and the emerging new aura around the Hasidic press did these books become a cherished and affordable commodity.

AFFORDING A BOOK

Books were a luxury for Jewish families. Few Jews could buy many books, and most Jews could afford just a couple. Some preferred purchasing books in installments, buying *kuntersin* (notebooks), unbound parts of books. Aron Zantberg, the owner of the only bookstore in Berdichev, was well aware of this situation. He purchased parts of his unbound stock from Madfis, the Sudilkov printer, including the prayer book *Seder tekhinot* for women, about 70 kopeks (0.7 rubles) apiece, and began selling parts of the book containing various blessings and prayers for anywhere between 7 and 30 kopeks.[39] A Jewish woman could spend such a sum on separate prayers, but the whole prayer book seems to have been out of her reach. She would thus purchase parts of the entire collection of women's prayers, and eventually have it bound.

Whatever their economic status, Jews purchased books. In the 1830s and 1840s, an Ashkenazic (Mitnagdic) or Sephardic (Hasidic) prayerbook cost 60–70 kopeks, the Pentateuch with Rashi cost 1–1.50 rubles, and a book on halakhah cost about 1.80–2 rubles. Kabbalah books would go for 1.50 rubles, a volume of Haim Vital would most likely be about 1.50–2 rubles, and a Hasidic homily and a tractate in ethics cost about 1.50–2 rubles.

These books were Hebrew *sifrei kodesh*—holy books. Purchasing them was not only a financial transaction but also a gesture of piety, the implementation of the commandment to spread the light of Jewish learning. However, buying books was always a challenge for ordinary shtetl dwellers.

For the price of one book, 60–75 kopeks, a Jew in the shtetl of Brailov could buy a simple wooden table, a cotton blanket, a copper samovar, or a goat. For the price of two books he could have two new chairs with calico seat covers, a thick feather blanket, or two goats. For three he could have an old gray cow, a four-door cupboard, or a good teacher for his son for half a year. For five books he could buy a young white cow, a mule, or a small wagon with four iron-coated wheels. Indeed, blankets, goats, and tables were more important commodities than books. The wealthier the shtetl, the more books Jews had. Nonetheless, shtetl Jews could get along without a goat or a cow, but a Jewish family had to have a book.

In addition to the intellectual and cultural impact, the 1836 closure of the printing presses had an immediate negative consequence: it brought prices up to the extent that the Shapiras remarked in 1845 that "people used to the old inexpensive prices would not be able to get used to new prices."[40] The era of cheap books of all sorts available in the marketplace came to an end. Even the newly established Zhitomir rabbinic seminary for future state-paid rabbis could not afford basic books, which were now 15 percent more expensive than before 1835, and the management had to rely on the generosity of the Galperins, the Berdichev bankers, to provide their students with books.[41]

Before the 1840s, books had been cheaper and some libraries huge. In 1776, even before the establishment of most Jewish presses, Podolia Jewish artisans—tailors, shoemakers, furriers, goldsmiths, winemakers, glaziers, bakers, and butchers—owned three to four books each. The wealthier and usually better educated cantors, wardens, store owners and leaseholders owned anywhere from seven to fifteen books each. Rabbis had about seventy, while synagogue preachers owned more than a hundred.[42] With the establishment of the Jewish press in the late 1780s to 1790s, the number of books grew. The wealthy Galician merchant Ber Birkentahl from Bolechów had more than 120 books in his library.[43] Rabbi Avraam Twersky, the *Trisker Rebbe*, had 447 books on his shelves.[44]

Pinhas Yosef Bromberg from Starokonstantinov, a purveyor of the Zhitomir military hospital, brought twenty Hebrew books with him to read while traveling from Volhynia to St. Petersburg on business.[45] The Tarashcha Rabbi Landa had more than forty books. The Radzivilov guild merchant Gartenshtein had 166 books in his library, assessed at about 300 silver rubles—the price of a four-room tile-covered stone house in his own shtetl.[46] Rabbi Mikhel Averbukh in the shtetl of Dunaevtsy had more than seven books in his house.[47]

Neither a rabbi nor a tsadik, Mordekhai Trifman was the son of a lease-holder from Lantskorun, and he had more than thirty-four titles in his collection. It included not only multivolume editions of the Hebrew Bible and Maimonides but also an impressive collection of kabbalistic books, such as the *Zohar* and Isaiah Horowitz's *Shnei lukhot ha-berit* (Two Tablets of Law) and several Hasidic volumes.[48] While Trifman's library is not representative thematically, it shows that a shtetl dweller had access to books from a wide variety of printing presses, both in Russia and Galicia, and could afford a library whose value at that time was about 100 silver rubles, equal to either ten horses, fifteen cows, one hundred goats, three to five fashionable winter fur coats, or seven black fox fur *shtraymls*.

Unlike those merchants who owned ten or more books and could keep them on the shelves for years, trading town dwellers, artisans, and housewives purchased only what they absolutely needed. Most likely, ordinary Jews would actually read, study, or pray from their books. Without relying on the biased informers and censors, yet following the data on book circulation, we shall now examine what it was that almost all Jews did indeed read.

AT THE TOP OF THE LIST

According to circulation figures, the Hebrew calendar was the common denominator of the Jews' reading list. Whatever one's prayer book, Hasidic and kabbalistic or traditional Ashkenazic, the calendar was one and the same for everybody, a real inter-cultural and interdenominational bridge. Its circulation of dozens of thousands far superseded even the most often reprinted books. Calendars were twelve to twenty pages long, palm-sized, user-friendly, pragmatically oriented, extremely cheap, and highly useful. A Polish traveler coming through Slavuta mentioned its Jewish press and its famous calendars.[49]

The calendar took Jews out of the shtetl and into the world. Calendars offered, as an introduction, more than thirty key events of human history, from the invention of boiled meat and music through the establishment of St. Petersburg, placed beside key events in Jewish history, from the Flood through Moshe Alshikh (1508–93), teacher of several renowned Safed mystics. Jewish time and gentile chronology was synchronized through the calendar, which gave the dates of the Hebrew months and days parallel to the dates and months of the gentile calendar. "One of the most didactical and polemical instruments of the age," to use Elisheva Carlebach's definition, the calendar trained the shtetl Jew to live among non-Jews.[50]

The calendar also taught political correctness. It included the birthdays of the ruling Romanov family on specially reserved pages, as an addendum to the birthday and the inauguration date of the present monarch on the first page (among the most important dates of gentile history) and alongside the dates of the creation of the legal codex *Shulkhan Arukh*. Thus, Jewish legalism and the Russian ruler faced one another in print. The dates for the establishment of the major Russian cities and the birthdays of Russian rulers worked both ways: they signaled Jewish loyalty to the regime and taught Jews to remember elementary facts about the Russian Empire, which would be appreciated by local clerks. The Russian bureaucrats would consider those who knew something about the Romanovs as the loyal subjects of His Majesty.

The shtetl Jew used the calendar as a guide to the liturgical year. The calendar marked all the fasts, festivals, and special occasions, provided a list of all the weekly Torah portions and additional Sabbatical readings, and meticulously recorded passages to be included or excluded from the daily liturgy and main prayers. The worshipper could also find detailed instructions, for example, on special readings during circumambulations (*hakafot*) during the intermediary days of the Tabernacle festivities (Sukkot).

Designed in parallel columns, the calendar gave all the dates for Christian holidays, indicating whether they were Catholic, Lutheran, or Eastern Orthodox. Starting from the September Elevation of the Holy Cross and the Nativity of Mary, the calendar took the reader through the entire gamut of Christian festivals and significant days, including St. Matthew and St. Francis, the Assumption and Simon of Trent, St. Barbara and

Thomas the Bishop. Most of these holidays appeared in Slavic transliterated in Yiddish or Hebrew, which, unlike Slavic religious notions translated into Yiddish or Hebrew, sounded less offensive to the Jewish ear. Corpus Christi was just Boże Ciało (in Hebrew letters); the Passions of Christ were conveyed through the Hebrew-Aramaic-Slavic blend *Inui de-Spas*, and Easter appeared as the Wielkanoc (Pol.: the Great Night). The original Slavic pronunciation allowed the Jew to learn the customs of potential customers, Christians of all denominations, whose holidays signified great joy for a Jew since they were also market days.[51]

Beside the Christian holidays, the Jewish reader saw the names of the biggest fairs happening on that day—from Frankfurt an der Oder to Kharkov. More important, every calendar gave a detailed list, sometimes alphabetized, of all the fairs and market days on which Jews could trade in all of East Europe. The shtetls were the foremost locations, with fairs in Tulchin, Ostrog, Korets, Polonnoe, Berdichev, Medzhibozh, Belaia Tserkov, Shepetovka, and Starokonstantinov. Shtetl merchants could also attend market days in Brody, Lemberg, Minsk, Druya, Liady, and Lubartów, and for the most ambitious, the calendar also listed market days in Leipzig, Neustadt, Breslau, Hamburg, Nikolsburg, Danzig, and Frankfurt an der Order.

Jewish calendars were also used as notebooks where people inscribed debts and debtors as well as the anniversaries of the deaths of relatives. Thus the calendar, a universal guide on East European trade, the Christian holiday cycle, Jewish liturgy, combined with a modicum of patriotism, was destined to be the bestseller among the traditional mercantile Jews, who knew much more about the surrounding Slavs than is usually assumed. These calendars revealed that Jews were well embedded in the Slavic environment and demonstrated their loyalty to the regime.

The second most important title to be found on the shelves of Jewish homes was the *siddur,* a prayer book—but a special one, which provided everyday ritual necessities (such as the prayers) and at the same time satiated the new intellectual curiosity (for Kabbalah). Among the many prayer books available, the most popular was *Sha'arei tsiyon* (Gates of Zion) compiled by the Podolia-born chronicler, preacher, and rabbinic judge Natan Neta Hanover in the third quarter of the seventeenth century.[52] Hanover added many kabbalistic comments to his prayer book, with many of them directly relying on the Lurianic Kabbalah.

This prayer book (generically called a *siddur*) had at least forty publications elsewhere in Europe over 150 years before finally reaching East European printers in the 1790s. Like any other prayer book, this one enjoyed wide circulation, and was also brought from abroad in disproportionately large quantities. For the printers in central Ukraine, however, *Sha'arei tsiyon* was special: it bridged Hasidic ideas on the centrality of prayer in the redemptive scenario, the kabbalistic concept of the intentionality of the process of praying, and the most routine Judaic everyday ritual of praying. The shtetl printers brought the book to press: between the 1790s and the 1830, some twenty reprints appeared, and each circulation was considerably larger than that of the Hasidic homilies or kabbalistic compilations.[53] The available numbers of *Sha'arei tsiyon* become even larger if we add more than half a dozen Belorussian and Polish publications and the additional four appearing in Zhitomir after the 1836 ban.

This prayer book, short, handy and published in large type to accommodate any reader, was highly recommended by none other than Avraam Yehoshua Heschel, the Apter Rebbe, a Hasidic master of superb popularity and authority.[54] This prayer book introduced liturgically shaped excerpts from the *Shnei lukhot ha-berit* (The Two Tablets of Law) by Isaiah Horowitz and from the *Zohar* (Book of Splendor), two formidable kabbalistic compendiums. What had been esoteric, elitist, and secretive was now available to anyone who was able to pray. This approach offered unparalleled uplift and a feeling of individual closeness to God, called *dvekut* in Kabbalah. Instead of portraying a praying individual as a "vessel filed with shame," it presented him or her as a "vehicle for the divine grace (*shekhinah*)."

Furthermore, the Hanover's prayer book spiritualized human physicality by revealing the secrets of the parts of the body, the Hebrew names of which were numerically—that is, in a secretive, mystical way—equivalent to functions and aspects of the divine. The prayer book also introduced key elements of the Sephardic liturgy, taken directly from the liturgical practices of Isaac Luria, a sixteenth-century kabbalistic luminary from Safed (Tzfat). Above all, it contained a kabbalistic version of the Kaddish (mourn-

10.5. The 1843 Juzefów re-edition of the Slavuta prayer book *Sha'arei tsiyon* (Gates of Zion) with the kabbalistic treatise "Sefer yetsirah" (Book of Creation) as the addendum.

ers' prayer), which asked God "to make the redemption flourish and bring in the Messiah," and also of the Kedushah (Sanctus), which compared the sanctification of the divine name by an individual to the "mystical utterings of the celestial beings," a much higher level of closeness to the divine than the traditional daily Sanctus previously offered. This Sanctus was used in the Ashkenazi synagogues only for the festive and Sabbath occasion, while this new prayer book made it into daily practice. Hasidic printers were right in putting this prayer book to press so often and popularizing it so widely: the new prayer style would pave the way for a wider acceptance of Hasidic customs and rites among East European Jews.

The third most popular title, not only in the shtetl but among the general Jewish readership throughout East Europe, was the *Tsene-rene*, known as the Jewish women's Bible. The book's author was Yaakov ben Isaac Ashkenazi, a preacher from Janów who lived in the late sixteenth and early seventeenth centuries. A talented preacher in his own right, he managed to weave together in a single uninterrupted narrative the biblical stories of the Pentateuch, the rabbinic Midrash, legal dicta, excerpts from the commentaries of Rashi and Bahya ibn Hlava (and through him also Nachmanides), deep psychological insights, local customs, and ethical parables. Perhaps under the impact of the German Reformation and translations of the Bible into vernacular language, Ashkenazi composed his work in Yiddish. Trying to create a book that would serve simultaneously as a biblical source and as a commentary on the Bible, Ashkenazi had no idea that his choice of language would open for him a vast and underestimated readership, Jewish women. Unlike Jewish men, Jewish women lacked solid Hebrew reading skills but could read in Yiddish. Thanks mainly to them, the book became an instant bestseller and was stylistically and linguistically adapted for different audiences throughout Europe, with more than 120 publications between the 1610s and the 1860s. We have already seen that the circulation of this book was unsurpassed by that of any other publication except certain prayer books and calendars.

The *Tsene-rene* was particularly popular in East Europe, where Yiddish was the mother tongue of the entire Jewish population. With its emphasis on female images, from Sarah to Miriam, the book uplifted female readers, presented them as pillars of the household, and advised them to respect their husbands and avoid scandal in the home—and divorce. The book inspired piety, modesty, and humility, emphasized the redemptive aspects of childbirth, and pointed out many positive features in the existing gender differentiation within the Jewish family. The book also explained how to understand a biblical verse, how to justify the behavior of a biblical character, and how to apply this understanding to everyday behavior. By bringing biblical characters alive and creating recognizable images, the book taught Jewish women to imitate the Book, and provided a useful framework to connect Holy Scripture and family life. In a way, the *Tsene-rene* became for thousands of readers a women's Bible, a women's *Shulkhan Arukh*, legal codex, and a women's Musar, ethical compendium, all in one.[55]

The three most popular publications—the calendar, the kabbalistic prayer book and the Yiddish Bible—were rather innocuous texts teaching ethics, gender roles, concentration, respect for non-Jews, and the importance of individual effort. However, the Russian authorities in the 1830s relied more on their enlightened perceptions of the Jews and Judaism than on empirical observation. The bias of the regime was reinforced by informers, while informers were either true enlightened thinkers or assumed an enlightened stance for pragmatic reasons. Thus the regime came to consider the Jews a mob of ignorant and gullible fanatics, worshippers of the anti-Christian Kabbalah and the offensive medieval Talmud. The Russian government felt the need to cure them of their obscurantist beliefs. Jewish censors—and kissing-up informers in the guise of enlighteners—helped the regime to attack Jewish traditionalism.

THE RUSSIAN GOVERNMENT AGAINST KABBALAH

Mysticism—any mysticism—irritated the enlightened Jewish censors and their high-ranking Russian bosses. Anyone who believed that the past was pregnant with esoteric miracles, the present concealed the promise of imminent redemption, and the future could be deciphered and predicted, if not influenced and brought closer, was for rational-minded Russian bureaucrats an obscurantist. The traditional piety of the shtetl, peppered with mystical beliefs, needed to be replaced by the enlightened rationalism of Russian-language education. The regime ruled that anyone involved in the publication of mystical books would lose his license.

Attempts to shut down Jewish presses began with what can be called the Ostrog case, which occurred ten years before the arrest of the Shapira brothers and closure of their press. At the center of the scandal was a book of Kabbalah: *Shivhei R. Haim Vital* (To Praise Rabbi Haim Vital).[56] This book triggered more controversy than many other mystical books earlier and later, and rightly so.

A close disciple of Isaac Luria, Vital had written a mystical diary, a self-asserting apologia, a spiritual will with elements of an autobiography.

The book betrayed Vital's deep feeling of personal failure: other Luria disciples apparently did not accept him as the head of their kabbalistic circle. To redeem himself, Vital resorted to self-aggrandizement in his dreams and visions, describing great kabbalists of the past, Isaac Luria included, sitting in the Paradise study house thirstily drinking in the holy words coming from his, Vital's, immortal lips. Vital portrayed Mohammad and Jesus as bogus leaders who were aware of their own failure and sent their followers to him, Haim Vital, the only expert in spiritual matters able to rectify people's souls.[57]

Aaron Klarfein, the Ostrog printer, obtained Vital's manuscript from Jerusalem and secured the endorsement of two rabbis. The book was published, sold, and made its way to one reader as far away as the province of Grodno, where the police confiscated it and sent it to Vilna. The censor examining the book was more in line with the state-established tolerance of various creeds than any anti-Jewish agenda. He was scandalized by Vital's anti-Christian and anti-Muslim innuendos, and requested a thorough investigation.

The police interrogated the printer in Ostrog, who gave elusive answers. As a result, in 1828 the authorities shut down Klarfein's press and reported it to Nicholas I. The Ostrog case created the blueprint for the Russian way of dealing with Jewish presses accused of printing Kabbalah. The government now instructed local authorities to be vigilant with regard to Jewish books and regularly report any illegal printing activity or book distribution.[58]

Trying to enhance their own importance, the censors incited the regime against Jewish printing presses, and the authorities adopted draconian measures to check the spread of Jewish mystical works. The anti-kabbalistic fervor of the Russian government was a reflection of the zeitgeist of the Nicholaevan regime, which used autocratic methods to inculcate the Russian version of the Enlightenment among its subjects. Attempts to keep Kabbalah books from publication went hand in hand with government efforts to prevent the spread of Christian Kabbalah and mysticism, from Jacob Boeme and Emmanuel Swedenborg to more contemporary Masonic writings.[59]

The new regulations issued for censors differed radically from the previous rules. For example, paragraph 24 of the 1804 statute delineated that if certain statements in a book could be understood in an ambiguous way, the censor was instructed to see them in positive light rather than expurgate them. This attitude, together with other benevolent measures, created unheard of opportunities for publishers. However, in the late 1830s to 1840s, censors received instructions to "prohibit entire books, the spirit and tendency of which did not coincide with the plans of the government, even if not every chapter of the book contained something reproachable."[60]

In newly approved instructions to the Jewish censors, the authorities also summarized what they saw as the reasons for such measures. Advised by informers, who acted in this particular case as biased but not necessarily misleading voluntary ethnographers, the authorities stated that the "local population, although it does not understand kabbalistic books, respects them to such a degree that on the days of repentance they read these books like they read prayerbooks and expect to earn redemption just for the act of reading."[61]

While the enigmatic suicide of Protagain in the Slavuta synagogue became a mere pretext for the closure of Jewish printing presses, it was above all the governmental antimystical drive that brought to life the governmental function as an expurgator of Jewish mysticism. Nicholas I approved drastic measures to impose strict control over Jewish books. Local police had warrants to search for and confiscate any suspicious books. Censorship control also became more rigorous. Books approved by local rabbis in the 1820s, those stamped by the Vilna censorship commission in the 1830s, and all those approved earlier in the century by the Riga censors all now fell under suspicion.

The police, the censors, and the local administration knew that the communal rabbis who had acted as voluntary censors were far too lenient. In some cases the administration issued complaints about the rabbis' negligence and even attempted to take them to court.[62] Local authorities, not without reason, accused Jews of forging a Vilna censorship stamp and stamping books on the list of banned publications. The informers, a rising subgroup of selfish Jewish sycophants, made themselves available to the local police and state administration.[63] They were most likely unhappy Jews, offended either by the elders of the community or by their own precarious situation, and were eager to denounce, for a small remuneration, the forbidden reading of their brethren. They considerably contributed to the end of the free printing era of the East European book.

OPEN SEASON ON KABBALAH

The persecution of Jewish book-print gives us a glimpse of the books on the shelves of the shtetl Jews. In one 1842 raid, the police confiscated twenty-four books from local houses. In most cases, town dwellers had two or three books, almost all of them standard Hebrew sources and prayer books. Jewish readers obtained their books from different printers, from Berdichev and Bratslav to Dyhernfurth and Ostrog. Most of them were published between the 1810s and 1820s. There were holiday prayer books, various editions of the Pentateuch, Maimonides, dirges, penitential prayers, and separate tractates of the Talmud. There were also, however, such editions as the Hasidic prayer book from Korets and a kabbalistic year-round prayer book from Żółkiew.[64] These books were in an absolute minority but the authorities were excited on discovering the two mystical books: aha, Jews do read that egregious Kabbalah!

In 1836, in the wake of the Slavuta case, the authorities confiscated eighteen books from the synagogue in Slavuta and also searched the homes of local Jews. Using a list of transliterated titles and comparing it to the transliterations on the title pages of the Hebrew books, the police confiscated five books from the guild merchant Rabinovich—one on ethics, two on Kabbalah, and two on Jewish law. Rabbi Kostiakovski had three books confiscated: a biblical commentary, a commentary on Judaic liturgy, and a book on ethics.[65] The town-dweller Zamonsky had about fifteen books at home, some of them on halakhah, most on Kabbalah, and one Hasidic.[66] In general, the police misspelled the titles of confiscated books, but sometimes they did not—and kabbalistic prayer books such as *Sha'arei tsiyon* did figure among them.[67]

In the village of Mozhenka, Cherkas district, a certain Krasnov had four books—responsa, ethics, Jewish law, and a collection of graveyard prayers. In Medvedovka, a certain Shpolianski had two books taken from him, one kabbalistic and one on ethics. Chernyshev and Dunaevsky from the same shtetl had one legal codex each. In the prayer house of the town of Medvedovka, there were twelve books, mostly legal codices and ethics. In Boguslav, Jewish readers showed the same pattern of preferences: one-third of books were legal codes, responsa, and homilies, one-third were on ethics, and one-third were on the Kabbalah and Hasidism.[68] This last third was the prize police catch.

The police were also glad to confiscate secular books—with the excuse that the books had been published abroad! Starting with Catherine, and especially under the patriotic Nicholas I, "abroad" in the public imagination came to signify "spiritually alien," "revolutionary," and "subversive." For example, in 1800, Dubno merchant Falkovich wanted to bring home eighteen volumes of French books on chemistry and was stopped.[69] This tendency, by no means ubiquitous in the 1800s, had become the rule by the late 1830s.

In 1836, Radzivilov merchant Daniel Gartenshtein complained that more than 150 books had been confiscated from him despite the local rabbi's approval of all of them. Gartenshtein had quite a library of French, German, and Hebrew books published abroad, including twelve dictionaries, various grammar books, a collection of Hebrew books on mathematics, medicine, and history, and also books published in Berlin on Jewish reforms. Yet his excellent and expensive collection of Jewish Enlightenment books was confiscated and burnt. Reading material from abroad was considered worse than mysticism and therefore harmful by default.[70]

The police searched far beyond the provinces of the Pale with their significant presence of Hasidim. In Grodno, a province much closer to Vilna than to Slavuta, local police intercepted 206 supposedly illegally published books and sent them to Vilna. The Vilna censors recorded that most of them were kabbalistic or Hasidic. Following this unpleasant discovery, an informer brought the police to the Romms' Vilna printing press for an unexpected search, where they found a number of books published elsewhere without approval. Among them were at least three prayer books illegally published in Ostrog, all of them with kabbalistic glosses, as well as several volumes of the *Zohar* and *Mifaʻalot Elokim* by Joel Baʻal Shem, approved by previous censors but also "unfortunately kabbalistic."[71] The government was up against something that, obliquely corroborated by other testimonies, constituted an increasingly popular reading among the Jewish scholarly elites throughout the Pale.[72]

CENSORS' LISTS CREATED

The sheer number of illegally published works available throughout the Pale (and even in Vilna) shocked the Vilna censors and the state clerks at the Ministry of Public Education. Following these discoveries, censor Tugenhold prepared his 1831 report for Count Benkendorf, the head of the Russian secret police, on the spread of illegal books, followed by a list of books to be prohibited. Tugenhold advised that certain books be absolutely forbidden from publication, such as *Noam Elimelekh*, the first book of Hasidic homilies by Elimelekh of Leżaysk; *Keter shem tov* (The Crown of the Good Name) and *Baʻal shem tov* (In Praise of the Besht), a collection of sayings of, and hagiographic stories on, the founder of Hasidism; *Likutei amarim*, the basic book of Habad Hasidism, and the anthology *Ein Yaakov*, because it included excerpts from kabbalistic texts such as the *Zohar* in the everyday study curriculum.

To justify his choices in the eyes of the authorities, Tugenhold mentioned six or seven books intercepted in Podolia and Volhynia from local Jews, all of them of kabbalistic or Hasidic origin.[73] The books on his list, however, seemed chosen at random. He did not include the books most often found among Jews, above all the ethical treatises, some with kabbalistic underpinnings. Tugenhold had composed his list based on what he himself had read, not on what the majority of Jews were reading. He realized that the government was after mysticism—and he provided his superiors with a list of blacklisted books that would please them. His recommendations reflected his serious engagement with the *Megaleh temirin* (Revealer of Secrets), an anti-Hasidic epistolary satirical novel by Joseph Perl, a Tarnopol-based enlightened scholar, writer, and teacher who had been praised by the Austrian authorities.[74]

Published in Vienna in 1819, *Revealer of Secrets,* the first Hebrew novel, had an enormous impact on the Jewish enlighteners in tsarist

Russia and subsequently on Hebrew book publishing. Perl's book mocked the pseudoepigraphic attribution of Jewish mystical books to an authority of the past. Perl portrayed himself as a mere compiler, presenting his novel as a collection of letters between various Hasidim. His Hasidim were searching feverishly for a certain *bukh*—a secular German-language book about Hasidism, denigrating and mistreating Hasidic piety and Hasidic masters. While trying to identify, locate, capture, and destroy this book—which was certainly Perl's own composition, *On the Nature of the Hasidic Sect*—Perl's imaginary Hasidim discuss pietistic rituals, Hasidic wonder-working masters, homilies, liturgy, the mystical meanings of the commandments, and the esoteric subtext of classical Jewish ideas—all, of course, in a derogatory and humorous manner.

Instead of criticizing Hasidism from the perspective of an enlightened Jew, Perl cleverly allowed his simpleton characters to reveal what he considered the foolishness of kabbalistic beliefs, the fake piety of the Hasidic masters, and the corruption of the movement. Most important, Perl's Hasidim discuss, evoke, refer to, and praise Hasidic books. The symbolic tension of the novel stems from the opposition of Hasidic books on the one hand, beatified by the charlatan pietists, and the traditional legalistic books of Jewish learning, scorned by them, on the other. To add insult to injury, Perl also appended a list of nineteen Hasidic texts with dates and place of publication, identifying the printing presses responsible for bringing these Hasidic books to light. In a sense, Perl's novel offered an inverse reader's digest—books that should not be purchased, read, owned, or studied by what Perl considered to be a normal Jew.[75]

The censors knew that the government suspected Hasidim and their followers of being a separatist, secretive, and fanatical sect, and they tried to substantiate this suspicion. They pointed a finger at what they thought would immediately trigger the reformist zeal of the government and erase the memory of the staunch Hasidic support of Russian political and military efforts. To say that in the 1820s and 1830s most Jewish readers were interested predominantly in books with Hasidic content is to follow the readers and admirers of Perl. The censors followed Joseph Perl's literary invention rather than the actual reading lists of Jews in the Pale. The Russian *Index librorum prohibitorum*—List of Forbidden Books—

canonized the thinking of the censors and successfully played to governmental suspicions.

Only later in the century did Jews begin purchasing and reading basic books written by the disciples of the Ba'al Shem Tov and his followers, exactly at the time when the Russian government announced its attack on Hasidic and kabbalistic books. Before that time, the emphasis on books by such spiritual masters as Rabbi Nachman of Bratslav or Schneour Zalman of Liady, allegedly read by thousands of Jews, was the product of the enlightened imagination of the Jewish censors. Instead of doing their homework and analyzing the rosters of confiscated books, they provided the government with misleading lists generated by their reading of anti-Hasidic sources such as *The Revealer of Secrets*, a "bibliographic" satire by Joseph Perl.

These lists of prohibited books, even more than the Slavuta case, contributed to the disruption of free Jewish printing. After the lists were dispatched, the police began confiscating mystical books, thinking that by confiscating these books, Jews would abandon their traditionalism. In 1840, in Ovruch, they confiscated two Hasidic books among eleven other titles. In 1845, they found a couple books on the Ba'al Shem Tov and by Rabbi Nachman of Bratslav in a number of unidentified shtetls in the Volhynia and Podolia provinces. The police confiscated a book by Schneour Zalman of Liady from a Kremenets Jew. This unimpressive number of books confiscated in the 1840s merely reflected the attempts of the regime to expurgate mystical writings first and foremost—and to follow the lists composed by the power-thirsty censors.[76]

THE END OF FREE PRINTING

Late in the eighteenth century, entrepreneurial East European Jews established several dozen printing presses and published hundreds of titles and thousands of books, many of them for the first time. This decentralized Jewish publishing effort took place with unheard-of freedom.

Paradoxically, it was the enlightenment desires of the Polish town-owners that brought about the establishment of the new Jewish presses in East Europe, which then turned to the publication of mystical books. Rising state-based Russian nationalism then turned the mystical book into an object of persecution. This book came to signify to the Russian regime not only the obscurantism of the Jews but also the legacy of the Polish past.

Neither the suicide of Protagain nor the arrest of the Shapira brothers in the Slavuta case triggered the closure of the Jewish printing presses; rather, it was the antimystical zeal of the government and the belief of enlightened Russian bureaucrats that mystical illusions caused disloyalty, separateness, subversion, and fanaticism—precisely what the government was trying to eliminate throughout the empire. The regime was already dealing with such fanaticism and subversion of the Poles in the western borderlands; Jews should be forbidden to join the same club of disloyal fanatics. Although the book-printing business that fed hundreds of the Jews and non-Jews in the shtetls and dozens of state clerks in the capitals was quite profitable, the regime chose ideology over economics. The "irrational" Kabbalah and Hasidism were no better in the eyes of the Russian administration than the revolutionary dreams of the Poles. Both belonged to what Nicholas I called "useless illusions" that contradicted the imperial vision of state-based enlightenment, the state-centered idea of useful service and rationalism.

The fact that the closed printing presses owed their establishment above all to the Polish magnates, who benefited financially from the Jewish printing enterprise, also played a role in its demise. Disrupting shtetl-based book manufacturing and moving it to government-controlled towns such as Zhitomir further undermined the Polish magnates and their towns and reinforced, at their expense, the urban centers controlled by and contributing to the Russian treasury.

The government's strategy achieved the opposite result: the suppression of books on mysticism, together with their authors and publishers, transformed the expurgated books into holy martyrs of the regime. The "suffering" of the Hasidic book facilitated its faster acceptance by shtetl readers and helped these books find their way deep into the shtetl. Suppressed in print, this material thus became firmly rooted in Judaic oral culture, which no regime could control.

In the late 1840s, already in Zhitomir, when the Shapiras managed to circumvent the zealous eye of the censor and publish a Hasidic book—such as the *Degel mahaneh Efraim* (The Banner of the Encampment of

Ephraim) by Efraim of Sudilkov, of which they printed an unimaginable 5,000 copies—there was no doubt that the book would be a best-seller.[77] At that time the Slavuta books became a commodity and business relations with the Slavuta press, a great honor. A contemporary Scottish theologian and biblicist passed in the mid-1820s through Volhynia and remarked that he had never seen a better edition of the Psalms than that of Slavuta publishers.[78] "Who in Germany has not heard of the deluxe printing house in Slavuta?" asked the German-Jewish newspaper *Der Orient* in 1840.[79] Avraam Ber Gottlober, one of the leading Russian enlighteners and a person sharply critical of anything Hasidic, still acknowledged that the Slavuta press was "the most beautiful and acclaimed among all the surrounding printing presses."[80] After the closure of this press, the Sudilkov publisher Ios Perlich took Juzefów books, glued on new title pages of Slavuta—priced very high on the market, owing to their status of a persecuted martyr—and sent them to the Iarmolintsy fair for sale.[81] Another Sudilkov printer, Shae Vaks, continued to sell in a clandestine manner Slavuta books, including *Sha'arei tsiyon*, the market for which had not been satiated.[82]

The appearance of the names of the new generation of Shapira publishers on Zhitomir books, for example, "Lipa Hanina Shapira from Slavuta," lent the books immediate prestige. In one of the Belorussian towns, the warden of the house of study hid a full set of the Zhitomir Talmud, published by the Shapiras "from Slavuta," away from those who were supposed to study it: "Hand over such a treasure!" he retorted.[83] Belief in the holiness of Slavuta books was corroborated by a legend that before printing a Hebrew book, the brothers Shapira would perform a ritual ablution of the type piece used to print it.

Seeing the impact of the printed book on the followers of the Hasidic masters, Rabbi Nachman of Bratslav became much more focused on his written work, calling the study of his books "the beginning of redemption" and arguing that the stability of the world depended on that reading and that the study of a Hasidic book enhanced spiritual reawakening and served as a blessing and a prayer, while his book could be used as a protective amulet in and of itself.[84] Kabbalistic books crossed the boundaries of the Hasidic communities: Abram Paperna from the Belorussian shtetl

Kopyl tells a story about certain Leibke, an admirer of Kabbalah. A well-to-do Jew, Leibke spent his free time studying the *Zohar*, with the help of which he sought to uplift himself to the status of a prophet. He used the kabbalistic reading codes to predict the fate of the Russian tsars and the outcome of the Crimean War.[85]

In the popular imagination, the piety of the Hasidim was projected onto the Hasidic book and made the book on Kabbalah a symbol of Hasidic mysticism in its entirety, of shtetl life, and of redemptive Judaic tradition in general. Honon, the would-be dybbuk from Ansky's namesake drama, considers the Talmud a "mighty, terrifying, endless" book "which does not elevate," whereas Kabbalah "opens up all the gates of heavens" and "illuminates with its radiating lightning thousands of worlds."[86]

In his short story, "A Book That Was Lost," S.Y. Agnon describes the fate of a manuscript of a certain Rabbi Shmaria. The narrator sent this manuscript from a shtetl post office to Jerusalem, but the text never made it there. Agnon discusses the nonencounter between shtetl Judaism and Jewish life in the Holy Land, but of importance to us is the fact that Rabbi Shmaria's lost book was a commentary on the *Magen Avraam* by the seventeenth-century Avraam Gombiner, who sought to infuse laws on everyday practices, halakhah, with deep kabbalistic meaning.[87]

Isaac Bashevis Singer in his short story "The Last Demon" has the Rabbi of Tishevitz use *The Book of Creation*—the classics of Kabbalah—to scare away a demon who sought to tempt him, and then makes the demon feed himself on the holiness of the kabbalistically reinterpreted Hebrew letters, the only survivors of the twentieth-century destruction of East European Jewry.[88]

Reading a kabbalistic or Hasidic book persecuted by the regime became for Jews what touching the Turin Shroud or kissing a healing icon was for a devoted Christian. The regime turned Kabbalah into a clandestine cultural pursuit, parallel to consuming smuggled vodka, wearing a dress made of contraband fabric, or helping Jews in the Holy Land.

CONCLUSION

THE END OF THE GOLDEN AGE

The golden age of the shtetl was over by the second half of the nine-teenth century, yet the shtetl did not disappear overnight. Let us make no mistake: Belaia Tserkov, Berdichev, Medzhibozh, Ostrog, Radzivilov, Shargorod, Shepetovka, Skvira, Slavuta, Talnoe, Uman, and Zaslav all remained where they had been before. Two hundred years later they are still there with now emphatically Ukrainian names such as Berdychiv, Bila Tserkva, Medzhybizh, Ostroh, Radyvyliv, Sharhorod, Shepetivka, Skvyra, and Iziaslav. Of course, these localities are very differ-ent now from what they were two hundred years ago. Their recognizable yet altered names do not convey the magnitude of the changes they have undergone.

FORCED DECLINE AND FALL

Scholars of Russian imperial history portrayed the geopolitical know-how of the Russian Empire, which by and large had less developed urban infrastructure, economic networks, financial system, and self-governing

341

institutions than the peoples in its western territories it conquered. Capturing new territories, the regime first empowered local elites and preserved the status quo of the institutions of local self-rule. Then it assimilated, ruined, and harnessed the elites and leveled local traditional social institutions, replacing them with the Russian administrative system.[1]

Russia thus suppressed and supplanted the Ukrainian autonomous Hetmanate on the left bank of the Dnieper River in the eighteenth century—and the imperial administration likewise subjugated, suppressed, and eliminated the Polish legacy on the right bank of the Dnieper River in the nineteenth century. The method was the same: not to assimilate Russian urban infrastructure into the social institutions in the newly appropriated territories but to bring those institutions down to the level of the underdeveloped and inefficient Russian administrative ones. Russian state-based nationalism and far-fetched ideological priorities had the upper hand over the country's immediate economic growth. Full control over the shtetl turned out to be more important than the shtetl's vigorous productivity. Paternalistic enlightenment of Catherine II transformed itself into the barrack enlightenment of Nicholas I.

Although in the western provinces the regime sought to put down the Poles and win over the Jews, Jews paid a high price in the Russian appropriation of its western lands. The regime radically limited the activities of the kahal in 1797 and then in 1844 curtailed it, getting rid of the communal umbrella organization not only as a corporate entity incompatible with the well-managed state but also as a legacy of the previous Polish regime. In 1827, Jews found themselves in the conscription pool—together with the Russian peasants, since Nicholas I saw the army as an institution teaching useful skills and reorienting Jewish loyalties from the Polish magnates to the Russian tsar. In 1836 the tsar outlawed the effervescent Jewish printing presses and introduced the strictest control and censorship over the only two state-endorsed printing presses. What had previously benefited the shtetl Jewish population—and, of course, the shtetl's Polish owners—now came to benefit the administrative towns such as Zhitomir in the southern and Vilna in the northern part of the Pale of Settlement.

The educational reforms of the 1840s, including the establishment of state schools and rabbinic seminaries, pursued the same goal: to transform what Moshe Rosman called "the lords' Jews," the Polish magnates' Jews, into Russian imperial Jews and useful subjects of His Majesty the Russian tsar. Included in these reforms was a not always successful yet consistent effort at squeezing the Jews out of the rural areas, a movement that took a particularly aggressive form in the 1840s and culminated in the 1880s, the setting of Sholem Aleichem's Tevye, who sells his belongings for pennies and leaves his beloved Anatevka for good.

These and many other reforms had multiple goals. The attempts of the regime to forcefully russify the Jews by integrating them into the Russian version of the well-managed state is only one of the contexts in which to consider the Jewish nineteenth-century transformation. Another context is Russia's no less consistent attempts to obliterate the Polish legacies—political, administrative, social, cultural, and economic—in the western provinces, particularly in such well-to-do ones as Kiev, Volhynia, and Podolia. These attempts became particularly intense after the 1863–1864 Polish rebellion, when the imperial officialdom incorporated the anti-Polish invectives of the Russian xenophobes, making them part of the government's political discourse.[2]

The regime used every opportunity to purchase the shtetls from the Polish magnates for the Russian treasury. It moved the trade centers and major annual fairs out of the previously thriving Polish towns in the Pale of Settlement and into interior Russia. It economically supported Russian administrative centers at the expense of the towns still in the possession of a Polish magnate. It put the towns in the western borderlands under the control of the Russian administration, if not the Russian gentry, organized mass resettlement of the impoverished members of the Polish szlachta, and broke the spine of the local economy, dependent on Jewish mediation between the rural and the urban. These measures were much more nationalistic than enlightened.

Russian industrialization also delivered a heavy blow to the shtetl. If a shtetl was lucky and had the newly established Russian railroad passing through, it would years later resemble a big village with some residual

11.1. The market square in Ozarintsy.
IA, f. 9, spr. 40, ark. 10. Courtesy of the Institute of Archaeology of the National Academy of Sciences of Ukraine.

urban infrastructure: a department store, a railway station and depot, and a couple of factories. The railroad communication relocated the market centers moving them elsewhere. If the shtetl did not get the railroad, it would turn into a village resembling Anatevka. Only the ruins of the magnate's castle, a desolate Catholic monastery, or a pompous synagogue building now functioning as a local museum are reminders of the shtetl's glorious past. Yet its industrious Jews, its inns and taverns, multiple stores and artisan shops, ubiquitous prayer houses, the pompous residence of the tsadik, and, of course, its bustling marketplace were no more. Of course, the shtetl had lost its unique economic status long before the two world wars, and the Holocaust finally stamped out its Jewish life.

The shtetl's fall from grace took almost another fifty years. The Russian regime managed to create robust internal markets, which competed with and in the long run suppressed the shtetl marketplace. The regime placed its bids on the state-owned towns that had never been in private Polish possession, even though they had been under the Polish-Lithuanian

Commonwealth. Instead of following the market, the Russian regime made the market follow the administration. The empire needed strong governmental centers entirely under its control; it abhorred the many independent towns with the dubious legacy of the previous regime and unruly economic potential. They were too Polish—and too Jewish. Besides, the Russian state capitalism of the second half of the nineteenth century did not like competition, particularly internal. Even without government-orchestrated political and economic regulations aimed at suppressing the burgeoning towns, the shtetl was doomed.

The regime forcibly moved the fair trade to administrative centers such as Kiev and Zhitomir, which successfully outplayed the surrounding shtetls economically, debilitating their markets and weakening trade networks. The introduction of rigid border controls, the disruption of Jewish-driven international trade, and the establishment of a new center on the Black Sea coast, Odessa, made trade move away from Brody, Dubno, Berdichev, and Uman southward, leaving the shtetls in dire straits. With the railroads connecting St. Petersburg, Moscow, Kiev, Kharkov, and Odessa, it was easier and more profitable to do business along the new transportation lines. Only the grain trade, now centered in the new international port of Odessa, still used the old Dnieper-based water routes.

Following the confiscation of their towns by the Russian imperial treasury, the Polish magnates with their lavish lifestyle and their entourages were seen no more. The shtetl market for French and Austrian goods disappeared. Numerous members of the Polish szlachta that had served the magnates in various administrative positions lost their livelihoods and had no better a fate than the impoverished Jewish urban dwellers who lost their trading opportunities. The Jewish elites who used to contribute to the urban development of the shtetls moved from Starokonstantinov to Zhitomir to Kiev and from Berdichev to Odessa. Those few who could pay the dues and join the merchants' first guild, those who obtained the exclusive rights of excise monopolists, and those who converted moved to Moscow or St. Petersburg. The market slowly declined, not only because of governmental restrictions but also as a result of the waning number of high-ranking consumers. Still, until the late nineteenth century the shtetl remained a key player in the exchange of agricultural products between rural areas and urban centers in the western provinces, and traded in grain as it had done for centuries. Of course, its market was no more a place where one could purchase "whatever one's heart desired."

Some shtetls, such as Shargorod, persevered in their capacity as centers of exchange between the town and the village, and their architecture retained (even today!) its unique shtetl flavor, whereas many more shtetls were obliged to follow the newly imposed architectural patterns and introduce brick buildings resembling any Russian provincial town.[3]

The Jews who were forced to obey the new law forbidding them from residing in rural areas resettled in the shtetl, contributing to its skyrocketing competition and further economic decline. The 1861 liberation of the Russian peasants slowly brought the Ukrainian peasants into the shtetls, where they became competitors of the Jews at the already decaying marketplace, which turned from a nineteenth-century version of a supermarket into a village bazaar. Thousands of Jews had to abandon trade and go into artisan labor, creating a growth of 30 percent in this economic sector, but they soon realized that the shtetl no longer provided them with a viable market, and their output could no longer compete with industrial mass-produced ready-made clothes, shoes, gloves, and hats. Jews took to the road, which led them to bigger towns and cities.

In the cities, often unable to establish themselves, Jews became blue-collar seasonal workers or red-shirt full-time proletarians, joining groups they previously had had little in common with. The introduction of the state monopoly on liquor production and the reclassification of hundreds of shtetls as villages where Jews were not allowed to reside pushed thousands of penniless Jews, artisans and petty merchants, tailors and watchmakers, leaseholders and tavernkeepers, out of the former shtetl in search of the means of survival—and about two million of them left for Argentina, South Africa, Canada, and the United States.

The Hasidim, together with their Hasidic masters, followed the market and moved to bigger cities, where they forged new identities combining urbanization and political orthodoxy. Although the same religious symbols were still visible on the shabby synagogue's Holy Ark, the shtetl no longer made its dwellers think of Jerusalem, particularly since the real

11.2. The Holy Arc in the Zaslav synagogue.
IA, f. 9, spr. 44, ark. 16. Courtesy of the Institute of Archaeology of the National Academy of Sciences of Ukraine.

Jerusalem had become a viable option, no longer just an unfeasible idea tantalizing the Jewish religious imagination.

The Jews who saw their towns descending into economic collapse were unable to protect themselves, let alone play their part in the daily model of shtetl violence of old. Previously billeted in the shtetls, the troops were moved into barracks, and no one but the undertrained, understaffed, and corrupt police were left in the shtetls to protect the Jews in the revolutionary times of mass violence. The ruined marketplace could not support extended Jewish families, and they either moved to more urbanized areas or turned into the shabbily dressed and strikingly poor Jews deftly portrayed on stage by S. Ansky, caught on camera by Roman Vishniac, and epitomized in *Fiddler on the Roof.*

In addition to these many economic and political causes, there was also a natural reason for this turn of events.

A NATURAL DISASTER

When things began changing for worse, there came the fire, to paraphrase a traditional Passover song, which swallowed the shtetl. The fire was a calamity that caused more damage than all the enforced integrationist reforms of Nicholas I or the segregationist, antisemitic laws of Alexander III put together. Unlike the government-imposed regulations, a fire in the shtetl left its dwellers with almost no choice and little, if any, hope. As a result of the fire, we can suggest the dates for the beginning of the end of the shtetl's golden age. For Shepetovka, Sudilkov, Gaisin, Litin, Yampol, Letichev, Balta, and Starokonstantinov, it happened around 1835. In other shtetls and towns, from Khmelnik to Makhnovka to Verbovets, it started several years later, in 1838 or in 1841, while in Chemerovtsy, Ostrog, and Zhvanets, it happened in the late 1840s.

In the aftermath of the fire, once the blaze had destroyed from half to two-thirds of the shtetl, the panicked townsfolk went to great lengths to find the guilty parties and bring them to justice. Sometimes the shtetl dwellers managed to catch a migrant worker, sometimes a runaway criminal. The wealthy merchants naturally suspected their debtors or rivals. The kahal did not hesitate to blame the communal outcasts, offenders of public morals, and informers, just to get rid of them by accusing them of arson.[4]

Documentary evidence proves that the causes of these fires were natural, and in most cases no arsonists were involved. Summer droughts and dry gusty winds, extremely flammable clay-coated wood, wooden shingles and straw-roofed houses—the very materials of which the shtetl was constructed—in combination with little fire control and the absence of appropriate tools to extinguish fires, brought much more devastation than any alleged scheming outcasts or underpaid hired workers. The fires, "part of the cycle of rural existence" in Russia, were also very much part of the shtetl cycle as well because of its unique semi-rural, semi-urban nature.[5]

As a rule, the first blaze sparked towing to a violation of elementary precautions. In Balta, somebody left an outdoor stove unattended. In Starokonstantinov, the chimney in one of the Jewish homes did not reach the roof, and the sparks flew straight into the straw stockpiled under the roof. In Bar, firewood piled near the monastery triggered a fire. In Shepetovka, someone in Gershko Kucher's house had apparently left red-hot coals near the heating stove.[6] The construction of the shtetl house, with its additions, hangars, dens, attached storage spaces for dry goods, grain, wood, and straw, fostered the rapid spread of an initial blaze.[7] For example, it took a fire just forty-five minutes to destroy more than forty houses in Medzhibozh.[8]

A fire could erupt at any moment, day or night, yet there were several patterns common to Volhynia, Podolia, and Kiev provinces. In most cases the fires started on hot and dry summer days, around evening time, when male Jews left for afternoon and evening prayers. Some fires occurred during the spring or fall holidays, when most Jews were warming food in the oven while they flocked to the Great Synagogue for the long prayer services.[9] When the fire spread to the roof of a house, be it in Makhnovka or in Khmelnik, the wind would pick it up from there and then continue, magnifying the disaster and consuming the town.

The police, fire brigade, and even specially deployed regiments could do little against the elements. Water pumps often did not work or produced insufficient water. The firefighters' horses, which dragged the wagons loaded with huge water barrels, did not want to go through the shtetl streets, which were in flames. Among the townsfolk there was no sense of a common task: people tried to save their own belongings, and the policemen were more often seen trying to save documents from blazing government buildings rather than checking the flames. Besides—and it appears in the primary sources as a profoundly tragicomic moment—the shtetl dwellers flocked to the scene of the fires, where they stood mesmerized by the magnitude of the disaster, watching the devastation as it happened, for example, in Radomyshl.[10] During his lifetime and in his multiple posthumous publications, the Maggid of Dubno scolded the Jews for reckless selfishness and the absence of a sense of a common task during the fire, but his rebukes could do only so much.[11] In addition to many other hindrances, the firefighters could not operate normally under these circumstances. Nor did they have adequate equipment, as was the case in Ostrog, where the administration stood idle and the blaze was not completely extinguished seven days after it had erupted. As a result, 25 percent of the town burned down.[12]

Unlike in rural fires, human casualties in the shtetls were relatively small, and most people managed to escape. However, three Jewish women and a Pole died in Sokal, two male Jews in Starokonstantinov, and two in Verbovets. One Jew lost his life and several unidentified people were badly burned in Kremenets, and one member of the Polish clergy and one Jewish woman perished in Khmelnik. Sometimes neighbors rescued Jews and Jewish children, as for example in Chemerovtsy, where the Pole Gaetski saved six Jewish children.[13]

Those who escaped witnessed the total devastation. In Ostrog, 160 houses burned down, resulting in a total of 230,000 silver rubles' damage. In Shepetovka, fire consumed forty-two Jewish houses, leaving 143 men and 150 women without shelter. The blaze destroyed forty Jewish houses, ten Christian ones, and ten various government buildings in Sudilkov. In Belogorodka, forty-two houses were destroyed in the blaze and eighty-nine families were left without a roof over their heads.[14]

In Yampol, a fire leveled thirty-eight houses, three hangars, and fifteen stalls and stores.[15] A devastating blaze in Khmelnik destroyed thirty-six Jewish houses, two prayer houses, a synagogue, a Catholic church, and the building of the town police, resulting in 11,840 rubles in damages to Jewish private property, 3,450 rubles in damage to Jewish public property, and 2,300 rubles in damage to Christian property.[16] During a fire in Litin, fifty-three houses and fifty-eight wooden stores burnt down, causing an estimated 122,120 rubles in damage.[17]

Since the fires destroyed not only homes but also stores and storages, it was not easy to rebuild the towns after the disasters. In Vladimir-Volynsk, about a thousand families were left without shelter, and several stores with between 1,200 and 4,000 rubles' worth of goods burned to the ground. Jews were enormously overrepresented among those victimized by the calamities: in the same town of Vladimir-Volynsk, 144 Jews and five Russians signed a petition asking for social relief.[18] The local administration was powerless, and the neighbors were also of little help. In Belogorodka, only sixteen houses in the town were untouched by the fire. Hence, other shtetl dwellers could not have physically accommodated victims of the fire even if they had wanted to.

The stockpiled goods in shtetl houses—textiles, grain, flour, groceries, wine, vodka, cattle, books—were irretrievably lost. More often than not the shtetl was able to rise from the ashes, yet the price its dwellers had to pay was exorbitant. Lutsk, although not a shtetl, is representative of what it meant for any town to survive a fire: before the fire its marketplace turnover was about 385,850 rubles; after the calamity, about 174,870 rubles.[19] A fire in the shtetl, like fires in rural areas, dramatically limited "the ability of communities of entire regions to move into a period of sustained economic development."[20]

The government ordered any deployed army battalions and the town administrators into the premises of nearby Catholic monasteries (if they were untouched by the fire), but the Jewish victims of the disaster had nowhere to go. The police reported hundreds of Jewish families left homeless with nothing to sustain themselves. They needed blankets, clothing, and bread. This kind of help took weeks to arrive, and when it did reach the victims it was sorely insufficient. Many Jewish families were allowed to resettle temporarily in nearby villages, but they had to leave these same villages soon, since the government did not want to see Jews resettling in the rural areas.[21]

The Sanguszkos and the Grocholskis, the Polish owners of the shtetls Shepetovka and Sudilkov, were nowhere close in terms of their wealth and influence to the eighteenth-century Polish magnates, who could defer Jewish taxes and even extend significant financial help to the Jews in their private towns. They provided one *korets* of grain per Jewish family (about eight to ten pounds) at best, and let Jews cut down trees in the forests they owned to rebuild their houses, but that was the most they could do.[22]

The Polish town-owners could no longer provide the help that was needed, whereas the Russian government did not rush to the rescue. The Russian administration was, of course, deeply saddened by the events, yet it was not particularly interested in rebuilding the shtetl economy, the backbone of the vanishing Polish presence in the Russian borderlands. After all, the worse the shtetl situation, the easier it would be to purchase the town from the bankrupt Polish gentry. It was a cynical but not an impractical decision.

11.3. Ruins of the magnates' castle in Korets.
CAHJP, P166, D23, no. 010. Courtesy of the Central Archives for the History of the Jewish People.

One also needs to remember that urban fires constituted about 8 percent of all Russia's fires in the mid-nineteenth century. Most of the fires in Russia—more than 90 percent—occurred in rural areas. Rebuilding the villages was a higher priority for the government. When informed of the shtetl fires, Nicholas and his minister of finance ordered Jewish debts deferred for five to ten years, but not cancelled. Interest-free loans were extended to the Jewish victims of the fires, but only to those who would rebuild in their towns. In most cases, they ordered to pay Jews three or four rubles in compensation for the damages. However, survivors complained to the governor that this assistance never reached them, as, for example, after devastating fires in Medzhibozh and Letichev.[23]

Some shtetls, especially the larger ones and those purchased by the government were actually rebuilt and regained their economic balance, but many more never recovered. Facing devastation of such enormous proportions, entire Jewish families preferred to leave their shtetl. Long before the industrialization of late imperial Russia ruined Jewish artisans, suppressed Jewish trade, and pushed thousands of Jews out of the shtetls to big towns and cities, it was a natural disaster like fire (and famine, in northern areas of the Pale of Settlement) that forced Jews to resettle.

The government, the military, and the financial administration still considered these Jews as members of their community of origin years after they had left, for tax and conscription purposes, registering them as the Derazhnia or Ostrog townsfolk, even though they had already lived for years in Berdichev and Kremenets, Zhitomir or Kamenets-Podolsk. The streets were wider there, sanitary conditions much better, and fire brigades more effective. Christians were also more influential and well-off in bigger towns, and as a rule, they were more eager to help, as for example in Kremenets, where local Christian authorities managed to raise 4,400 rubles for eleven Jewish families who had lost their belongings and homes in a fire.[24] But that was already a different story about Jewish encounters with urban spaces beyond the shtetl.

A CULTURAL ARTIFACT

Once the energetic and entrepreneurial Jews left the shtetl, it turned into a real village, with small Jewish grocery and kerosene stores surrounding the empty marketplace, which was filled with puddles and mud. Other shtetls were purchased by the crown treasury and became district or province centers, growing into towns that no longer depended on the marketplace, and with an infrastructure very different from that of the shtetl. The shtetl lost its Poles and its Jews—and the incoming Christian, predominantly Ukrainian, population reinforced the shtetl's rural elements but reaped no benefit from retaining its urban features.

With a few very rare exceptions, these towns today have almost nothing in common with the shtetls they once were. Only the name of the shtetl is still a reminder of its past. We now evoke the shtetl names with reverence and fascination, as the Jews of the shtetls once evoked the names of the great Hasidic masters. The shtetl irreversibly turned into a cultural artifact, a magic lantern with faded pictures of the lives of the Jewish forefathers.

Mendele Moykher Sforim used to say that every Jew had Glupsk in his veins—Glupsk was for him a quintessential and imaginary shtetl. Indeed,

11.4. A well in a shtetl.

CAHJP, P166, D27, no. 011. Courtesy of the Central Archives for the History of the Jewish People.

wherever the Jews arrived, they brought their shtetl with them. And with the shtetl came its idiosyncratic Slavic features, which shaped the Jewish identity for a century to come. In Jaffo, Buenos Aires, or New York, they were convinced that if the laws of a country went against common sense, then doing things illegally would not only make sense but also prove that they were smart. They realized that to survive in austere circumstances, Jews needed to be multitaskers, and that alacrity was the key to success in any economic or social pursuit. They also realized that petty crime was bad but organized crime was better. Even in what one can call civilized countries they retained their Slavic predilection for the forbidden.

The shtetl Jews had lost their inns, but gossiping at the dinner table on any subject became an embedded tradition. The family remained for them one of the highest positive values, while being a bachelor, one of the most negative—to the extent that remarrying became a kind of sport, second only to gossiping. Even if they could neither read nor understand them, Jews knew that Hebrew books, particularly on Kabbalah and Hasidism, had redemptive value, and they kept them on their shelves. Jews could move as far as Johannesburg, yet they still added the summer blessing over dew to their winter prayers, because for them the sky was always over the land of Israel. They readily raised funds for their brethren in the land of Israel—but were in no rush to join them there. And a good drink for them was, naturally, a precious moment of freedom, particularly when it coincided with the spiritual uplift of the Sabbath day.

The shtetl and its Jews did not disappear but entered a new era, a new iron age with anti-Jewish violence, political and practical antisemitism, revolutions, wars, and the total extinction of the Jewish presence in the shtetl. This era firmly associated the shtetl, the *mestechko,* with provincialism and backwardness. The shtetl as we have seen it at its height was no longer there. It vanished, like an East European Atlantis, together with its unique dwellers, their pursuits, their material culture, and their dreams.

We can, and perhaps will, mourn its demise, its descent into oblivion, its complete destruction in the fires of the Holocaust. We will cherish the precious fragments of memories retained by the few survivors, but we can also tell stories of the shtetl's greatness, of its vibrant life and fascinating verve. We can—and should—explore what the shtetl was in its moment of glory, which is exactly what this book is all about.

ABBREVIATIONS

AGAD	*Archiwum Główne Akt Dawnych*, Central Archive of Old Documents, Warsaw
ark.	*arkush*, page
BHT	*Beit Hatfutsot*, Museum of the Jewish People (Diaspora Museum), Tel Aviv
BN	*Biblioteka Narodowa*, National Library, Warsaw
CAHJP	Central Archives for the History of the Jewish People, Jerusalem
CJA	Center for Jewish Art at Hebrew University, Jerusalem
d.	*delo, dilo,* file
DAKO	*Derzhavnyi Arkhiv Kyivskoi Oblasti*, State Archive of Kyiv Region, Kyiv
DAKhO	*Derzhavnyi Arkhiv Khmelnytskoi Oblasti*, State Archive of Khmelnytskyi Region, Khmelnytskyi, Ukraine
DAPO	*Derzhavnyi Arkhiv Kamianets-Podilskoi Oblasti*, State Archive of Kamianets-Podilskyi Region, Kamianets-Podilskyi, Ukraine
DATO	*Derzhavnyi Arkhiv Ternopilskoi Oblasti*, State Archive of Ternopil Region, Ternopil, Ukraine
DAVO	*Derzhavnyi Arkhiv Vynnytskoi Oblasti*, State Archive of Vynnytsia Region, Vynnytsia, Ukraine
DAZHO	*Derzhavnyi Arkhiv Zhytomyrskoi Oblasti*, State Archive of Zhytomyr Region, Zhytomyr, Ukraine
f.	*fond*, collection
GARF	*Gosudarstvennyi arkhiv Rossiiskoi Federatsii*, Moscow
IA	*Instytut Arkheolohii Natsionalnoi Akademii Nauk Ukrainy*, Institute of Archaeology of the National Academy of Sciences of Ukraine, Kyiv

IR	*Instytut Rukopysu*, Institute of Manuscript at the Vernadsky National Library of the Academy of Sciences of Ukraine, Kyiv
JNUL	Jewish National and University Library, Jerusalem
l.	*list*, page
LKhG	*Lvivska khudozhnia galereia*, Lviv Art Gallery, Lviv, Ukraine
LME	*Lvivskyi muzei etnohrafii ta khudozhnioho promyslu*, Lviv Museum of Ethnography and Crafts, Lviv
LNB	*Lvivska naukova biblioteka im. V. Stefanyka*, Stefanyk Library of the National Academy of Sciences of Ukraine, Lviv
LNM	*Lvivskyi natsionalnyi muzei*, Lviv National Museum, Lviv
LVIA	*Lietuvos Valstybes Istorijos Archyvas*, Lithuanian State Historical Archives, Vilnius
MIK	*Muzei istorychnykh koshtovnostei Ukrainy*, Museum of Historical Treasures of Ukraine, Kyiv
MN	*Muzeum narodowe*, National Museum, Warsaw
MNB	*Muzeum narodowe*, Bochnia, Poland
MNK	*Muzeum narodowe*, Kraków
NBU	*Natsionalna Biblioteka Ukrainy im. V.I. Vernadskoho*, Vernadsky National Library of the National Academy of Sciences of Ukraine, Kyiv
NPA	*Nacionalinis spaudos archyvas*, National Press Archive, Vilnius
op.	*opis', opys*, inventory
PNB	*Polska Biblioteka Narodowa*, Polish National Library, Warsaw
PSZ	*Polnoe sobranie zakonov Rossiiskoi Imperii*, Complete collection of laws of the Russian Empire
RGADA	*Rossiiskii gosudarstvennyi arkhiv drevnikh aktov*, Russian State Archive of Old Documents, Moscow
RGIA	*Rossiiskii gosudarstvennyi istoricheskii arkhiv*, Russian State Historical Archive, St. Petersburg
RGVIA	*Rossiiskii gosudarstvennyi voenno-istoricheskii arkhiv*, Russian State Military and Historical Archive, Moscow
SPb.	St. Petersburg
spr.	*sprava*, file
TAMA	Tel Aviv Museum of Art, Tel Aviv

TB   Babylonian Talmud
TsDIAU   *Tsentralnyi derzhavnyi istorychnyi arkhiv Ukrainy*, Central
            Historical Archive of Ukraine, Kyiv
YIVO   *Yidisher visnshaftlekher institut*, Institute for Jewish Research,
            New York

NOTES

INTRODUCTION: WHAT'S IN A NAME?

1. I leave aside the encounter of East European Jews with the Kievan Rus as it was centuries before the Russian Empire—and Muscovy—came into being and because the idea of uninterrupted continuity between Kievan Rus and Muscovy is a self-serving baroque age legend, invented by Kievan church clerics in the Russian court service. On Jews in Kievan Rus, see Alexander Kulik, "Jews from Rus in Medieval England," *Jewish Quarterly Review* 102, no. 3 (2012): 371–403; idem, "The Jews of 'Slavia Graeca': The Northern Frontier of Byzantine Jewry?," *Jews in Byzantium* (2012): 297–314; idem, "Judeo-Greek legacy in Medieval Rus," *Viator* 39, no. 1 (2008): 51–64.

2. On the Pale of Jewish Settlement and its formation and development as a sociopolitical and legal institution, see John Klier, *Russia Gathers Her Jews: The Origins of the "Jewish Question" in Russia* (Dekalb, IL: Northwestern Illinois University Press, 2011), and Alessandro Cifariello, "Ebrei e 'zona di residenza' durante il regno di Alessandro II," *Studi Slavistici* 7 (2010): 85–109.

3. See, for example, some regional works containing comparative data: S. M. Karetnikov, *Volynskaia guberniia. Geografichesko-istoricheskii ocherk gubernii i opisanie uezdov* (Kremenets: V. Tsvik, 1910); A. I. Baranovich, *Magnatskoe khoziaistvo na iuge Volyni v XVIII v.* (Moscow: Izdatel'stvo Akademii Nauk SSSR, 1955); Max Boyko, *Economic and Social Problems in the History of Volhynia* (Bloomington, IN: Oseredok Bibliohrafii Volyni, 1971).

4. Galina Nosova, "Ob izmeneniiakh v finansovo-ekonomicheskom polozhenii zapadnykh gubernii Rossii v 1812 godu," in *1812 god. Liudi i sobytiia velikoi epokhi: Materialy Mezhdunarodnoi nauchnoi konferentsii* (Moscow: Kuchkovo pole, 2010), 67–98, esp. 69–72.

5. David Assaf, Gadi Sagiv, "Ha-hasidut be-Rusya ha-tsarit: hebetim historiim ve-hevratiim," in Il'ia Lurie, ed., *Toldot yehudei Rusya* (Jerusalem: Zalman Shazar, 2012), 75–112, here 81–85.

6. Marvin Herzog, ed., *The Language and Culture Atlas of Ashkenazic Jewry*, 3 vols. (Tübingen: Max Niemeyer Verlag, 2000), 290, map 117.

7. See Leo Wiener, "On the Judaeo-German Spoken by the Russian Jews," *American Journal of Philology* 14, no. 1 (1893): 41–67, and Max Weinreich, *History of the Yiddish Language* (Chicago: University of Chicago Press, 1980), 481–482, 578–590, 593–594, 637–638. For the Ukrainian influence on Yiddish, see ibid., 587–593.

8. Henceforth I use contemporary Russian administrative terms for all geographic localities. This decision has been necessitated by a historical context—the book portrays the time when what today is Ukraine was incorporated into the Russian Empire

politically and administratively. This russification is an important background to my story. Also, the decision is necessitated by a pure convenience. Most shtetls had their Yiddish names different from Polish, Russian, and Ukrainian names (e.g., *Zvil* for Novokrad-Volynskyi; *Trisk* for Turiisk; *Bardychev*, first syllable stressed, for Berdychiv, second syllable stressed), modern Ukrainian names are different from the contemporary Russian administrative names and were not used in the period described in the book (e.g., Zaslav vs. Iziaslav), while the subsequent renaming of the shtetls and their transformation into villages makes it impossible to connect a modern locality in Ukraine with a historical shtetl in the Russian Empire.

9. See in more detail Yohanan Petrovsky-Shtern and Antony Polonsky, eds., *POLIN*, vol. 26 (2013), 3–5 and Dan Shapira, "The First Jews of Ukraine," ibid., 65–77.

10. Antony Polonsky, *The Jews in Poland and Russia*, 3 vols. (Oxford: Littman Library of Jewish Civilization, 2010), 1:7–39, 68–90.

11. For the most important works touching on the sociocultural profile of the shtetl, see David Assaf, *The Regal Way: The Life and Times of Rabbi Israel of Ruzhin* (Stanford, CA: Stanford University Press, 2002); Israel Bartal, *The Jews of Eastern Europe, 1772–1881* (Philadelphia: University of Pennsylvania Press, 2005); Arthur Eisenbach, *The Emancipation of the Jews in Poland, 1780–1870* (Oxford: Institute for Polish-Jewish Studies, 1991); David Fishman, *Russia's First Modern Jews: The Jews of Shklov* (New York: New York University Press, 1995); Gershon Hundert, ed., *The YIVO Encyclopedia of Jews in Eastern Europe*, 2 vols. (New Haven, CT: Yale University Press, 2008); John Klier, *Rossiia sobiraet svoikh evreev: Proiskhozhdenie evreiskogo voprosa v Rossii* (Moscow, Jerusalem: Mosty Kultury/Gesharim, 2000); Antony Polonsky, *The Jews in Poland and Russia*, 3 vols. (Oxford: Littman Library of Jewish Civilization, 2010), esp. vol. 1; Nancy Sinkoff, *Out of the Shtetl: Making Jews Modern in the Polish Borderlands* (Providence, RI: Brown Judaic Studies, 2004); Michael Stanislawski, *Tsar Nicholas I and the Jews: The Transformation of Jewish Society in Russia, 1825–1855* (Philadelphia: Jewish Publication Society of America, 1983); Shaul Stampfer, *Families, Rabbis and Education: Traditional Jewish Society in Nineteenth-Century Eastern Europe* (Oxford: Littman Library of Jewish Civilization, 2010). Henceforth I will quote only the most relevant sources and avoid long footnotes.

12. Berl Kagan, ed., *Luboml: The Memorial Book of a Vanished Shtetl* (Hoboken, NY: Ktav, 1997), 1.

13. Lawrence A. Coben, *Anna's Shtetl* (Tuscaloosa: University of Alabama Press, 2007), 9; see here an accurate critique of the scholarship on the shtetl, 201.

14. S. Y. Abramovitsh, *The Wishing-Ring: A Novel* (Syracuse, NY: Syracuse University Press, 2003), 1–2.

15. On literary images of the shtetl as a construction that has hardly anything to do with its historical verisimilitude, see Katarzyna Więcławska, *Zmartwychwstałe miasteczko: Literackie oblicza sztetl* (Lublin: Wydawnictwo Uniwersytetu Marii Curie Skłodowskiej, 2005). On the literary constructions of the shtetl, see Dan Miron, *Image of the Shtetl and Other Studies of Modern Jewish Literary Imagination* (Syracuse, NY: Syracuse University Press, 2001), 1–48.

16. Yisroel Aksenfeld, *The Headband*, in *The Shtetl*, trans. and ed. by Joachim Neugroschel (Woodstock, NY: Overlook Press, 1989), 49 and 57. Neugroschel deftly captures Axenfeld's irony; see "khoche in aza *shtetl* (ikh hob aroysgekhapt, hot nit faribl)—in aza *shtot* vi Loyhoyopoli"; see Yisroel Aksenfeld, *Dot* [Dos] *shterntikhl un Der Ershter yiddisher rekrut* (Buenos Aires: YIVO, 1971), 32.

17. Alana Newhouse, "A Closer Reading of Roman Vishniac," *New York Times Sunday Magazine,* April 4, 2010, MM36.

18. Eva Hoffman, *Shtetl: The Life and Death of a Small Town and the World of Polish Jews* (Boston: Houghton Mifflin, 1997), 12.

19. Paul Kriwaczek, *Yiddish Civilization: The Rise and Fall of the Forgotten Nation* (London: Weidenfeld and Nicholson, 2005), 19.

20. Abraham Joshua Heschel, "The Eastern European Era in Jewish History," *YIVO Bleter,* vol. 25 (1945): 1–21.

21. Steven Zipperstein, "Underground Man: The Curious Case of Mark Zborowski and the Writing of a Modern Jewish Classic," *Jewish Review of Books* 2 (Summer 2010): 38–42, here 38.

22. Mark Zborowski and Elizabeth Herzog, *Life Is with People: The Culture of the Shtetl.* Foreword by Margaret Mead, introduction by Barbara Kirshenblatt-Gimblett (New York: Schocken Books, 1995), xiv, 61.

23. Israel Bartal, "Imagined Geography: The Shtetl, Myth, and Reality," in Steven T. Katz, ed., *The Shtetl: New Evaluations* (New York: New York University Press, 2007), 187–191.

24. Gershon Hundert, "The Importance of Demography and Patterns of Settlement for an Understanding of the Jewish Experience in East-Central Europe," in Steven T. Katz, ed., *The Shtetl: New Evaluations* (New York: New York University Press, 2007), 29–38.

25. See Gershon David Hundert, *Jews in Poland-Lithuania in the Eighteenth Century: A Genealogy of Modernity* (Berkeley: University of California Press, 2004); Moshe Rosman, *The Lords' Jews: Magnate-Jewish Relations in the Polish-Lithuanian Commonwealth during the Eighteenth Century* (Cambridge, MA: Harvard University Press for the Center for Jewish Studies, Harvard University and the Harvard Ukrainian Research Institute, 1990); Adam Teller, *Kesef, koah, ve-hashpaʻah: ha-Yehudim be-aḥuzat bet Radzʼivil be-Lita ba-meʼah ha-18* (Jerusalem: Merkaz Zalman Shazar, 2006).

26. Isaac Levitats, *The Jewish Community in Russia, 1772–1844* (New York: Columbia University Press, 1943).

27. John Doyle Klier, "What Exactly Was the Shtetl?," in Gennadi Estraikh and Mikhail Krutikov, eds., *The Shtetl: Image and Reality. Papers of the Second Mendel Friedman International Conference on Yiddish* (Oxford: Legenda, 2000), 23–35, here 26–28.

28. Samuel Kassow, "Introduction," in Steven T. Katz, *The Shtetl: New Evaluations* (New York: New York University Press, 2007), 1–28, here 3; idem, "Shtetl," in Gershon D. Hundert, ed., *The YIVO Encyclopedia of Jews in Eastern Europe* (New Haven, CT: Yale University Press, 2008), 2:1732–1739.

29. For example, in 1799 Minkovtsy officially had fifty-three houses yet was considered a shtetl, even though the nearby villages boasted between 164 and 180 houses. DAKO, f. 333, op. 1, spr. 2 ("Vedomost o dorogakh Skvirskogo uezda," 1799), ark. 1–2.

30. DAKO, f. 1, op. 336, spr. 4051 ("Svedenia o kolichestve muzhskogo i zhenskogo evreiskogo naselenia," 1848), ark. 256–256. Berdichev, the biggest of these towns, was classified as *mestechko* as late as the 1870s; see, for example, CAHJP, HM2/9308.2 (original—TsDIAU, f. 442, op. 548, spr. 50, "O vvedenii gorodovogo polozheniia 1870 goda v Podolskoi gubernii i o zhalobe evreev Bara na mestnoe gorodskoie pravlenie," 1879), ark. 82.

31. DAKO, f. 1, op. 351, spr. 8 ("Vedomosti kolichestva naselenia v uezdakh," 1802), ark. 3–5.

32. DAKO, f. 1, op. 336, spr. 3376 ("Po predlozheniiu Kievskogo Voennogo Gubernatora ob otkrytii v m. Belaia Tserkov iarmarkov," 1840), ark. 11–14.

33. TsDIAU, f. 442, op. 1, spr. 1198 ("Vedomosti o kolichestve naselennykh punktov, naselenia, promyshlennykh predpriiatii, uchebnykh zavedenii i pr. po Podol'skoi gubernii," 1832), ark. 8–9.
34. Figures of the 1860s. See P. P. Chubinskii, *Trudy etnografichesko-statisticheskoi ekspeditsii v Zapadno-russkii krai* (St. Petersburg: Geograficheskoe obshchestvo, 1872), 178–179.
35. Zipperstein, "Underground Man," 41.
36. CAHJP, HM2/5735 (original—Woewódzkie Archiwum Kraków, Archiwum Sanguszkow, sygn. 546, "Rachunki ekonomiczne roznych dobr: Porządek synagogi zasławskiej według inwentarza opisany," 1740), no pagination, par. 22.
37. Quoted in Gershon David Hundert, "From the Perspective of Progress: Travelers and Foreigners on Jews in Poland and Lithuania in the Eighteenth and Early Nineteenth Centuries," in David Assaf and Ada Rapoport-Albert, eds., *Yashan mipney hadash: Mehkarim be-toldot yehudey mizrakh eropa u-ve-tarbutam* (Jerusalem: Zalman Shazar, 2009), 115–135, here 120.
38. In an ongoing debate among various scholars regarding the parameters of the "marriage of convenience" between Jews and magnates, I accept its positive assessment by Moshe Rosman and Gershon Hundert only with the limitations and caveats put forward by Adam Teller. See, for example, Adam Teller, "'In the Land of Their Enemies'? The Duality of Jewish Life in Eighteenth-Century Poland," *Polin* 19 (2007): 431–446.
39. In the 1850s, the shtetls of Kiev province belonged to various gentry, both Eastern Orthodox and Catholic: Obukhov belonged partially to the state treasury, partially to General Berdiaev; Borodianka to landlord Poniatowski, Gostomel to Colonel Berezovski, Kagarlyk to Major General Trashchinski, Rzhishchev to Duchess Dravinska, Belaia Tserkov and Rokitna to Counts Branicki, Fastov to the state treasury, Boiarka to Branicka, Rymanovka to landlord Abramova, Ekaterinopol to the state treasury, Boguslav to Branicki, Kozin to Colonel Montrezor, Korsun to Count Lopukhin, Trakhtomirov to Colonel Levkovich, Dashev to Duchess Potocka, Priskov to landlord Kolysko, Korostyshev to Count Olizer, Malin to Prince Radziwiłł, Novofastov to landlord Lubovicki, Khodarkov to Swidzinski, Khoshevate to landlord Mladecki, Zhashkov to Tarnovecki, Talnoe to Duchess Naryshkina, Smela to Duchess Bobrinska, Bililovka to the state treasury, and Makhnovka to various gentry members. See DAKO, f. 35, op. 14, spr. 8 ("Po predlozheniu nachalnika gubernii o priglashenii zemlemera," 1854–1857), ark. 24–31.
40. CAHJP, HM2/9531.2 (TsDIAU, f. 490, op. 3, spr. 10, "O prieme v kaznu m. Zhvanets," 1861–69), ark. 21; CAHJP, HM2/9531.3 (TsDIAU, f. 490, op. 13, spr. 44, "O liustratsii zinkovskogo imeniia," 1843), ark. 2–3.
41. For example, in the 1870s and 1880s, such towns as Lutsk, Kovel, Vladimir-Volynsk, Kremenets, Ovruch, Novograd-Volynsk, Zaslav, Ostrog, Starokonstantinov, and Dubno still were considered *vladel'cheskii*, privately owned towns.
42. CAHJP, HM8969.1 (original—TsDIAU, f. 442, op. 1, spr. 7890, "O predstavlenii svedenii o mestechkakh Kievskoi gubernii, v kotorykh litsam evreiskoi natsional'nosti razreshaetsia arendovat korchmy," 1849), ark. 62–72, 74–80.
43. Ibid., ark. 82.
44. See tables arranged according to the name of the shtetl, province, and district, its owner and reasons, for it to be called that way, ibid., ark. 62–72, 74–82, 159–166.
45. CAHJP, HM2/9316.23 (original—RGIA, f. 1268, op. 1, d. 300, "Po pros'bam pomeshchikov raznykh gubernii o pereimenovanii selenii v mestechki," 1807), ll. 1, 8, 27, 78–79, 183–185, 260–262.

46. CAHJP, HM2/7959.3 (original—TsDIAU, f. 442, op. 550, spr. 43, "O zamoshchenii ulits Balty iz sum koroboshcnogo sbora," 1895), ark. 37–38.

47. For more detail on this, see Gregory Freeze, "The *Soslovie* (Estate) Paradigm and Russian Social History," *American Historical Review* 91, no. 1 (1986): 11–36.

48. CAHJP, HM2/7959.3 (original—TsDIAU, f. 442, op. 550, spr. 43, "O zamoshchenii ulits Balty iz sum koroboshcnogo sbora," 1895), ark. 104–105.

49. Precisely because the shtetl was not "ethnically Jewish" I disagree with the conceptualization of the shtetl by Ben-Cion Pinchuk, who projects the 1897 statistics onto the entire period of the shtetl history; see his "The Shtetl: An Ethnic Town in the Russian Empire," *Cahiers du Monde Russe* 41, no. 4 (2000): 495–504.

50. CAHJP, HM8969.1 (original—TsDIAU, f. 442, op. 1, spr. 7890, "O predstavlenii svedenii o mestechkakh Kievskoi gubernii, v kotorykh litsam evreiskoi natsional'nosti razreshaetsia arendovat korchmy," 1849).

51. NBU, Orientalia Department, Pinkasim collection, or. 3, n. 2 ("*Pinkas de-hevrah kadisha,*" Burial society, ca. 1752–ca. 1871).

52. Avraam Ber Gottlober, *Zikhronot u-masa'ot,* 2 vols. (Jerusalem: Mosad Byaliḳ, 1976), 2:55, 62, 64.

53. For the pinkasim from Baranovka, Bar, Balta, Berdichev, Letichev, Medzhibozh, and other localities identifying as a town (*ir*) their places of origin, see NBU, Orientalia Department, Pinkasim collection, f. 321, op. 1, d. 3 (OR 4); d. 5 (OR 7); d. 6 (OR 8); d. 50 (OR 91); d. 60 (OR 105); d. 86 (OR 29).

54. Nosson Sternhartz, *Haye MOHARA"N* (Jerusalem: Meshekh ha-nahal, 1982), 112 (siman 114).

55. "*Pinkas shel hevrah ahavat re'im,*" NBU, Orientalia Department, f. 321, op. 1 (OR 17).

56. Arye Leib(ush) ben Eliyahu Bolechover, *Arugot ha-bosem* (Vilna: Yosef Reuven Rom, 1870), part 2: *Even ha-ezer,* siman 5, d. 6b–7a.

57. Israel Isser ben Zeev Wolf, *Sefer sha'ar mishpat* (Mogilev, 1810), siman 15, d. 31.

58. In his Hebrew homilies, published posthumously, Maggid of Dubno (d. 1804) included his famous parables, which he had originally presented in Yiddish and in which he used the terms *shtot* ('*ir*) and *shtetl* ('*ir ktanah*) indiscriminately, sometimes interchangeably. The Yiddish version of his parables, taken from his homiletic texts and translated back into the original language of oral sermon, also uses these two terms indiscriminately and interchangeably. Both shtetl and shtot have *parnasim* (oligarchs of the community), a synagogue warden, a rich philanthropist, a rabbi, a wise man, and a fool. See Yaakov Kranz, *Ohel Yaakov* (Warsaw: Goldman, 1874), 1:18, 24, 28, 41, 43, 57, 71, 76–77, 97, 107–108, 121, 131, esp. 137, and idem, *Ale mesholim fun Dubner maggid,* 2 vols. (New York: Hebrew Publishing Co., 1925), 1:34, 38, 64, 68, esp. 11; 2:25, 27, 50–51, 77.

59. Yekhezkel Segal ha-Levy Landau, *Noda bi-yehudah* (Jerusalem: Jerusalem Institute, 1994), vol. 2: *Even ha-ezer,* siman 115, d. 282–283.

60. Alla Sokolova, "Evreiskie mestechki pamiati: lokalizatsiia shtetla," in V.A. Dymshits et al., *Shtetl: XXI vek* (St. Petersburg: Peterburgskaia Iudaika, 2008), 29–64.

CHAPTER 1: RUSSIA DISCOVERS ITS SHTETL

1. A. A. Glagolev, *Zapiski russkogo puteshestvennika,* 4 vols. (St. Petersburg: Rossiiskaia Akademiia Nauk, 1837), 1:107, 111–114.

2. RGADA, f. 16, op. 1, d. 748 ("Donesenie general-gubernatora Mikhaila Krechetnikova o Kievskoi gubernii,"), ll. 45, 141–142, 191; RGADA, f. 16, op. 1, d. 622 ("Donesenie

gubernatora Fedora Berkhmana o Bratslavskoi gubernii," 1793), ll. 1–3; RGADA, f. 16, op. 1, d. 706 ("Donesenie gubernatora Vasiliia Sheremetieva o Iziaslavskoi gub.," 1793), ll. 1–5; RGADA, f. 16, op. 1, d. 747 ("Donesenie gubernatora Semena Shirkova po Kievskoi gubernii," 1793), ll. 1–6.

3. RGADA, f. 1239, op. 3, d. 65010 ("Zhurnal vysochaishikh povelenii po delam s Pol'sheiu, po chasti upravliaemoi Generalom-Ad'iutantom Platonom Zubovym," 1792), 4–5, 8, 44–47; RGADA, f. 1239, op. 3, d. 65018 ("Zhurnal vysochaishim poveleniiam po delam s Pol'sheiu," 1793), ll. 2–4, 67, 10–12, 23–24, 27–28, 56–57.

4. For Catherine II (the Great), see Robert K. Massie, *Catherine the Great: Portrait of a Woman* (New York: Random House, 2011); Isabel de Madariaga, *Catherine the Great: A Short History* (New Haven, CT: Yale University Press, 1990), and John LeDonne, *Ruling Russia: Politics and Administration in the Age of Absolutism, 1762–1796* (Princeton, NJ: Princeton University Press, 1984).

5. RGADA, f. 1239, op. 3, d. 65041 ("Zhurnal vysochaishim poveleniiam po delam s Polsheiu," 1794 g.), ll. 27, 30–32, 135.

6. DAKO, f. 1, op. 336, spr. 4 ("Raporty gorodnichikh vladel'cheskikh gorodov," 1790), ark. 13–14, 48–49.

7. DAKO, f. 1, op. 336, spr. 4 ("Raporty gorodnichikh vladel'cheskikh gorodov," 1790), ark. 14–19; DAKO, f. 2, op. 3, spr. 410 ("Perepiska kievskoi kazennnoi palaty," 1797–1798), ark. 4; for some fifty years after the second partition of Poland in 1793, the denizens of the western provinces and of the Kingdom of Poland (also under Russian control) used both ruble and złoty, often preferring złoty to ruble. While the official złoty to ruble exchange rate was 6.6:1, quite often (as the grassroots documents testify) the rate was 4:1. On the russification of Polish currency, see Ekaterina Pravilova, "From the zloty to the ruble: the Kingdom of Poland in the monetary politics of the Russian empire," in Jane Burbank, Mark von Hagen, and Anatolyi Remnev, eds., *Russian Empire: space, people, power, 1700–1930* (Bloomington: Indiana University Press, 2007), esp. 298–317.

8. DAKO, f. 2, op. 3, spr. 376 ("Perepiska po voprosu o preobrazovanii Kievskoi gubernii," 1797), ark. 17, 44–47, 98–101, 127, 136.

9. RGADA, f. 1239, op. 3, d. 65051 ("Zhurnal imennym ukazam," 1795), ark. 19–20, 38, 60–62, 73, 76, 82, 86–87.

10. DAKO, f. 2, op. 3, spr. 379 ("O preobrazovanii Kievskoi gubernii i razdelenii ee na uezdy," 1797–1798), ark. 16, 53, 72–73.

11. CAHJP, H2/9453.15 (original—TsDIAU, f. 442, op. 789a, spr. 298, "Po predstavleniiu Zhitomirskogo voennogo gubernatora o vrede i neudobnosti imet uezdnye goroda v prinadlezhashchikh chastnym vladel'tsam pomest'iakh," 1839), ark. 2–3.

12. Ibid., 4–5.

13. CAJHP, HM9529.12 (original—TsDIAU, f. 442, op. 346, spr. 26, "O prodazhe goroda Dubno v kaznu," 1841), ark. 127.

14. TsDIAU, f. 442, op. 533, spr. 183 ("O sostoianii Podol'skoi gubernii za 1879 g."), ark. 8.

15. On the cartographers (called land surveyors, *zemlemery*) as the most important clerks in care of collecting basic data, see DAKO, f. 2, op. 3, spr. 379 ("O preobrazovanii Kievskoi gubernii i razdelenii ee na uezdy," 1797–1798), ark. 1–3.

16. RGADA, f. 12, op. 1, d. 223 ("O rasporiazheniiakh po upravleniiu oblastei vnov priobretennykh ot Pol'shi. Iz bumag kn. Platona Zubova"), ll. 1–3; DAKO, f. 2, op. 3, spr. 375 ("O sostoianii umanskogo uezda," 1797), ark. 8.

17. These cartographers were trained in the military, served at the Main Headquarters of the Russian troops in the Ukraine, and were commissioned to collect the data by the Governor-General M.M. Krechetnikov, see Mykola Barmak, *Formuvannia vladnykh instytutsii Rossiis'koi imperii na pravoberezhnii Ukraini: kinets' XVIII—persha polovyna XIX st.* (Ternopil: Aston, 2007), 151–153.

18. For western travelers to East Europe and their travelogues, see Wendy Bracewell, ed., *Orientations: An Anthology of East European Travel Writing, ca. 1550–2000* (Budapest and New York: Central European University Press, 2009); Wendy Bracewell and Alex Drace-Francis, eds., *Under Eastern Eyes: A Comparative Introduction to East European Travel Writing on Europe* (Budapest and New York: Central European University Press, 2008); Larry Wolff, *Inventing Eastern Europe: The Map of Civilization on the Mind of the Enlightenment* (Stanford, CA: Stanford University Press, 1994). Several descriptions of the Jews by western travelers do not fit the general stereotype and we will use them in due course, among them those assembled by Gershon Hundert, see his "From the perspective of progress: travelers and foreigners on Jews in Poland and Lithuania in the eighteenth and early nineteenth centuries" in David Assaf and Ada Rapoport-Albert, eds., *Yashan mipney hadash: Mehkarim be-toldot yehudey mizrakh eropa u-ve-tarbutam* (Jerusalem: Zalman Shazar, 2009), 115–135.

19. CAHJP, HM2/8870 (original—DAKhO, f. 115, op. 4, spr. 2, "Topograficheskoe opisanie Bratslavskogo uezda," 1799), ark. 1–4.

20. DAKO, f. 2, op. 3, spr. 341 ("Perepiska gorodskikh dum o stroitel'stvakh v gorodakh," 1796), ark. 1–3.

21. CAHJP, HM3/9385.1 (original—DAPO, f. 115, op. 2, spr. 2, "Kameral'noe i topograficheskoe opisanie Letichevskogo uezda," 1812), ark. 6–7, 23–28, 166–170; CAHJP, H2/9385.2 (DAPO, f. 115, op. 2, spr. 5, "Topograficheskoe opisanie Vinnitskogo uezda," 1797–1806), ark. 5–7, 118; CAHJP, HM2/9385.3 (DAPO, f. 115, op. 2, spr. 6, "Kameralnoe i topograficheskoe opisanie mestechek i selenii Kamenetskogo uezda," 1796–97), ark. 4–7, 38, 46.

22. CAJHP, HM2/8870 (original—DAKhO, f. 115, op. 4, spr. 2, "Topograficheskoe opisanie Bratslavskogo uezda," 1799), ark. 11–13, 42.

23. CAJHP, HM2/8870 (original—DAKhO, f. 115, op. 4, spr. 2, "Topograficheskoe opisanie Bratslavskogo uezda," 1799), ark. 1–4.

24. A.U. Bolotnikov, N. Ia. Ozertsovskii, "Dnevnik. 1782–1783," in S. A. Kozlov, *Russkii puteshestvennik epokhi Prosveshcheniia* (St. Petersburg: Istoricheskaia illiustratsiia, 2003), 277–356, here 347.

25. Ivan M. Dolgorukov, "Slavny bubny za gorami ili Puteshestvie moe koe-kuda 1810 goda," *Chteniia v Imperatorskom Obshchestve Istorii i Drevnostei Rossiiskikh*, kn. 2 (1869): 1–170, here 209.

26. See Andreas Kappeler, "*Mazepintsy, Malorossy, Khokhly*: Ukrainians in the Ethnic Hierarchy of the Russian Empire," in Andreas Kappeler, Zenon E. Kohut, Frank E. Sysyn, Mark von Hagen, eds., *Culture, Nation, and Identity: The Ukrainian-Russian Encounter (1600–1945)* (Edmonton and Toronto: Canadian Institute of Ukrainian Studies Press, 2003), 162–181, here 162–163.

27. On the history of Kamenets-Podolsk in general and its Jewish community in particular, see Ion Vinokur, Hryhorii Khotiun, *Kamianets'-Podil'skyi derzhavnyi istoryko-kul'turnyi zapovidnyk* (Lviv: Kameniar, 1986); Avraam Rosen et al., eds., *Kaminits-Podolsk u-sevivatah* (Tel Aviv: Irgun yots'ei Kaminits-Podolsk u-sevivatah be-Yisrael, 1965), available in English: Abraham Rosen, ed., *Kaminits-Podolsk and Its Environs*

(Bergenfield: Avotaynu, 1999); Ia. Shulman, *Goroda i liudi evreiskoi diaspory v vostochnoi evrope do nachala XX veka* (Moscow: TLS Faktors, 2002), 89–109. For the history of non-Jewish guilds in the town, see *Tsekhova knyha bondariv, stel'makhiv, kolodiiv, stoliariv mista Kam'aintsia-Podil'skoho vid 1601 do 1803 r.* (Kyiv: Vseukrains'ka akademia nauk, 1932).

28. *Polnoe sobrante zakonov Rossiiskoi imperii* (St. Petersburg: Tipografiia II otdelenia sobstvennoi E. I. V. kantseliarii, 1830–1916), (hereafter PSZ), vol. 24, no. 18, 132; (Levanda V.O. *Polnyi khronologicheskii sbornik zakonov i polozhenii kasaiushchikhsia Evreev, ot ulozheniia Tsaria Alekseia Mikhailovicha do nastoiashchego vremeni, ot 1649–1873 g.* (St. Petersburg: K. V. Trubnikov, 1874), 43 (no. 51).

29. This religious aspect of the traditional Jewish historiographic sources is analyzed at length in Yosef Hayim Yerushalmi, *Zakhor: Jewish History and Jewish Memory* (Seattle: University of Washington Press, 1982), see esp. 81–103, and for the ahistorical character of Jewish communal record and memory books, see ibid., 46.

30. The Vernadsky Library of the National Academy of Sciences of Ukraine, *Orientalia* Department, Pinkasim collection, f. 231, op. 1, no. 33 [or. 61], f. 2a. For a commented translation of this document, see my "Russian Legislation and Jewish Self-Governing Institutions: The Case of Kamenets-Podolsk" and "The Minute-book of the Kamnits (Kamenets) Burial Society," in *Jews in Russia and Eastern Europe* 56, no. 1 (2006): 107–130.

31. Here I disagree with the opposite view about the impact of the Polish magnate culture on the Hasidic masters: Poland did not know the opulent Hasidic courts whereas Russia did. Cf. Adam Teller, "Hasidism and the challenge of geography: the Polish background to the spread of the hasidic movement," *AJS Review* 30, no. 1 (2006): 1–29.

32. Nehemia Polen, "Rebbetzins, Wonder-Children and the Emergence of the Dynastic Principle in Hasidism," in Steven T. Katz, ed., *The Shtetl: New Evaluations* (New York: New York University Press, 2007), 76–123. For Israel of Ruzhin, see David Assaf, *The Regal Way: The Life and Times of Rabbi Israel of Ruzhin* (Stanford, CA: Stanford University Press, 2002).

33. For more detail, see my "The Enemy of the Humanity: The Anti-Napoleon Paradigm in Russian Imagination and the Genesis of the *Protocols of the Elders of Zion*," in Esther Webman, ed., *The Global Impact of the Protocols of the Elders of Zion: A Century-old Myth* (Milton Park, Oxon, UK: Routledge, 2011), 44–66.

34. Esther 6:13.

35. Menahem Gerlits, *Am le-vadad yishkon* (Bnei Brak: Maim hayim, 2000), 158–160, 172–180, 186–190.

36. Binyamin Lukin, "'Sluzhba naroda evreiskogo i ego kagalov': Evrei i Otechestvennaia voina 1812 goda," *Lehayim* 11, no.187 (2007): 38–42.

37. Sergei Volkonskii, *Zapiski* (Irkutsk: Vostochno-sibirskoe knizhnoe izdatel'stvo, 1991), 228.

38. GARF, f. 1165, op. 1, d. 113 ("Donesenia Volynskogo grazhdanskogo gubernatora o zagranichnykh slukhakh i proisshestviiakh," o zaderzhanii podozritel'nykh lits, o khode evakuatsii Volynskoi gubernii," 1812), l. 56.

39. L. E. Gorizontov, *Paradoksy imperskoi politiki: poliaki v Rossii, Russkie v Pol'she* (Moscow: Indrik, 1999), 19, 38–39, 44–45, 62–63, 80–81, 100–101, 124–125.

40. RGADA, f. 204 (Kab. Pavla), op. 1, d. 1 ("Raporty kamenets-podol'skogo voennogo gubernatora A. Bekleshova Pavlu I o pogranichnykh delakh s Avstriei i Pol'shei," 1797), ll. 1–8, 15, 23.

41. GARF, f. 1165, op. 1, d. 113 ("Donesenia Volynskogo grazhdanskogo gubenatora …"), l.7.

42. GARF, f. 1165, op. 1, d. 149 ("Delo po nabliudeniiu za politicheskim nastroeniem zhitelei gubernii, prisoedinennykh ot Pol'shi"), ll. 1, 7, 10, 16–17, 22–24, 40–41.

43. Volkonskii, *Zapiski*, 201.

44. GARF, f. 1165, op. 1, d. 6 ("Delo o rassledovanii slukhov o gotovivshikhsia v Vilenskoi, Minskoi gub. i Belostokskoi obl. evreiskikh pogromakh," 1813), ll. 3–4, 6–8, 16.

45. GARF, f. 1165, op. 1, d. 113 ("Donesenia Volynskogo grazhdanskogo gubernatora …"), ll. 6–7, 10, 55–56, 63–64.

46. S. Shuazel-Guf'ie, *Istoricheskie memuary ob imperatore Aleksandre I ego dvore* (Moscow: Gosudarstvennaia istoricheskaia publichnaia biblioteka Rossii, 2007), 94.

47. Baron Korf, who meticulously collected all the biographic data on Nicholas, thought that this was a genuinely Nicholas's idea, not prompted by anybody in his coterie. See GARF, f. 728, op. 1, d. 2271, ch. I, vol. 1 ("Materialy dlia biografii Nikolaia I"), l. 118; also see N. K. Shilder, *Imperator Nikolai I: ego zhizn i tsarstvovanie*, 2 vols. (St. Petersburg: Suvorin, 1903), 1:68.

48. CAHJP, HM2/9445.1 (original—RGIA, f. 1269, op. 1, spr. 2, "Ob ustroistve evreev," 1840), l. 66 (this file is a collection of earlier documents, including the 1820s reports of the Warsaw Jewish committee on various Jewish reforms).

49. CAHJP, HM2/9558.3 (original—RGADA, f. 1239, op. 3, d. 55352, "Pismo ravvina Shargoroda Davida Gertsenshteina Pavlu I," 1798), l. 1; CAHJP, HM2/8863.1 (f. 224, op. 1, spr. 24, "O nagrazhdenii evreiia Ios Aizika Rabinovicha medal'iu za userdie," 1833), ark. 1–3.

50. DAKO, f. 1, op. 336, spr. 449 ("Po zhalobe umanskogo kuptsa Girshberga na grafa Pototskogo za otkaz v vozvrate vremenno vydannogo emu denezhnogo vekselia," 1802), ark. 1–5.

51. Yisroel Aksenfeld, "The Headband," in Joachim Neugroschel, ed., *The Shtetl* (Woodstock, NY: Overlook Press, 1989), 49–172, here 83.

52. CAHJP, HM2/9455.3 (original—TsDIAU, f. 442, op. 1, spr. 1597, "Perepiska s shefom korpusa zhandarmov Benkendorfom," 1834), ark. 91–92.

53. A. A. Glagolev, *Zapiski russkogo puteshestvennika* , 4 vols. (St. Petersburg: Rossiiskaia Akademiia Nauk, 1837), 1:110.

54. DAKO, f. 2, op. 1, spr. 7434 ("Po otnosheniiu Kievskoi gubernskoi pochtovoi kontory," 1837), ark. 1, 12, 14.

55. DAKO, f. 1, op. 336, spr. 2117 ("Delo ob otkaze gruppy kuptsov i meshchan v arende pocht," 1835), ark. 9–10.

56. The analysis of the dearth of clerks in the newly acquired provinces prompts speculation that the empowerment of Jews might have been urged for pragmatic reasons. See Barmak, *Formuvannia vladnykh instytutsii,* 115.

57. CAHJP, HM2/9315.13 (original—RGIA, f. 1286, op. 1286, spr. 69, "O evreiakh, izbrannykh v magistratskie chleny," 1806), ll. 1–6.

58. TsDIAU, f. 946, op. 1, spr. 2 ("Opis zhurnala volynskogo gubernskogo magistrata," 1796–97), ark. 11–13, 53–55, 57. See also the data for other Jewish members of the province council, TsDIAU, f. 946, op. 1, spr. 6 ("Protokoly zasedanii volynskogo gubernskogo magistrata").

59. DAKO, f. 3, op. 1, spr. 75 ("Po zhalobe kuptsa Rabinovicha na zloubotrebleniia v Zvenigorodskom magistrate," 1811), ark. 6–7.

60. See Sh. Ettinger and Ch. Shmeruk, "Le-toldot ha-yeshuv ha-yehudi be-Kremenets," in Avraam Shmuel Shtein, ed., *Pinkas Kremnits: Sefer zikaron* (Tel Aviv: Hotsa'at irgun 'ole Kremnits be-Yisrael, 1954), 17–45, here 30.

61. Barmak, *Formuvannia vladnykh instytutsii*, 289–290.

62. CAHJP, HM2/8924.5 (original—TsDIAU, f. 442, op. 1, spr. 1441, "O predstavlenii svedenii o litsakh evreiskoi natsional'nosti, ne priniavshikh pravoslavie i nakhodiv-shikhsia na gosudarstvennoi sluzhbe," 1833), ark. 7, 13–19. See also CAHJP, HM2/8968 (original—TsDIAU, f. 442, op. 1, spr. 3329, "Po predstavleniiu podol'skogo gu-bernskogo pravleniia ob osvobozhdenii evreev, zanimaiushchikh dolzhnosti po goro-dskim vyboram," 1840), ark. 8–8, 21–21.

63. John Klier, *Imperial Russia's Jewish Question* (Cambridge: Cambridge University Press, 1995), 300–331.

64. Ivan M. Dolgorukov, "Puteshestvie v Odessu i Kiev 1810," *Chtenia v Imperatorskom Obshchestve Istorii i Drevnostei rossiiskikh*, kn. 3 (1869), 171–350, here 208 and 217.

65. Olimpiada Shishkina, *Zametki i vospominaniia russkoi puteshestvennitsy po Rossii v 1845 g.*, 2 vols. (St. Petersburg, E. I. V. Tipografiia, 1848), 1: 262.

66. A. N. Muraviev, *Sochineniia i pis'ma*, edited by Iu. I. Gerasimov and S.V. Dumin, (Irkutsk: Vostochno-sibirskoe knizhnoe izdatel'stvo, 1986), 68–71.

67. *Otechestvennaia voina 1812 g. v vospominaniakh sovremennikov* (Moscow: Gosu-darstvennaia publichania istoricheskaia biblioteka Rossii, 2008), 105.

68. RGVIA, f. Voenno-uchenyi arkhiv, d. 18944 ("Opisanie mestechek Podolskoi guber-nii," 1831).

69. Józef Ignacy Kraszewski, *Wspomnienia Wołynia, Polesia i Litwy*, edited by Stanisław Burkot (Warsaw: Ludowa Spółdzielnia Wydawnicza, 1985), 27–28.

70. A. E. Rozen, *Zapiski dekabrista*, edited by G. A. Nevelev (Irkutsk: Vostochno-sibirskoe knizhnoe izdatel'stvo, 1984), 86.

71. Ebenezer Henderson, *Biblical researches and travels in Russia* (London: J. Nisbet, 1826), 206, 214.

72. Nikolai Basargin, *Vospominaniia, rasskazy, stat'i*, edited by I. V. Porokh (Irkutsk: Vostochno-sibirskoe knizhnoe izdatel'stvo, 1988), 269–270.

CHAPTER 2: LAWLESS FREEDOM

1. Massie, *Catherine the Great*, 539–545.

2. On Catherine II's economic policy in the context of her tolerant attitudes to internal Russian religious minorities (such as Old Believers), see Aleksandr Pyzhikov, *Grani russkogo raskola: zametki o nashei istorii ot XVII veka do 1917 goda* (Moscow: Drev-lekhranilishche, 2013), 147–183.

3. RGADA, f. 1239, op. 3, d. 65051 ("Zhurnal imennym ukazam," 1795), ll. 86–87.

4. RGADA, f. 397, op. 1, d. 285 ("O sbore poshlin v novopriobretennykh ot Pol'shi oblastiakh"), ll. 10–16. Note that Catherine II allowed, among other things, silver and gold buttons and canes and buttons with precious stones, something that only the top level aristocracy could afford.

5. V. Iu. Saiapin, *Tamozhennaia sluzhba (v dvukh knigakh). Kniga I. Myto i mytniki* (Grodno: Grodnenskaia tipografiia, 2005), 232.

6. John Doyle Klier, *Russia Gathers Her Jews: The Origins of the "Jewish Question" in Russia, 1772–1825* (DeKalb, IL: Northern Illinois University Press, 1986), 96–97.

7. RGADA, f. 397, op. 1, d. 775 ("Reestr podlinnym zhurnalam 1794 g."), ll. 3–3b, 10b, 32–36, 40–42.

8. RGADA, f. 276, op. 2, d. 254 ("Po raportu Gusiatinskoi pogranichnoi tramolzhni," 1798), ll. 2–9.

9. RGADA, f. 276, op. 3, d. 1441 ("Ob osvidetel'stvovanii i perekleivanii vo vsekh prio-bretennykh ot Polshi gorodakh i torgovykh mestechkakh tovarov," 1797), ll. 59–60.

10. RGADA, f. 15, op. 22, d. 34, l. 402.

11. RGADA, f. 276, op. 3, d. 1441 ("Ob osvidetel'stvovanii i perekleivanii vo vsekh prio-bretennykh ot Polshi gorodakh i torgovykh mestechkakh tovarov," 1797), ll. 23, 30, 59, 60, 64, 148–149b, 158–159, 223–227, 308–309.

12. V. Iu. Saiapin, *Tamozhennaia sluzhba (v dvukh knigakh). Kniga II. Bor'ba s kontraban-doi* (Grodno: Grodnenskaia tipografiia, 2005), 41.

13. CAHJP, HM2/9308.6 (original—TsDIAU, f. 210, op. 2, spr. 14, "Spisok kuptsov, pro-ezzhavshikh cherez volochiskuiu, gusiatinskuiu i radzivilovskuiu tamozhni," 1796), ark. 4–6.

14. CAHJP, HM2/9480.2 (original—TsDIAU, f. 444, op. 1, spr. 118, "Berenshtein David Mendelevich donosit o vyvozimoi za granitsu Satanovskimi evreiami Rossiiskoi sere-brianoi monety," 1824, raport of 1817), ark. 212.

15. CAHJP, HM2/7928.5 (original—TsDIAU, f. 533, op. 1. spr. 452, "Po zhalobe kuptsov evreev na nespravedlivuiu konfiskatsiiu tovarov i vekselei," m. Zlatopol, 1804), ark. 1–3.

16. RGADA, f. 276, op. 3, d. 1698a (["On smuggling in Proskutov District"], 1799), ll. 6, 8, 10, 18–19.

17. CAHJP, HM2/9556.3 (original—DAPO, f. 120, op. 1, spr. 350, "Po obvineniu Benia Maerkovicha v provoze kontrabandnykh tovarov," 1804–12), ark. 1–5, 9, 71–72.

18. CAHJP, HM2/9481.1 (original—TsDIAU, f. 444, op. 3, spr. 167 (2), "Kontrabandy po volynskoi gubernii," 1826), ark. 165.

19. DAKO, f. 2, op. 1, spr. 2704 ("O vysylke v Novomirgorod k sledstviiu o kontrabandnykh tovarakh evreev Haima Iampol'skogo, Mendelia Chernogo, Gershka Chernomazova, Aria Leibu Lokteva i o vziatii v sekvestr imenii ikh," 1827), ark. 1–2, 7–8, 10–11, 30.

20. CAHJP, HM2/9480.2 (original—TsDIAU, f. 444, op. 1, spr. 118, "Berenshtein David Mendelevich donosit o vyvozimoi za granitsu Satanovskimi evreiami Rossiiskoi sere-brianoi monety," 1824, raport of 1817), ark. 144.

21. CAHJP, HM2/9386A (original—DAPO, f. 297, op. 1, spr. 5, "O evree Iose Kel'mane, sudimom za vodvorenie kontrabandnykh tovarov," 1837), ark. 1–2, 26–27, 48, 61, 192–194.

22. CAHJP, HM2/9458.10 (original—TsDIAU, f. 442, op. 782, spr. 368, "O provezennykh chrez neizvestnogo evreia kontrabandnykh tovarakh," 1832).

23. CAHJP, HM2/9480.3 (original—TsDIAU, f. 444, op. 1, spr. 139, "Uchrezhdennoi po vysochaishemu poveleniiu sekretnoi komissii dlia poimki kontrabandy," 1824), ark. 143, 146, 204b, 239.

24. GARF, f. 109, 2-ia eksp, op. 58, d. 85 ("O zhelanii Berdichevskogo kuptsa Ruvina Rubinshteina lichno vstretitsia s gosudarem imperatorom dlia donesenia o nekoto-rykh vazhnykh zloupotrebleniiakh," 1828), ll. 24–45.

25. CAHJP, HM2/9556.3 (original—DAPO, f. 120, op. 1, spr. 350, "Po obvineniiu Benia Maerkovicha v provoze kontrabandnykh tovarov," 1804–1812), ark. 82.

26. CAHJP, HM2/9480.3 (original—TsDIAU, f. 444, op. 1, spr. 139, "Uchrezhdennoi po vysochaishemu poveleniiu sekretno komissii dlia poimki kontrabandy," 1824), ark. 29–30.

27. V. Iu. Saiapin, *Tamozhennaia sluzhba (v dvukh knigakh). Kniga II. Bor'ba s kontraban-doi* (Grodno: Grodnenskaia tipografiia, 2005), 45–47, 58, 65.
28. CAHJP, HM/9481.1 (original—TsDIAU, f. 444, op. 3, spr. 167 (2), "Kontrabandy po volynskoi gubernii," 1826), ark. 385–392.
29. CAHJP, HM2/9482.1 (original—TsDIAU, f. 442, op.1, spr. 2172, "O vyselenii lits evre-iskoi natsional'nosti s pogranichnoi territorii," t.1, 1836), ark. 48–51.
30. CAHJP, HM2/9480.6 (original—TsDIAU, f. 444, op. 3, spr. 167, "Ob uchrezhdennoi v Berdicheve komissii dlia izsledovania taino vvozimykh tovarov," 1824–1828), ark. 1–2, 15–16.
31. CAHJP, HM2/9522.2 (original—GARF, f. 109, 2-ia eksp. 3 otd., d. 50, "O donose titu-liarnogo sovetnika kniazia Gorchakova," 1826), l. 4.
32. HM2/9812.18 (original—GARF, f. 1717, op. 1, d. 108, "Delo o rozyske zhandarmskim polkovnikom Freigangom lits, zanimavshikhsia provozom kontrabandy," 1826), ark. 5, 8.
33. CAHJP, HM2/8924.13 (original—TsDIAU, f. 442, op. 1, spr. 1505, "O rozyske i zader-zhanii kontrabandnykh tovarov i kontrabandistov v pogranichnykh mestechkakh Radzivilovskogo tamozhennogo okruga," 1833), ark. 28.
34. CAHJP, HM2/8924.11 (original—TsDIAU, f. 442, op. 1, spr. 1503, "O priniatii mer po bor'be s kontrabandistami, 1831), ark. 1–15; CAHJP, HM2/8924.12 (original—TsDIAU, f. 442, op. 1, spr. 1504, "O pribytii chinovnika ministerstva finansov de-Lafonena dlia otyskaniia skladov s kontrabandnymi tovarami," 1833–1834), ark. 1–9.
35. CAHJP, HM2/8923.12 (original—TsDIAU, f. 442, op. 1, spr. 2015, "O kuptse Baratse i ego prikazchikakh, zanimaiushchikhsia kontrabandnoi torgovlei," 1835), ark. 1–4.
36. HM2/9812.7 (original—GARF, f. 109, 3 eks., op. 143, d. 175, "O vysylke avstriiskikh poddannykh evreev Noikha Vainshteina, ego zheny, i Iudy Leiby Gal'perina za gran-itsu"); CAHJP, HM2/8924.13 (original—TsDIAU, f. 442, op. 1, spr. 1505, "O rozyske i zaderzhanii kontrabandnykh tovarov i kontrabandistov v pogranichnykh mestech-kakh Radzivilovskogo tamozhennogo okruga," 1833).
37. CAHJP, HM2/8927.5 (original—TsDIAU, f. 442, op. 1, spr. 1506, "O rozyske i zader-zhanii kontrabandistov i kontrabandnykh tovarov na territorii Radzivilovskogo tamozhennogo okruga," 1833), ark. 22–24.
38. CAHJP, HM2/9452.8 (original—TsDIAU, f. 442, op. 783, spr. 79, "Po pis'mu kuptsa Falieva i po pokazaniiu Brodskogo evreiia Iakuba Altera o proizvodiashcheisia perepiske zdeshnikh zhitelei," 1834), ark. 1–5, 21.
39. CAHJP, HM 9265.1 (original—TsDIAU, f. 442, op. 1, spr. 2191, "O zapreshchenii v"ezda v Rossiiu kuptsam Hasseliu I., Stel'tseru M., Gintsbergu N., i dr., prozhivaiushchim v g. Brody i zanimaiushchimsia kontrabandnoi torgovlei," 1836), ark. 1–3, 9, 20–21, 67–68.
40. CAHJP, HM2/9480.5 (original—TsDIAU, f. 444, op. 3, spr. 425, "V sviazi s navetom M. Kandelia na ustiluzhskikh evreev ob izgotovlenii fal'shivykh shtempelei i kleime-nii imi kontrabandnykh tovarov," 1826), ark. 1–3, 79, 90.
41. RGADA, f. 276, op. 3, d. 1580 ("Po raportu isakovskoi tamozhni," 1799), ll. 1–6; RGADA, f. 276, op. 1, d. 1525 ("Delo po soobscheniiu volynskogo gubernskogo prav-leniia," 1799), ll. 1–3.
42. According to at least one report, peasants and other Christians participated in the contraband even on a larger scale than the Jews, which might be accurate regarding the quantity of the participants but not regarding the importance of their dealings for the regional economy, see Nahum Sharon, ed., *Sefer Lutsk* (Tel Aviv: Yirgun yots'ei Lutsk be-Yisrael, 1961), 36.

43. CAHJP, HM2/8992.11 (original—RGADA, f. 261, op. 6, spr. 693, "Dva pis'ma moskovskogo pocht-direktora Iv. Pestelia k prezidentu kommerts-kollegii Vorontsovu," 1789–1790), ll. 1–9.

44. CAHJP, HM2/8265.12 (original—DAKO, f. 533, op. 1. spr. 1388, "Ob arestovannykh u romenskogo meshchanina Iankelia Shpigelia mednykh deneg i tovarov," 1811).

45. CAHJP, HM2/8924.13 (original—TsDIAU, f. 442, op. 1, spr. 1505, "O rozyske i zaderzhanii kontrabandnykh tovarov i kontrabandistov v pogranichnykh mestechkakh Radzivilovskogo tamozhennogo okruga," 1833), ark. 50–52.

46. RGADA, f. 276, op. 3, d. 1698a (["O kontrabandakh v Proskurovskom uezde"], 1799), l.16.

47. RGADA, f. 276, op. 3, d. 1446 ("Ob otstranenii ot dolzhnosti chinovnikov i tamozhennogo inspektora Volynskoi gubernii Petrova," 1797), 122, 143–44, 188.

48. CAHJP, HM/9481.1 (original—TsDIAU, f. 444, op. 3, spr. 167 (2), "Kontrabandy po volynskoi gubernii," 1826), ark. 67.

49. CAHJP, HM2/9480.6 (original—TsDIAU, f. 444, op. 3, spr. 167, "Ob uchrezhdennoi v Berdicheve komisssii dlia izsledovaniia taino vvozimykh tovarov," 1824–1828), ark. 23.

50. CAHJP, HM2/9480.2 (original—TsDIAU, f. 444, op. 1, spr. 118, "Berenshtein David Mendelevich donosit o vyvozimoi za granitsu Satanovskimi evreiami Rossiiskoi serebrianoi monety," 1824; report of 1817), ark. 154.

51. RGADA, f. 276, op. 3, d. 1912 ("Po zapiske gospodina ministra kommertsii," 1804), ll. 2, 4, 10–10b, 27, 39, 49–50.

52. CAHJP, HM2/9316.17 (RGIA, f. 1286, op. 2, d. 252, "Po predstavleniiu Volynskogo grazhdanskogo gubernatora ob isprashivaemom tamoshnim evreiskim obshchestvom dozvoleniia prislat ot sebia deputata v St. Peterburg," 1817), ll. 1–16.

53. CAHJP, HM2/8924.14 (TsDIAU, f. 442, op. 1, spr. 1508, "O sostavlenii ravvinami iugo-zapadnykh gubernii kliatvy, zapreshchaiushchei evreiam uchastvovat v kontrabandnoi torgovle," 1833), ark. 2–4, 15.

54. CAJHP, HM2/9656.3 (original—DAVO, f. D-391, op. 1, spr. 662, "Po obvineniiu evreiki iz Berdicheva v zavoze kontrabandnykh tovarov," 1848), ark. 1–6, 10, 13.

55. CAHJP, HM2/8924.13 (original—TsDIAU, f. 442, op. 1, spr. 1505, "O rozyske i zaderzhanii kontrabandnykh tovarov i kontrabandistov v pogranichnykh mestechkakh Radzivilovskogo tamozhennogo okruga," 1833), ark. 38.

56. CAJHP, HM2/9565.1 (original—DAVO, f. D-391, op. 1, spr. 656, "Delo po raportu chastnogo pristava Greitsa o kontrabandakh," 1848), ark. 5.

57. CAHJP, HM2/8924.13 (original—TsDIAU, f. 442, op. 1, spr. 1505, "O rozyske i zaderzhanii kontrabandnykh tovarov i kontrabandistov v pogranichnykh mestechkakh Radzivilovskogo tamozhennogo okruga," 1833), ark. 1–2, 13.

58. CAHJP, HM2/9480.6 (original—TsDIAU, f. 444, op. 3, spr. 167, "Ob uchrezhdennoi v Berdicheve komisssii dlia issledovania taino vvozimykh tovarov," 1824–28), ark. 142.

59. CAHJP, HM/9481.1 (original—TsDIAU, f. 444, op. 3, spr. 167 (2), "Kontrabandy po volynskoi gubernii," 1826), ark. 67, 76, 115–122.

60. Calculated on the basis of the following files and documents: DAKO, f. 450, op. 1, spr. 1 ("Kniga registratsii poshlin, vzimaemykh s kuptsov za provozimye tovary. Vasil'kovskaia tamozhnia," 1791); CAHJP, HM2/9308.6 (original—TsDIAU, f. 210, op. 2, spr. 14, "Spisok kuptsov, proezzhavshikh cherez volochinskuiu, gusiatinskuiu i radzivillovskuiu tamozhni," 1796); RGADA, f. 276, op. 2, d. 254 ("Po raportu Gusiatinskoi pogranichnoi tamozhni," 1798); RGADA, f. 276, op. 2, d. 475 ("Po raportu

raznykh tamozhen," 1809); RGADA, f. 276, op. 3, d. 1592 ("Po raportam Podol'skogo tamozhennogo inspektora Iushnevskogo: Tsekhinovskaia and Gusiatinskaia tamozhni," 1799); CAHJP, HM2/8924.13 (original—TsDIAU, f. 442, op. 1, spr. 1505, "O rozyske i zaderzhanii kontrabandnykh tovarov i kontrabandistov v pogranichnykh mestech-kakh Radzivilovskogo tamozhennogo okruga," 1833); CAHJP, HM/9481.1 (original—TsDIAU, f. 444, op. 3, spr. 167 (2), "Kontrabandy po volynskoi gubernii," 1826); GARF, f. 109, 3-ia eksp., op. 113, d. 4 ("O vydache pasportov po Volynskoi gubernii," 1828); HM2/8924.11 (original—TsDIAU, f. 442, op. 1, spr. 1503, "O priniatii mer po bor'be s kontrabandistami, 1831); HM2/9453.12 (original—TsDIAU, f. 442, op. 789a, spr. 120, "Po otnosheniiu ministerstva finansov s prilozheniem spiska priezzhaiush-chikh v Brody dlia zakupki tovarov," 1839).

61. HM2/9453.12 (original—TsDIAU, f. 442, op. 789a, spr. 120, "Po otnosheniiu minis-terstva finansov s prilozheniem spiska priezzhaiushchikh v Brody dlia zakupki tova-rov," 1839), ark. 2–2b, 8–9.
62. Barbara Kirshenblatt-Gimblett, "Contraband: Performance, Text and Analysis of a Purimshpiel," *Drama Review* 24, no. 3 (1980): 5–16.
63. Brat'ia Bulgakovy, *Perepiska*, 3 vols. (Moscow: Zakharov, 2010), 2:339.
64. Isaak Babel, *Sobranie sochinenii v chetyrekh tomakh* (Moscow: Vremia, 2006), 1:64–65.
65. In the original, "*dobroe delo, khoroshee delo*." E. Bagritskii, *Stikhotvoreniia i poemy* (St. Petersburg: Akademicheskii proekt, 2000), 37–40, here 37.
66. In the original, "angel voruiushchii." See O. E. Mandel'shtam, *Sobranie sochinenii v 2-kh tt.* (Moscow: Khudozhestvennaia literatura, 2000), 1:251.

CHAPTER 3: FAIR TRADE

1. GARF, f. 1165, op. 1, d. 141 ("Perepiska s Volynskim grazhdanskim gubernatorom, glavnokomanduiushchim v Peterburge i dr., o neobkhodimosti priniatiia mer dlia vosprepiatstvovaniia namereniiu frantsuzskogo pravitel'stva zakupit v Rossii loshadei i medi dlia voennykh nuzhd," 1813–1814), ll. 1–9.
2. TsDIAU, f. 442, op. 790a, spr. 2 ("O delakh chinovnikov sekretnykh poruchenii i rasporiazheniiakh po doneseniiam ikh," 1840–1841), ark. 12–14, 29–30, 32–33.
3. See Bek's report in TsDIAU, f. 442, op. 1, spr. 2054, ch. 1 ("Po raportu korpusa zhan-darmov polkovnika Beka o raznykh proisshestviakh, sluchivshikhsia na berdichev-koi iarmarke," 1836), ark. 1–42. For Bek as a trustworthy, serious and well-balanced Russian clerk, see GARF, f. 109, 1-ia eksp., op. 15, d. 137 ("O donose evreia Golden-berga na evreev Abelia Nasenbeina i Haima Shmulia Cherta, v peresylke zagranich-noi perepiski Pol'skikh vykhodtsev k raznym litsam v Volynskoi gubernii," 1840), ll. 1–4; GARF, f. 109, 1-ia eksp., op. 10, d. 164 ("O zhelanii evreia Girshki Kopersh-mita otkryt' izvestnuiu emu tainu," 1835), l. 7.
4. I. Aksakov, *Issledovanie o torgovle na ukrainskikh iarmarkakh* (St. Petersburg: Tipo-grafiia Imperatorskoi Akademii Nauk, 1858), 36.
5. Shpilevsky travelled through Belorussia in the 1840s; his famous travelogue appeared in 1853. See Pavel Shpilevskii, *Puteshestvie po Poles'iu i Belorusskomu kraiu* (Minsk: Polym'ia, 1992), 91.
6. O. M. Ivashchenko and Iu. M. Polishchuk, *Evrei Volyni: kinets XVIII-pochatok XX stolittia* (Zhytomyr: Volyn, 1998), 46.

7. TsDIAU, f. 442, op. 1, spr. 1198 ("Vedomosti o kolichestve naselennykh punktov, nas-elenia, promyshlennykh predpriiatii, uchebnykh zavedenii i pr. po Podol'skoi guber-nii," 1832), ark. 1–3.

8. Ivashchenko, *Ievrei Volyni*, 47–48.

9. Ignacy Schiper, *Dzieje handlu żydowskiego na ziemiach polskich* (Warsaw: Nakładem Centrali Związku kupców w Warszawe, 1937), 413.

10. TsDIAU, f. 442, op. 44, spr. 678 ("Raport statskogo sovetnika Krainskogo Podol'skomu, Volynskomu i Kievskomu gubernatoru Aleksandru Bezaku," 1865), ark. 40–55.

11. CAHJP, HM2/9264 (original—TsDIAU, f. 442, op. 1, spr. 1197, "O podgotovke k priezdu Nikolaia I v Kiev," 1831), 3, 11, 26.

12. N.N. Varadinov, *Istoriia ministerstva vnutrennikh del*, 8 vols. (St. Petersburg: Tipogafiia Ministerstva vnutrennikh del, 1859), 2/1: 183.

13. Robert Jones, "Ukrainian Grain and Russian Market in the Late Eighteenth and Early Nineteenth Centuries," in Iwan S. Koropeckyj, ed., *Ukrainian Economic History: Interpretive Essays* (Cambridge, MA: Harvard University Press for Harvard Ukrainian Research Institute, 1991), 210–227, here 213.

14. DAKO, f. 1, op. 351, spr. 45 ("Raporty Makhnovskoi gorodskoi politsii o povyshenii tsen na produkty," 1824), ark. 2–3.

15. See P. P. Chubinskii, ed., *Trudy etnografichesko-statisticheskoi ekspeditsii v Zapadno-russkii krai*, 7 vols. (St. Petersburg: V. Bezobrazov, 1872), 7:84–85.

16. This process began in 1789, when Sanguszko supported the claims of local urban dwellers against the Jews, thus triggering the decline of the town economy. See Sh. Ettinger and Ch. Shmeruk, "Le-toldot ha-yeshuv ha-yehudi be-kremements," in Avraam Shmuel Shtein, ed., *Pinkas Kremnits: Sefer zikaron* (Tel Aviv: Hotsa'at irgun 'ole Kremnits be-Yisrael, 1954), 17–45, here 25.

17. Volhynia (87,000 male and 74,000 female); Podolia (66,000 male and 86,000 female); Kiev (42,000 male and 31,000 female). In 1835, the Ministry of the Interior reported 50,000 Jews in Vitebsk province, 195,000 in Volhynia, 83,000 in Grodno, 4,000 in Ekaterinoslav, 105,000 in Kiev, 23,000 in Kurliandia, 97,000 in Minsk, 87,000 in Mogilev, 157,000 in Podolia, 14,000 in Poltava, 3,000 in Taurida, 16,000 in Kherson, 18,000 in Chernigov, 36,000 in Bessarabia, 36,000 in Belostok. For the official data, see Varadinov, *Istoriia ministerstva vnutrennikh del*, 3/1: 557 (data covering the early 1830s), and ibid., 3/2: 139 (covering 1835).

18. Ralph S. Clem, "Population Change in the Ukraine in the Nineteenth Century," in Koropeckyj, *Ukrainian Economic History*, 234–240; Varadinov, *Istoriia ministerstva vnutrennikh del*, 2/2:101–102, 155 (data covering 1820–1824); 3/1:26 (data covering 1826).

19. DAKO, f. 185, op. 1, spr. 632 ("Delo o prederzhatel'stve voennogo dezertira Rein-barg," 1835–1836), ark. 1–5.

20. The marketplace distinguished the shtetl and single it out among the surrounding villages not only everywhere in Ukraine and Lithuania, but also in the Kingdom of Poland. See Ruszard Kołodziejczyk, *Miasteczka Polskie w XIX–XX wieku: Z dziejów formowania się społeczności* (Kielce: Kieleckie towarzystwo naukowe, 1992), 85.

21. L. P. Marnei and N. V. Piotukh, "Prostranstvennaia struktura razmeshcheniia torgovo-ekonomicheskikh tsentrov: Stolichnye i provintsial'nye iarmarki v Rossii i Korolevstve Pol'skom v pervoi treti XIX veka," *Stolitsa i provintsiia v istorii Rossii i Pol'shi* (Moscow: Nauka, 2008), 133–148, here 133.

22. CAHJP, HM2/9532.4 (original—TsDIAU, f. 442, op. 1, spr. 2176, "Po obvineniiu evreev Bazalii v kontrabande i perepravke dezertirov zagranitsu, a takzhe o vyselenii lits evreiskoi natsional'nosti s pogranichnoi territorii, t. 5, Kamenets-Podolsk, gubernskii gorod," 1836–1838), ark. 93.

23. Gershon Hundert, "The Importance of Demography and Patterns of Settlement for an Understanding of the Jewish Experience in East-Central Europe," in Steven T. Katz, ed., *The Shtetl: New Evaluations* (New York: New York University Press, 2007), 29–38, here 35.

24. Nahum Sharon, ed., *Sefer Lutsk* (Tel Aviv: Yirgun yots'ei Lutsk be-Yisrael, 1961), 37.

25. CAJHP, HM2/8870 (original—DAKhO, f. 115, op. 4, spr. 2, "Topograficheskoe opisanie Bratslavskogo uezda," 1799), ark. 5–9, 28–38, 102–103. For a very similar pattern of trade in Balin, Smotrich, Chechel'nik, and Orynin, see CAHJP, HM2/9385.3 (DAPO, d. 115, op. 2, spr. 6, "Kameral'noe i topograficheskoe opisanie mestechek i selenii Kamenetskogo uezda," 1796–1797), ark. 4, 17, 38, 46.

26. DAKO, f. 185, op. 1, spr. 441 ("O torguiushchikh meshchanakh, 1825 g.," 1825), ark. 1–264.

27. CAHJP, H2/9385.2 (original—DAPO, f. 115, op. 2, spr. 5, "Topograficheskoe opisanie Vinnitskogo uezda," between 1797 and 1806), ark. 5–7.

28. DAKO, f. 35, op. 14, spr. 311 ("Mezhevaia vedomost Umanskogo uezda," 1860), ark. 1–6.

29. Christine Ruane, *The Empire's New Clothes: A History of the Russian Fashion Industry, 1700–1917* (New Haven, CT: Yale University Press, 2009), 14.

30. The book by Luzzatto was reprinted several times in East Europe and its circulation was two times higher than regular commentaries or ethical works—on a par with the circulation of the basic prayer books. See CAHJP, HM2/8345.3 (original—DAZhO, f. 396, op. 1, spr. 8, "Kniga dlia zapiski i polnoty rukopisei, postupaiushchikh k pechataniiu v Zhitomirskuiu evreiskuiu tipografiiu," 1847), ark. 2–5.

31. In the original, "*bi-zrizut gadol ke-darko.*" See Nosson Sternhartz, *Haye MOHARA"N* (Jerusalem: Meshekh na-nahal, 1982), 420 (siman 338).

32. TB Hagigah 17a, Rosh ha-shanah 4b.

33. TB Ketubot 24b.

34. Ignaz Bernstein, *Jüdische Sprichwörter und Redensarten: Im Anhang Erotica und Rustica* (Hildesheim: Georg Olms, 1969), 333 (no. 51).

35. DAKO, f. 450, op. 1, spr. 1 ("Kniga registratsii poshlin, vzimaemykh s kuptsov za provozimye tovary. Vasil'kovskaia pogranichnaia tamozhnia," 1791), n. p.

36. Esther Juhasz in her otherwise insightful article on guild embroideries wrongly states that it was used exclusively by Jews for their ritual objects; see Sarah Harel Hoshen, ed., *Treasures of Jewish Galicia: Judaica from the Museum of Ethnography and Crafts in Lviv, Ukraine* (Tel Aviv: Beth Hatfutsot, 1996), 151.

37. CAHJP, HM3/9385.1 (original—DAPO, f. 115, op. 2, spr. 2, "Kameral'noe i topograficheskoe opisanie Letichevskogo uezda," 1812), ark. 5–6, 120–123, 166–170.

38. RGADA, f. 276, op. 3, d. 1592 ("Po raportam Podol'skogo tamozhennogo inspektora Iushnevskogo: Tsekhinovskaia i Gusiatinskaia tamozhni," 1799), ll. 2–9, 47, 87, 100.

39. DAKO, f. 2, op. 1, spr. 4510 ("O prodazhe iz konfiskovannogo Umanskogo imeniia vodki," 1833), ark. 1–3.

40. Prov. 15:16. See Eccl. 4:6.

41. CAHJP, HM2/9452.6 (original—TsDIAU, f. 442, op. 783, spr. 60, "Po raportu Kremenetskogo politsmeistera, s naidennymi v Krementse v evreiskikh domakh i lavkakh porokha, puliakh i drobi," 1833), ark. 8.

42. CAHJP, HM2/9891.14 (original—TsDIAU, f. 442, op. 152, spr. 898, "Po donosheniiu kievskogo gubernatora o prodazhe evreem Moshko Varshavskim (on zhe Poliak) raznogo roda voennogo oruzhiia," 1843), ark. 1–12, 16, 18, 44.

43. AGAD, Archiwum Radziwiłłow. Dz. 34, sygn. 291, ll. 1–2.

44. This claim is made by Ukrainian historians, see Ivashchenko and Polishchuk, *Ievrei Volyni*, 53.

45. L. L. Rokhlin, *Mestechko Krasnopolie (Mogilevskoi gub.): opyt statistiko-ekonomicheskogo opisaniia tipichnogo mestechka cherty osedlosti* (St. Petersburg: Sever, 1908), 12.

46. I. Kandelaki, *Rol' iarmarok v russkoi torgovle* (St. Petersburg: Ministerstvo finansov, 1914), 46.

47. CAHJP, HM2/9263.4 (original—TsDIAU, f. 442, op. 1, spr. 2055, "Ob izmenenii sroka iarmarok, proiskhodiashchikh v imenii Krasinskogo v Dunaevtsakh"), ark. 5.

48. Aksakov, *Issledovanie o torgovle na ukrainskikh iarmarkakh*, 19.

49. Fernand Braudel, *Civilization and Capitalism, 15th–18th Century: The Wheels of Commerce* (Berkeley: University of California Press, 1992), 2:30–44.

50. Sternhartz, *Haye MOHARA"N*, 357 (siman 591).

51. TsDIAU, f. 442, op. 790a, spr. 2 ("O delakh chinovnikov sekretnykh poruchenii i rasporiazheniakh po doneseniam ikh," 1840–1841), ark. 34–36.

52. Varadinov, *Istoriia ministerstva*, 2/2: 410–411, 3/1: 265–266.

53. For comparative figures of the turnover on Belorussian fairs, see Ina Sorkina, *Miastechki Belarusi w kantsy XVIII—pershai palove XIX st* (Vilnius: Evropeiskii gumanitarnyi universitet, 2010), 112–130.

54. Bohdan Sushins'kyi, *Balta: Misto, osviachene vichnistiu. Istorychni ese* (Odesa: Druk, 2005), 175.

55. RGADA, f. 1239, op. 3, d. 54555 ("[Matvei Radziwiłł to Pavel I]," April 20, 1797), ll. 1–2.

56. TsDIAU, f. 442, op. 789a, spr. 89 ("Ob uravnenii berdichevskikh i zhitomirskikh kuptsov i o perevode berdichevskoi iarmarki v Kiev," 1839–1841), 2–18.

57. B. Lukin, A, Sokolova, B. Khaimovich, eds., *Sto evreiskikh mestechek Ukrainy* (St. Petersburg: Alexander Gersht, 2000), 161–162.

58. Varadinov, *Istoriia ministerstva*, 2/1: 224, 539 (the comparative data cover 1818–1819), also 3/1: 446–447.

59. TsDIAU, f. 442, op. 1, spr. 2532 ("O torgovykh oborotakh na byvshei v m. Berdicheve Onufrievskoi iarmonke," 1838), ark. 1, 3–13, 15.

60. AGAD, Zb. Czołowskiego, sygn. 449 (M 39056, "Summariusz intrat," 1790–1791), l. 10.

61. Zvi Kaminsky, *Geven amol a shtot Berdichev* (Paris: Kaminski, 1952), 50–52.

62. Rabbi Pinhas of Korets [Pinhas ben Avraam Aba Shapira], "Sha'ar avodat ha-shem," siman 18, in his *Imrei Pinhas ha-shalem*, 2 vols. (Bnei Brak: Yehezkel Shraga Frenkel, 2003), 2:329.

63. Aksakov, *Issledovanie o torgovle*, 22.

64. CAHJP, HM2/9529.6 (original—TsDIAU, f. 442, op. 80, spr. 201, "O 92 lavkakh, nakhodiashchikhsia v Berdicheve na starom bazare," 1847), ark. 2–12.

65. DAKO, f. 1, op. 336, spr. 3377 ("Po predlozheniiu Kievskogo, Podol'skogo i Volynskogo general-gubernatora ob uchrezhdenii v Umani iarmarkov," 1840), ark. 1–2, 13.

66. DAKO, f. 1, op. 336, spr. 3376 ("Po predlozheniiu Kievskogo Voennogo Gubernatora ob otkrytii v m. Belaia Tserkov iarmarkov," 1840), ark. 1–3, 11–13, 15–18.

67. DAKO, f. 2, op. 3, spr. 4712 ("Svedeniia departamenta manufaktury vnutrennei torgovli ministerstva finansov," 1824), ark. 8–10.

68. Such important early modern towns as Lutsk, Rovno and Kovel rapidly declined in the nineteenth century. Lutsk lost its medieval glitter and went from 50,000 to 11,000 inhabitants, also losing its economic centrality in the region. See Józef Kraszewski, *Szkice obycajowe i historyczne* (Warszawa: Gebethner i Wolff, 1882), 145–147.

69. CAHJP, HM2/9531.5 (original—TsDIAU, f. 442, op. 1, spr. 1195, "Otchety Kievskogo, Podol'skogo i Volynskogo grazhdanskikh gubernatorov," 1832), ark. 66–67.

70. CAHJP, HM2/9455.4 (original—TsDIAU, f. 442, op. 1, spr. 1816, "Perepiska s Kievs-kim grazhdanskim gubernatorom o predostavlenii svedenii o kontraktovoi iarmarke v Kieve," 1835), ark. 1; DAKO, f. 2, op. 1, spr. 6184 ("Po prosheniiu torguiushchikh v g. Kieve khlebom promyshlennikov, zhaluiushchikhsia, chto evrei privoziat v g. Kiev raznogo roda khleb i proch., ssypaiut v naemnykh ambarakh i proizvodiat onym tor-govliu, delaia podryv," 1836), ark. 1–3, 5–6; Israel Nahum Dorevsky, *Lekorot hayehu-dim be-kiev* (Berdichev: Sheftel, 1902), 75–80.

71. CAHJP, HM2/9264.5 (original—TsDIAU, f. 442, op. 1, spr. 2178, "O razreshenii evreiam-kuptsam 1 i 2 gildii priezzhat v Kiev na Kreshchenskuiu iarmarku," 1835–1836), ark. 1.

72. CAHJP, HM2/9306.4 (original—TsDIAU, f. 442, op. 1, spr. 4030, "Perepiska s kievs-kim gubernskim pravleniem ob otkrytii kharcheven vo vremia kontraktovoi iarmarki v g. Kieve dlia priezzhaiushchikh evreev," 1841), ark. 1–8.

73. TsDIAU, f. 442, op. 789a, spr. 89 ("Ob uravnenii berdichevskikh i zhitomirskikh kuptsov v uravnenii gil'deiskikh povinnostei i o perevode berdichevskoi iarmarki v Kiev," 1839–1841), ark. 1–2, 6, 18–19, 23.

74. CAHJP, HM2/8267.8 (original—TsDIAU, f. 442, op. 789-A, spr. 267, "Delo o perevode prisutstvennykh mest iz mestechka Letichev v Medzhibozh," 1839), ark. 1–2.

75. V. Lukin and B. Khaimovich, *100 evreiskikh mestechek Ukrainy. Istoricheskii putevodi-tel.* Vyp. 1: *Podoliia,* 2nd ed. (Kharkov: Tarbut la'am, 1998), 120–122.

76. Mordechai Nadav, *The Jews of Pinsk, 1506 to 1880,* edited by Mark Jay Mirsky and Moshe Rosman (Stanford, CA: Stanford University Press, 2008), 331–334.

77. *Regesty i nadpisi: svod materialov dlia istorii evreev rossii (80 g.-1800 g.),* 3 vols. (St. Petersburg: Obshchestvo dlia rasprostraneniia prosvechsheniia mezhdu evreiami Rossii, 1899–1913), 3: 64, 101–102, 103 (nos. 1973, 2058, 2060).

78. TsDIAU, f. 442, op. 1, spr. 1260 ("Po prosheniiu berdichevskogo evreiskogo meschan-skogo obshchestva ob uchrezhdenii magistrata ili ratushi v Berdicheve, volynskoi gubernii," 1832–1834), ark. 2–4, 7–14, 19–23, 33–37.

79. David Assaf, *The Regal Way: The Life and Times of Rabbi Israel of Ruzhin* (Stanford, CA: Stanford University Press, 2002), 35–36.

80. TsDIAU, f. 442, op. 1, spr. 4982, ch. 1 ("Po prosheniiu Berdichevskogo evreiskogo obschestva ob okazanii sodeistviia v uchrezhdenii v g. Berdichev nekotorykh prisut-stvennykh mest," 1843), ark. 1, 4–7, 10–11, 15–19, 26–27.

81. TsDIAU, f. 442, op. 1, spr. 4982, ch. 4 ("Po prosheniiu Berdichevskogo evreiskogo obshchestva ob okazanii sodeistviia v uchrezhdenii v g. Berdichev nekotorykh prisu-tstvennykh mest," 1843), ark. 289, 370–374.

82. DAKO, f. 35, op. 14, spr. 8 ("Po predlozheniiu nachal'nika gubernii o priglashenii zemlemera," 1854–1857), ark. 118.

83. A prominent Polish Jewish social historian pointed to the decline of Berdichev trade in the 1840s, which he claimed was a result of the new laws on smuggling and higher taxes on import goods. His figures showed that Berdichev turnover was about 3.2 million rubles in 1827, 1.8 million rubles in 1836, and about 600,000 rubles in 1846.

While the significance of Berdichev trade might have really declined, yet it was far less evident, and the reasons might lie in elsewhere. See Ignacy Schiper, *Dzieje handlu żydowskiego na ziemiach polskich* (Warsaw: Nakładem Centrali Związku kupców w Warszawe, 1937), 427.

84. *Journey to a Nineteenth-Century Shtetl: The Memoirs of Yekhezkel Kotik*, edited. by David Assaf (Detroit, MI: Wayne State University Press, 2002), 342.

85. This type of loan the Jews called *viderkauf.* On this borrowing practice, see J. Kalik, "Hafkadah, viderkauf bepe'ilutam hakalkalit shel yehudei mamlekhet polin-lita," in Ran Aharonsohn and Shaul Stampfer, eds., *Yazamut yehudit be'et hahadashah, mizrakh eropah ve'erets yisra'el* (Jerusalem: Magnes, 2000), 25–47.

86. These newly established funds were called *fundusz edukacyjny.* The following documents prove that the Jews made loans in the 1740s to 1770s and, after having paid the interest for fifty or sixty years, still were required to pay back the principle in the 1810s to 1820s: RGADA, f. 1603, op. 1, d. 625 ("O summach po Dominikanach Pod-kamieneckich po Kapitule Zamoyskiei od synagogi wołynskiei"), ll. 55–33; RGADA, f. 1603, op. 2, d. 675 ("Dzieło o długu na Kahalie Korylnickiem"), ll. 5–11; RGADA, f. 1603, op 2, d. 684 ("Dzieło o summe"), ll. 5–10; RGADA, f. 1603, op. 2, d. 857 ("Dzieło o summe pojezuickiey"), ll. 22–23; RGADA, f. 1603, op. 2, d. 788 ("Dzieło o summe pojezuickiey, zl. 1000"), ll. 17–18; RGADA, f. 1603, op. 2, 828 ("Dzieło o 4 roznych summach"), ll. 80–81.

87. TsDIAU, f. 442, op. 790a, spr. 2 ("O delakh chinovnikov sekretnykh poruchenii i ra-sporiazheniakh po doneseniam ikh," 1840–1841), ark. 12–14, 28–29, 30–31.

88. Max Weinreich et al., eds., *Yidishe filologye,* vol. 1 (1924): 398.

89. Nahum Stutchkoff, *Der oytser fun der Yidisher schprach* (New York: YIVO, 1950), 175, 429, 499, 502.

90. For Repnin's reaction in his capacity as a military governor to the report submitted by Minister of Finance Kankrin: "Izvlechenie iz zapiski," *Chteniia v Imperatorskom Ob-shchestve istorii i drevnostei rossiiskikh,* bk. 2 (April–June 1864): 131–142, here 133.

91. See, for example, an important study of one of the first Minister of Finance Kankrin reforms, Wayne Dowler, "Merchants and Politics in Russia: The Guild Reform of 1824," *Slavonic and East European Review* 65, no. 1 (1987): 38–52.

92. See Chubinskii, *Trudy etnografichesko-statisticheskoi ekspeditsii,* 7:211.

93. On the dynamics of salaries and expenses in interior Russia, see Boris Mironov, "Wages and Prices in Imperial Russia, 1703–1913," *Russian Review* 69, no. 1 (2010): 47–72, here 59.

94. For Krestovsky's antisemitism, see in more detail the chapter "The Russian Army's Jewish Question" in my *Jews in the Russian Army, 1827–1917: Drafted into Modernity* (Cambridge: Cambridge University Press, 2008), 275–280.

95. Nikolai Leskov, *Sobranie sochinenii v 11-ti tt.* (Moscow: Khudozhestvennaia litera-tura, 1957), 6:103.

96. In the original, *sushcheiu zhidovkoi.* See Fedor Dostoevsky, *Brat'ia Karamazovy,* in his *Polnoe sobranie sochinenii v 30-ti tt.* (Leningrad: Nauka, 1976), 14:311 (line 30).

97. Anton Chekhov, "Shampanskoe," in his *Polnoe sobranie sochinenii i pisem v 30 tt.* (Moscow: Nauka, 1976), 4:282.

98. V. I. Lenin, *Polnoe sobranie sochinenii v 55 tt.,* 5th ed. (Moscow: Politizdat, 1967), 36:192.

99. In the original, *"torgash-provokator, kotoryi na ubiistve i predatel'stve delal 'gesheft' svoei posmertnoi slavy."* See Valentin Pikul, *Nechistaia sila* (Moscow: Sovremennik, 1992), 300.

100. L. V. Belovinsky, *Entsiklopedicheskii slovar' russkoi zhizni i istorii XVIII-nachalo XX v.* (Moscow: OLMA Press, 2003), 142.

101. See Yuri Slezkine, *The Jewish Century* (Princeton, NJ: Princeton University Press, 2004), 4–39.

CHAPTER 4: THE RIGHT TO DRINK

1. Yekhezkel Kotik, whose grandfather had held a liquor monopoly, explains in his memoir how it worked: "This is how excise duty used to be levied: an excise official working in the brewery supervised the amount of liquor sold to the tavern keepers. If the buyers bought along a barrel, the supervisor measured the number of pails [should be buckets—*YPS*] it was likely to hold, stamped it with the customs seal, and issued a certificate for that amount. Then he would record the number of pails sold. Once a month, the duty on it was forwarded by the distillery owner to the excise office in Brisk. There was another inspector at work in the town whose task it was to ensure that the vodka sold by the tavern keepers came solely from the barrels stamped with the custom seal. If he came upon a barrel that had not been stamped, there was no doubt that its contents had been smuggled in." See Kotik, *Journey to a Nineteenth-Century Shtetl*, 191–193, here 192.

2. DAKO, f. 3, op. 5, spr. 800 ("Delo o Khodorkovskom i Liubarskom," 1821), ark. 1–2, 11–12b.

3. Arcadius Kahan, *Russian Economic History: The Nineteenth Century* (Chicago: University of Chicago Press, 1982), 108.

4. Jacob Goldberg, "Tavernkeepers," in *The YIVO Encyclopedia of Jews in Eastern Europe*, 2 vols. (New Haven, CT: Yale University Press, 2008), 1849–1852, here 1849.

5. Ivan Pyzhov, *Istoriia kabakov v Rossii* (Moscow: Volf, 1868), 264–274; William Eugene Johnson, *The Liquor Problem in Russia* (Westerville, OH: American Issue Publishing Co., 1915), 19–20, 113, 117.

6. CAHJP, HM2/8969.2 (original—TsDIAU, f. 442, op. 1, spr. 8025, "O khranenii kontrabandnykh tovarov korchmariami Dubenskogo uzeda Brizgalom, Galatsom, Veinerom i dr.," 1849), ark. 8–9.

7. CAHJP, H2/9453.15 (original—TsDIAU, f. 442, op. 789a, spr. 298, "Po predstavleniiu Zhitomirskogo voennogo gubernatora o vrede i neudobnosti imet uezdnye goroda v prinadlezhashchikh chastnym vladel'tsam pomest'iakh," 1839), ark. 4–5.

8. DAKO, f. 35, op. 14, spr. 8 ("Po predlozheniu nachal'nika gubernii o priglashenii zemlemera,"1854–1857), ark. 118–119.

9. This seems to be an increase in comparison with the prepartitioned Poland, where liquor leases constituted about 69 percent of all the leaseholding contracts of a magnate. See Gershon Hundert, *The Jews in a Polish Private Town. The Case of Opatov in the Eighteenth Century* (Baltimore, MD: Johns Hopkins University Press, 1992), 66. On the predominance of Jews in innkeeping, see also Hundert, *Jews in Poland-Lithuania*, 20. A historian of Pinsk argues that after 1760s, the liquor lease became entirely Jewish; see Mordechai Nadav, *The Jews of Pinsk, 1506 to 1880* (Stanford, CA: Stanford University Press, 2008), 287. For the situation in the Kingdom of Poland after the partitions, see Glenn Dynner, *Yankel's Tavern: Jews, Liquor, and Life in the Kingdom of Poland* (New York: Oxford University Press, 2013).

10. DAKO, f. 1, op. 336, spr. 331 ("Vedomosti Lipovetskogo nizhnego suda o shinkakh," 1800), ark. 1–9; DAKO f. 2, op. 3, spr. 4711 ("Vedomosti o kolichestve shinkov, gosti-

nits, kofeen i drugikh piteinykh zavedenii, sostoiashchikh na otkupe v uezdnykh gorodakh Kievskoi gubernii," 1825), ark. 4, 8, 36, 55, 72; DAKO, f. 2, op. 1, spr. 2465 ("Vedomost o shinkakh v Umanskom povete sostoiashchikh," (1825), ark. 1–8, 11–12; DAKO, f. 2, op. 1, spr. 2466 ("Vedomost o shinkakh, v radomysl'skom povete sostoiashchikh," ([1825]), ark. 1–22; DAKO, f. 2, op. 1, spr. 2468 ("Delo o shinkakh, sostoiashchikh v Makhnovke," 1825), ark. 1–11.

11. DAKO, f. 2, op. 1, spr. 2464 ("O sostoianii v Kievskoi gubernii v pomeshchich'ikh imeniakh shinkakh," 1825), ark. 1–2, 4–5, 17–18.

12. CAHJP, HM2/9567.3 (original—DAVO, f. 391, op. 3, spr. 11, "Po ukazu podol'skoi kazennoi palaty s kopieiu kontrakta ob otdannykh piati gerberakh," 1807), ark. 1; CAHJP, HM2/8267.2 (original—TsDIAU, f. 442, op. 77, spr. 34, "Po otnosheniiu komanduiushchim svodnym artilleriiskim okrugom," 1844), ark. 10–11; DAKO, f. 2, op. 1, spr. 4958 ("O prodazhe doma i korchmy," 1834), ark. 1–4.

13. CAHJP, HM2/8267.2 (original—TsDIAU, f. 442, op. 77, spr. 34, "Po otnosheniiu komanduiushchim svodnym artilleriiskim okrugom," 1844), ark. 10–11.

14. DAKO, f. 2, op. 1, spr. 4958 ("O prodazhe doma i korchmy," 1834), ark. 1–4.

15. Arthur Eisenbach, *The Emancipation of the Jews in Poland, 1780–1870* (Oxford: Institute for Polish-Jewish Studies, Oxford University, 1991), 96. It does not seem, however, that Jews were in fact forced from tavernkeeping in the Ukraine at that time; see Hundert, *Jews in Poland-Lithuania*, 215–216.

16. PSZ I, no. 22,651.

17. Glenn Dynner, "Legal Fictions: The Survival of the Rural Jewish Liquor Trade in the Kingdom of Poland," *Jewish Social Studies* 16, no. 2 (2010): 28–66.

18. Salo W. Baron and Arcadius Kahan, *Economic History of the Jews* (Jerusalem: Keter, 1975), 136–137.

19. PSZ I, no. 27,963.

20. CAHJP, HM2/9307.12 (original—TsDIAU, f. 442, op. 1, spr. 5167, "Delo o rozyske lits, privezshikh kontrabandnye tovary v korchmu s Maloi Volintsy," 1843), ark. 1–3.

21. N. I. Lorer, *Zapiski dekabrista*, edited by by M.V. Nechkina (Irkutsk: Vostochnosibirskoe knizhnoe izdatel'stvo, 1984), 82.

22. TsDIAU, f. 442, op. 790a, spr. 2 ("O delakh chinovnikov sekretnykh poruchenii i rasporiazheniakh po doneseniam ikh," 1840–1841), ark. 45–46.

23. DAKO, f. 1099, op. 1, spr. 60 ("Delo o privlechenii k sudu korchemnogo muzykanta rimsko-katolicheskogo veroispovedaniia Fomu Iankovskogo za igru v shinkakh i na evreiskikh svad'bakh v prazdnichnye i postnye dni za 1830 god," 1830), ark. 1–3.

24. DAKO, f. 2, op. 1, spr. 4171 ("Po prosheniiu evreiki Feigi Portnoi," 1833), ark. 1–2.

25. CAHJP, HM2/9567.3 (original—DAVO f. 391, op. 3, spr. 11, "Po ukazu podol'skoi kazennoi palaty s kopieiu kontrakta ob otdannykh piati gerberakh," 1807), ark. 2–3.

26. Pinhas ben Avraam Aba Shapira, *Imrei Pinhas ha-Shalem*, 2 vols. (Bene Brak: Y. S. Frankel, 2003), 2:101 ("Sha'ar torat adam," 8).

27. Nosson Sternhartz, *Haye MOHARA"N* (Jerusalem: Meshekh ha-nahal, 1982), 117–118 (chaps. 116–117).

28. DAKO, f. 2, op. 3, spr. 374 ("Raporta o sostoianii uezdov i gorodov Kievskoi gubernii," 1797), ark. 49.

29. CAHJP, HM9532.4 (original—TsDIAU, f. 442, op. 1, spr. 2176, "Po obvineniiu evreev Bazalii v kontrabande i perepravke dezertirov zagranitsu a takzhe o vyselenii lits evreiskoi natsional'nosti s pogranichnoi territorii, t. 5, Kamenets-Podolsk, gubernskii gorod," 1836–1838), ark. 408–409.

30. DAKO, f. 3, op. 5, spr. 800 ("Delo o Khodorkovskom i Liubarskom," 1821), ark. 12–15.

31. A. P. Chekhov, *Polnoe sobranie sochinenii i pisem v 30 tt.* (Moscow: Nauka, 1975), 7:30–32.

32. Hanna Barvinok [Oleksandra Bilozers'ka-Kulish], *Tvory u dvokh tt.* (Lviv: BaK, 2011), 1:28–34, esp. 29.

33. CAHJP, HM2/9316.31 (original—RGIA, f. 1269, op. 1, d. 17, "Delo ob uluchshenii byta evreev," 1843), l. 4.

34. DAKO, f. 1, op. 336, spr. 3069 ("Delo o zakrytii korchem i shinok, podryvavshikh gosudarstvennuiu torgovliu," 1836–1844), 65, 105.

35. CAHJP, HM2/9651.2 (original—TsDIAU, f. 442, op. 1. spr. 2246, "Ob issledovanii kachestva vodki i trav, naidennykh u soderzhatelia korchmy v m. Shepetovke," 1836), ark. 1–2, 5–7, 13–14.

36. CAHJP, HM2/9567.3 (original—DAVO f. 391, op. 3, spr. 11, "Po ukazu podol'skoi kazennoi palaty s kopieiu kontrakta ob otdannykh piati gerberakh," 1807), ark. 9.

37. CAHJP, HM2/9211.2 (original—DAVO, f. 321, op. 3, spr. 27, "Po prosheniiu zhitelei mestechka Rzhishcheva Itskovicha i Leibovicha," 1794), ark. 2–3.

38. The old Polish system of leasing wineries, beer breweries, and taverns to the Jews survived also in the Kingdom of Poland, particularly on the landowner's estates; see Dynner, "Legal Fictions."

39. DAKO, f. 2, op. 1, spr. 2404 ("Po raportu soderzhatelia v gorode Zvenigorodke piteinogo otkupa Elisavetgradskogo kuptsa Leiby Barskogo," 1824), ark. 1–3.

40. Pyzhov, *Istoria kabakov v Rossii*, 274.

41. DAKO, f. 2, op. 1, spr. 2404 ("Po raportu soderzhatelia v gorode Zvenigorodke piteinogo otkupa Elisavetgradskogo kuptsa Leiby Barskogo," 1824), ark. 5–7.

42. DAKO, f. 1, op. 336, spr. 499 ("Delo o vzyskanii deneg s otkupshchikov vinnoi prodazhi," 1803), ark. 1–4, 10.

43. DAKO, f. 2, op. 1, spr. 3219 ("Po zhalobe soderzhatelia Tarashchanskogo piteinogo otkupa kuptsa 2-oi gil'dii Froima Zaslavskogo," 1829), ark. 1–5, 8–10.

44. DAKO, f. 2, op. 1, spr. 4544 ("Po predpisaniiu Ministra finansov o dostavlenii svedenii, kasatelno slozheniia s Grosmana i Berenshteina nedoimki," 1833), ark. 1–3.

45. CAHJP, HM2/8969.4 (original—TsDIAU, f. 422, op. 1, spr. 8027, "O nezakonnom uchrezhdenii konnoi strazhi soderzhatelem piteinoi arendy v m. Troianove kuptsom Berliandom," 1849), ark. 1–39.

46. CAHJP, HM2/8924.10 (original—TsDIAU, f. 442, op. 1, spr. 1499, "Po zhalobe pomeshchika Radzivilla i arendatorov piteinogo otkupa Berdicheva Rubinshteina A. i G. na Berdichevskoe meshcanskoe obschestvo za otkaz ot pokupki arendnoi vodki," 1833), ark, 1–3, 6, 20–21, 34.

47. G. Orshanskii, *Russkoe zakonodatel'stvo o evreiakh. Ocherki i issledovaniia* (St. Petersburg: Landau, 1877), 389.

48. GARF, f. 109, 1-ia eksp., op. 11, d. 220 ("Po donosu berdichevskogo meshchanina Ushera Dubenskogo," 1836), ark. 1–7; CAHJP, HM2/9482.4 (original—TsDIAU, f. 442, op. 147, spr. 565, "Po raportu korpusa zhandarmov podpolkovnika Beka o raznykh zloupotrebleniiakh po Berdichevskomu otkupu pitei," 1838), ark. 1–4, 51–52, 124–125.

49. CAHJP, HM2/8977.4 (original—DATO, f. 37, op. 3, spr. 48, "Sledstvennoe delo o poiskakh sostavitelei pisma s prizyvom k evreiskomu naseleniiu g. Krementsa ne upotrebliat vodku," 1835), ark. 1–2, 11–12, 14, 78–80.

50. DAKO, f. 1, op. 336, spr. 3069 ("Delo o zakrytii korchem i shinok, podryvavshikh gosudarstvennuiu torgovliu," 1836–1844), 28, 31, 35, 47–61, 179–184, 601–606.

51. Ibid., ark. 15.

52. CAHJP, HM2/9307.4 (original—TsDIAU, f. 422, op. 1, spr. 5087, "Perepiska s kievskim, podol'skim i volynskim grazhdanskim gubernatorom o zapreshchenii litsam evreiskoi natsionalnosti arendovat sel'skie i traktovye korchmy," 1843), ark. 9, 14.

53. For the biased accounts that blame Jews in peasants' drinking habits, see A. Kirkor, "Etnograficheskii vzgliad na Vilenskuiu guberniiu," *Etnograficheskii sbornik Geograficheskogo obshchestva* 3 (St. Petersburg, 1858); 175; anon., "Byt malorusskogo krest'ianina (preimushchestvenno v Poltavskoi gubernii)," *Etnograficheskii sbornik Geograficheskogo obshchestva* 3 (1858): 19–47; see the Galician popular ironic blessing of vodka that "makes everybody a Jewish subject" in P. Efimenko, *Sbornik malorossiiskikh zaklinanii* (Obshchestvo istorii i drevnostei Rossiiskikh, 1874), 3.

54. Rogger, *Jewish Policies and Right-Wing Politics*, 156.

55. Original: "Hey, nalyvaite povnii chary, / Shchob cherez vintsia lylosia. / Shchob nasha dolia nas ne tsuralas', / Shchob krashche v sviti zhylosia." See M. Shevchenko, ed., *Naikrashchi pisni Ukrainy* (Kiev: Demokratychna Ukraina, 1995), 80.

56. Sholom Aleichem, *Tevye's Daughters*, trans. Frances Butwin (New York: Crown, 1965), 163.

57. [Solomon Schechter], "*Sihot hani tsintra de-dehava*," *Ha-shahar*, vol. 8 (1877), pp. 324–327, 416–419, 460–463.

58. Adam Mickiewicz, *Pan Tadeusz* (Warsaw: Czytelnik, 1966), 102–105, here 104 (lines 219–220).

59. Alexander Blok, "Dvenadtsat'," in his *Sobranie sochinenii*, 8 vols. (Moscow and Leningrad: Gosudarstvennoe izdatel'stvo khudozhestvennoi literatury, 1960), 3:354.

60. Vladimir Maiakovsky, "Sergeiu Eseninu," in his *Polnoe sobranie sochinenii*, 13 vols. (Moscow: Gosudarstvennoe izdatelstvo khudozhetsvennoi literatury, 1958), 7:100.

61. Czeslaw Milosz, *The Collected Poems, 1931–1987* (New York: Ecco Press, 1988), 451.

62. Venedict Erofeev, *Moscow to the End of the Line*, trans. William Tjalsma (Evanston, IL: Northwestern University Press, 1994), 27.

63. Igor Guberman, *Gariki na kazhdyi den'* (Moscow: Emiia, 1992), 175.

CHAPTER 5: A VIOLENT DIGNITY

1. CAHJP, HM2/8351.5 (original—TsDIAU, f. 533, op. 2, spr. 323, "Po obvineniu zhitelia Ilinets Kievskoi gubernii Voronovitskogo G.," 1828), ark. 1–8.

2. DAKO, f. 2, op. 1, spr. 4185 ("Po prosheniiu evreev Kholodenka i Usherenka," 1833), ark. 1.

3. DAKO, f. 1, op. 336, spr. 2302 ("Delo po zhalobe meshchanina Shekhtmana na izbienie i ograblenie ego starshinami berdichevskogo pekarskogo tsekha," 1827), ark. 1–2. See a similar case of physical violence against the Kiev dweller Liumarsky, beaten, arrested, and put in chains by the head of Kiev artisan guild Novokhatsky, allegedly for challenging the monopoly of the guild: DAKO, f. 1, op. 336dop., spr. 1801 ("Delo po soobshcheniiu gubernskogo prokurora o neobosnovannom areste i nalozhenii tsepei na meshchanina evreia Liumarskogo," 1823), ark. 1–3.

4. DAKO, f. 2, op. 1, spr. 4171 ("Po prosheniiu evreiki Feigi Portnoi," 1833), ark. 1–2, 3–5.

5. DAKO, f. 3, op. 5, spr. 1172 ("O radomysl'skikh evreiakh Shmuile Tsesarike i Shae Shkolnike," 1824), ark. 1–5.

6. DAKO, f. 3, op. 1, spr. 1211 ("Po prosheniiu radomysl'skogo meshchanina Monashka [Menashe] Burshteina," 1824), ark. 1–11.

7. DAKO, f. 185, op. 1, spr. 658 ("Delo o privlechenii k otvetstvennosti meshchanina Tenenboimova za soderzhanie v svoem dome traktirnoi torgovli i prederzhatel'stva v svoem dome begloi krestianki Mimrinkovoi i beglogo kantonista," 1836–1844), ark. 39, 41–42, 122–123, 148, 182.

8. DAKO, f. 185, op. 1, spr. 745 ("Delo o meshchanine Srule Rashkovskom za pokushenie na zhizn meshchanina Iudki Zatulovskogo," 1841), ark. 1–5, 110–113.

9. DAKO, f. 1, op. 336, spr. 245 ("Delo po zhalobe umanskikh meshchan na gorodnichego za izbienie i zloupotrebleniia pri sbore podatei, 1800), 29.

10. NBU, Orientalia Department, Pinkasim collection [or. 81], n. 45. *Pinkas shel ha-hevrah kadisha shel gomlei hasadim*, Burial society, 1744–1893, ff. 56–59.

11. CAHJP, HM9452.25 (original—TsDIAU, f. 442, op. 786, spr. 230, "Po raportu Volynskogo gubernskogo prokurora s predstavleniem prosheniia evreia Arona Finkel'shteina o trebovanii ego v Kiev," 1836), ark. 4–6.

12. NBU, Orientalia Department, Pinkasim collection [or. 99], n. 64, *Pinkas shel hevrah kadisha*, Miropol, 1790–1925.

13. NBU, Orientalia Department, Pinkasim collection [or. 103], n. 23. *Pinkas shel hevrah po'alei tsedek*, Society of Righteous Workers, Miastkovka, 1765–1913.

14. RGADA, f. 1239, op. 3, d. 62331 ("Vypiska iz prosheniia, poluchennogo pod kuvertom gubernatora Ryleeva," 1696), ll. 1–2.

15. DAKO, f. 2, op. 1, spr. 5872 ("Po prosheniiu meshchanki Anny Pleshakovoi," 1835), ark. 2.

16. DAKO, f. 1, op. 336, spr. 676 ("Delo po zhalobe meshchanina Mordkovicha na Moshenskoe evreiskoe obshchestvo," 1804), ark. 1–4.

17. CAHJP, HM2/8351.2 (original—TsDIAU, f. 533, op. 2, spr. 72: "Ob izbienii kagalnym m. Beloi Tserkvi Kievskoi gub. Grachom E. meshchanina Bondarenko," 1827), ark. 1–8.

18. CAHJP, HM2/9892.14 (original—TsDIAU, f. 442, op. 151, spr. 541, "Delo o rassmotrenii zhaloby lits g. Balta ob izbienii ikh ravvinom Balty," 1842), ark. 1–2, 10.

19. NBU, Orientalia Department, Pinkasim collection [or. 81], n. 45. *Pinkas shel hahevrah kadisha shel gomlei hasadim*, Burial society, Letichev, 1744–1893, ff. 62, 150.

20. Nohum Stutchkoff (and Zvi Hirsch Smolyakov), *Nit keyn foyglen, nor bafliglt: frazeologishe oysdrukn* (Tel Aviv: I.L. Printing House, 2002), 34.

21. DAKO, f. 185, op. 1, spr. 673 ("Delo po prosheniiu belotserkovskikh meshschan ob udalenii tsirul'nika (fel'dshera) Grinberga iz ikh obshchestva za neuzhivchivost'," 1837–1839), ark. 1–3; DAKO, f. 185, op. 1, spr. 823 ("Po obvineniiu tsirulnika Grinberga v lechenii krovopuskaniem bez vrachebnogo nabliudeniia," 1848), ark. 9–10.

22. CAHJP, HM2/8351.9 (original—TsDIAU, f. 533, op. 2, spr. 522, "Po raportu Makhnovskogo zemskogo ispravnika o zhiteliakh m. Vakhnovka [Kelman] Bitmana i [Iosel] Abramovicha"), ark. 1–2.

23. CAHJP, HM2/8265.9 (original—DAKO, f. 533, op. 1, spr. 1310, "O ratmane zvenigorodskogo magistrata [Berko] Rabinoviche," 1811), ark. 1–2, 6.

24. Michael Stanislawski, *Tsar Nicholas I and the Jews: The Transformation of Jewish Society in Russia, 1825–1855* (Philadelphia: Jewish Publication Society of America, 1983), 128–129.

25. GARF, f. 109, 4-ia eksp., op. 166, d. 126 ("O vozmushchenii evreev v gorode Starokonstantinove pri ob'iavlenii im ukaza o obrashchenii ikh k ispravleniiu rekrutskoi povinnosti," 1827), ark. 1–2, 7, 13.

26. DAKO, f. 3, op. 5, spr. 295 ("Ob oslushnosti Gershka Plotnitskogo protivu zasedatelia Nikolenkova," 1816), ark. 1–3.

27. DAKO, f. 2, op. 3, spr. 375 ("O sostoianii umanskogo uezda," 1797), ark. 14.

28. CAHJP, HM2/9553.1 (original—DAKhO, p. 120, op. 1, spr. 34, "Po obvineniiu meshchanina Mikuly Abramovicha v oskorblenii gorodnichego Dushenkevicha," 1798–1800), ark. 1–2.

29. Kotik, *Journey to a Nineteenth-Century Shetl*, 195.

30. DAKO, f. 3, op. 1, spr. 307 ("Otnoshenie Kievskomu gubernskomu pravleniiu o raporte Boguslavskogo uezdnogo striapchego po delam o Kagane i Umanskom," 1834), ark. 1–2.

31. DAKO, f. 185, op. 1, spr. 409 ("Delo o meshchanine Mordukhe-Reisfove, zanimavshegosia izlecheniem venericheskoi bolezni," 1824), ark. 1–6.

32. CAHJP, HM2/9966.6 (original—GARF, f. 109, op. 1828, 1-ia eksp., d. 156, "Ob estafetakh, otpravliaemykh iz Galitsii v Berdichev," 1827–1828).

33. Gavin Langmuir, "At the Frontiers of Faith," in Anna Sapir Abulafia, ed., *Religious Violence between Christians and Jews: Medieval Roots, Modern Perspectives* (New York: Palgrave, 2002), 138–156, here 153.

34. In this 1837 blood libel case several Jews including Itsek Malakh, Shaya Shopnik, Shliomo Furman, and Biniamin Reznik were arrested for allegedly cutting the tongue of Prokop Kozak for ritual purposes, see O. M. Ivashchenko and Iu. M. Polishchuk, *Evrei Volyni: Kinets XVIII-pochatok XX stolittia* (Zhytomyr: Volyn, 1998), 116.

35. Simon Dubnow, *History of the Jews in Russia and Poland*, 3 vols. (New York: Ktav, 1975), 1:396–401.

36. On *Aleiynu* and censors, see Amnon Raz-Krakotzkin, *The Censor, the Editor, and the Text*, trans. Jackie Feldman (Philadelphia: University of Pennsylvania Press, 2007), 164. On *Aleinu* as a prayer of Jewish martyrs who rejected Christianization, see Stefan Reif, *Judaism and Hebrew Prayer. New Perspectives on Jewish Liturgical History* (Cambridge: Cambridge University Press, 1993), 209. For multiple examples of sacrilegious treatment of Christian symbols, including expectoration among Jews, see Elliot Horowitz, *Reckless Rites: Purim and the Legacy of Jewish Violence* (Princeton, NJ: Princeton University Press, 2006), 149–212.

37. CAHJP, HM2/9553.8 (original—DAPO, f. 120, op. 1, spr. 121, "Po obvineniu Duvida Shlemovicha i Rakhmana Mikhelevicha v bogokhul'stve," 1802), ark. 26.

38. TsDIAU, f. 442, op. 150, d. 82 ("Po zhalobe starokonstantinovskogo meshchanina Moshki Blanka" 1841), ark. 1–2b.

39. CAHJP, HM2/9417.2 (original—DAPO, f. 228–57e, op. 1, spr.1543, "Delo po ubiistvu Shvartsmana i Oksmana," 1836), ark. 62–64.

40. DAKO, f. 3, op. 5, spr. 812 ("Po prosheniiu Umanskogo evreiskogo obshchestva o povorovannykh ponomarem iz evreiskoi sinagogi veshchei," 1821), ll. 1–2, 5–6.

41. CAHJP, HM2/9553.2 (original—DAKhO, f. 120, op. 1, spr. 41, "Po obvineniiu Shmulia Tsinera, Borukha Moshkovicha i dr. v krazhe tserkovnykh veschei," 1800–1801), ark. 26, 27, 72.

42. DAKO, f. 2, spr. 1, op. 3533 ("O vorovstve meshchaninom Borokhom Bukovskim tserkovnykh veshchei," 1831), ark. 1–3.

43. DAKO, f. 3, op. 1, spr. 152 ("Spiski zakliuchennykh, soderzhashchikhsia po Kievskoi gubernii za 1825 god," t. 2), ark. 77–82.

44. Horowitz, *Reckless Rites*, 184.

45. CAHJP, HMF 790A-B (original—GARF, f. 109, spr. 335: "Po bezymiannomu donosu o tom, chto nekotorye evrei Polonnogo v netrezvom vide pozvolili sebe poruganiia nad khristianskoiu religieiu," 1854), ll. 1–2, 6, 16, 21, 27, 34, 37, 41, 44.
46. Ivashchenko and Polishchuk, *Evrei Volyni*, 34.
47. CAHJP, HM2/9452.8 (original—TsDIAU, f. 442, op. 783, spr. 79, "Po pis'mu kuptsa Falieva i po pokazaniiu Brodskogo evreiia Iakuba Altera o proizvodiashcheisia perepiske zdeshnikh zhitelei," 1834), ark. 47–48, 58, 68.
48. CAHJP, HM2/9146.5 (original—TsDIAU, f. 442, op. 1, spr. 2767, "Ob udalenii na piatidesiativerstnoe rasstoianie ot granitsy meshchanina m. Podberezhets, Volynskoi gubernii," 1838), ark. 9–13.
49. CAHJP, HM2/9452.8 (original—TsDIAU, f. 442, op. 783, spr. 79, "Po pis'mu kuptsa Falieva i po pokazaniiu Brodskogo evreiia Iakuba Altera o proizvodiashcheisia perepiske zdeshnikh zhitelei," 1834), ark. 68.
50. CAHJP, HM/9481.1 (original—TsDIAU, f. 444, op. 3, spr. 167 (2), "Kontrabandy po Volynskoi gubernii," 1826), ark. 131–132, 230.
51. John Klier and Shlomo Lambrosa, eds., *Pogroms: Anti-Jewish Violence in Modern Russian History* (Cambridge: Cambridge University Press, 1992), 143, 328.
52. In the wake of the 1812 Napoleonic invasion the Russian secret police arrested several dozen suspected Poles in Minsk and Vilna provinces as soon as it established that they had plotted an anti-Jewish pogrom; see GARF, f. 1165, op. 1, d. 6 ("Delo o rassledovanii slukhov o gotovivshikhsia v Vilenskoi, Minskoi gub. i Belostokskoi obl. evreiskikh pogromakh," 1813), ll. 7–8, 16.
53. David Nirenberg, *Communities of Violence: Persecution of Minorities in the Middle Ages* (Princeton, NJ: Princeton University Press, 1996), 231.
54. John Doyle Klier, "Christians and Jews and the 'Dialogue of Violence' in Late Imperial Russia," in Anna Sapir Abulafia, ed., *Religious Violence between Christians and Jews: Medieval Roots, Modern Perspectives* (New York: Palgrave, 2002), 157–170, here 158.
55. Kotik, *Journey to a Nineteenth-Century Shetl*, 113. On Polish landlords humiliating Catholics and Christian Orthodox, see ibid., 114–115, 118–119, 124.
56. Chone Shmeruk, "Majufes," *POLIN: The Jews in Poland*, vol. 1 (1992): 463–474.
57. AGAD, Archiwum Radziwiłłow. Dz. XI, sygn. 210, ll. 1–20.
58. DAKO, f. 2, op. 1, spr. 3865 ("Po vedomosti Makhnovskogo uezdnogo suda ob arestantskikh delakh," 1832), ark. 3.
59. CAHJP, HM2/7927.4 (original—TsDIAU, f. 442, op. 136, spr. 315, "Po zhalobe Skvirskogo meshchanina Itska Kurlabkina o prinesennykh pomeshchikom Strashinskim poboiakh i soderzhanii v kolodkakh," 1833), ark. 1–2.
60. CAHJP, HM2/9554.3 (original—DAPO, f. 120, op. 1, spr. 198, "Po zhalobe zhitelei mestechka Sharovki na obidy, uchinennye pomeshchikom Dul'skim," m. Sharovka, 1804), ark. 1–49.
61. DAKO, f. 185, op. 1, spr. 342 ("Ukaz Kievskogo gubernskogo pravleniia o rassledovanii dela po zhalobe meshchanina Kagana na ekonoma Novosel'skogo," 1822), ark. 5–10.
62. DAKO, f. 219, op. 2, spr. 9 ("Po predpisaniiu gubernskogo prokurora," 1819), ark. 1–4.
63. DAKO, f. 2, op. 1, spr. 5729 ("O prichinennykh evreiu Kaganskomu ekonomom Beliavskim zhestokikh poboev," 1835), ark. 1–3.
64. Taras Shevchenko, *Zibrannia tvoriv*, 6 vols. (Kyiv: Naukova dumka, 2003), 1:265–278, 699–706, here 273.

65. CAHJP, HM2/9479.5 (original—TsDIAU, f. 444, op.1, spr. 88, "Po pros'be tsekhovykh starshin evresikogo obshchestva g. Bara," 1823), ark. 1–31.
66. CAHJP, HM2.9554.4 (original—DAKhO, f. 120, op. 1, spr. 201, "Po obvineniiu baltskogo kvartal'nogo nadziratelia Sakhnovskogo v nanesenii poboev evreiskim kagalnym," 1803), ark. 4.
67. G. Bogrov, *Zapiski evreia*, 3 vols. (Odessa: Sherman, 1912), 3:149–152.
68. DAKO, f. 2, op. 1, spr. 6565 ("O nizhnikh chinakh Ukrainskogo egerskogo polka," 1835), ark. 1–2.
69. CAHJP, HM2/9306.27 (original—TsDIAU, f. 442, op. 1 spr. 4809, "Ob izbienii i ograblenii meshchan Dantsiga, Shulmana i dr., vozvrashchavshikhsia s iarmarki v g. Zhitomir, soldatami Zhitomirskogo vnutrennego garnizonnogo bataliona," 1842), ark. 1–2.
70. John Doyle Klier, *Russians, Jews, and the Pogroms of 1881–1882* (Cambridge: Cambridge University Press, 2011), 115–116.
71. Mendele Moykher Sforim (S. Y. Abramovitsh), *Ale verk. Fishke der krumer* (New York: Hebrew Publishing Co., 1920), 7:11.
72. Michael Wex, *Just Say Nu* (New York: Harper, 2007), 145–155.
73. Erika Timm, Gustav Adolf Beckmann, *Etymologische Studien zum Jiddischen* (Hamburg: Helut Buske, 2006), 110.
74. Jabotinsky, *Samson Nazorei* (Odessa: Optimum, 2001), 114.
75. Dov Levin, "Lekert, Hirsh," in *The YIVO Encyclopedia*, 2:1012.
76. Abraham Ascher, "Interpreting 1905," in Stefani Hoffman and Ezra Mendelsohn, eds., *The Revolution of 1905 and Russia's Jews* (Philadelphia: University of Pennsylvania Press, 2008), 15–30, here 27–28.
77. Jonathan Frankel, *Prophecy and Politics: Socialism, Nationalism, and the Russian Jews, 1862–1917* (Cambridge: Cambridge University Press, 1981), 368–370.
78. See Michael Stanislawski, *A Murder in Lemberg: Politics, Religion, and Violence in Modern Jewish History* (Princeton, NJ: Princeton University Press, 2007), 114–120.

CHAPTER 6: CRIME, PUNISHMENT, AND A PROMISE OF JUSTICE

1. Reconstructed on the basis of DAKO, f. 3, op. 5, spr. 1230 ("O evree Itske Leiboviche," 1824), ark. 1–3.
2. Jonathan Daly, "Russian Punishment in the European Mirror," in Susan P. McCaffray and Michael Melancon, eds., *Russia in the European Context, 1789–1914. A Member of the Family* (New York: Palgrave, 2005), 161–188, here 176.
3. N.F. Dubrovin, *Russkaia zhizn v nachale XIX veka* (St. Petersburg: DNK, 2007), 156–157, 161, 178.
4. B.N. Mironov, *Sotsial'naia istoriia Rossii perioda imperii (XVIII—nachalo XX v.)*, 2 vols. (SPb.: Dmitrii Bulanin, 1999), 2: 83–90, 96.
5. DAKO, f. 2, op. 1, spr. 6941 ("Po prosheniiu evreia Benisha Finkel'shteina o vorovstve u nego veshchei na 18 tysiach rublei," 1837–1840), ark. 4–40.
6. DAKO, f. 2, op. 1, spr. 7014 ("Po prosheniiu evreia Abrama Fridlianda s zhaloboiu na vasil'kovskikh evreev," 1837), ark. 1–5.
7. CAHJP, HM2/475/1/339 (DAVO, f. 472, op. 1, spr. 332, "Delo po obvineniiu [Duvida] Shliomovicha i [Rahmiel] [Mikhel]evicha v antireligioznykh deistviiakh," 1801–1802), ark. 19–30.

8. See Adam Teller, "Tradition and Crisis? Eighteenth-Century Critiques of the Polish-Lithuanian Rabbinate," *Jewish Social Studies* 17, no. 3 (Spring/Summer 2011): 1–39.

9. PNB, Microfilms Department, Rps. BJ 4513 ("Księga wyroków w r. 1800 Izby Cywilnej Kijowskiei sądu Głownego 2-go Departamentu"), ll. 71–72, 74–75, 163–167, 295–297, 416–419, 603–604.

10. In the northern parts of the Pale of Settlement, in Lithuania, the courts also quite often made decisions in favor of the Jews suing the members of Polish szlachta; see, for example, an insightful sociocultural and legal analysis in Eugene M. Avrutin, "Jewish Neighbourly Relations and Imperial Russian legal Culture," *Journal of Modern Jewish Studies* 9, no. 1 (2010): 1–16.

11. Poles also turned to the Russian legal system seeking justice. For example, landlord Bogucki from Vasilkov district could not use either his bygone power or his clout with the authorities. He found himself in need to request a paper from the Russian court that would allow him to settle accounts with one Satanovski-Cherny from Tarashcha, who had allegedly "took by tricks" Bogucki's silverware and money. See DAKO, f. 2, op. 1, spr. 2948 ("Po zhalobe dvorianina Boguckogo o nedache rascheta Tarashchanskim zhitelem evreem Avrumom Satanovskim," 1826), ark. 1–5.

12. DAKO, f. 2, op. 3, spr. 410 ("Perepiska kievskoi kazennoi palaty," 1797–1798), ark. 188–190.

13. DAKO, f. 2, op. 1, spr. 3865 ("Po vedomosti Makhnovskogo uezdnogo suda ob arestantskikh delakh," 1832), ark. 2–3.

14. DAKO, f. 185, op. 1, spr. 342 ("Ukaz Kievskogo gubernskogo pravlenia o rassledovanii dela po zhalobe meshchanina Kagana na ekonoma Novosel'skogo," 1822), ark. 5–10.

15. CAHJP, HM9894.31 (original—TsDIAU, f. 533, op. 1, spr. 1184, "O zakhvate imushchestva, prinadlezhashchego krestianinu s[ela] Dubievka Gunke arendatorom [Iudka] Eliovichem," 1810), ark. 1–12.

16. DAKO, f. 1, op. 336, spr. 2942 ("Po predlozheniiu Kievskogo voennogo gubernatora o postupkakh Chigirinskogo zemskogo ispravnika," 1835–1845), ark. 1–2, 48, 113–116.

17. DAKO, f. 1, op. 370, spr. 1b ("Delo po rassmotreniiu Skvirskim sudom pretenzii raznykh lits ob oplate sledovavshikh im deneg," 1848–1850), ark. 56, 62, 94.

18. DAKO, f. 3, op. 5, spr. 1022 ("Po prosheniiu evreia [Tsalia] Rozenfelda o vzyskanii," 1823), ark. 1–3.

19. DAKO, f. 3, op. 5, spr. 1134 ("Po predpisaniiu gospodina ministra [Gorenshtein i Bernshteinova]," 1824), ark. 1–9.

20. DAKO, f. 2, op. 1, spr. 7022 (["Smelianskogo kagala evreika Rivka Golda Balak-leiska"]), ark. 1, 5, 7–8.

21. Mironov, *Sotsial'naia istoriia*, 2:87.

22. DAKO, f. 2, op. 1, spr. 4843 ("Delo o dostavlenii svedenii o evreiakh," 1834), ark. 1–2.

23. CAHJP, HM2/9417.1 (original—DAPO, f. 228–57, op. 1, spr. 1542, "Po donosu evreev Oksmana i Shvartsmana o propushchennykh po revizii dushakh," 1836), ark. 13.

24. CAHJP, HM2/9547.3 (original—DAPO, f. 228–57c, spr. 8831, "Delo ob ubiistve Shiromvarom i ravvinami Fridmanom i Menelem evreev Shvartsmana i Oksmana"), ark. [85].

25. CAHJP, HM 9265.1 (original—TsDIAU, f. 442, op. 1, spr. 2191, "O zapreshchenii vyezda v Rossiiu kuptsam Hasseliu I., Steltseru M., Gintsbergu N., i dr., prozhivaiushchim v g. Brody i zanimaiushchimsia kontrabandnoi torgovlei," 1836), ark. 9.

26. DAKO, f. 2, op. 3, spr. 3746 ("O prodovol'stvii kvartiruiushchikh voisk drovami," 1817). The title of the case should be "On raising funds for Jewish deputies in St. Pe-

tersburg among the kahal members of Kiev province," 1816, ark. 66–70, 78, 79, 83, here 89.

27. DAKO, f. 1, op. 351, spr. 4 ("Delo o ssylke v Sibir' i nakazanie plet'mi korchmaria Leibovicha," 1797), ark. 1–2.

28. DAKO, f. 2, op. 1, spr. 2563 ("Ob otobrannykh Zvenigorodskim zemskim ispravnikom u prestupnikov Ioselia i Fankelia Kanevskikh 1300 rublei," 1826), ark. 3.

29. DAKO, f. 3, op. 5, spr. 621 ("Imennye vedomosti ob arestantakh, soderzhashchikhsia v Kievskoi gubernii za maiskuiu sego goda tret'," 1820), ark. 1–10, 11–16, 17–21, 67–93; DAKO, f. 3, op. 5, spr. 623 ("O soderzhashchikhsia pod strazheiu kolodnikakh," 1820).

30. DAKO, f. 3, op. 1, spr. 154 ("Vedomost' o zakliuchennykh i podsudimykh po lipovets-komu povetu," 1825), ark. 61–64, 121–129.

31. DAKO, f. 3, op. 1, spr. 155 ("Vedomosti o zakliuchennykh i podsudimykh po Makh-novskomu povetu," 1825–1826), ark. 6, 25–30, 236–241, 145–148.

32. DAKO, f. 3, op. 1, spr. 152 ("Spiski zakliuchennykh, soderzhashchikhsia po Kievskoi gubernii za 1825 god," t. 2), 1–2, 5–6, 14, 29, 49, 56, 63, 73, 77–82, 89–94, 101–104, 128. Also, in 1815, there were two Jews detained among forty-eight arrested and kept in Old Kievan prison; in 1817, there were seven Jews among ninety-one detainees: two Jews were incriminated in melting Russian copper coin and making forged money, two in minor stealing and two in burglary, and another Jew was punished by flogging for an unknown crime. See DAKO, f. 2, op. 3, spr. 3339 ("Obozrenie gubernii Kievs-kim grazhdanskim gubernatorom," 1817), ark. 72.

33. CAHJP, HM2/9479.3 (original—TsDIAU, f. 444, op. 1 spr. 38, "Gubernii podol'skoi reviziia," 1823), ark. 34–38, 60–61.

34. Several other reports from the district courts in the shtetls of Kiev district covering 1805 through 1808 and 1818 testify to the low, if any, Jewish presence in the peniten-tiary system, among considerable Orthodox Christian peasants, soldiers, and Catho-lic Polish townsfolk. See the data on Vasilkov district court prison, DAKO, f. 1099, op. 1, spr. 35 ("Resheniia suda za 1805–1808") and DAKO, f. 1099, op.1, spr. 36 ("Resh-eniia suda za 1818 god," 1818).

35. CAHJP, HM2/9556.1 (original—DAPO, f. 120, op. 1, spr. 305, "Po obvineniiu Voli Gershkovicha v pokupke kradenykh veshchei," 1803), ark. 1–2.

36. DAKO, f. 2, op. 1, spr. 5249 ("Po otnosheniiu podpolkovnika Lenkevicha kasatel'no evreia Iosia Maslovskogo," 1835), ark. 1, 12.

37. DAKO, f. 185, op. 1, spr. 735 ("Vedomosti o podsudimykh, nakhodiashchikhsia v vasil'kovskom magistrate," 1841), ark. 25–30.

38. This picture of the Jewish criminality does not fit in the general picture of crime in the empire with one exception. Most crime in Russia entailed attempts against the state property, individual life, and private ownership. By Jews it was different: most crime was directed against private property, while murder was negligible and state property violation nonexistent. The only offence as rarely attested among the Jews as among the Christians was sexual, perhaps because it remained largely underreported. See Mironov, *Sotsial'naia istoriia Rossii*, 2:90–95.

39. See, for example, data on the Jewish delinquents accused of forty-four cases of mur-der attested in 1811 in one province (Kiev). See DAKO, f. 1, op. 336, spr. 1132 ("Sve-deniia gorodskikh i zemskikh politsii o kolichestve zavodov stekol'nykh, zheleznykh, faiansovykh," 1811), ark. 5, 8.

40. DAKO, f. 3, op. 1, spr. 43 ("Otnoshenie Poltavskogo gubernskogo prokurora o sode-istvii v reshenii dela Leizera Mailovicha," 1808), ark. 1.

41. DAKO, f. 3, op. 1, spr. 115 ("Perepiska s Poltavskim gubernskim prokurorom i Skvir-skim povetovym striapchim o vysylke svedenii o zakliuchennom Shkol'nike," 1820–1821), ark. 2; DAKO, f. 3, op. 1, spr. 155 ("Vedomosti o zakliuchennykh i podsudi-mykh po Makhnovskomu povetu," 1825–1826), ark. 25–30; DAKO, f. 3, op. 1, spr. 307 ("Otnoshenie Kievskomu gubernskomu pravleniiu o raporte Boguslavskogo uezdnogo striapchego po delam o Kagane i Umanskom," 1834), ark. 1–2.

42. DAKO, f. 3, op. 5, spr. 404 ("O vysylke v zhitomirskii nizhnii sud evreia Gershkovi-cha," 1816), ark. 1–3; DAKO, f. 3, op. 5, spr. 357 ("O vysylke v Bratslavskii nizhnii sud evreia Leizera Goldenberga," 1816), ark. 1–11; DAKO, f. 3, op. 5, spr. 1025 ("Ob ares-tante evree Ienkele Duvidoviche Brilianchike," 1824), ark. 5–6.

43. Nahum Stutchkoff, *Der oytser fun der Yidisher shprakh* (New York: YIVO, 1950), 491, 493.

44. Fernand Braudel, *Civilization and Capitalism, 15th–18th Century: Structures of Every-day Life*, 3 vols. (Berkeley: University of California Press, 1992), 1:324.

45. DAKO, f. 3, op. 5, d. 179 ("O podsudimykh evree Kol'mane Gal'perine, Shliome Krechko i Khaime Ostrogradskom," 1816), ark. 1–2; DAKO, f. 3, op. 5, spr. 357 ("O vysylke v Bratslavskii nizhnii sud evreia Leizera Gol'denberga," 1816), ark. 1–11; DAKO, f. 3, op. 5, spr. 1025 ("Ob arestante evree Ienkele Duvidoviche Brilianchike," 1824), ark. l. 5–6; DAKO, f. 185, op. 1, spr. 374 ("Delo o Vasil'kovskom meshchanine Sheinise, podozrevaemogo v podzhoge domov drugikh meshchan," 1823), ark. 2–11; DAKO, f. 219, op. 1, spr. 37 ("Perepiska s Kievskoi gubernskoi prokuraturoi o sniatii pokazaniia s zhtelia m. Zvenigorodka Portnogo," 1820), ark. 2–4; DAKO, f. 2, op. 1, spr. 7064 ("O masterovom 18-go ekipazha Khaime Rudnikove za vorovstvo u evreiki Gel'manovoi golovnogo ubora," 1837), ark. 1; DAKO, f. 2, op. 1, spr. 7022 (["Smelian-skogo kagala evreika Rivka Golda Balakleiska"]), ark. 1–5; DAKO, f. 3, op. 1, spr. 115 ("Perepiska s Poltavskim gubernskim prokurorom i Skvirskim povetovym striap-chim o vysylke svedenii o zakliuchennom Shkol'nike," 1820–21), ark. 1–2; DAKO, f. 2, spr. 1, op. 3533 ("O vorovstve meshchaninom Borokhom Bukovskim tserkovnykh veshchei," 1831), ark. 1–3.

46. Stutchkoff, *Der oyster fun der Yidisher shprakh*, 496.

47. CAHJP, HM2/9553.2 (original—DAKhO, f. 120, op. 1, spr. 41, "Po obvineniiu Shmu-lia Tsinera, Borukha Moshkovicha i dr. v krazhe tserkovnykh veshchei," 1800–1801), 26–27, 73.

48. DAKO, f. 2, op. 1, spr. 7236 ("O dosledovanii dela o evree Froime Nossoviche," 1837), ark. 1–13.

49. DAKO, f. 2, op. 1, spr. 6975 ("Ob evree Itsko Provornom," 1837–1838), ark. 7–9.

50. DAKO, f. 3, op. 1, spr. 152 ("Spiski zakliuchennykh, soderzhashchikhsia po Kievskoi gubernii za 1825 god," t. 2), 14–15.

51. CAHJP, HM2/8968.8 (original—TsDIAU, f. 442, op. 1, spr. 4307, "Delo ob ubiistve meshchanina g. Tomashpolia Sapozhnika," 1841), ark. 1–10.

52. This kind of intercultural delinquency was typical not only of the shtetl: it was at-tested to elsewhere in Europe. See, for example, Paulus Adelsgruber, Laurie Cohen, and Börries Kuzmany, *Getrennt und doch verbunden: Grenzstädte zwischen Österreich und Russland 1772–1918* (Vienna: Böhlau, 2011), 113–126; Rudolf Glanz, *Geschichte des niederen jüdischen Volkes in Deutschland: Eine Studie über historisches Gaunertum, Bettelwesen und Vagantentum* (New York, n.p., 1968), 85–102.

53. DAKO, f. 2, op. 1, spr. 6925 ("O evreiakh Vol'ke Modnom i Avrume Sheigetse," 1838), ark. 1–2, 5–6.

54. Stealing uniforms for resale seems to have been a relatively safe and lucrative business. Consider, f.e., the case of three Jews, Galperin, Krechko and Ostrogradsky, who stole uniform from the house of praporshchik Bragin and later ran away from prison. See DAKO, f. 3, op. 5, d. 179 ("O podsudimykh evree Kolmane Galperine, Shliome Krechko i Khaime Ostrogradskom," 1816), ark. 1–3.

55. DAKO, f. 3, op. 5, spr. 12 ("Po otnosheniiu Volynskogo gubernskogo prokurora o Ienkele Gumennom, podozrevavshemsia v vorovstve," 1813), ark. 1–2, 8–10.

56. DAKO, f. 3, op. 5, spr. 473 ("Po otnosheniiu poltavskogo prokurora," 1817), ark. 19.

57. CAHJP, HM2/9566.9 (original—DAVO, f. D-391, op. 1, spr. 752, "Delo po obvineniu Berkovich Krintsy v krazhe veschei," 1844–1845), ark. 1–18.

58. Stutchkov, *Der oytser fun der Yidisher schprach*, 496.

59. DAKO, f. 2, op. 1, spr. 2563 ("Ob otobrannykh Zvenigorodskim zemskim ispravnikom u prestupnikov Ioselia i Fankelia Kanevskikh 1300 rublei," 1826), ark. 3–28.

60. HM2/9561.5 (original—GARF, f. 109, 2-ia eksp. , op. 63, d. 188, "O razboinicheskikh shaikakh v Malorossiiskikh guberniiakh, sostoiavshikh po bolshei chasti iz evreev," 1833), ll. 1–10.

61. See three major Ukrainian novels dedicated to Karmaniuk that portray him as a romantic and tragic Byron-esque national character, the enemy of serfdom, and the champion of the poor. Mykhailo Staryts'kyi, *Karmeliuk: Istorychnyi roman* (Kyiv: Dnipro, 1871); Vasyl Kucher, *Ustym Karmaliuk: Roman* (Kyiv: Derzhavne vydavnytstvo khudozhnioi literatury, 1957); and Volodymyr Hzhyts'kyi, *Opryshky; Karmaliuk: Istorychni romany* (Lviv: Kameniar, 1971).

62. See Volodymyr Liubchenko, "Karmeliuk chy Karmaniuk?" *Ukrains'kyi istorychnyi zhurnal* 1 (1997): 122–127; idem, "Evrei Podolii i Ustim Karmaniuk (Karlmaliuk): Analiz vzaimootnoshenii," *Vestnik Evreiskogo universiteta* 15 (1997): 36–45; also see K. Huslystyi and P. Lavrov, *Ustym Karmaliuk: Zbirnyk dokumentiv* (Kyiv: Akademiia nauk Ukrainy, 1948). Valerii Diachok, however, uncovered new archival sources and offered a much more sober interpretation of Karmaniuk relations with the Jews than Liubchenko; see his "Ustym Karmaliuk (Karmaniuk) ta rozbiinyts'tvo na Podilli: Konkretno-istorychnyi ta dzhereloznavchyi aspekty," *Naukovi zapysky: Istorychni nauky* 12 (Ostroh: Ostroz'ka Akademiia, 2008): 175–201.

63. CAHJP, HM9483.3 (original—TsDIAU, f. 442, op. 149, spr. 94, "Po prosheniiu evreev Iosia Faishteina i Gershki Kotliara o priostanovlenii reshenia obshchego sobraniia pravitel'stvuiuschego Senata po delu ob ograblenii [Magdaleny] Paplinskoi," 1840), ark. 12–14, 55.

64. GARF, f. 109, op. 2, d. 428 ("O evreiakh Goldblate, Zemane, Leventale, Iakobsone, Godshalke i Levi kasatel'no fal'shivyh assignatsii," 1822), ll. 1–2.

65. CAHJP, HM2/9524.3 (original—GARF, f. 109, op. 4-ia eksp., d. 74, "O fal'shivoi monete i assignatsiiakh," 1935), ark. 1–25.

66. CAHJP, HM2/9483.7 (original—TsDIAU, f. 442, op. 150, spr. 182b, "O evreiakh, delaiushchikh v Zhitomire monetu iz nizkoprobnogo serebra," 1845), ark. 1, 7, 47–48, 119–120.

67. DAKO, f. 2, op. 1, spr. 4348 ("O poimannom v Kievskom uezde evree Gol'dmane," 1833), ark. 1–3, 6–8, 12–14, 31–35.

68. CAHJP, HM2/9891.5 (original—TsDIAU, f. 442, op. 152, spr. 46, "Po donosu evreia Shmulia Iufima na nepravilnoe budto by primenenie ego k delu o naidennoi u berdichevskogo evreia Korifa fal'shivoi monety," 1843), ark. 1–2.

69. Moshe Haim Efraim [of Sudilkov], *Degel Mahane Efraim* (Jerusalem: Mir, 1995), 260.

70. For the legal and religious segregation of Poles throughout the nineteenth century, see Daniel Beauvois, *La bataille de la terre en Ukraine, 1863–1914: Les Polonais et les conflits socio-ethniques* (Lille: Presses universitaires de Lille, 1993); idem, *Pouvoir russe et noblesse polonaise en Ukraine: 1793–1830* (Paris: CNRS, 2003); and a productive critique of these books in Gorizontov, *Paradoksy imperskoi politiki*, 63–81.

71. [Dov Baer ben Samuel of Linits], *In Praise of the Baal Shem Tov*, transl. and ed. Dan Ben-Amos and Jerome R. Mintz (Northvale: Jason Aronson, 1994), 23–24 (no. 11).

72. Dantik Baldaev, *Slovar blatnogo vorovskogo zhargona: v dvukh tomakh* (Moscow: Kampana, 1997); Mikhail Grachev, *Istoriko-etimologicheskii slovar vorovskogo zhargona* (St. Petersburg: Folio-Press, 2000); Wilhelm von Timroth, *Russische und sowjetische Soziolinguistik und tabuisierte Varietäten des Russischen (Argot, Jargons, Slang und Mat)* (München: Sagner, 1983); M. M. Fridman, "Evreiskie elementy 'Blatnoi muzyki,'" in *Iazyk i literatura*, vol. 7 (Leningrad: Nauchno-issledovatel'skii institut rechevoi kul'tury, 1931): 131–138. On a similar criminal argot of the Jewish underworld on eighteenth- to nineteenth-century German lands, see Glanz, *Geschichte des niederen jüdischen Volkes*, 197–207.

73. Lesia Stavyts'ka, *Argo, zhargon, sleng: Sotsial'na dyfferentsiatsiia ukrains'koi movy* (Kyiv: Krytyka, 2005), 103–105.

74. Dov Baer ben Samuel, *In Praise of the Baal Shem Tov*, 127–128 (no. 127).

CHAPTER 7: FAMILY MATTERS

1. DAKO, f. 1099, op. 1, spr. 12 ("Delo po obvineniiu meshchanina Lazebnika v iznasilovanii nesovershennoletnei docheri odnodvortsa Rakotnogo," 1835), ark. 3, 8, 18–19, 61.

2. This chapter draws from the Hebrew-language rabbinic responsa literature, supporting it with archival Russian-language findings. Although responsa are a *prescriptive* type of source involving the suggestions and advice of a rabbi, this chapter makes use primarily of the questions the responsa seek to answer. These questions are valuable and trustworthy *descriptive* sources, if of an unusual nature. "By their nature," insightfully explains Shaul Stampfer, "responsa deal with exceptional cases rather than with common ones for which standard answers are available. Still, they are useful. The questions posed shed light on popular values, desires, and what questioners feel is right." See his *Families, Rabbis, and Education: Traditional Society in Nineteenth-Century Eastern Europe* (Oxford: Littman Library of Jewish Civilization, 2010), 66.

3. Calculated on the basis of CAHJP, HM2/9211.3 (original—DAVO, f. 521, op. 3, spr. 35, "Spiski evreiskikh semei, zhitel'stvuiushchikh v uezdakh Bratslavskoi gub., Borshchagovka, Novofastov, Pavoloch, Ruzhin, Skvira, Khodorovka," 1795), ark. 1–31.

4. CAHJP, HM2/9159 (original—DAKhO, f. 225, op. 19, spr. 501–504, "Spiski evreiskikh obshchin mestechek Podol'skoi gubernii. Perepis' evreiam Podol'skoi gubernii mogilevskogo poveta Barskogo kagala," 1806), no pagination.

5. In my discussion of "premature" marriages I am relying on the analysis provided by Shaul Stampfer in *Families, Rabbis, and Education*, 7–25, especially 8–15.

6. CAHJP, HM2/8872.7 (original—DAKhO, f. 225, op. 1, spr. 505, "Perechnevye vedomosti evreev ushitskogo uezda," 1806), 253 half folios, nonpaginated.

7. Solomon Maimon, *An Autobiography* (Kessinger Publ., 2006), 74–78.

8. CAHJP, HM2/9315.1 (original—RGIA, f. 18, op. 4, d. 493, "Spiski kuptsov po guberniiam," 1832), ll. 70–71.

9. CAHJP, HM2/9158.1 (original—DAKhO, f. 226, op. 79, spr. 2690, "Vedomosti tserkovnosluzhitelei goroda Nemirova, chinshevoi shliakhty," 1795), ark. 200–205.

10. CAHJP, HM2/6602 (original—Archiwum Państwowe, Kraków. Archiwum Sanguszków, Teki tzw. Arabskie. Teka 505, "Akta Sanguszków Zasławskie miejskie żydowskie sprawy," 1790), ark. 5–6.

11. CAHJP, HM2/9211.3 (original—DAVO, f. 521, op. 3, spr. 35, "Spiski evreiskikh semei, zhitel'stvuiushchikh v uezdakh Bratslavskoi gub., Borshchagovka, Novofastov, Pavoloch, Ruzhin, Skvira, Khodorovka," 1795), ark. 107.

12. Stampfer, *Families, Rabbis, and Education*, 33–34, 125–126.

13. B. N. Mironov, *Sotsial'naia istoriia Rossii perioda imperii (XVIII—nachalo XX v.)* (St Petersburg: Dmitrii Bulanin, 1999), 2:234.

14. CAHJP, HM2/9158.1 (original—DAKhO, f. 226, op. 79, spr. 2690, "Vedomosti tserkovnosluzhitelei goroda Nemirova, chinshevoi shliakhty," 1795), ark. 200–205.

15. CAHJP, HM2/9211.3 (original—DAVO, f. 521, op. 3, spr. 35, "Spiski evreiskikh semei, zhitel'stvuiushchikh v uezdakh Bratslavskoi gub., Borshchagovka, Novofastov, Pavoloch, Ruzhin, Skvira, Khodorovka," 1795), ark. 107.

16. See an extensive table containing data on 43 towns in DAKO, f. 1, op. 336, spr. 4051 ("Svedenia o kolichestve muzhskogo i zhenskogo evreiskogo naselenia," 1848), ark. 256. The data foreshadow the data on the late nineteenth-century migrations overseas, which also singled Jews out as a group migrating with families.

17. BT, Gittin 52a.

18. Mendele Moykher Sforim, "Shloyme Reb Khaims," in *Ale shriftn* (New York: Hebrew Publishing Co., 1910), 2:32.

19. Arye Leib Bolechover, *Shem aryeh*, 2 vols. (Vilna: Romm, 1873), siman 62, 72b.

20. Olimpiada Shishkina, *Zametki i vospominaniia russkoi puteshestvennitsy po Rossii v 1845 g*, 2 vols. (St. Petersburg: E.I.V. Tipografiia, 1848), 1:249.

21. Edward Morton, M.B., *Travels in Russia, and a Residence at St. Petersburg and Odessa, in the Years 1827–1829* (London: Longman, 1830), 157.

22. Kotik, *Journey to a Nineteenth-Century Shtetl*, 113, 210, 315.

23. This is a testimony of Adam Neale, quoted in detail in Gershon D. Hundert, "From the Perspective of Progress: Travelers and Foreigners on Jews in Poland and Lithuania in the Eighteenth and Early Eighteenth centuries," in David Assaf and Ada Rapoport-Albert, eds., *Yashan mipney hadash: Mehkarim be-toldot yehudey mizrakh eropa u-vetarbutam* (Jerusalem: Zalman Shazar, 2009), 1:115–135, here 122.

24. Józef Ignacy Kraszewski, *Wspomnienia Wołynia, Polesia i Litwy*, 2 vols. (Wilno: T. Glücksberg, 1840), 1:132.

25. DAKO, f. 923, op. 1, spr. 6 ("Po raportu nizhnego zemskogo piriatinskogo suda," 1782), ark. 2–3.

26. See the etching in Iwo Pogonowski, *Jews in Poland: A Documentary History: The Rise of Jews as a Nation from Congressus Judaicus in Poland to the Knesset in Israel* (New York: Hippocrene Books, 1993), 288.

27. DAKO, f. 923, op. 1, spr. 6 ("Po raportu nizhnego zemskogo piriatinskogo suda," 1782), ark. 1–2.

28. Reconstructed on the bases of the lists provided in CAHJP, HM2/9480.3 (original—TsDIAU, f. 444, op. 1, spr. 139, "Uchrezhdennoi po vysochaishemu poveleniiu sekretno komissii dlia poimki kontrabandy," 1824); CAHJP, HM2/8927.5 (original—TsDIAU, f. 442, op. 1, spr. 1506, "O rozyske i zaderzhanii kontrabandistov i kontrabandnykh tovarov na territorii radzivilovskogo tamozhennogo okruga," 1833); CAHJP, HM2/8926.4

(original—TsDIAU, f. 442, op. 1, spr. 1366, "Po doneseniam iz razlichnykh naselennykh punktov o pozharakh i pr.," 1833); CAHJP, HM/9265.1 (original—TsDIAU, f. 442, op. 1, spr. 2191, "O zapreshcheni vyezda v Rossiiu kuptsam Hasseliu I., Stel'tseru M., Gintsbergu N., i dr. prozhivaiushchim v g. Brody i zanimaiushchimsia kontrabandnoi torgovlei," 1836); CAHJP, HM2/9386A (original—DAKhO, f. 297, op. 1, spr. 5, "O evree Iose Kelmane, sudimom za vodvorenie kontrabandnykh tovarov," 1837).

29. The "color" aspect of the Jewish material culture remains an underexplored matter. For some interesting observations on Jewish multicolored fabric, see Liudmyla Baibula, "Kolektsiia ievreis'kykh vybiiok u L'vivs'komu muzei etnohrafii ta khudozhnioho promyslu," in V. Shashkevych, ed., *Zbirnyk materialiv naukovykh konferentsii 'Zberezhennia ievreis'koi istoryko-kul'turnoi spadshchyny' ta 'Ukraino-ievreis'ky vzaiemyny'"* (Lviv: Naukovyi tsentr iudaiky im. F. Petriakovoi, 2010), 1:17–29.

30. CAHJP, HM2/8926.4 (original—TsDIAU, f. 442, op. 1, spr. 1366, "Po doneseniiam iz razlichnykh naselennykh punktov o pozharakh i pr.," 1833), ark. 122.

31. Moshe Rosman, "Hakdamat '*Tehinah immahot*' le-Sarah Rivkah Rachel Leah Horowitz," in Yosef Hacker and Yaron Harel, eds., *Lo-yasur shevet mi-Yehuda: hanhagah, rabanut ve-kehilah be-toldot yisrael* (Jerusalem: Mossad Byalik, 2011), 301–316.

32. Carol Herselle Krinsky, *Synagogues of Europe: Architecture, History, Meaning* (New York: Dover Publications, 1985), 47–52, esp. plates nos. 77–79, 82–85, 94–96.

33. Arye Leib Bolechover, *Shem aryeh*, 2 vols. (Vilna: Romm, 1873), vol. 1, siman 6, d. 6–6a.

34. Stampfer, *Families, Rabbis, and Education*, 43–49.

35. Haim ben Dov ha-Kohen Rapaport (d. 1839) was the son of the head of the rabbinic court in Medzhibozh and served as the head of the rabbinic court in Ostrog. He answered questions from rabbinic scholars and rabbis from Lokhvitsa, Olyka, Slavuta, Annipol, Mezhirich, Shepetovka, Radzivilov, Helm, Lemberg (Lviv), Minsk, and Dubno, including the requests of such famous rabbinic figures as Efraim Zalman Margolioth (Margolis; 1762–1828) from Brody.

36. Haim ben Dov ha-Kohen Rapaport, *Maim haim: She'elot u-teshuvot* (Zhitomir: Brothers Shapira, 1857), part 2, siman 3, d. 3.

37. Until 1833, Yosef Landa was the head of the rabbinic court in Litin (Podolia), then until his death, in Jassy. Among his correspondents whose questions he answered were Israel Isser of Vinnitsa, Yudl Landa from Sadigora, Moshe of Savran, Isaac Meir ben Avraam Yehoshua Heschel of Medzhibozh, and Israel of Ruzhin.

38. Yosef Landa, *Sefer birkat Yosef* (Jerusalem: H. M. Landa, 1999; copy of the Lemberg: Uri Zev Wolf edition), siman 46, d. 17 (erroneous pagination in this edition throughout).

39. NBU, Orientalia Department, Pinkasim collection, n. 45 [or. 81]. *Pinkas shel ha-hevrah kadisha shel gomilei hasadim*, Burial society record book. 1744—1893, Letichev (Podolia), [ark. 31].

40. NBU, Orientalia Department, Pinkasim collection, or. 58, n. 29. *Pinkas shel ha-hevrah kadisha*, 1785—1830, Zaslav.

41. Bolechover, *Shem aryeh*, vol. 1, siman 63, d. 64.

42. Reconstructed on the basis of a description in CAHJP, HM9532.4 (original—TsDIAU, f. 442, op. 1, spr. 2176, "Po obvineniiu evreev Bazalii v kontrabande i perepravke dezertirov zagranitsu, a takzhe o vyselenii lits evreiskoi natsional'nosti s pogranichnoi territorii," 1836–38), ark. 78.

43. CAHJP, HM2/8871.5 (original—DAPO, f. 115, op. 1, spr. 959, "O postroike bani evreiskikh obshchin v Gaisine," 1839), ark. 1–2.

44. S. O. Gruzenberg, "O fizicheskom sostoianii evreev, v sviazi s usloviiami ikh zhizni, sanitarnyi ocherk," *Evreiskoe obozrenie* 2 (1884): 21–39, 3 (1884): 53–74.

45. DAKO, f. 2, op. 1, spr. 7168 ("Po prosheniiu evreiki Perly Pearovskoi ob osvobozhdenii muzha ee za dachu pristanishcha kakomu-to evreiu," 1837), ark. 1–4.

46. CAHJP, HM2/8977.3 (original—DATO, f. 37, op. 3, spr. 20, "Delo po obvineniiu evreiskikh dukhovnykh pravvikov v mestechke Radzivilov v vynesenii nepravil'nykh prigovorov chlenam evreiskogo kagala," 1826), ark. 1–5, 7–9.

47. CAHJP, HM2/9459.2 (original—TsDIAU, f. 442, op. 278, spr. 26a, "Protokoly, raporty, perepiska i drugie materialy o rassledovanii dela ob ubiistve v Slavute Leizera Protogaina i areste Pinkhasa i Abby Shapiro," 1835–1836), ark. 300b–315.

48. CAHJP, HM7928.21 (original—TsDIAU, f. 533, op. 1, spr. 616, "Po zhalobe mestnogo evreia na gorodnichego," 1804), ark. 4–5.

49. DAKO, f. 1, op. 336, spr. 245 ("Delo po zhalobe umanskikh meshchan na gorodnichego za izbienie i zloupotrebleniia pri sbore podatei, 1800), ark. 13, 15–16, 22.

50. NBU, Orientalia Department, Pinkasim collection, or. 58, n. 29. *Pinkas shel ha-hevrah kadisha*, 1785–1830, Zaslav.

51. Yosef Landa, *Sefer birkat Yosef* (Jerusalem: H.M. Landa, 1999; copy of the Lemberg: Uri Zev Wolf, edition), chapter 2 (*Even Ha-ezer*), siman 4, p. 2b.

52. Bolechover, *Shem aryeh*, siman 10, d. 13–14.

53. Arye Leib Bolechover (active in the 1820s–1860), an amazingly tolerant and sensitive *posek*—rabbinic judge and legal authority—was born in Satanov and served as the head of the rabbinic court in Zaslav. He answered questions of rabbinic scholars, scribes, and butchers from Satanov, Kamenets, Smela, Zhabotin, Belogorodka, Rovno, Medzhibozh, Olyka, Studenitse, Starokonstantinov, Ostrog, Kanev, Polonnoe, Korets, Mogilev-Podolsk, Vinnitsa, Tarnorud, Krasilov, and Yampol. He answered questions of illustrious scholars such as Yosef Shaul Natanzon from Lemberg (Lviv), Levy Isaac from Berdichev, and Yaakov Halberstam from Mogilev.

54. TB Shabbat 134a, Hullin 47b, Yevamot 64b.

55. Arye Leib Bolechover, *Shem Aryeh*, siman 31, d. 43–43b.

56. See, for example, the cases of Khaia Oislenderova, who considered the Gutgarts family accountable for her own health, financial, and family problems: DAKO, f. 2, op. 1, spr. 7776 ("Po prosheniiu evreiki Khai Oislenderovoi, s zhaloboiu na evreia Gutgartsa i zhenu ego za isporchenie ee glaz," 1837), ark. 1–2; and Moshko Blank, who sued distant relatives and the sons of people who had allegedly ruined him twenty years before: TsDIAU, f. 442, op. 144, spr. 46 ("Po zhalobe starokonstantinovskogo meshchanina evreia Shmuelia Toporovskogo za nepravilnoe zavladenie doma evreem Moshko Blankom," 1836), ark. 1–3; TsDIAU, f. 442, op. 144, spr. 47 ("Delo po zhalobe Starokonstantinovskogo kuptsa Shliomy Chatskisa za nepravilnoe zavladenie evreem Moshko Blankom lavkoiu i polovinoiu kamennogo pogreba," 1836), ark. 1–3. See also the discussion of Jewish real estate disputes in chapter 8.

57. Nachman of Bratslav, *Likutei MOHARA"N*, 2:108.

58. Bolechover, *Shem aryeh*, siman 15.

59. Rapaport, *Maim haim*, siman 77, d. 49b.

60. See Matt Goldish, ed., *Spirit Possession in Judaism: Cases and Contexts from the Middle Ages to the Present* (Detroit, MI: Wayne State University Press, 2003), 45–54, 59–64.

61. Rapaport, *Maim haim*, part. 2, siman 7, d. 6–7.

62. Rapaport, *Maim haim*, siman 15, d. 11.

63. Rapaport, *Maim haim*, siman 6, d. 5.
64. Yekhezkel Segal ha-Levy Landau, *Noda bi-yehudah* (Jerusalem: Jerusalem Institute, 1994), siman 33, d. 237–244.
65. Bolechover, *Shem aryeh*, siman 32, d. 45b.
66. Israel Isser ben Zeev Wolf (ca. 1750–1828) served as the head of the rabbinic court in Vinnitsa and Nemirov. Between 1780 and 1828 he answered questions from Brailov, Litin, Satanov, Bratslav, Berdichev, Belopolie, and Tulchin.
67. Israel Isser, *Sefer sha'ar mishpat*, dd. 54–70; Aryeh Leb ben Shemuel, *Yeriot ha-ohel: she'selot u-teshuvot* [Mezyrow: s.n., 1794], she'elah 19. d. 37 (this author was the head of the rabbinic court in Satanov); Abraham Moses ben Asher, ha-Levi. *Maim kedoshim ... uve-sof she'elot u-teshuvot* (Mezhirov, 1810), 113–116b.
68. Israel Isser, *Sefer sha'ar mishpat*, siman 24, d. 56–62.
69. Yekhezkel Segal ha-Levy Landau (1713–1793), was one of the foremost rabbinic thinkers, he studied in Brody and Vladimir-Volynsk, served as the head of the rabbinic court in Yampol, later in Prague. He wrote answers to questions from the major European communities, including Glogau, Berlin, and London. He answered questions from Galicia and Volhynia while serving in Yampol.
70. Landau, *Noda bi-yehudah*, siman 29, d. 73–77.
71. Rapaport, *Maim haim*, siman 9, d. 9.
72. Israel Isser ben Zeev Wolf, *Sefer sha'ar mishpat* (Mogilev: 1810), siman 31.
73. TsDIAU, f. 1163, op. 1, spr. 1 ("Berdichevskii ravvinat; metricheskaia kniga"), ark. 67, 77, 86, 192.
74. CAHJP, HM2/8004.8 (original—TsDIAU, f. 442, op. 1, spr. 6231: "Vedomosti o kolichestve evreiskogo naseleniia, kagalov, sinagog etc.," 1845), ark. 4b–5, 6b–7; CAHJP, HM2/9306.2 (original—TsDIaU, f. 442, op. 1, spr. 4027, "Vedomosti o kolichestve evreiskogo naselenia, kagalov, sinagog, molitvennykh shkol, Kievskoi, Podol'skoi i Volynskoi gubernii," 1841), ark. 6b–9, 15–16; CAHJP, HM9306.20 (original—TsDIAU, f. 442, f. 1, spr. 4629, "Vedomosti o chisle kagalov, sinagog, molitvennykh shkol, dolzhnostnykh lits po Kievskoi gub.," 1842), ark. 2–5 (1842), 6–9, 14–17.
75. Eric Haberer, *Jews and Revolution in nineteenth century Russia* (Cambridge: Cambridge University Press, 1995), 55–56; Pauline Wengeroff, *Rememberings: the world of a Russian-Jewish woman in the nineteenth century*. Ed. by Bernard D. Cooperman (Bethesda, MD: University Press of Maryland, 2000), 210–212.
76. For the detailed analysis of the "unmaking" of Jewish family, see ChaeRan Freeze, *Jewish Marriage and Divorce in Imperial Russia* (Hanover, NH: University Press of New England, 2002); for a broader discussion of Jewish women's history, see Moshe Rosman, *How Jewish Is Jewish History?* (Oxford: Littman Library of Jewish Civilization, 2007), 168–181.
77. See my entry "Demons," in *The YIVO Encyclopedia of Jews in Eastern Europe*, 1:222–223.
78. See my essay "'We Are Too Late': Shloyme Ansky and His Paradigm of No Return," in Gabriella Safran and Steven Zipperstein, eds., *The Worlds of S. Ansky: A Russian-Jewish Intellectual at the Turn of the Century* (Stanford, CA: Stanford University Press, 2006), 83–102.
79. See "Sabbath Meal," the 1920s, in Hillel (Grigorii) Kazovskii, *Khudozhniki Vitebska: Yegudah Pen i ego ucheniki* (Moscow: Imidzh, 1991), n.p.
80. Ignaz Bernstein, *Jüdische Sprichwörter und Redensarten. Im Anhang Erotica und Rustica* (Hildesheim: Georg Olms, 1969), 89 (1299), 89 (1301), 270 (3691), 332 (5, 13), 333 (21, 26, 30, 33, 34), 335 (64), 336 (75, 80, 82, 90), 337 (94, 102, 103), 338 (115), 343 (200).

81. Braudel, *Civilization and Capitalism,* 2:75.
82. See his two novellas, "A Penalty Soldier" and "An Inherited Candlestick," in Osip Rabinovich, *Sochineniia,* 3 vols. (St. Petersburg: Landau, 1880), 1:3–74. For an analysis of these stories in the context of Russian Jewish discourse on russification, see Yohanan Petrovsky-Shtern, *Evrei v russkoi armii, 1827–1914* (Moscow: Novoe literaturnoe obozrenie, 2003), 361–370.
83. Alexander Kuprin, *Sobranie sochinenii v 5-ti tt.* (Moscow: Pravda, 1982), 2:167–186, here 184.
84. Vassili Rozanov, *Kogda nachal'stvo ushlo* (Moscow: Respublika, 1997), 206–208, 224–226, 278–281, 440–441, 544–546; idem, *Nesovmestimye kontrasty zhitiia* (Moscow: Iskusstvo, 1990), 483–487.
85. Franz Kafka, *Letters to Milena* (Harmondsworth: Penguin, 1983), 24–25, 53–54, 136–137.
86. See my preface to the Ukrainian version of Agnon's Nobel Lecture in "Ї": *nezalezhnyi kul'turolohichnyi chasopys* (2008).
87. Vassili Grossman, *Sobranie sochinenii v 4-kh tt.* (Moscow: Vargius, 1998), 2:414.

CHAPTER 8: OPEN HOUSE

1. CAHJP, HM2/9209 (original—DAVO, f. 391, op.1 spr. 397, "O prodazhe imushchestva zhitelei Brailova evreev 20 khoziaev," 1847), ark. 76.
2. CAHJP, HM2/9194 (original—DAVO, f. 473, op. 1, spr. 654, "Delo po obvineniiu Elkunovicha Duvida i Abramovicha Falka v ukrytii bezhavshego iz poseleniia v Sibiri Gorbyka Nikolaia," 1836), ark. 3–4.
3. CAHJP, HM2/9896.1 (original—DAKO, f. 533, op. 5, spr. 1075, "Po prosheniiu evreia Mendelia Froimovicha Blekhera o zagrablennykh u nego umanskimi arendatorami raznykh veshchei," 1827), ark. 1–2.
4. Iwan S. Koropeckyj, ed., *Ukrainian Economic History. Interpretive Essays* (Cambridge, MA: Harvard University Press for Harvard Ukrainian Research Institute, 1991), 296–297.
5. CAHJP, HM2/9206.5 (original—DAVO, f. 391, op. 1, od. zb., 440, "Delo o prodazhe imushchestva iuzvinskogo evreiskogo obshchestva dlia pogashenia dolga," 1853), ark. 40–46.
6. L.L. Rokhlin, *Mestechko Krasnopol'ie (Mogilevskoi gub.): opyt statistiko-ekonomicheskogo opisaniia tipichnogo mestechka cherty osedlosti* (St. Petersburg: Sever, 1908), 38–39.
7. DAKO, f. 185, op. 1, spr. 593 ("Delo o meshchanine Mote Darzane, obviniaemom v ukryvatel'stve beglykh krestian," 1833), ark. 17–28.
8. DAKO, f. 2, op. 1, spr. 6832 ("Otnositel'no ustroistva evreiskikh korobochnykh sborov," 1837), ark. 11.
9. DAKO, f. 1, op. 336, spr. 3015 ("Po raportu Zvenigorodskogo magistrata o nedoimkakh Ol'shanskogo obshchestva," 1836), ark. 1–3.
10. CAHJP, HM2/9219.1 (original—DAVO, f. 222, op. 2, spr. 6, "Delo po zhalobe Mezhirovskogo evreiskogo obshchestva na pomeshchika Orlovskogo Severina," 1847), ark. 24.
11. David Grupper and David Klein, *The Paper Shtetl: A Complete Model of an East European Jewish Town* (New York: Schocken Books, 1984), pp. F and D.
12. The uniqueness of the shtetl house has been in the focus of several innovative studies of Alla Sokolova. See, for example, her "Evreiskie mestechki pamiati: Lokalizatsiia

shtetla," in V. A. Dymshits et al., eds., *Shtetl: XXI vek* (St. Petersburg: Peterburgskaia Iudaika, 2008), 29–64; idem, "Domostroitel'naia traditsiia shtetlov Podolii v pamiat-nikakh i pamiati," *Etnograficheskoe obozrenie* 6 (2009): 38–57, and her dissertation, "Traditsionnaia arkhitektura shtetlov Podolii: XVIII—nachalo XX vv." (St. Peters-burg: Dissertatsiia na soiskanie uchenoi stepeni kandidata nauk, 2001).

13. CAHJP, HM9532.4 (original—TsDIAU, f. 442, op. 1, spr. 2176, "Po obvineniiu evreev Bazalii v kontrabande i perepravke dezertirov zagranitsu, a takzhe o vyselenii lits evreiskoi natsionalnosti s pogranichnoi territorii," 1836–1838), ark. 35.

14. CAHJP, HM2/9457.1 (original—TsDIAU, f. 442, op. 1, spr. 7524, "O zapreshchenii v'ezda v Rossiiu i konfiskatsii imushchestva bezhavshego za granitsu ravvina m. Ruzhina," 1848), ark. 4, 28, 81.

15. CAHJP, HM 9265.1 (original—TsDIAU, f. 442, op. 1, spr. 2191, "O zapreshchenii v'ezda v Rossiiu kuptsam Hasseliu I., Stel'tseru M., Gintsbergu N., i dr., prozhivaiush-chim v g. Brody i zanimaiushchimsia kontrabandnoi torgovlei," 1836), ark. 21.

16. *Sefer kerem beit yisrael: Ruzhin, Sadigora* (Jerusalem: Kiryat Melekh, 2002), 125–126.

17. CAHJP, HM2/9386A (original—DAPO, f. 297, op. 1, spr. 5, "O evree Iose Kel'mane, sudimom za vodvorenie kontrabandnykh tovarov," 1837), ark. 192–194.

18. CAHJP, HM2/9451.20 (original—TsDIAU, f. 293, op. 1, spr. 230, "Protokoly, perepiska, i dr. materialy o tsenzurnom prosmotre nadpisei pod pechatnymi portretami pro-roka Moiseia," 1854), ark. 122.

19. P. P. Chubinskii, ed., *Trudy etnografichesko-statisticheskoi ekspeditsii v Zapadno-Russkii krai*, 7 vols. (St. Petersburg: Bezobrazov, 1872), 7:22.

20. DAKO, f. 2, op. 1, spr. 6328 ("Po zhalobam lits za otiagoshchenie postoem," 1836), ark. 6–7.

21. Ina Sorkina, *Miastechki Belarusi w kantsy XVIII—pershai palove XIX st* (Vilnius: Ev-ropeiskii gumanitarnyi universitet, 2010), 321–322; Alla Sokolova, "'Belyi gospodin' v poiskakh ekzotiki: Evreiskie dostoprimechatelnosti v putevykh zapiskakh i iskusst-vovedcheskikh ocherkakh (XIX–nachalo XX veka)," in O. Budnitskii et al., eds., *Russko-evreiskaia kultura* (Moscow: Rosspen, 2006), 406–436, here 410–413; O. M. Ivashchenko, Iu. M. Polishchuk, *Evrei Volyni: kinets XVIII-pochatok XX stolittia* (Zhy-tomyr: Volyn, 1998), 42. See also Albert Kaganovich, *Rechitsa: Istoriia evreiskogo mes-techka Iugo-Vostochnoi Belorussii* (Jerusalem: n.p., 2007), 66.

22. Unlike urban dwellers or peasants, who had to go to church to partake of holy sacra-ments, the Jews needed a single holy artifact, the Torah scroll, which turned any group of ten male Jews above thirteen into a legitimate prayer quorum and the room into an ad hoc synagogue. For the quote, see CAHJP, HM3/9385.1 (original—DAPO, f. 115, op. 2, spr. 2, "Kameral'noe i topograficheskoe opisanie Letichevskogo uezda," 1812), ark. 166–170.

23. Ivashchenko and Polishchuk, *Evrei Volyni*, 32.

24. Sokolova, "'Belyi gospodin' v poiskakh ekzotiki," 420.

25. This multifunctionalism was characteristic not only of central Ukrainian shtetls but also of Belorussian ones. See an insightful observation in Sorkina, *Miastechki Belar-usi*, 323.

26. CAHJP, HM9532.1 (original—TsDIAU, f. 442, op. 1, spr. 2176, "Po obvineniu evreev Bazalii v kontrabande i perepravke dezertirov zagranitsu a takzhe o vyselenii lits evreiskoi natsionalnosti s pogranichnoi territorii," 1836–1838), ark. 79.

27. Ibid., ark. 72–78.

28. Ibid., ark. 408.

29. Comparatively speaking, fewer rich Jews lived in Uman in the 1820s than rich Christians; the same number of middle-class Jews as middle-class Christian townsfolk (but much more than middle-class Christian peasants); more poor Jews than poor Christian townsfolk and fewer than poor Christian peasants. Here are the numbers on which the discussion is based: szlachta had twenty good houses (21% of total), fifty satisfactory houses (53% of total), and twenty-five unsatisfactory houses (26% of total), for ninety-five houses in all; Christian dwellers had ten good houses (22%), twenty-five satisfactory houses (54%), and eleven unsatisfactory houses (24%), for forty-six altogether; Jews had respectively 100 (16%), 300 (48%), and 220 (36%), for 620 houses total; peasants had respectively forty-five (24%), seventy (37%), and seventy-five (39%), for 190 houses total. See DAKO, f. 2, op. 3, spr. 4745 ("Vedomosti o chisle zhitelei v gorode Umani i o chisle lits, platiashchikh podati," 1827), ark. 19–20.

30. CAHJP, HM2/9194 (original—DAVO, f. 473, op. 1, spr. 654, "Delo po obvineniiu Elkunovicha Duvida i Abramovicha Falka v ukrytii bezhavshego iz poseleniia v Sibiri Gorbyka Nikolaia," 1836), ark. 3–4.

31. N.L. Pushkareva, L.V. Bessmertnykh, *"A se grekhi zlye, smertnye …" Russkaia semeinaia i seksual'naia kul'tura glazami istorikov, etnografov, literatorov, fol'kloristov, pravovedov i bogoslovov," XIX–nachala XX veka, 3 vols.* (Moscow: Ladomir, 2004), 1:289–291.

32. P. P. Chubinskii, *Trudy etnografichesko-statisticheskoi ekspeditsii,* 7:22.

33. Haim Chemerinsky, *Ayarati Motele* (Jerusalem: Magness Press, 2002), 157.

34. CAHJP, HM2/9209 (original—DAVO, f. 391, op.1 spr. 397, "O prodazhe imushchestva zhitelei Brailova evreev 20 khoziaev," 1847), ark. 176; cf. with the same pattern of ten poor Jewish households in Slobodkovets: CAHJP, HM2/9386A (original—DAPO, f. 297, op. 1, spr. 5, "O evree Iose Kelmane sudimom za vodvorenie kontrabandnykh tovarov," 1837), ark. 192–194.

35. NBU, Institute of Manuscript, f. 278 (Stefan Taranushchenko, "Notatky pro ukrains'ku khatu"), nos. 1–100, 1286–1326.

36. DAKO, f. 333, op. 1, spr. 75 ("Perepiska ob otvode zhiteliam g. Radomyshlia mesta dlia postroiki domov," 1848), ark. 1–4.

37. CAHJP, HM2/8872.1 (DAPO, f. 115, op. 2, spr. 164, "Po ukazu gubernskoi stroitelnoi komissii o nabliudenii za postroikoi v gorode Bratslave doma evreem Nahmanom Rechisterom," 1833), ark. 1–5; DAKO, f. 333, op. 1, spr. 75 ("Perepiska ob otvode zhiteliam g. Radomyshlia mesta dlia postroiki domov," 1848), ark. 1–4; for the standard architectural designs of the houses of various types, see CAHJP, HM2/9316.23 (original—RGIA, f. 1268, op. 1, d. 300: "Po pros'bam pomeshchikov raznykh gubernii o pereimenovanii selenii v mestechki," 1807), ll. 183–185.

38. CAHJP, HM2/8872.1 (original—DAPO, f. 115, op. 2, spr. 164, "Po ukazu gubernskoi stroitel'noi komissii o nabliudenii za postroikoi v gorode Bratslave doma evreem Nahmanom Rechisterom," 1833), ark. 4–5.

39. HM2/7959.5 (original—TsDIAU, f. 442, op. 75, spr. 18, "Po zhalobe evreia zhitelia Bara na deistviia mestnogo politsmeistera," 1842), ark. 7–8.

40. DAKO, f. 2, op. 3, spr. 1174 ("Raporta Kievskogo gorodovogo arkhitektora," 1803), ark. 6–7.

41. DAKO, f. 333, op. 1, spr. 54 ("Perepiska ob otvode mesta zhiteliam Skviry dlia postroek," 1846), ark. 31, 40, 46, 48.

42. Ibid., ark. 9, 13. 20, 24–25.

43. DAKO, f. 333, op, 2, spr. 80 ("Perepiska ob otvode zhiteliam Skviry zemli dlia postroek," 1848), ark. 15, 29, 40, 82.
44. DAKO, f. 2, op. 1, spr. 5268 ("Po prosbe evreiki [Rukhlia] Sakhnovskoi otnositelno doma ee, nakhodiashchegosia v Rozheve," 1835), ark. 4–5.
45. DAKO, f. 2, op. 1, spr. 6541 ("Po prosheniiu kantseliarista Ilnitskogo," 1836), ark. 2.
46. DAKO, f. 333, op. 1, spr. 54 ("Perepiska ob otvode mesta zhiteliam Skviry dlia postroek," 1846), ark. 31–40.
47. CAHJP, HM2/9453.8 (original—TsDIAU, f. 442, op. 32, spr. 293, ("Ob uchrezhdenii v Kamenets-Podol'skom evreiskoi bol'nitsy," 1855), ark. 1–2.
48. DAKO, f. 2, op. 1, spr. 7255 ("Po prosheniiu vasil'kovskogo 3-ei gil'dii kuptsa Mordekhaia Shmuliovicha Polkovskogo," 1837), ark. 1.
49. DAKO, f. 2, op. 1, spr. 7389 ("O dozvolenii evreiu Khaimu Borishpolskomu pochinit' na sobstvennyi schet shalash," 1837), ark. 1–10.
50. DAKO, f. 2, op. 1, spr. 5093 ("O naime v Makhnovke doma evreia Rabonovicha dlia gorodskoi bolnitsy," 1835), ark. 1–2. In the mid-1840s, Balta had 13,000 people, had one pharmacy, the closest were forty to fifty miles away, see TsDIAU, f. 442, op. 1, spr. 10760 ("Ob otkrytii apteki v Balte," 1853), ark. 1–6.
51. DAKO, f. 2, op. 1, spr. 5505 ("Ob otpuske Makhnovskomu kuptsu Shtakmanu deneg za naem doma ego pod pomeshchenie prisutstvennykh mest," 1835), ark. 1–2.
52. TsDIAU, f. 442, op. 85, spr. 68 (I) ("Opisanie gorodskoi bol'nitsy," 1854), ark. 41.
53. CAHJP, HM2/9670.2 (original—DAVO, f. 496, op. 1, spr. 12), "Kniga po chasti maklera po zapisi kontraktov," 1826), ark. 1–3. A similar process of shtetl urbanization took place in the Kingdom of Poland, too. In some forty-three shtetls in Podliasie, post offices, military hospitals, paved marketplaces, renovated bridges, and brick streets appeared in the mid-1820s, apparently on a faster pace than in the central provinces of the Pale. See Josef Kazimierski, *Miasta i miasteczka na Podlasiu: zabudowa—ludność—gospodarka* (Warsaw: Archiwum Państwowy, 1994), 30–33, 37–38.
54. TsDIAU, f. 442, op. 78, spr. 165 ("O postroike v gorode Balte pomeschenii dlia iarmarok," 1845–1859), ark. 1, 11, 17, 26, 40, 46, 54–55, 132–133, 169, 233, 261–263.
55. CAHJP, HM2/9453.21 (original—TsDIAU, f. 442, op. 67, spr. 362, "O postroike dereviannykh lavok v Kamentse," 1835), ark. 1–3, 17, 20, 43, 55, 128, 180.
56. CAHJP, HM2/9566.4 (original—DAVO, f. 391, op. 1, spr. 27, "Kniga aktov kupchikh krepostei i dolgovykh obiazatelsyv," 1827), ark. 29.
57. CAHJP, HM2/9670.4 (original—DAVO, f. 496, op. 1, spr. 5, "Aktovaia kniga," 1824), ark. 1; CAHJP, HM2/9670.2 (DAVO, f. 496, op. 1, spr. 3, "Kniga Litinskogo gorodskogo magistrata," 1826), ark. 1–4; CAHJP, HM2/9566.4 (original—DAVO, f. 391, op. 1, spr. 27, "Kniga aktov kupchikh krepostei i dolgovykh obiazatel'stv," 1827), ark. 29, 50, 60, 64; CAHJP, HM2/9670.1 (original—DAVO, f. 496, op. 1, spr. 2, "Aktovaia kniga litinskogo gorodovogo magistrata," 1820), ark. 449, 452, 455, 463, 466; CAHJP, HM2/9670.3 (original—DAVO, f. 496, p. 1, spr. 4, "Kniga aktov litinskogo gorodovogo magistrata," 1823), ark. 9.
58. DAKO, f. 185, op. 1, spr. 747 ("Delo o nasledstvennom dome, prinadlezhashchem Duvidu Slobodianskomu," 1841–1847), ark. 19–142.
59. DAKO, f. 185, op. 1, spr. 748 ("Delo o pred'iavlenii iska meshchankoi Brisoi Shtenbergovoi k meshchaninu Grutmanu," 1841), ark. 1–14, 27–32.
60. CAHJP, HM2/9206.2 (original—DAVO, f. 392, op. 1, spr. 359, "Delo po isku Mezhirovskogo Srulia," 1843), ark. 1–3. It seems that the destabilizing process ruining family relations in more urbanized environment affected also traditional spiritual

hierarchies. See, for example, a conflict between a rich dweller Moshe ben Isaac ha-Levy from Jassy and Avraam Yehoshua Heschel, the Rabbi of the town, around the shared place between their real estate, *Iggrot ha-Ohev Israel* (Jerusalem: Merkaz Torani Ohev Israel, 1981), 40–42.

61. CAHJP, HM2/9206.1 (DAVO, f. 391, op. 1, spr. 352, "Delo po isku Guskelei Aizika i Nukhima k sestram Khane i Sane za dom i lavku," 1835), ark. 1–3.

62. DAKO, f. 185, op. 1, spr. 743 ("Po isku Leiby na brata Duvida Sandlera o nasledtsvennom dome," 1841), ark. 1–4.

63. DAKO, f. 2, op.1, spr. 6218 ("O perevode 3-ei sapernoi brigady iz doma vasil'kovskogo kuptsa Epelboima v drugoi evreia kuptsa Gufelda," 1836), ark. 7; for a similar case, see DAKO, f. 2, op. 1, spr. 7433 ("O razreshenii evreiu Gurinu snesti sobstvennyi dom, gde pomeshchaetsia gauptvakhta," 1837), ark. 1–2.

64. DAKO, f. 2, op. 1, spr. 5124 ("Delo o pochinke stroenii v Umani i uezde," 1835), ark. 12.

65. DAKO, f. 2, op. 1, spr. 5421 ("Ob udobnom stroenii dlia razmeshcheniia parkov," 1835), ark. 1–5; DAKO, f. 2, op. 1, spr. 5199 ("Ob otvode kvartiry general-maioru Karneevu i brigadnomu ego shtabu," 1835), ark. 1–3; DAKO, f. 219, op. 2, spr. 6 ("O kvartirakh v Kieve," 1819–1824), ark.1–2.

66. DAKO, f. 2, op. 1, spr. 2499 ("O udovletvorenii zhitel'nitsy Gurovichevoi za zaniatie ee doma," 1825), ark. 1–7.

67. DAKO, f. 1238, op. 1, spr. 728 ("O voznagrazhdenii makarovskikh evreev za postoi podvizhnogo zapasnogo parka no. 10," 1848), ark. 5–7.

68. DAKO, f. 2, op. 1, spr. 2602 ("Perepiska o naznachenii v dome evreia Gershberga kvartiry dlia generalov," 1825), ark. 2, 7, 9.

69. GARF, f. 109, op. 2a, d. 283 ("Zapiska ofitsera ob antipravitel'stvennom nastroenii poliakov v Volynskoi gub.," 1836), ll. 1–3.

70. DAKO, f. 2, op. 1, spr. 2347 ("O zaplate deneg po umanskomu povetu," 1823), ark. 1–3, 5, 13.

71. DAKO, f. 2, op. 1, spr. 2339 ("Delo o zaplate deneg," 1823), ark. 5.

72. TsDIAU, f. 442, op. 68, spr. 149 ("Delo po prosheniiu vladel'tsa Berdicheva kn. Frantsa Radzivila po prosheniiu berdichevskikh zhitelei," 1836–1838), ark. 1–3.

73. DAKO, f. 2, op. 1, spr. 6328 ("Po zhalobam lits za otiagoshchenie postoem," 1836), ark. 11–12.

74. DAKO, f. 1238, op. 1, spr. 267 ("Na pochinku doma Kushnira," 1840), ark. 1–2.

75. DAKO, f. 1238, op. 1, spr. 728 ("O voznagrazhdenii makarovskikh evreev za postoi podvizhnogo zapasnogo parka no. 10," 1848), ark. 17.

76. For the description of this episode of quartered troops, see Grigorii Bogrov, *Zapiski evreia*. 3 vols. (Odessa: Sherman, 1912), 3:149–152.

77. DAKO, f. 1, op. 336dop., spr. 2785 ("Delo po zhalobe skvirskogo gorodnichego na beschinstva Irkutskogo gusarskogo polka, raskvartirovannogo v g. Skvira," 1833), ark. 2, 26, 32–35, 62, 66, 68.

78. RGADA, f. 276, op. 3, d. 2041 ("Po soobschcheniiu volynskogo gubernskogo pravleniia o vzyskanii s Tarasova i kazakov 465 chervontsev za zabraniie imi u evreiia Iankeliovicha loshadei," 1809), ll. 1–3.

79. CAHJP, HM2/7928.7 (original—DAKO, f. 533, op. 1, spr. 436, "Po prosheniu poverennogo evreiskoi obshchiny Boguslava," 1804), ark. 3.

80. DAKO, f. 2, op. 1, spr. 5091 ("O razorenii doma Umanskogo evreia Mordka Rozenberga voinskim postoem," 1835), ark. 1–3.

81. DAKO, f. 2, op. 1, spr. 6328 ("Po zhalobam lits za otiagoshchenie postoem," 1836), ark. 1–2, 3–4.

82. CAHJP, HM2/8267.5 (original—TsDIAU, f. 442, op. 650, spr. 102, "Perepiska s Ministerstvom vnutrennikh del i podol'skim gubernskim pravleniem o vydelenii sredstv iz sum korobochnogo sbora na privedenie v poriadok ulits Medzhibozha," 1897), ark. 1.

83. CAHJP, HM2/7959.3 (original—TsDIAU, f. 442, op. 648, spr. 149, "Ob otpuske 30,000 iz summy Baltskogo korobochnogo sbora na zamoshchenie Balty," 1895), ark. 1–5.

84. [Pekhotnogo 45-go Azovskogo E. I. V. Velikogo kniazia Borisa Vladimirovicha polka], Poruchik N. Ziuts, *Opisanie goroda Starokonstantinova ot nachala osnovaniia do nashikh dnei (1561–1884)* (Starokonstantinov: S. Arenberg, 1884), 21–22.

85. Mendele Moykher Sforim, "Shloyme Reb Khayim's" in his *Ale shriftn* (New York: Hebrew Publishing Co., 1910), 2:3–73, here 10–12; see also in English translation, *A Shtetl and Other Yiddish Novellas*, edited with introduction and notes by Ruth Wisse (Detroit, MI: Wayne State University Press, 1986), 281–284.

CHAPTER 9: IF I FORGET THEE

1. CAHJP, HM2/9651.2 (original—TsDIAU, f. 442, op. 1. spr. 2246, "Ob issledovanii kachestva vodki i trav, naidennykh u soderzhatelia korchmy v m. Shepetovke," 1836), ark. 13.

2. See Omri Shasha, "Ben Ish Hai: At the Crossroads of Modernity," *Segula Magazine* 2 (2011): 12–24.

3. Maimonides in his *Mishneh Torah*, Hilkhot Melakhim 5:4 mentions this custom derived from TB Ketubot 35b and based on an interpretative reading of Deut. 32:43: "*ve-khiper adamah et amo*" (and the earth will atone for its people). Jewish custom of putting some earth from the land of Israel into the grave on the forehead of the deceased was introduced most likely by Hasidei Ashkenaz who reacted to a Catholic custom of putting a bag with some earth from the grave under the head of the deceased. See Daniel Sperberg, *The Jewish Life Cycle: Custom, Lore and Iconography. Jewish Customs from Cradle to the Grave* (Ramat Gan: Bar-Ilan University Press/ Oxford: Oxford University Press, 2008), 466–467, n. 7. See also the sources in Daniel Sperberg, *Minhagei Israel: Mekorot ve-toldot* (Jerusalem: Ha-rav Kook, 1998), 6:99–100, n31.

4. Pinhas ben Avraam Aba Shapira, *Imrei pinhas ha-shalem*, 2 vols. (Bnei Brak: Yehezkel Shraga Frenkel, 2002), 1:470 (*Sha'ar Olam* 55).

5. Nachman of Bratslav, *Likutei MOHARA"N* (Jerusalem: Meshekh ha-nakhal, 1999), 2:43 (siman 116).

6. Moshe Haim Efraim of Sudilkov, *Degel mahaneh Efraim* (Jerualem, MIR, 1995), 163.

7. Moshe Tsvi of Savran, *Likutei shoshanim* (Jerusalem: Ginzei shoshanim, 2008), 155.

8. Israel of Ruzhin, *Yirin kadishin ha-shalem*, edited by Naftali Flintenstein, 3 vols. (Jerusalem: Siftei Tsadikim, 2009), 2:472.

9. The metaphor is based on Ezek. 11:16.

10. George K. Loukomski, *Jewish Art in European Synagogues* (London: Hutchinson and Co., 1947), 169.

11. Ex. 39:30. See Franz Landsberger, "The Origin of European Torah Decorations," in Joseph Gutmann, ed., *Beauty in Holiness: Studies in Jewish Customs and Ceremonial*

Art (New York: Ktav, 1970), 87–121. The editor of the volume claims that although the association of Torah decorations (breast-piece, frontlet) with the Temple is widely accepted it has no foundation in rabbinic sources; see Gutmann, "Torah Ornaments, Priestly Vestments, and the King James Bible," in Gutman, *Beauty in Holiness*, 122–124. For the sacred meanings of the Torah scroll ornaments and "garments" in a wider Judaic religious context, see a different view of Bracha Yaniv, *Ma'aseh hoshev: ha-tik le-sefer torah ve-toldotav* (Ramat Gan: Universitat Bar-Ilan, 1997); idem, "The mystery of the flat Torah finials from East Persia," *Padyavand* 1 (1996): 63–74; idem, "Synagogue ceremonial textiles: Based on the Lviv Museum of Ethnography and Artistic Craft Collection," in *Visnyk kharkivs'koi derzhavnoi akademi dyzainu i mystetstv* 8 (2010): 165–178; and idem, "'This Is the Table That Stands before the Lord': On the Synagogue 'Bimah' or 'Teivah' Cover," *Review of Rabbinic Judaism* 14, no. 2 (2011): 208–220.

12. Based on Hoshea 14: 3.

13. As quoted in Mendel Piekarz, *Ha-hanhagah ha-hasidit* (Jerusalem: Mossad Byalik, 1999), 228.

14. Yaakov Yosef of Polonnoye, *Tsofnat pa'aneah*, edited with an introduction and notes by Gedalyah Nigal (Jerusalem: Makhon le-heker ha-sifrut ha-hasidit, 1988), 59:4.

15. For the Temple and the land imagery on the altars, see also Maria and Kazimierz Piechotka, *Heaven's Gates: Wooden Synagogues in the Territories of the former Polish-Lithuanian Commonwealth* (Warsaw: Krupski, 2004), 23–24, 90.

16. The saying comes from "The Will of Rabbi Eliezer the Great" and most likely draws from TB Berakhot 28b.

17. This quote from the morning liturgy appearing in Judaic prayer books is from Ps. 5:7.

18. Bracha Yaniv, "The Sun Rays on Top of the Torah Ark: A Dialogue with the Aureole, the Christian Symbol of the Divinity on Top of the Altarpiece," in Marcel Poorthuis et al., eds., *Interaction between Judaism and Christianity in History, Religion, Art and Literature* (Leiden: Brill, 2009), 477–493, here 485.

19. Ilia Rodov, "'The King of the Kings' Images of Rulership in Late Medieval and Early Modern Christian Art and Synagogue Design," in Poorthuis et al., *Interaction between Judaism and Christianity in History, Religion, Art and Literature*, 457–475, here 463.

20. Ilia Rodov, "Dragons: A Symbol of Evil in European Synagogue Decoration?," *Ars Judaica* 1 (2005): 63–84, here 82.

21. Tamar Shadmi, "From Functional Solution to Decorative Concept: Stages in the Development of Inscribing Liturgical Texts on Synagogue Walls," *Ars Judaica* 6 (2010): 69–80.

22. On two greatest East European ethnographers, see Maksymiljan Goldstein, *Kultura i sztuka ludu żydowskiego na ziemiach polskich: Zbiory Maksymiljana Goldsteina. Z przedmową* Majera Bałabana (Warszawa: Wydawn. Artystyczne i Filmowe, 1991); Gabriella Safran and Steven Zipperstein, eds., *The Worlds of S. An-sky: A Russian Jewish Intellectual at the Turn of the Century* (Stanford, CA: Stanford University Press, 2006), esp. 266–280.

23. See Gen. 44:18–45:15, and Midrash Rabbah, Gen. 93:2.

24. For unicorn and lion fighting, see for example a photo from an East European wooden synagogue in Maria i Kazimierz Piechotkowie, *Krajobraz z Menora: Żydzi w miastach i miasteczkach dawnej Rzeczpospolitej* (Wrocław: Zakład Ossolińskich, 2008), f. 107. For the messianic context of the encounter between the unicorn and the lion, see Shalom Sabar, "The harmony of the Cosmos: The Image of the Ideal Jewish

World according to Venetian *Ketubbah* Illuminators," in Mauro Perani, ed. *I Beni Culturali Ebraici in Italia: Situazione attuale, problemi, prospettive e progetti per il futuro* (Ravenna: Longo, 2003), 195–215.

25. Dan. 6:10.
26. Ps. 16: 8.
27. Efraim of Sudilkov, *Degel mahaneh Efraim*, 65.
28. See Rabbi Nachman of Bratslav, *Likutei MOHARA"N* (Jerusalem: Meshekh ha-nakhal, 1999), 1:115a–b, siman 234.
29. Pinhas ben Avraam Aba Shapira, *Imrei Pinhas ha-shalem*, 2 vols. (Bnei Brak: Yehezkel Shraga Frenkel, 2002), 1:297 (*Sha 'ar Tefillah* 53).
30. Esther Juhasz, "Ha-'shiviti-menorah'—bein mufshat le-homrey iyunim be-yatsug ha-kodesh," Ph.D. diss., Hebrew University, 2004, pp. 30–36, 78–96.
31. Israel Bartal, "Merkaz ba-shulayim: temurot bi-mekomah shel Yerushalayim be-todaat ha-yehudim," in Israel Bartal, Hayim Goren, *Sefer Yerushalayim 1800–1917* (Jerusalem: Yad Ben Tsvi, 2010), 63–72, here 65–66.
32. Shalom Sabar, *Masel Tov: Illuminierte jüdische Eheverträge aus der Sammlung des Israel Museum* (Berlin: Jüdische Verlangsanstalt, 2000), 44–53.
33. 2 Chron. 2:7.
34. Ezk. 20:6.
35. Ex. 19:4.
36. Gen. 49:8–10.
37. Pirkei Avot 5:24.
38. On the redemptive scenario in Amidah (Eighteen Benedictions) prayer, see Reuven Kimelman, "The Daily 'Amidah and the Rhetoric of Redemption," *Jewish Quarterly Review* 79, nos. 2/3 (1988–1989): 165–197.
39. Joseph and Yehudit Shadur, *Traditional Jewish Papercuts: An Inner World of an Art and Symbol* (Hanover, NH: University Press of New England, 2002), 29–31, 52–58, 63, 80–81, 97, 107, 126.
40. Shalom Sabar, "Domestic Wall decorations and Folk Papercuts," in Sarah Harel Hoshen, ed., *Treasures of Jewish Galicia: Judaica from the Museum of Ethnography and Crafts in Lviv, Ukraine* (Tel Aviv: Beth Hatfutsot, 1996), 137–147, here 137–138.
41. Ps. 91:1.
42. This part of the chapter is inspired by my mentor, Arthur Green. See his essay "The Zaddiq as Axis Mundi in Later Judaism," *Journal of the American Academy of Religion* 45, no. 3 (1977): 327–347, esp. 330 and 341.
43. Moshe Tsvi of Savran, *Likutei shoshanim*, 174.
44. Ex. 25:30.
45. For the description of this practice, see Samuel Aba Horodetzky, *Ha-hasidut ve-hahasidim*. 4 vols. (Tel Aviv: Devir, 1953), 3:92.
46. See Haviva Pedaya, "Le-hitpathuto shel ha-degem ha-hevrati-dati-kalkali ba-hasidut: ha-pidiyon, ha-havurah, veha-'aliyah le-regel," in Menahem Ben-Sasson, ed., *Dat ve-kalkalah: yahasei gomlin* (Jerusalem: Zalman Shazar, 1995), 311–373.
47. Haggai 2:8.
48. Avraam Yehoshua Heschel, *Ohev Yisrael ha-shalem* (Jerusalem: Siftei Tsadikim 1996), 133b–134a.
49. See, for example, Menahot 72b–73a, Ta'anit 26b.
50. Ps. 27:8–9.

51. Israel Fridman [of Ruzhin], *Yirin kadishin ha-shalem*. 3 vols., edited by Naftali Flin-tenstein (Jerusalem: Siftei Tsadikim, 2009), 1:56, 2:367–328, 655.

52. Avraam Yehoshua Heschel, *Ohev Yisrael ha-shalem* (Jerusalem: Siftei Tsadikim 1996), 62, 116–117, 132–134, 156–157, 173, 185, 203, 208.

53. Levy Isaac of Berdichev, *Kedushat Levy ha-shalem* (Jerusalem: Torat ha-netsakh, 1978), 48.

54. Israel Fridman [of Ruzhin], *Yirin kadishin ha-shalem* 2:464–466.

55. Arthur Green, *Tormented Master: A Life of Rabbi Nahman of Bratslav* (Tuscaloosa: University of Alabama Press, 1979), 63–93; see also Martin Cunz, *Die Fahrt des Rabbi Nachman von Brazlaw ins Land Israel (1798–1799): Geschichte, Hermeneutik, Texte* (Tübingen: J.C.B. Mohr-Siebeck, 1997).

56. Rabbi Nachman of Bratslav, *Likutei MOHARA"N* (Jerusalem: Meshekh ha-nakhal, 1999), 1:8, siman 1:12, siman 9:5; 1:32, siman 22:8; 1:49, siman 35:5; 1:56, siman 48; 1:93b, siman 80; 94a, siman 81; 1:102b, siman 129; 1: 105b, siman155; 2:1a, siman 1:4; 2:25b–26a, siman 40; 2:30b–31a, siman 67; 2:36a–b, siman 78; 2 43a, siman 116.

57. *Degel mahaneh Efraim*, 181.

58. All four places were the sites of the great rabbinic scholars and of the *kivrei tsadikim*, the graves of the righteous, highly revered by the traditional Jews throughout Dias-pora. Safed was the place connected to Shimon bar Yohai, the legendary author of the *Zohar*, and also to the most important sixteenth-century mystics (Yosef Karo, Shlomo Alkabetz, Isaac Luria, Haim Vital, and others). Tiberias most likely served as a place for the last meetings of the Sanhedrin and the codification of the Mishnah by Yehuda ha-Nasi, if not of the codification of the Palestinian Talmud. Hebron hosted the cave of Mahkpelah, with the graves of the biblical Avraam, Sarah, Isaac, Rebecca, Jacob, and Leah. Jerusalem hosted the ruins of the Second Temple and the graves of the biblical prophets and kings. The nineteenth-century vision of the land of Israel (*Erets Yisroel*) was centered in these communities and sites and did not imply a continuous geographic entity or polity, even in biblical terms.

59. Yehiel Gernshtein, *Erets Yisrael shel malah: Aliyatam shel gedolei Yisrael le-erets Yis-rael*, 2 vols. (Tel Aviv: Pe'er, 1985), 2–3.

60. Assaf, *The Regal Way*, 206.

61. Nathaniel Deutsch, *The Maiden of Ludmir: A Jewish Holy Woman and Her World* (Berkeley: University of California Press, 2003), 197–202.

62. Avraam Yaari, *Iggrot Erets Yisrael* (Ramat Gan: Massada, 1971), 328–337.

63. Dov Ber Rabinovitz, ed., *Iggrot ha-rav ha-kadosh mi-Ruzhin u-vanav*, 3 vols. (Jerusa-lem: Mishkenot ha-roim, 2003), 1:205–206; 2: 101.

64. David Assaf, *The Regal Way: The Life and Times of Rabbi Israel of Ruzhin* (Stanford, CA: Stanford University Press, 2002), 205–206.

65. Meir Menahem Rotshild, *Ha-halukah ke-bitui le-yahasah shel yahadut ha-golah leyi-shuv hayehudi be-Erets Yisrael ba-shanim 1810–1860* (Jerusalem: Reuven Mas, 1986), 18.

66. Gernshtein, *Erets Yisrael shel malah*, 2:6–9; Avraam Yaari, *Shlukhei Erets Yisrael: toldot ha-shlikhut me-arets la-golah*, 2 vols. (Jerusalem: Ha-rav Kook, 1997), 2:625.

67. Yaari, *Shlukhei Erets Yisrael*, 2:616–617, 620, 621–622, 624, 627–629.

68. Avraam Yaari, *Iggrot Erets Yisrael* (Ramat Gan: Massada, 1971), 328–337.

69. Yaari, *Iggrot Erets Yisrael*, 336–337, 383, 397. For an interesting literary depiction which combined sympathy to the messenger of the Jewish community in Palestine with

elements of anti-Hasidic mockery, see Yisroel Aksenfeld, "The Headband," in Joachim Neugroschel, ed., *The Shtetl* (Woodstock, NY: Overlook Press, 1989), 135–136.

70. For a significant association of the Hurvah synagogue and the Temple, see Shalom Sabar, "Mi-vet ha-mikdash le-vet ha-kneset 'ha-Hurvah,'" in Reuven Gafni et al., *Ha-Hurvah: Shesh me'ot shanim shel hityashvut yehudit bi-Yerushalayim* (Jerusalem: Yad Ben-Zvi, 2010), 111–132.

71. CAHJP, HM2/8925 (TsDIAU, f. 442, op. 1, spr. 2221, "Ob areste v Zhitomire turetsk-ogo evreia Arona Alkalaia po podozreniiu v antikhristianskoi propagande," 1836), ark. 1–5, 30, 36–37.

72. According to the data available, Plonsky died in prison; see Avraam Yaari, *Shlukhei Erets Yisrael: toldot ha-shlikhut me-arets la-golah,* 2 vols. (Jerusalem: Ha-rav Kook, 1997), 2:763.

73. CAHJP, HM2/8004.1 (original—TsDIAU, f. 442, op. 1, spr. 2446, "O sbore evreiami g. Vladimira deneg na postroiku sinagogi v Ierusalime," 1837), ark. 47.

74. Siegfried Justus I, *Der Mensch als Bürger im Reiche Gottes: Sieben Sendschreiben von Zion nebst einigen Noten aus einem diplomatischen Aktenstuck, das Reich Gottes betreffend* (Mainz: C. G. Kunze, 1832).

75. GARF, f. 109, op. 12, d. 126 ("O poluchennom iz Leipziga vozzvanii k izrail'skim obshchestvam o vozobnovlenii Ierusalimskogo khrama," 1837), ll. 1–2.

76. GARF, f. 109, op. 12, d. 221 (1837), 10, 15.

77. CAHJP, HM2/7774.9 (original—RGIA, f. 821, op. 8, spr. 502 ("O razreshenii sbora sredi evreev Rossii dobrovol'nykh pozhertvovanii v pol'zu ikh edinovertsev v Palestine na stroitelstvo sinagogi v Ierusalime," 1859), ll. 5, 33.

78. For more detail on the increasing Russian geopolitical presence in the Holy land early in the nineteenth century, see I. Smirnova, "Religioznoe protivostoianie velikikh der-zhav v Sviatoi zemle v 1830-kh godakh," *Rossiiskaia istoriia* 1 (2012): 44–59.

79. CAHJP, HM2/8927.4 (original—TsDIAU, f. 442, op. 1, spr. 2446, "O sbore zhiteliami g. Krementsa i Vladimira Rabinovichem, Lektenshteinom i dr. deneg sredi evreisk-ogo naseleniia etikh gorodov na postroiku sinagogi v Ierusalime," 1838), ark. 5–8.

80. Meir Menahem Rotshild, *Ha-halukah ke-bitui le-yahasah shel yahadut ha-golah leyi-shuv hayehudi be-Erets Yisrael ba-shanim 1810–1860* (Jerusalem: Reuven Mas,1986), 24, 27–31, 70–71.

81. Shaul Stampfer, *Families, Rabbis, and Education: Traditional Society in Nineteenth-Century Eastern Europe* (Oxford: Littman Library of Jewish Civilization, 2010), 102–120, here 112.

82. CAHJP, HM2/8004.1 (original—TsDIAU, f. 442, op. 1, spr. 2446, "O sbore evreiami g. Vladimira deneg na postroiku sinagogi v Ierusalime," 1837), ark. 45–47. A rabbi of Voronovitsy in Vinnitsa region introduced, although later in the century, a special regulation requiring from each Jew under the penalty of excommunication to set aside money gained from sale or purchase of yeast—and send the raised funds to the land. See CAHJP, HM2/7929.8 (original—TsDIAU, f. 442, op. 52, spr.158, "Materialy sledstviia po donosu gruppy voronovitskikh evreev v sviazi s konfliktom mezhdu raznymi gruppami evreiskogo obschestva," 1872), ark. 1–19.

83. CAHJP, HM2/8927.4 (original—TsDIAU, f. 442, op. 1, spr. 2446, "O sbore zhiteliami g. Krementsa i Vladimira Rabinovichem, Lektenshteinom i dr. deneg sredi evreisk-ogo naseleniia etikh gorodov na postroiku sinagogi v Ierusalime," 1838), ark. 18.

84. CAHJP, HM2/7774.8 (original—RGIA, f. 821, op. 8, spr. 506: "Po prosheniiu bankira I. Galperina o razreshenii sbora sredi evreiskogo naseleniia Rossii pozhertvovanii v

polzu Palestinskikh evreev v sviazi s postigshim Palestinu neurozhaem," 1858), ark 1–3.

85. CAHJP, HM2/9051.29 (original—RGIA, f. 777, op. 1, d. 777, "Delo o predstavlenii popechitelem Vilenskogo uchebnogo okruga vedomostei o evreiskikh knigakh," 1828), l. 77.

86. GARF, f. 109, op. 12, d. 126 ("O poluchennom iz Leiptsiga vozzvanii k izrail'skim obshchestvam o vozobnovlenii Ierusalimskogo khrama," 1837), ll. 1–5, 15–16.

87. Haim Yosef David Azulay's works enjoyed enormous popularity among the Jews in East Europe: in addition to Żolkiew and Lemberg, they regularly appeared in the Slavuta, Polonnoe, Sudilkov typographies, and later in Grodno, Vilna, and Warsaw.

88. Jody Myers, *Seeking Zion: Modernity and Messianic Activism in the Writings of Tsevi Hirsch Kalischer* (Oxford: Littman Library of Jewish Civilization, 2003).

89. RGADA, f. 4, op. 1, d. 182 ("Pis'ma imperatora Iosifa II Velikomu kniaziu Pavlu I," 1781–1790), l. 9; on this trip, see also A.M. Peskov, *Pavel I* (Moscow: Molodaia gvardiia, 2003), 301–302.

90. Shakhna Zvi Likhtman, *Harei besamim* (Berdichev: Sheftel, 1897), s. 82.

91. Haim ben Dov ha-Kohen Rapaport, *Maim haim: she'elot u-teshuvot* (Zhitomir: Brothers Shapira, 1857), 32 (part 2, siman 42).

92. Yehoshua Heschel Rabinovits, *Masekhet avot im biur Torat avot* (New York, 1926), 10.

93. Lev. 16:10 and 22.

94. A. Sokolova, "Arkhitektura shtetla v kontekste traditsionnoi kultury," in V. Lukin et al., eds., *100 evreiskikh mestechek Ukrainy. Istoricheskii putevoditel.* Vyp. 2: *Podoliia* (St. Petersburg: Gersht, 2000), 69.

95. Dan Ben-Amos and Jerome Mintz, eds., *In Praise of the Baal Shem Tov* (Northvale, NJ: Jason Aronson, 1993), 23–24 (tale 11).

96. Levy Isaac of Berdichev, *Kedushat Levy ha-shalem*, 533.

CHAPTER 10: THE BOOKS OF THE PEOPLE

1. See Joel Mokyr, "Mercantilism, the Enlightenment, and the Industrial Revolution," in Ronald Findlay et al., eds., *Eli Heckscher, International Trade, and Economic History* (Cambridge, MA: MIT Press, 2006), 269–303.

2. CAHJP, HM2/8925.3 (original—TsDIAU, f. 442, op. 1, spr. 2349), ark. 88.

3. On Minkovtsy, see Avraam Yaari, "Likutim bibliografiim. Ha-defus ha-ivri be-minkovets," *Kiryat sefer* 19 (3) (1942): 267–276; Veniamin Lukin, "Evrei—poddannye gosudarstva Min'kovetskogo (k istorii evreiskogo knigopechataniia na Ukraine)," *Paralleli* 10–11 (2009): 535–560.

4. David Fishman, *Russia's First Modern Jews: The Jews of Shklov* (New York: New York University Press, 1995), 5.

5. CAHJP, HM2/8925.3 (original—TsDIAU, f. 442, op. 1, spr. 2349), ark. 89.

6. On the beginning of the Jewish book printing in late eighteenth-century eastern Poland, see Yitshak Rivkind, "Le-toldot ha-defus ha-ivri be-Polin," *Kiryat sefer* 11, no. 1 (1934–1935): 95–104; Saul Ginzburg, "Tsu der geshikhte fun yidishen druk-vezen," *Historishe verk*, 3 vols. (New York: Saul Ginzburg 70-yoriger yubilei komitet, 1937), 48–62; Avraam Yaari, "Tosefot le-bibliografya shel defusei Polin-Rusya," *Kiryat sefer* 21, no. 3 (1944): 296–301; Haim Dov Friedberg, *Toldot ha-defus be-polanyah* (Tel Aviv: Barukh Fridberg, 1950); Zeev Gries, "Printing and Publishing before 1800," and Kenneth Moss, "Printing and Publishing after 1800," in *The YIVO Encyclopedia of*

Jews in Eastern Europe, 2:1454–1458, 1459–1468, and the substantial bibliography amassed there.

7. See Yeshayahu Vinograd, *Otsar ha-sefer ha-ivri* (Jerusalem: Institute for Computerized Bibliography, 1993), index.

8. Identifying these books as kabbalistic or Hasidic is not a trivial task. Yeshayahu Vinograd in his seminal catalogue quite often does not differentiate between Hasidic and kabbalistic, while Ben Yaakov's and Friedberg's catalogues do not tag book titles. See Isaac Benjacob, *Otsar ha-sefarim*, 3 vols. (Vilna: Romm, 1880); Bernard Friedberg, *Bet eked sefarim*, 4 vols. (Tel Aviv: ha-mimkar ha-rashi, 1951–1956).

9. *Mishnayot: Seder Nezikin* (Slavuta: Moshe Shapira, 1806), title page.

10. Yaakov ben Asher, *Tur: Even ha-ezer* (Medzhibozh, 1821), title page, verso.

11. CAHJP, HM2/9777.13 (original—LNHA, f. 378, d. 1791), ll. 1–2.

12. Here Tugenhold reveals his knowledge of *Megaleh temirin* which he read in its first Vienna 1820 edition. He uses Joseph Perl's work to depict all the evils and intrigues of Hasidim and urges the government to look at the Austrian experience in dealing with Hasidim, see CAHJP, HM2/9777.13 (original: LSHA, f. 378, d. 1791, "Po otnosheniu ministra Vnutrennikh Del o merakh po unichtozheniiu vrednykh mezhdu evreiami khassidskikh sochinenii," 1834), ll. 1–2, 11b–13; the reference to Joseph Perl is on l. 12b.

13. CAHJP, HM2/9459.1 (original—TsDIAU, f. 442, op. 278, d. 26a, "Protokoly, raporty, perepiska i drugie materially o rassledovanii dela ob ubiistve v Slavute Leizera Protogaina i areste Pinkhasa i Abby Shapiro," 1835–1836), ark. 300.

14. CAHJP, HM2/7779.30 (original—RGIA f. 1374, op. 2, d. 1426, "O zapreshchenii pechatat evreiskie knigi v mestechkakh Slavute, Koretse, Novodvore, Shklove i Grodno bez razresheniia rizhskoi evreiskoi tsenzury," 1798), ll. 1–2.

15. GARF, f. 1165, op. 1, d. 245 ("Doneseniia gubernatorov v Ministerstvo politsii o kolichestve tipografii i knizhnykh lavok po guberniiam," 1811), l. 3.

16. Reconstructed on the basis of the 1842 Sudilkov printing press described by local police. Visibility was directly linked to the number of people involved. Authorities knew about Slavuta less because of its printers than because of its paper manufacture factory, which employed twenty-four Christians and ten Jews. See CAHJP, HM2/9892.10 (original—TsDIAU, f. 442, op. 151, spr. 303, "Delo ob obnaruzhenii pechatnogo stanka i nelegal'noi literatury u lits Sudilkova Zaslavskogo uezda Perlicha Sh.," 1842), ark. 1–10, 118.

17. On the late nineteenth century, see Hagit Kohen, *Be-hanuto shel mokher ha-sefarim: hanuyot yehudiyot shel sefarim be-mizrakh eropa ba-mahatsit ha-shniya shel ha-me'ah ha-tesha' 'esre* (Jerusalem: Magnes, 2006), and Jeffrey Veidlinger, *Jewish Public Culture in Late Imperial Russia* (Bloomington: Indiana University Press, 2009).

18. On the shtetl fairs, see my "'The Marketplace in Balta: Aspects of Economic and Cultural Life," *East European Jewish Affairs* 37, no. 3 (2007): 277–298.

19. CAHJP, HM2/9885.8 (original—TsDIAU, f. 293, op. 1, spr. 63, "O knigakh i bumagakh, otobrannykh u evreev Sudilkova," 1842), ark. 1–2.

20. CAHJP, HM2/8925.3 (original—TsDIAU, f. 442, op. 1, spr. 2349, "Po prosheniiam evreiskikh kuptsov i obshchinnykh deiatelei ob otkrytii evreiskoi tipografii v Kieve," 1836), ark. 78, 88, 89.

21. On the Shapiras (or Shapiros; both forms are used in contemporary documents), see David Assaf, "Shapira Family," in *YIVO Encyclopedia*, 2:1701–1702; on the Romms, see Zeev Gries, ibid., 2:1588–1589. On the controversy, see Michael Stanislawski, "The

"Vilna Shas" and East European Jewry," in Sharon Liberman and Gabriel Goldstein, eds., *Printing the Talmud. From Bomberg to Schottenstein* (New York: Yeshiva University Museum, 2005), 97–102.

22. See Saul Ginsburg, *The Drama of Slavuta*. Transl. by Ephraim Prombaum (Lanham: University Press of America, 1991); Dmitrii Eliashevich, *Pravitel'stvennaia politika i evreiskaia pechat v Rossii. 1797-1917. Ocherki istorii tsenzury* (St. Petersburg: Gesharim, 1999), 175–179.

23. GARF, f. 109, 1-ia eksp., op. 12, d. 108, "Po bezymennym donosam o protivuzakonnykh deistviiakh evreev Zeiberlinga i Mandelshtama a takzhe chinovnika Dukshinskogo," 1837, ll. 25–26.

24. CAHJP, HM2/9051.21 (original—RGIA, f. 772, op.1, d. 233, "Po predstavleniiu vilenskogo tsenzurnogo komiteta o evreiskikh knigakh, napechatannykh bez odobreniia," 1830), l. 1–1a.

25. CAHJP, HM2/9789.10 (original—LNHA, f. 567, op. 6, spr. 218, "Perepiska s upravleniem Vitebskogo, Mogilevskogo i Smolenskogo general-gubernatora ob obnaruzhenii khasidskikh sochinenii v nezakonnoi tipografii Shepelia Slavina v m. Kopysi," 1853), ll. 1–2, 30.

26. CAHJP, HM2/9892.10 (original—TsDIAU, f. 442, op. 151, spr. 303, "Delo ob obnaruzhenii pechatnogo stanka i nelegal'noi literatury u lits Sudilkova Zaslavskogo uezda Perlicha Sh.," 1842), ark. 1–10.

27. TsDIAU, f. 442, op. 786, d. 211 ("Bumagi, prinadlezhashchie Iakovu Lipsu," 1836), ark. 14.

28. CAHJP, HM2/9451.14 (original—TsDIAU, f. 293, op. 1, d. 93, "O evreiskikh knigakh, predstavlennykh v tsenzurnyi komitet," 1844), ark. 13.

29. TsDIAU, f. 442. op. 803, d. 319, ll. 1–4.

30. CAHJP, HM2/9308.3 (original—GARF, f. 109, 1-ia eksp., op. 11, d. 306, "O nevypolnenii Vysochaishe utverzhdennogo polozheniia otnositel'no unichtozheniia evreiskikh tipografii i o zloupotrebleniiakh so storony tsenzury evreiskikh knig," 1836), ark. 2–2b.

31. On the attitudes of the Habsburg Empire toward Hasidim in the Austrian Galicia, see a short summary in Polonsky, *The Jews in Poland and Russia*, 1:257–260; a more detailed analysis in Raphael Mahler, *Hasidism and the Jewish Enlightenment: Their Confrontation in Galicia and Poland in the First Half of the Nineteenth Century* (Philadelphia: Jewish Publication Society of America, 1985); and the critique of Mahler's book in Nancy Sinkoff, *Out of the Shtetl: Making Jews Modern in the Polish Borderlands* (Providence, RI: Brown Judaic Studies, 2004), 210–211.

32. CAHJP, HM2/8968.11 (original—TsDIAU, f. 442, op. 1, spr. 4658, "Po zhalobe radzivilovsogo kuptsa [Danielia] Gartenshteina na Volynskoe gubernskoe pravlenie za konfiskatsiiu i sozhzheniie prinadlezhavshikh emu knig na evreiskom iazyke," 1842), ark. 7–8.

33. CAHJP, HM8925.3 (original—TsDIAU, f. 442, op. 1, spr. 2349, "Po prosheniiam evreiiskikh kuptsov i obshchinnykh deiatelei ob otkrytii evreiskoi tipografii v Kieve," 1836–1840), ark. 82–86.

34. CAHJP, HM2/9739.10 (original—LNHA, f. 567, op. 2, d. 5380, "O Vilenskoi evreiskoi tipografii," 1844–1864), ll. 2, 13–23, 377–378. Cf. the circulation in the 1850s, ll. 377–378; Also cf. Pinhas Kon, "Menahem Man Romm na'ase toshav ve-nikhtav be-vilna," *Kiryat sefer* 12, no. 1 (1935–1936): 109–115.

35. CAHJP, HM2/8345.3 (original—DAZhO, f. 396, op. 1, spr. 8, "Kniga dlia zapiski i polnoty rukopisei postupoaiuschikh k pechataniu v Zhitomirskuiu evreiskuiu

tipografiiu," 1847), ark. 2–5. The number of titles published in Zhitomir decreased and went from 48 titles in 1847 and 37 in 1848, to 21 in 1849, 29 in 1850, 16 in 1851, and 18 in 1852.

36. Nosson Sternhartz, *Haye MOHARA"N* (Jerusalem: Meshekh ha-nahal, 1982), siman 88, 91, 175–176, 184, 346–349, 351.

37. Pinhas ben Avraam Aba Shapira, *Imrey Pinhas ha-shalem*, 2 vols. (Bnei Brak: Yehezkel Shraga Frenkel, 2002), 1:506–507 (*Sha'ar sipurim*, 48).

38. RGADA, f. 276, op. 2, d. 475 ("Po raportu raznykh tamozhen," 1809), ll. 10–12.

39. CAHJP, HM2/8927.1 (original—TsDIAU, f. 442, op. 1, spr. 2367, "Ob otdache pod sud vladel'tsa tipografii v m. Sudilkove [Itsko] Madfisa za napechatanie knig bez dozvoleniia tsenzury," 1837), ark. 3–5, 25.

40. CAHJP, HM2/7987.1 (original—TsDIAU, f. 707, op. 87, d. 1153, "O evreiskoi tipografii, prednaznachennoi k uchrezhdeniiu v Zhitomire," 1845), ark. 121–124, 194–199.

41. Compare to Soloviev's *History of Russia*, 3 rubles for the first volume, 2.50 for the second; 9 rubles for the *History of Civic Laws* by Nevolin; 4 rubles for *Physics* by Shcheglov; 2 rubles for the *History of Nicholas I's Reign*; 1.25 for Sreznevsky's *Research into Paganism*; 2.85 for the *History of Ancient and New Literature* by Schlegel; 1.50 for the *History of Jews*, by Modestov; 4 rubles for Vilman's *History of Medieval Literature* (all titles in Russian); 1.30 for the German Bible with Ludwig Fillipson's commentaries. See CAHJP, HM2/8347, "O snabzhenii biblioteki evreiskimi raznymi knigami," 1852 (original—DAZhO, f. 396, op. 2, d. 57), ark. 44, 188. Maskilic books were of the same price ranging between 0.75 and 1.50 per book: the seminary's director Eichenbaum approved of the purchase of following books, paying 1 ruble for Eichel's *Toldot Mendelson*, 50 kopeks for Reifman's *Pesher davar*; 1 ruble for Mapu's *Ahavat Tsiyon*; 75 kopeks for Luzzatto's *Migdal oz*, 1 ruble for De Rossi's *Meor einayim*, and 75 kopeks for the periodical *Tsiyon*. See CAHJP, HM2/8347.13 (original—DAZhO, f. 396, op. 2, d. 85, "O pokupke knig dlia biblioteki uchilishcha," 1854).

42. CAHJP, HM/7423 ("Stempowane książki hebrajskie w Wojewódstwie Podolskiem," 1776), ll. 16–17 (X–XI).

43. Ber of Bolechow, *The Memoirs of Ber of Bolechow (1723–1805),* translated and with an introduction by M. Wishnitzer (London: Humphrey Milford, 1922), 100.

44. CAHJP, HM2/9423 (original—GARF, f. 109, 1-ia eksp., op. 1846, d. 277, "Po donisu evreia Avruma Kuperbanta o prestupnykh zamyslakh evreev protiv gosudaria imperatora," 1846), l. 23.

45. GARF, f. 109, op. 13, d. 241 (1838 [Bromberg]), l. 17–17a.

46. CAHJP, HM2/8968.11 (original—TsDIAU, f. 442, op. 1, spr. 4658, "Po zhalobe radzivilovskogo kuptsa [Danielia] Gartenshteina na Volynskoe gubernskoe pravlenie za konfiskatsiiu i sozhzheniie prinadlezhavshikh emu knig na evreiskom iazyke," 1842), ark. 1–8.

47. CAHJP, HM2/9548.1 (original—DAKPO, 228–57/8832, "Delo po obvineniiu gruppy lits 82 chelovek v ubiistve donoschikov Oksmana i Shvartsmana," 1836), ark. 39.

48. CAHJP, HM2/8967.10 (original—TsDIAU, f. 442, op. 1, spr. 2746, "O meshchanine Liantskorunia, Kamenetskogo uezda, Trifmana M., zanimaiushchegosia tolkovaniem evreiskikh religioznykh knig i podozrevaiushchegosia v zaniatiiakh gadaniem i predskazaniem," 1838), ll. 1–3, 8; CAHJP, HM2/9551.1 (original—DAKhO, f. 228, op. 1, spr. 8838, "Delo po obvineniiu Zelmana, Gershteina i dr. v ubiistve Tilmana Nukhima," 1838–1839), ark. 114–116.

49. In the original: "kalendarzy dlia izraelitów całego Wołynia," see Józef Ignacy Kraszewski, *Wspomnienia Wołynia, Polesia i Litwy*, 2 vols. (Wilno: T. Glücksberg, 1840), 1:200.

50. Elisheva Carlebach, *Palaces of Time: Jewish Calendar and Culture in Early Modern Europe* (Cambridge, MA: Belknap Press of Harvard University Press, 2011), 36.

51. Calendars are taken from the following collections: LNA (Nac. Spaud. Archivas), BKC 258174, *Luah ha-shanah mishnat taka"a im nosaf luah ha-lev* (Tarnopol: n. p., 1815); *Luah mishnat taktsa"a* (Vilna and Grodna: Zymel Nochimowicz, 1825); JNUL, Scholem Collection, R PV 3595, *Luah mishnat tara"h* (Zhitomir: Shapiro Brothers, 1847); JNUL, Scholem Collection, R 89 A 520 *Luah mishnat taktsa"v* (Minsk: Blonshtein, 1836).

52. On the historiography of Natan Neta Hanover (or Hannover) , see Gershon Bacon, "'The House of Hannover':'Gezeirot Tah' in Modern Jewish Historical Writing," *Jewish History* 17, no. 2 (2003): 179–206, and Adam Teller, "Jewish Literary Responses to the Events of 1648–1649 in the Creation of a Polish-Jewish Consciousness," in Gabriella Safran and Benjamin Nathans, eds., *Culture Front* (2008): 17–45, esp. 26–35.

53. The 1847 report of the brothers Shapira to the committee on censorship shows 2,000 copies of *Sha'arei tsiyon* published, see CAHJP, HM2/8345.3 (original—DAZhO, f. 396, op. 1, spr. 8, "Kniga dlia zapiski i polnoty rukopisei, postupaiushchikh k pechataniu v Zhitomirskuiu evreiskuiu tipografiiu," 1847), ark. 2–5. The next most popular prayer book was *Korban minhah,* which enjoyed only three to four reprints over the same period of time.

54. See his *haskamah*, rabbinic endorsement, on the first page of the Ostrog (1823) edition.

55. I rely here on the work of my student Marcy Blattner, "Tsena U'Rena: The Least Famous Bestseller," thesis, Northwestern University, 2012, and the secondary sources she reviewed here.

56. The book is known today under the title *Sefer ha-hezyonot* (The Book of Visions), see its English-language edition, *Jewish Mystical Autobiographies: Book of Visions and Book of Secrets:* (New York: Paulist Press, 1999).

57. Haim Vital, *Sefer ha-hezionot. Darkhei haim* (Jerusalem: Shuvi nafshi, 2002), 95–96 (no. 29).

58. CAHJP, HM2/9051.29 (RGIA, f. 777, op. 1, d. 777, "Delo o predstavlenii popechitelem Vilenskogo uchebnogo okruga vedomostei o evreiskikh knigakh," 1828), ll. 30–78.

59. Andrei Zorin, *Kormia dvuglavogo orla ... Literatura i gosudarstvennaia ideologiia v Rossii v poslednei treti XVIII—pervoi treti XIX veka* (Moscow: Novoe literaturnoe obozrenie, 2001), 68–94. See Konstantin Burmistrov, "Kabbalah and Secret Societies in Russia (Eighteenth to Twentieth Century)," in Boaz Huss et al., eds., *Kabbalah and Modernity: Interpretations, Transformations, Adaptations* (Leiden: Brill, 2010): 79–105.

60. CAHJP, HM2/9885.19 (original—TsDIAU, f. 293, op. 1, spr. 162, "Po otnosheniiu MNP k sostavleniiu proekta instruktsii dlia tsenzorov evreiskikh knig"), ark. 5.

61. Ibid., ark. 21.

62. See, for example, a complaint of the Volhynia provincial authorities of rabbi Roitenberg from Rovno. CAHJP, HM2/9891.10 (original—TsDIAU, f. 442, op. 152, d. 366, "Po predstavleniiu Volynskogo gubernskogo pravleniia ob oslushnosti Rovenskogo ravvina Roitenberga, uklonivshegosia ot peresmotra evreiskikh knig," 1843). On the leniency of local rabbis and their reluctance to expurgate harmful books, see also a

denunciation of certain Kagin, a convert from Judaism: GARF, f. 109, 1-ia eksp., op. 13, d. 232 ("O donose perekreshchentsa iz evreev Kagina," 1838), ll. 1–2.

63. For the discussion of the phenomenon of informers, see my *Lenin's Jewish Question* (New Haven, CT: Yale University Press, 2010), 56–61.

64. CAHJP, 9885.7 "Po otnosheniiu volynskogo gubernskogo pravleniia o razsmotrenii 24 evreiskikh knig. 1842," ll. 4–5.

65. *Seder ha-yom*, Żółkiew, 1830; *Tokef ha-nes*, commentary on the book of Esther, Lemberg, 1797; and a foreign edition of *Avodat ha-kodesh*, either by Meir ibn Gabbai or by Haim Yosef David Azulai.

66. *Sha'ar gan eden*, Korets, 1803, another three books from Korets, the Żółkiew-published kabbalistic prayer book *Seder tefilah al-derekh ha-sod*, 1781; Azulai's *Hesed Avraam*, Slavuta, 1794; *Ketonet passim* by Yaakov Yosef of Polonnoe; *Sefer haredim* by Eliezer Azikri, Żółkiew, 1796; *Sefer ha-Rokeah* by Eliezer of Worms, Berdichev, 1817.

67. DAKO, f. 2, op. 1, spr. 6724 ("O zaderzhannykh s evreem Khaskelem Galbirom sumnitelnykh evreiskikh knig," 1836), 7–24.

68. Most Hasidic books found in the area covered by the primary documents which I had consulted, were *Ramzei tora* (Or torah) by Dov Ber, the Maggid of Mezrich; *Kol arye* by Arie Leib ha-Maggid mi-Polonnoe, *Beit ha-Levy* by Yeruham Haim mi-Dolina, and the Kapust-printed books by Dov Ber Schneerson. Among kabbalistic books there were *Or ha-hokhmah*, *Pardes rimonim*, *Sha'ar gan eden*, *Shefa tal*, *Hesed le-Avraam*, *Kanfei Yona* and kabbalistic prayer books such as *Yisod ve-shoresh ha-avodah* and *Sha'arei tsiyon*.

69. CAHJP, HM2/7779.24 (original—RGIA, f. 1374, op. 3, d. 2409, "Perepiska s ucherezhdennoi pri radzivilovskoi tamozhne tsenzuroi o knigakh, zapreshchennykh k vvozu i rasprostraneniiu, v t.ch. o tainom provoze knig cherez m. Gusiatino," 1800), l. 1.

70. CAHJP, HM2/8968.11 (original—TsDIAU, f. 442, op. 1, spr. 4658, "Po zhalobe radzivilovsogo kuptsa [Danielia] Gartenshteina na Volynskoe gubernskoe pravlenie za konfiskatsiiu i sozhzheniie prinadlezhavshikh emu knig na evreiskom iazyke," 1842), ark. 1–8.

71. CAHJP, HM2/9051.21 (original—RGIA, f. 772, op.1, d. 233, "Po predstavleniiu vilenskogo tsenzurnogo komiteta o evreiskikh knigakh, napechatannykh bez odobreniia," 1830), ll. 23–26.

72. See Zeev Gries, *The Book in the Jewish World, 1700–1900* (Oxford: Littman Library of Jewish Civilization, 2007), 69–90.

73. CAHJP, HM2/9051.21 (original—RGIA, f. 772, op. 1, d. 233, "Po predstavleniiu vilenskogo tsenzurnogo komiteta o evreiskikh knigakh, napechatannykh bez odobreniia," 1830), ll. 11–13, 23–26, 93–96.

74. Eliashevich points to the direct contacts between Tugenhold and Perl (see his *Pravitel'stvennaia politika i evreiskaia pechat'*, 153), yet misses the impact of Perl's *Megaleh temirin* on Tugenhold.

75. Joseph Perl, *Revealer of Secrets. The First Hebrew Novel*, translated with an Introduction and notes by Dov Taylor (Boulder, CO: Westview Press, 1997), Prologue, 14–20, 32, 34, 39, 45–46; letter 8, n4, letter 13: 54, 58; letter 15: 108–109, 114; letter 16: 96–97; letter 34:19, letter 51:19, letter 56: 22; letter 61: 67–85, 93–94; letter 76:29; letter 76, n1–7; letter 109: 25–28; letter 121: 27. For the list of books, see pp. 245–246. For the discussion of Perl's book, see Sinkoff, *Out of the Shtetl*, 238–241.

76. CAHJP, HM2/9885.19 (original—TsDIAU, f. 293, op. 1, sp. 162, "Po otnosheniiu MNP k sostavleniiu proekta instruktsii dlia tsenzorov evreiskikh knig," 1852), ark. 21.
77. CAHJP, HM2/8345.3 (original—DAZhO, f. 396, op. 1, spr. 8, "Kniga dlia zapiski i polnoty rukopisei, postupaiushchikh k pechataniiu v Zhitomirskuiu evreiskuiu tipografiiu," 1847), ark. 2–5.
78. Henderson, *Biblical researches*, 213.
79. Published by Julius Fürst between 1840 and 1851 in Leipzig. The quote is from Saul Ginsburg, *The Drama of Slavuta* (Lanham, MD: University Press of America, 1991), 30–31.
80. Avraam Ber Gottlober, *Zikhronot u-masa'ot*. 2 vols (Jerusalem: Byalik, 1976), 1: 185.
81. CAHJP, HM2/9892.10 (original—TsDIAU, f. 442, op. 151, spr. 303, "Delo ob obnaruzhenii pechatnogo stanka i nelegal'noi literatury u lits Sudilkova Zaslavskogo uezda Perlicha Sh.," 1842), ark. 46–47.
82. CAHJP, HM2/9451.14 (original—TsDIAU, f. 293, op. 1, spr. 93, "O evreiskikh knigakh, predstavlennykh v tsenzurnyi komitet," 1844), ark. 9–10.
83. Kotik, *Journey to a Nineteenth-Century Shtetl*, 322.
84. Nosson Sternhartz, *Haye MOHARA"N* (Jerusalem: Meshekh ha-Nahal, 1982), siman 88, 91, 175–176, 184, 346–349, 351.
85. A. I. Paperna, "Iz nikolaevskoi epokhi," in V. Kelner, ed., *Evrei v Rossii. XIX vek* (Moscow: Novoe literaturnoe obozrenie, 2000), 27–176, here 38–39.
86. S. Ansky, "Dibbuk: mezh dvukh mirov," *Yehupets* 10 (2002): 167–247.
87. S. Y. Agnon, *A Book that was Lost and Other Stories* (New York: Schocken, 1995), 128–135.
88. Isaac Bashevis Singer, *The Collected Stories* (New York: Farrar Straus & Giroux, 1982), 179–187.

CONCLUSION: THE END OF THE GOLDEN AGE

1. John LeDonne, *Grand Strategy of the Russian Empire, 1650–1831* (New York: Oxford University Press, 2004), 209–218.
2. On squeezing the Polish szlachta out of Russia's western provinces, see Gorizontov, *Paradoksy imperskoi politiki*, 146–152; on the negative images of Poles in the Russian nationalistic discourse, see Roman Bobryk and Jerzy Faryno, *Polacy w oczach Rosjan— Rosjanie w oczach Polaków, Zbiór studiów* (Warsaw: Slawistyczny ośrodek wydawniczy, 2000), 118–119, 142–148.
3. Alla Sokolova, "Brick as an instrument of innovative assault: the transformation of the house-building tradition in the 'shtetls' of Podolia in the late 19th and early 20th centuries," in Jurgita Šiaučiunaitė-Verbickienė, and Larisa Lempertienė, eds., *Central and East European Jews at the Crossroads of Tradition and Modernity* (Vilnius: Centre for the Study of Culture and History of Eastern European Jews 2006), 188–219.
4. For a communal outcasts accused of arson, see CAHJP, HM2/9146.2 (original— TsDIAU, f. 442, op. 1, spr. 1769, "O rozyske lits, podbrosivshykh vosplameniaiushchiesia veshchestva k domam berdichevskikh meschan (Volko) Harlaka (Beila) Fizonovoi i Shepsy," Aug 14, 1834), ark. 1–2; for a competitor accused of arson, see CAHJP, HM2/8967.14 (original—TsDIAU, f. 442, op. 1, spr. 2772, "O pozharakh v Podolskoi gubernii za aprel-noiabr," 1838), ark. 5–6, 10; for the case of a local Christian boy blamed, see CAHJP, HM2/9146.3 (original—TsDIAU, f. 442, op. 1, spr. 1770, "Raport mogilevskogo politsmeistera," 1834), ark. 1–2.

5. Cathy A. Frierson, *All Russia Is Burning! A Cultural History of Fire and Arson in Late Imperial Russia* (Seattle: University of Washington Press, 2002), 65. On this subject matter, see also Nigel A. Raab, *Democracy Burning? Urban Fire Departments and the Limits of Civil Society in Late Imperial Russia, 1850–1914* (Montreal: McGill–Queen's University Press, 2011). On the long overdue reform of the firefighters' departments, see A. D. Sheremetev, *Proekt pozharnoi reformy v Rossii* (St. Petersburg: Tipo-lit. D. Semeniukova, 1895).

6. TsDIAU, f. 442, op. 1, spr. 2236 ("O pozhare, proisshedshem v Starokonstantinove, Volynskoi gubernii," 1836–1838), ark. 1–2, 9; HM2/9263.1 (original—TsDIAU, f. 442, op. 1, spr. 1776, "O pozhare, proisshedshem v gorode Bare," 1834), ark. 1–2; CAHJP, HM89/8267.1 (original—TsDIAU, f. 442, op. 66, spr. 310, "Po prosheniiu evreev Iarmolinets," 1834), l. 1–2;

7. CAHJP, HM2/8967.1 (original—TsDIAU, f. 442, op. 1. spr. 2020, "Delo o pozhare v Gaisine," 1835), ark. 1; CAHJP, HM2/8926.4 (original—TsDIAU, f. 442, op. 1, spr. 1366, "Po doneseniam iz razlichnykh naselennykh punktov o pozharakh i pr.," 1833), ark. 1–122.

8. CAHJP, HM2/4778.25 [9306.25] (original—TsDIAU, f. 442, op. 1, spr. 4778, "Donesenie o pozhare v m. Medzhibozh Letichevskogo poveta Podolskoi gub.," 1842), ark. 1–3.

9. CAHJP, HM2/9263.1 (original—TsDIAU, f. 442, op. 1, spr. 1352, "O pozhare, proisshedshem v g. Verbovtse," 1832), ark. 2–3, 14; CAHJP, HM2/9266.14 (original—TsDIAU, f. 442, op. 36, spr. 1394, "Po raportu ushitskogo suda o pozhare v Zhvanchike," 1859), ark. 1–2.

10. CAHJP, HM2/9530.5 (original—TsDIAU, f. 707, op. 87, spr. 215, "Po doneseniiu shtatnogo smotritelia radomyshl'skogo uezdnogo uchitelia Butovicha," 1836), ark. 1–7.

11. Yaakov ben Wolf Kranz, *Ale mesholim fun Dubner Magid,* 2 vols. (New York: Tashrak, 1925), 2:34.

12. CAHJP, HM2/9529.3 (original—TsDIAU, f. 442, op. 1, spr. 7628, "O vydache posobii postradavshim ot pozhara zhiteliam gg. Ostroga, Kovlia, Teofilia i Krementsa," 1848), ark. 1–6, 36, 45–47, 54, 107.

13. CAHJP, HM2/9263.10 (original—TsDIAU, f. 442, op. 1, spr. 6812: "O vydache pokhvalnogo lista dvorianinu Gaetskomu za spasenie shesti detei vo vremia pozhara v m. Chemerovtsakh, Podol'skoi gubernii," 1846), ark. 1–2.

14. CAHJP, HM2/8967.5 (original—TsDIAU, f. 442, op. 1, spr. 2024, "Delo o pozharakh, proisshedshikh v m. Shepetovke, Sudilkove i Belogorodke," 1835), ark. 1–6; CAHJP, HM2/8967.6 (original—TsDIAU, f. 442, op. 1, spr. 2025, "Delo o razreshenii zhiteliam g. Belgorodki pereselitsia v derevni," 1835), ark. 1–3.

15. CAHJP, HM2/8967.13 (original—TsDIAU, f. 442, op. 1, spr. 2771, "O pozharakh v Volynskoi gubernii," 1838), ark. 40.

16. CAHJP, HM2/9306.16 (original—TsDIAU, f. 442, op. 1, spr. 4254, "O pozhare v Khmelnike, Podol'skoi," August 1841).

17. CAHJP, HM2/8967.3 (original—TsDIAU, f. 442, op. 1, spr. 2022, "Delo o pozhare v Litin," 1835), ark. 3–15.

18. CAHJP, HM2/8006 (original—TsDIAU, f. 1423, op. 1, spr. 29: "Po prosbe evreiskogo vladimirskogo obshchestva," 1833), ark. 1–2.

19. CAHJP, HM2/9316.15 (original—RGIA, f. 1286, op. 1, d. 205, "Po pros'be poverennykh ot Lutskikh evreev Meizlisha i Goldfarba o ssude im 10,000 rublei," 1808), ll. 1–9, esp. 11.

20. Frierson, *All Russia Is Burning*, 67.

21. CAHJP, HM2/8967.2 (original—TsDIAU, f. 442, op. 1, spr. 2021, "Delo o pozhare v m. Iaryshevke," 1835), ark. 1–3.

22. CAHJP, HM2/8967.5 (original—TsDIAU, f. 442, op. 1, spr. 2024, "Delo o pozharakh, proisshedshikh v m. Shepetovke, Sudilkove i Belogorodke," 1835), ark. 5–6.

23. CAHJP, HM2/8266.10 (original—TsDIAU, f. 442, op. 72, spr. 127, "Perepiska s letichevskim zemskim sudom o proshenii evreev mestechka Medzhibozh o vydelenii denezhnoi pomoshchi dlia postroiki domov evreiam, postradavshim ot pozharov," 1839), ark. 1–2; CAHJP, HM2/8967.7 (original—TsDIAU, f. 442, op. 1, spr. 2026, "Delo po prosheniu zhitelei Leticheva o materialnoi pomoshchi," 1835).

24. CAHJP, HM2/8967.4 (original—TsDIAU, f. 442, op. 1, spr. 2023, "Delo o pozhare, proisshedshem v g. Krementse," 1835).

ACKNOWLEDGMENTS

It took me fifteen years to find the sources for this book, three years to write it, and two to find a publisher. Everybody with whom I have discussed the subject matter of this book over the last twenty years should be mentioned here, including my students, friends, editors, publishers, interlocutors, peers, senior colleagues, and family members. Since this is hardly feasible, I must apologize that I am not able to thank each and every one who helped me bring my shtetl to life.

Before I realized that I wanted to change my career and become a historian, Menahem Feldman, Binyamin Richler, and Barry Walfish taught me elements of Hebrew paleography and helped me understand the significance of the newly declassified East European depositories of Jewish manuscripts, particularly the collections of record books of East European Jewish communities and confraternities.

The opportunity to translate lecture series and full-length courses taught by Gershon Hundert and Moshe Rosman attuned me to different styles of historical thinking, and my Ramot Bet Friday morning seminars with Shaul Stampfer shaped me as a scholar obsessed with the quantitative, social, demographic, and economic aspects of history.

The key mantra of Antony Polonsky, "context is everything," revealed to me that in order to contextualize one has to know the context, while Art Green's motto "read the text," had me revisit again and again every bit of evidence I collected.

The archival research for this book, conducted in five countries, brought me in contact with dozens of archivists who guided me through their holdings as Virgil guided Dante, explaining what I could or could not find, how the system works and what a bottomless pit their archive was. My particular thanks to Volodymyr Danylenko and Olha Muzychuk from Kyiv, Tatiana Burmistrova, Olga Edelman, Dmitrii Feldman, Aleksei Litvin, Sergei Mironenko from Moscow, Larissa Lempertas from Vilnius, Hanna Węgrzinek from Warsaw, Hadassa Assoulin and Binyamin Lukin from Jerusalem.

Special thanks to my colleagues Timothy Breen, John Bushnell, Harry Fox, François Guesnet, Mikhail Krutikov, Boerris Kuzmany, Joel Mokyr, Derek Penslar, Adam Teller, and Andrew Wachtel who read parts of or the entire manuscript, pointed out my inconsistencies, helped me to make my story more nuanced and taught me how to tighten up my narrative, initially twice as long as its present incarnation.

I was blessed with multiple opportunities to read parts of my book, presenting it to different audiences at the University of Alberta in Edmonton, the College of Charleston in South Carolina, University of Illinois at Urbana Champaign, Northwestern University, University of Oxford, University College London, University of Vienna, and Hebrew University in Jerusalem. I am grateful to the organizers of my presentations but especially thankful to my listeners whose critical and enthusiastic feedback made me enthusiastic and critical about my story.

I am indebted to Anatoly Alekseev, Israel Bartal, Judith Kalik, Alexander Kulik, Andrei Orlov, Alexander Pereswetoff-Morath, Moshe Rosman, Dan Shapira, Shaul Stampfer, Moshe Taube, my colleagues at the Institute for Advanced Studies at Hebrew University, Jerusalem, who read and discussed several chapters of the manuscript at the seminars of the Institute.

I received the excellent advice of Ken Alder, Thomas LeBien, Rodger Kamenetz, Marshall Poe, and Jonathan Sarna, who shared their insights into writing and publication strategies.

The funding provided by my endowed chair initially came from Lester Crown, whose amazing generosity allowed me to devote my time entirely to productive research and writing. Additional financial help came from the Fulbright Foundation, the National Endowment for the Humanities, the Memorial Foundation for Jewish Culture (twice), Northwestern University research grants (twice), and the Institute for Advanced studies at Hebrew University (twice).

Ex ungue leonem, as the Latin proverb says. By looking "at the claws of the lion," hidden behind the curtain, we can recognize his majestic whole. Of course I know who the two anonymous reviewers were who painstakingly went through the entire manuscript and whose recommendations I accepted with humility and admiration. I cannot name them here for security reasons yet want to thank them from the depth of my heart.

The team of Brigitta van Rheinberg from Princeton University Press, including Claudia Acevedo, Ellen Foos, and Dimitri Karetnikov took my paper shtetl from me and turned it into a robust final product with a beautiful design, attractive look, and, I hope, some intellectual and spiritual value.

As far as the writing process is concerned, I am perennially indebted to Annette Ezekiel Kogan, who made my golden age shtetl speak idiomatic English with no Yiddish or Slavic accent.

My wife Oxana and my children, Sara Sofiya and Shlomo Efraim stoically withstood my long absences while on archival trips to East Europe and Israel. They gave me their infallible support and inspiration, and always believed that I could accomplish what I was planning to accomplish, even when I seriously doubted that I could. Their love and dedication transformed my existence as a blue-collar intellectual into the life of a proud *pater familias* and resident of the golden age shtetl not to be confused with the West Rogers Park, Chicago.

INDEX

Hoffman, Eva 10
Hotin 230
house (in the shtetl) 245–256, 250, compared to a peasant hut 250, 255, in travelogues and literature 268–271, its architecture and multi-functionalism 246–252, 255–256, its interior 249–252, its quality 252–253, its urban ethos 253–255. *See also* trade
Hundert, Gershon David 12

Ialutorovsk 202
Ianovka 17
Iarmolintsy 97, 338
Iasnogrodka 266
Ilintsy 151
Isaac Mickhal, rabbi 81–83
Israel of Ruzhin *see* Fridman
Issakhar Ber of Zaslav, rabbi 291
Issakhar Ber of Złoczów rabbi, 291
Isser, Israel rabbi 24, 236
Istanbul 288
Ivanovo 100

Jabotinsky, Ze'ev (Vladimir) 180
Janów 328
Jerusalem 27, 42, 88, 156, 196, 223, 232, 275, 277–297, 299–303, 330, 339, 346–347. *See also* land of Israel
Jesenska, Milena 241
Jews 6, 8, 10, 13–15, 20–22, 25, 27, 32, 48, 50, 60, 91, 137, 155, 182, 190, 200, 342, 353, as artisans 54, 93, 115, 128, 151, 173, 176–177, 203, 205–208, 216, 218, 250, 262–269, 322–323, 344, 346, 352, as cabmen (*balagolas*) 91–92, as economically most active 39–40, as efficient tradesmen 96–102, 109–110, as international traders 63–66, 87, as merchants in proportion to Christian 93–94, as middlemen (*faktors*) 92–93, 98, as robust and physically capable people 171–173, as smuggles 67–89, as stereotypical criminals 209, as stereotypical innkeepers 123, 145–146, as stereotypical people of the *gesheft* 118–119, child mortality and out-of-wedlock births among 228, divorces among 237–238, fighting for the real estate 261–263, in prison 190–197, mocking Christianity 151–152, portrayed in police documents 188–190, promiscuity and adultery among 228–237, rebelling against liquor trade monopolists 139–144, sharing values with non-Jews 77–81, their attire 220–222, their attitude to courts 184–188, their charity boxes for the land of Israel 297–299, their domestic animals 243–245, their family structure 216–219, their loyalty toward Russia 42–51, 82, 165–171, their sexual mores 224–228. *See also* shtetl
Joel Ba'al Shem, rabbi 334
Judaism 45, 151–153, 162, 164–166, 168, 173, 200, 202, and excommunication from 139, and family 214–216, 228–233, 230–231, and family conflicts 228–239, and funeral rituals 273–275, and sexual relations 224–228, as reconfirmed through inter-religious violence 168–169, burial laws in 176, dietary laws in 139, its attitudes to Christian theology 151, 165. *See also* Jews, Hasidism, Mitnagdim
Jusefów 327, 338

Kabbalah (Judaic mysticism) 278–279, 309–312, 314, 317–318, 325–326, 329–334, 336–339. *See also* Judaism, Hasidism
Kafka, Franz 241
Kagarlyk 126
kahal (communal elders) 12, 15, 22–23, 49, 79, 81, 97, 113, 116, 157–157, 159–162, 175–176, 184, 185, 187, 209, 214, 226–227, 229–230, 237, 249, 332, 342, 348
Kalinovka 227
Kalisher, Tsvi Hirsch, rabbi 300
Kalisk 291
Kamenets-Litovsk 115, 217, 220
Kamenets-Podolsk 5, 14, 22, 34, 41, 48, 51, 65, 78, 94, 187, 191, 202, 238, 246–247, 257, 259–260, 353
Kamenka 126
Kampenhausen, Baltasar 87
Kankrin, Egor 71–74, 77, 82, 86, 110, 137, 139, 144,

Zhabotin 16
Zhashkov 18
Zhelekhov 67
Zhidichin 17
Zhinkov 17, 38
Zhinkovets 22, 41
Zhitomir 34, 47, 49, 81, 107, 110–111, 165,
    193, 196–199, 205–206, 295, 313, 345,
    353, as the administrative center
    134–135, 140, 141, 143, competing
    with Berdichev 111–116, divorce rate
    in 238, 273, brothers Shapira printing

press in 318–322, 326, 337–338, 342.
    See also Berdichev
Zholkver, Usher 45
Zhornitsa 244, 253
Zhvanets 17, 41, 58, 78, 100, 251, 348
Zionism 275, 295
Zlatopolie 22, 53, 61, 184, 186
Złoczów 291
Żółkiew 284, 309, 332
Zolotonosha 190, 192, 200
Zvenigorodka 50, 129, 137, 161, 191, 193,
    207